Princeton Theological Monograph Series

Dikran Y. Hadidian

General Editor

40

EVANGELICALISM AND KARL BARTH

*His Reception and Influence in
North American Evangelical Theology*

EVANGELICALISM
and
Karl Barth

His Reception and Influence in North American Evangelical Theology

PHILLIP R. THORNE

PICKWICK PUBLICATIONS
An imprint of *Wipf and Stock Publishers*
199 West 8th Avenue • Eugene OR 97401

Pickwick Publications
An imprint of Wipf and Stock Publishers
199 W 8th Ave, Suite 3
Eugene, OR 97401

Evangelicalism and Karl Barth
His Reception and Influence in North American Evangelical Theology
By Thorne, Phillip R.
Copyright©1995 by Thorne, Phillip R.
ISBN: 1-55635-028-7
Publication date 1/1/1995

TO MY WIFE

Whose loving sacrifice
made this dream come true

CONTENTS

Contents vii
Preface xi
Introduction xiii
Relevant Literature and Scholarly Contribution xvii

**Chapter One: The Identity of American
                 Evangelicalism** 1

**From Evangelical Heritage to Fundamentalist
Experience** 3
    Contours of a Consensus 3
    Pressures Upon the Consensus 5
    Theological Pressures.. 5
    Social Pressures 8
    Conservative Coalitions 9
Four Dominant Traditions 10
    Northern Fundamentalist Evangelicalism 10
    The Holiness-Pentecostal Tradition 12
    Reformed Confessionalism 13
    Southern Evangelicalism 15
**From Fundamentalist Experience to Evangelical
Resurgence** 16
    Fundamentalist Pattern, Fundamentalist Image 16
    Separation and Success 17
    A New "Evangelicalism" 20
    A New "New Evangelicalism" 22
        Dwelling In and Breaking Out 23
        Converging Conservatisms 25
A Changing Evangelical Mosaic 27

Chapter Two: Fundamentalist Evangelicalism: Barth Reception within a Dominant Paradigm 31

Cornelius Van Til: Establishing an Interpretive Paradigm 33
   Barth Reception 35
   The New Modernism 35
   Christianity and Barthianism 39
Orthodox Reformed Theologians 41
   The Christian Reformed Church 41
      Louis Berkhof 42
      Fred Klooster 43
   Orthodox Presbyterianism 44
      An Early Encounter 45
      Francis Schaeffer 46
      Gordon Haddon Clark 49
      Barth Reception 51
   Carl F.H. Henry: Evangelical Spokesman 54
      Barth Reception 58
      God, Revelation and Authority 60
Other Fundamentalist Evangelical Interpreters 62
   Evidentialist Orthodox Apologists 63
      John Warwick Montgomery 63
      John Gerstner and R.C. Sproul 65
      Clark Pinnock 66
      Kenneth Kantzer 67
      Charles Caldwell Ryrie 69
   Pietistic Fundamentalist Evangelicalism 70
      H. Orton Wiley 71
      E. Y. Mullins and W. T. Connor 72

Chapter Three: Beyond Fundamentalist Evangelicalism: New Evangelical Reception in the Reformed Traditions 79

Bromiley and Berkouwer: Early Influences, Enduring Models 81
   Geoffrey Bromiley 81

> Barth Reception 83
>> G. C. Berkouwer 86
>> Barth Reception 89
>> The Triumph of Grace 90
>> Sin, Election and Reconciliation 91
>> Cornelius Van Til 94
>
> **Fuller Seminary: Flagship of Evangelical Identity** 95
>> The Vassady Incident 96
>> Edward John Carnell: Evangelical Pioneer 99
>> New Evangelicalism at Fuller 103
>> Colin Brown 104
>> Paul King Jewett 107
>> James Daane 112
>> Ray Sherman Anderson 117
>
> **Bernard Ramm: Model of Fundamentalist Transition** 123
>> The Reception of Barth and the Reappraisal of Evangelical Theology 125
>> After Fundamentalism: The Future of Evangelical Theology 129
>
> **Donald Bloesch: Converging Mainline Evangelical** ... 133
>> Barth Reception 137
>>> Methodology 139
>>> Soteriology 141
>
> **Concluding Comment** 143

Chapter Four: New Evangelical Reception in the Pietistic Traditions 149

> **Southern Baptist Evangelicalism** 151
>> The Southern Baptist Theological Seminary 152
>> Eric Rust 153
>> Dale Moody 155
>>> The Word of Truth 158
>> David L. Mueller 159
>
> **The Holiness-Pentecostal Tradition** 164
>> J. Rodman Williams 164
>> The Wesleyan Theological Society 165

Laurence Wood	166
Donald W. Dayton	167
The Anabaptist Evangelical Tradition	171
John Howard Yoder	172
Barth Reception	173
Concluding Comment	174

| **Chapter 5: Conclusion** | 177 |

A Basic Historical Pattern	177
A Fundamentalist Evangelical Paradigm	177
Beyond Fundamentalist Evangelicalism	178
A General Pattern and a Basic Divide	179
Other Patterns	179
Differences Between Traditions	179
Shifting Issues and Growing Sophistication	181
Whither Evangelicalism?	182

| **Bibliography** | 185 |
| **Subject Index** | 233 |

PREFACE

Doctoral dissertations are written for many and complex reasons. But without a doubt, the driving motivation for this one has been personal: the critical evaluation of a religious and theological tradition which I call my own. I am an American Evangelical who has been deeply influenced by the Fundamentalist Evangelicalism of my forebears and the New Evangelicalism of my own generation. This study is in part, therefore, an exercise in self-evaluation.

The specific choice of topic—the reception and influence of Karl Barth—is, on one hand, logical. It provides a revealing lens for viewing the complex and changing nature of Evangelical religion and a sharp tool for analyzing Evangelical theology. The depth and richness of Barth's own thought also makes the study of Evangelical interaction worthwhile.

But the decision to investigate the interchange between Barth and the Evangelical tradition has a more personal dimension. It began with Dr. Ronald Thiemann, my revered Professor at Haverford College from 1977 to 1981. It was from him that I first learned of Karl Barth, and it was largely because of him that the relationship between Barth and Evangelical theology became lodged near the center of my own theological pilgrimage. Professor Thiemann was, and is, a great teacher. I hope he will regard this dissertation as partial payment of the debt of gratitude I owe.

During the writing of this work I have developed other debts as well. To Bishop Stephen Sykes I owe more than I can say. No person could have had a wiser, more caring doctoral mentor than I. Without his careful criticism this work would have been decidedly inferior; and without his pastoral care it would never have been completed. To Professor Ray Anderson, who supervised me while stateside, I am also thankful. His insight into both Barth and the nature of American Evangelicalism, especially at Fuller, have been extremely helpful—as have his words of encouragement during a long and painful process.

But to one person, and one person alone, I owe the debt of love. Without her costly sacrifices—more than a person should have to pay—this dissertation would not have been started or finished. To her, therefore, I dedicate this book.

INTRODUCTION

The story of American Evangelicalism contains many ironies. But the most ironic may be its present experience of resurgence and fragmentation. At a time in history when the social power and intellectual respectability of the burgeoning movement has been widely acknowledged, astute observers are also chronicling tensions and conflicts which threaten its cohesion. In 1976, *Time* magazine's "Year of the Evangelical," Carl Henry even spoke of an "identity crisis":

> While he is still on the loose, and still sounding his roar, the Evangelical lion is nonetheless slowly succumbing to an identity crisis. The noteworthy cohesion that American Evangelicals gained in the sixties has been fading in the seventies through multiplied internal disagreements and emerging counterforces (Henry, 1976, 22).

While possibly overstating the cohesion present during the sixties, Dr. Henry voices the opinion of many when he identifies the presence of internal disputes and the absence of comprehensive integrating structures or leaders as sources of growing confusion. That this confusion amounts to a crisis is a matter of more personal concern.

One personally concerned theologian is Dr. Bernard Ramm. From his perspective, however, the crisis stems not from a recent loss of cohesion but from a long-term theological failure underlying the fragmentation. This failure is modern Evangelicalism's captivity to a Fundamentalist theology that has failed to respond adequately to post-Enlightenment rationality. But there is hope; and that hope is to be found in Karl Barth. Only by following the centrist course Barth has charted between the Scylla of capitulating Liberalism and the Charybdis of rigidifying Fundamentalism can Evangelical theology meet the Enlightenment challenge without compromising its identity. At least this is the thesis of Ramm's 1983 book, *After Fundamentalism*.

Ironically, the fact that an established Evangelical theologian has proposed such a course is itself symptomatic of the disease to which Carl Henry points. There was a time when such a proposal was, if not unthinkable, certainly unwelcome. But the suggestion and use of Barth as a model has been on the rise within Evangelicalism since the sixties. And this is due, not only to the growing familiarity that recent translations and secondary studies have facilitated, but also to changes within American Evangelicalism itself.

Barth has become an increasingly influential dialogue partner in the theological development of American Evangelicalism, and the study of how he has been received should provide a valuable perspective on the nature of this religious tradition. In fact, if Bernard Ramm is right, understanding how Barth has been received, and why, could play a significant role in the future of Evangelical theology. But American Evangelical theologians (and those interested in engaging them) have yet to receive a comprehensive and critical analysis of the reception of Barth within their tradition. Therefore, it will be the purpose of this study to provide such an analysis.

The study itself is composed of five chapters, along with a brief introduction. In the first chapter a descriptive analysis of American Evangelicalism is offered. It is defined as a mosaic of traditions that share a parallel narrative history and consequent family resemblances; and the story that emerges through a retelling of the narrative history provides an interpretive framework for the rest of the study.

In chapters two through four the reception of Barth is then analyzed. On the basis of a comprehensive study of American Evangelical comment, essential aspects of important Evangelical evaluations are identified and interpreted. Each theologian is identified as a representative of a basic paradigm, a pattern of Barth reception rooted in a characteristic theology and typical social history. The paradigm of chapter two is designated "Fundamentalist Evangelical," while in chapters three and four the interpreters are described as "New Evangelical." This results in a two-fold typology which corresponds to the most important distinction that can be made between Evangelical interpreters: those who espouse an orthodox apologetic paradigm and those who maintain more mediating approaches. In this distinction the powerful and persistent influence of the fundamentalist experience within Evangelical history is portrayed.

Of course, such a simple typology cannot stand alone. Beyond these basic distinctions, therefore, various differentiations are proposed to explain more precisely the contours of Barth interpretation. These differences include not only the specific arguments of the various interpreters, but also their broader theological positions and historical traditions. Fundamentalist Evangelicals, for example, manifest a polemic approach to Barth, based upon strict adherence to a perceived orthodoxy and a well-defined theory of revelation and rationality. But theories of rationality differ between theologians, and the importance of these theories decreases as one moves from the reformed centers of scholarship into the more pietistic traditions. Furthermore, some Fundamentalist Evangelicals combine their polemic with qualified notes of praise, especially those, like Carl Henry and Kenneth Kantzer, who have played influential roles in the postwar resurgence of Evangelical religion.

These differences, among others, are observed and interpreted in chapter two. Likewise, the similarities and differences between the various New Evangelical responses to Barth are discussed in chapters three and four, with an eye to both theological argument and historical locus. In fact, the division itself between chapters three and four represents a separation between reformed New Evangelicals and the varieties of New Evangelicalism found among the more pietistic Southern Baptists, Wesleyans and Pentecostals. In all these distinctions—between Fundamentalist and New Evangelical, pietist and reformed, Southern Baptist, Wesleyan and Pentecostal—the historical analysis of chapter one continues to make its presence felt.

RELEVANT LITERATURE
AND SCHOLARLY CONTRIBUTION

The primary contribution of this book is to provide a comprehensive interpretation of the reception of Barth within North American Evangelicalism. On the basis of a study of every notable theologian within American Evangelicalism (since 1920), a descriptive analysis has been written to identify the essential aspects of influential evaluations of Barth and locate them in the context of each interpreter's theology and history. This interpretive exercise has required the author to investigate, not only Evangelical theology, but its history, as well, and to develop his own conclusions about how the story of American Evangelical religion is to be told.

Only three general studies have been written on the subject of Barth's reception among American Evangelicals: Harold John Loewen's 1976 dissertation on Barth's doctrine of inspiration (which treats Evangelical response at length), Gregory Bolich's 1980 book, *Karl Barth and Evangelicalism*, and Richard Albert Mohler Jr.'s 1989 dissertation, "Evangelical Theology and Karl Barth: Representative Models of Response." To this, one may add brief articles by Geoffrey Bromiley and Donald Dayton—which discuss both Evangelical and non-Evangelical reception—and a restatement by Loewen of one aspect of his dissertation (Bromiley, 1988; Dayton, 1974, 1985; Loewen, 1987). On the reception of Barth among English speaking theologians, three other important essays have been written, but none of them engage American Evangelical comment (Sykes, 1979; Roberts, 1989; Voskuil, 1980).[1]

Of these studies, Dr. Mohler's dissertation is the most germane. The others suffer from limitations of scope that undermine their ability to portray the full range of Evangelical reception or to interpret it with sufficient depth. Indeed, such comprehensive depiction is not their purpose. Loewen's study, for example, concentrates upon Barth's doctrine of Scripture, and although he begins with a description of American Evangelical response, his singular focus precludes comprehensive analysis. But even within these confines, the four categories of Evangelical response by which he organizes the introduction fail to reveal the essential features of Barth's reception. Thus, it is not Ryrie's "dispensationalism" that determines his response to Barth, but rather his apologetic orthodoxy, which he holds in common with most of the "philosophical," "reformed" and "irenic" Evangelicals Loewen describes. Furthermore, to identify Reformed Evangelical response with Cornelius Van Til, which Loewen does, is to reduce the tradition to a particular representative and to obscure important lines of theological development (Loewen, 1976, 1-92).

In a subsequent article, however, Loewen drops his fourfold categorization, and speaks instead of a single "Evangelical Type" that dominates postwar reception (Loewen, 1987). Represented by Henry, Clark and Van Til, this paradigm is characterized by a philosophical criticism of Barth's doctrine of revelation that is rooted in its own philosophically controlled theory of inspiration. While making no claims to comprehensive depiction, this later study does make a helpful contribution: it highlights the basic divide in Evangelical Barth reception and identifies essential features of the most influential early paradigm.

Bolich's book, published for a more general audience, makes this basic divide its fundamental interpretive category. Following the lead of Cornelius Van Til and G. C. Berkouwer, "the Evangelical response to Barth has seen the alignment of scholars along two lines": those who regard him as a "foe of Evangelical faith" and those who see in him a "potential friend" (Bolich, 1980, 98,77,87). This alignment, according to Bolich, corresponds to two different kinds of Evangelicalism: a "critical" theology, rooted in the Fundamentalist experience of the early twentieth century, and a more "constructive" theology that manifests less rigidity in defining Evangelical boundaries and greater willingness to dialogue with other points of view.

But there are limitations to Bolich's study. His review of Evangelical response is contained within forty-two pages of a book devoted to another purpose: proposing Barth as a "model and guide" for the "renewal and reform" of Evangelical theology (Ibid.,187). The result is a survey with limited exposition of Evangelical interpretations and limited analysis of the theological traditions within which these occur. This leads to the omission of important features of Evangelical reception, as well as the commission of at least one serious error, misplacing Carl Henry along the Evangelical divide. Bolich's book is, however, one widely read example of an Evangelical call to consider Barth a model for theology.

Dr. Mohler's dissertation constitutes a significant advance upon all previous studies. Focusing his attention directly upon the reception of Barth within the American Evangelical tradition, he avoids the problems that stem from both Loewen's and Bolich's limitation of scope. He treats a broad range of Evangelical theologians and engages in significant exposition of their interpretations of Barth's theology. Furthermore, Mohler relates this reception in many cases to the theologian's view of Evangelical identity and his locus within the Evangelical tradition.

Mohler concludes that Evangelical response to Barth manifests a basic three-fold typology, and this typology provides the general structure for his analysis. "The Evangelical Rejection of Barth" represented primarily by Cornelius Van Til and Carl Henry, comprises Evangelicals who consider Barth's theology a "rival to the Evangelical faith" and who exclude him from the clearly defined boundaries of orthodoxy (Ibid., 7, 13-134). "Evangelicals in Critical Dialogue," on the other hand, manifest a "dialectical" reading (Ibid., 135-229). "Unwilling to call for the appropriation of Barth as a model," men like Donald Bloesch and Berkouwer still discern in his writings "possibilities for a theological dialogue that could impact in some manner the form and content of Evangelical theology" (Ibid., 7, 136-7). Finally, "The Evangelical Appropriation of Barth," seen in Geoffrey Bromiley, Donald Dayton, Bernard Ramm and Thomas Torrance, moves one step further: it considers Barth a theological model to guide Evangelicals as they mediate between the twin commitments of historic continuity and contemporary engagement (Ibid., 230-98). Within this three-part framework Dr. Mohler offers meaningful analysis of both Barth reception and Evangelical identity.

There are, however, important ways in which the present study differs from Dr. Mohler's work. In the first place, Mohler's three-fold typology is not considered helpful. While there are differences among various "New Evangelical" interpreters, these differences do not represent different categories of response or theological paradigms. Rather, every American Evangelical theologian who departs from a Fundamentalist paradigm engages in a dialectical reading, both criticizing Barth and constructively appropriating, or at least affirming, elements of his theology. Dr. Mohler seems to admit as much when he returns in the conclusion of his study to a basic two-fold division among Evangelical Barth interpreters (Ibid., 308-13).[2]

Another contrast between the present study and Dr. Mohler's work can be found in the role historical interpretation plays. While considerable historical comment is present in Mohler's book, he does not provide a comprehensive analysis of American Evangelicalism that allows the history of the tradition to shape his study. Instead, he approaches the issue of reception through "representative models" of response and discusses Evangelical identity in terms of the views expressed by these theologians. But the failure to provide such an analysis produces negative consequences in Dr. Mohler's presentation. It does not allow him, for example, to display the historical contours of American Evangelical reception of Barth, or to explain, as effectively as he might, the nature and causes of that reception. It also leads to the ommission of important representatives of Evangelical thinking, especially the theologians at The Southern Baptist Theological Seminary, Mohler's alma mater, or the most influential Christian Reformed theologian in America during the first half of the twentieth century, Louis Berkhof. Equally surprising for a study that centers on the resurgent Evangelical movement in postwar America is Dr. Mohler's decision to include an extended discussion of Thomas Torrance, while devoting limited space to Geoffrey Bromiley.

For these reasons, among others, the present study contends that Barth reception among Evangelicals is best interpreted through a sustained correlation of historical and theological explanation, and that this requires, from the beginning, an historically informed definition of Evangelical identity.

NOTES

1. Hutchens' comparative study of Carl Henry and Karl Barth is indirectly relevant (Hutchens, 1989).

2. Mohler's typology must be questioned when it is used to suggest that the appropriation of Barth by Bernard Ramm or Geoffrey Bromiley is more extensive, or less critical, than that of Donald Bloesch. It would also seem that the interpretive categories have been inapropriately applied when Carnell is discussed among those who appropriate Karl Barth as a model for theology, or when Kenneth Kantzer is distinguished from Carl Henry's fundamentally critical response.

1

THE IDENTITY OF AMERICAN EVANGELICALISM

Providing a definition of American Evangelicalism is no simple matter. Both popular and technical literature on the subject reveals a remarkable difference of opinion, a disparity that parallels the diversity of those to whom the label has been applied: strictly confessional Presbyterians who separated from a culturally dominant denomination, and culturally dominant Southern Baptists who have resisted creedal definition; Holiness and Pentecostal denominations originating in the lower socio-economic strata of society, and charismatic Episcopalians who occupy a significantly higher economic plane; independent Bible Church dispensationalists and Evangelical lobbies in mainline denominations; ethnic Reformed traditions and Black "Bible-Believing" churches—all these, and more, have been placed under the Evangelical banner. A diverse lot, indeed! They live in different sections of the country, belong to different socio-economic groups, participate in different denominations with diverse confessional heritages, and espouse differing theologies.

Such diversity has even caused some to question the existence of a coherent Evangelicalism (Dayton,1991). But among those who continue to claim an identifiable unity, there is recognition of the need to employ terms that capture both the unity and diversity of the subject. "Mosaic" (Anderson, 1989b), "kaleidoscope" (Smith, 1986), "movement" (Ellingsen, 1988), "coalition" (Marsden, 1986), even "mood" (Bloesch, 1973) and "circus tent" (Murphy, 1981) have been used.[1]

George Marsden provides a helpful orientation to the discussion when he recognizes three basic uses of the term: Evangelicalism as a theological category, a broad religious movement, and a more narrowly defined historical community (Marsden, 1986, ix-xvi). As a theological designation, Evangelicals are those who hold a high view of Scripture and a generally conservative theology, often profess a conversion experience and usually place high priority on evangelism and personal sanctification (Shelley, 1967, 14; Quebedeaux, 1974, 3-4; Marsden, 1986; Smith, 1986; Bloesch, 1983b, 5, 17; Ellingsen, 1988). As a religious movement, Evangelicalism is a theologically conservative continuation of the missions-oriented Protestantism associated with the Anglo-Saxon Awakenings of Whitfield, Wesley and Finney.[2] When indicating a specific historical community, the term typically denotes the coalition of transdenominational schools, societies, publishing houses, and constituencies, with roots in turn-of-the-century Fundamentalism, which has provided the institutional matrix and leadership center for the postwar Evangelical resurgence (Marsden,1986, vii-xix; Carpenter,1984, 5-6).

Any comprehensive interpretation of the Evangelical phenomenon must utilize all three categories, for broad religious movements encompass people living in communities who identify themselves, in part, by theological description. And failure to distinguish between movement, community and theology has often hampered effective interpretation. Consider, for example, James Barr's identification of inerrancy and conversionism as the controlling ideas of Fundamentalism (which he equates with "conservative Evangelicalism" in America and Great Britain). The obvious question is, "What communities or leaders within the movement are aptly described by this generalization?" Evangelicalism may indeed be the unrealized ideal and Fundamentalism the operative reality among most Evangelicals, as Barr suggests (Barr, 1980, preface). But the complexity of the situation burdens this interpretation with a *prima facie* implausibility. Biblical inerrancy, for example, is a contested doctrine among modern Evangelicals, and may not even be the majority opinion (Johnston, 1979, 15-47; Hunter, 1987, 20-33).To define Evangelical identity in these terms, therefore, is to be guilty of a theological reduction that fails to appreciate the actual diversity present.[3]

This theological reduction is paralleled by, and often rooted in, an historical one. Failing to distinguish between the Evangelical movement and the communities which participate in the movement, many observers have reduced Evangelicalism to one or more of its constitutive traditions. The most common of these is the restriction of Evangelicalism to Fundamentalism, and Fundamentalism to the coalition formed between dispensational premillenialists and Old School Presbyterians at the turn of the century. Although qualified by its originator, and seriously challenged by subsequent interpreters (Sandeen, 1970; Marsden, 1980, 199-205; Moore, 1988), this proposal continues to be influential (Rudnick, 1966; Hinson, 1983). Certainly no community within the Evangelical mosaic can be understood apart from a fundamentalist experience, but that experience has also been more diverse than is typically recognized.

One of the challenges for any interpretation of American Evangelicalism, therefore, is to account for the broad-based coalition which the Evangelical movement represents while distinguishing between the historical communities that comprise the movement; and this must be done with due regard for the beliefs by which the participants define themselves. In this study the strategy employed will be to identify American Evangelicalism as a *mosaic of traditions which share a parallel narrative history* and certain *family resemblances*. The parallel history includes a formative heritage in nineteenth century Protestantism, a countermodern orientation during the twentieth century fundamentalist experience, and a positive identification with the postwar resurgence of religion that appropriated the name Evangelical. Arising from this shared history are an identifiable set of family resemblances which have enabled these diverse communities and traditions to form coalitions, engage in common actions, and be recognized by each other as members of a common movement. An Evangelical, therefore, is someone who identifies the Evangelical narrative as his or her own story and manifests, consequently, some or all of the family resemblances that mark the traditions within the mosaic.[4]

For the sake of focus not every Evangelical community will be discussed in this study. But the author contends that any adequate analysis requires the recognition of four dominant traditions which have exerted significant influence upon the public perception and development of the whole movement: 1) Northern Fundamentalist Evangelicalism, a complex of interdenominational organizations and leaders which has arisen out of the Fundamentalist coalition of (mostly) northern Presbyterians and Baptists, and has drawn conservatives into united action during the Fundamentalist movement and the postwar Evangelical resurgence; 2) the Holiness and Pentecostal tradition, arising out of common historical sources but separated denominationally and theologically in the present situation; 3) Reformed Confessionalism, mostly Orthodox Presbyterian and Dutch Reformed; and 4) Southern Evangelicalism, predominantly the Southern Baptist Convention. Around these central traditions have gathered a diverse array of distinguishable people and communities, not the least important of which are the numerous mainline conservatives who have identified with Evangelical beliefs and participated in Evangelical causes.[5]

In the study that follows, these dominant traditions and the narrative history they share will provide the map upon which the reception of Barth is placed. The purpose of the rest of this chapter will be to draw the map.

From Evangelical Heritage to Fundamentalist Experience.
Contours of a Consensus

The story begins in the nineteenth century, for it was in this period that a conservative Protestantism which described itself as Evangelical became the dominant cultural and religious force in America. In this day of pluralism and secularity, it is difficult to comprehend the "remarkable consensus" of religious thought that existed within the major denominations or the influence it exerted upon American culture (Marsden, 1980, 13). The words of William McLoughlin seem overstated, but informed participants and contemporary historians confirm the claim that "the story of American Evangelicalism is the story of America itself in the years 1800-1900" (McLoughlin, 1968, 1).

It was during this century, for example, that the Puritan ideal of a "Christian America" became the dominant cultural myth, achieving a *de facto* establishment of Evangelical religion (Handy, 1984; Marty, 1971). Generally committed to the "lively experiment" of religious voluntarism entailed in the disestablishment of religion, American churches capitalized on the new competitive situation by multiplying voluntary organizations—denominations and interdenominational societies—and engaging in revivalistic and reforming activities (Mead, 1963; Marty, 1971; Foster, 1960). Driving this revivalism was a genuine missionary zeal with millennial overtones; and providing its unique cultural context was the political and social shift toward a more radical democratization and the movement of both religion and culture into the frontier (Handy, 1984; Smith, 1956).

The converging rise of Jacksonian democracy and Evangelical revivalism at the beginning of the 19th century became, therefore, a determinative event in American history (Marty, 1971; Mead, 1963). The result was the cultural dominance of Evangelical religion. The fact that this hegemony was maintained by Protestants who shared a generally reformed heritage (Calvinist-Puritan-Wesleyan) and a common Scottish Enlightenment rationality did not hinder Evangelical progress either (May, 1976; Bozeman, 1977; Marsden, 1980). A common rationality, a broad theological consensus, and successful participation in revivalistic and reforming enterprises formed a strong cultural base for Evangelical unity and identity. Modern American Evangelicalism originated, if anywhere, in this experience.[6]

And this experience has become its enduring heritage. Most of the family resemblances that exist within the modern Evangelical mosaic maintain, in modified form, the distinguishing characteristics of the nineteenth century movement. These family resemblances include: a *biblicism* that expressed itself in both restorationist and conservative confesssional forms; a *conversionist gospel* that tended toward *perfectionism*; a *custodial ideal* for American civilization, typically expressed in *millennial* terms; and a *generally reformed and realistic conceptual framework* that bore witness to America's Puritan founding and the influence of the Scottish Enlightenment. Nineteenth century Evangelicalism bears the marks, therefore, of *a revivalist movement in a reformed framework within a particular American situation.*

What the American situation provided, besides its Puritan founding, was the shaping impulses of freedom and the frontier. Located on the edge of a limitless frontier, relatively unencumbered by layers of European tradition, and propelled forward by its post-revolutionary democratic vision, America and its people manifested an elevation of the individual and an orientation toward the future. Because revivalism converged with these broader cultural emphases, it found a receptive climate for rapid expansion. What it expanded into, and somewhat reshaped, was a predominantly reformed culture that had absorbed the impact of the Enlightenment by means of Scottish realism. Committed to freedom, Evangelicalism tended toward a low-church, anti-historical emphasis on exclusive biblical authority and personal conversion. Oriented toward the future and steeped in biblical realism, it tended toward millennialism. Intertwined with culture, this millennialism was often identified with an American custodial ideal. As various interpreters have noted, these or something like these, were nineteenth century Evangelicalism's unifying characteristics during a period of widespread consensus.[7]

Pressures Upon the Consensus

But this Evangelical consensus, while impressive, was far from monolithic. There was contained within the unity an unstable and expanding diversity that would eventually produce, under pressure, a more fragmented mosaic of religion in America. Martin Marty identifies the Civil War as the "Beginning of the End" for the "Protestant Empire", while Robert Handy locates the decisive loss of the custodial ideal in the "Second Disestablishment" of religion after the First World War (Handy, 1984; Marty, 1971). But whether viewed from the beginning or the end, one must conclude that between these wars a seismic transformation occurred in American religion.

Crashing into the cultural shores of the 1920s as the prohibition crusade and the Modernist-Fundamentalist controversies, the tidal wave of nineteenth century Evangelicalism lost its force. But prior to these events an undertow of forces had been pulling in contrary directions, undermining its power, and ultimately causing Evangelicalism to become a crashing wave rather than a land engulfing flood. Of these contrary forces, three merit particular attention: the demise of calvinist theology, the impact of modernization upon society, and the division of the country into warring sections. Together these constitute the fundamental pressures upon the Evangelical consensus that produced the controversies and new coalitions which characterize the twentieth century situation.

Theological Pressures

Nineteenth century theology, especially after the Civil War, was in a state of flux, marked by internal tensions and broad transitions. The central event in this period of change was the century-long demise of calvinist dominance, for the reformed conceptual framework had provided the basic context for religious discourse and united action since the Puritan founding (Ahlstrom, 1975; Kuklick, 1984). The liberalizing of theology by turn-of-the-century modernists is one aspect of the story, while the influence of arminian traditions is another. Distinguishable yet interrelated events, together they form the story of the loss of Reformed orthodoxy as the dominant intellectual framework for Evangelical religion.

Liberalism is a term used to describe a religious tradition in America distinguished by its opposition to regnant orthodoxies in the name of intellectual integrity. Originating with the critical rationalism of the Boston Unitarians and influenced by the American transcendentalists, liberalism became a powerful force in the Evangelical denominations toward the end of the nineteenth century through the seminal works of men like Newman Smyth (1902), William Newton Clark (1898), Henry Churchill King (1901) and William Adams Brown (1902, 1906). Proponents of a new, reconstructed, or progressive theology, these self-described "Modernists" were convinced that the old orthodoxies needed to be modified to incorporate modern insights. Generally speaking, they imbibed the optimistic views of evolutionary progress current within post-Darwinian culture and applied them to theology. God was viewed as immanent, and his activities were often identified with the progress of nature and culture. Protestant Orthodoxy's doctrine of revelation came under severe criticism, and Scripture was often interpreted as an historically conditioned report of religious experience (Hutchison, 1976; Marty, 1986; Cauthen, 1962; Kuklich, 1984).

These revisions, however, were not offered as attacks upon Christianity, but rather as sincere attempts to reinterpret the faith in ways that would allow modern men to believe. The form was being changed so the essence could be preserved. When the historical impact of two World Wars and a major depression forced the liberal tradition to jettison its optimistic commitment to evolutionary progress, and as thinkers like Reinhold Niebuhr reintroduced depravity into the theological vocabulary, turn-of-the-century modernism was changed. But the essential distinguishing characteristic of liberalism was maintained: a revisionist program arising out of a basic commitment to the methods and agreed-upon conclusions of modern scientific rationality.

The impact of this liberal tradition upon the Evangelical Protestant denominations was felt in a series of heresy trials and contested appointments that occurred between 1870 and 1910. Although most early decisions favored the conservative parties, by the second and third decades of the twentieth century a more tolerant position toward those labeled modernist had been taken. Only in the Presbyterian and Northern Baptist denominations were conservative coalitions able to mount a serious battle for power, and these conflicts became the Modernist-Fundamentalist controversies of the 1920s.

By the twentieth century, therefore, Reformation orthodoxy

had been modified, or replaced, by a revisionist liberal tradition within the educational centers of the dominant denominations, creating a division within the Protestant house between conservative and liberal, Fundamentalist and Modernist. Of course these distinctions were neither absolute nor static, but the institutional separations that arose from them have preserved and extended their relevance into the present day (Marsden, 1980; Cole, 1931; Szasz, 1980; Marty, 1971).

Coterminous with and contributing to the rise of modernist thought was the modification of Evangelical theology under the influence of revivalism. Labelled the "Methodist Age" by William Warren Sweet (1944), the nineteenth century witnessed a progressive disposition of the Congregational-Presbyterian-Episcopalian triumvirate as the numerically dominant Protestant presence. Intensive revivalist activity by circuit preachers and frontier evangelists established Methodist dominance in the central regions of the United States and Baptist hegemony in the South—a pattern that has persisted to the present day. In the North, where Baptists and Methodists made significant gains as well, the more established Presbyterians and Congregationalists engaged in successful revivalist activities of their own. But the success of revivalism exerted an arminian pressure upon theology. Not only did it allow the confluence of arminian and pietistic traditions with reformed and confessional ones, but the practice of revivalism actually shifted the focus of theology. Intense revivalism highlighted the activity of man rather than the sovereignty of God, and conducted on the frontier by lay evangelists with only the rudiments of theological education, it led to a diminished focus upon doctrinal precision and denominational distinctives. The result was a kind of pragmatic Evangelicalism (Smith, 1956; McLoughlin, 1968; Matthews, 1977).

These developments were epitomized in the person and work of Charles G. Finney, who with Lyman Beecher and Nathaniel Taylor captured the spirit of the age and provided leadership within the Congregational-Presbyterian context as it moved toward this pragmatic Evangelicalism. Although officially a Presbyterian until just prior to the dissolution of the Plan of Union (in 1837), Finney adopted optimistic views of human ability, perfectionist doctrines of Spirit baptism, and an anti-authoritarian bias in tension with traditional Presbyterian Calvinism. His "New Measures" revivalism, codified in the *Lectures on Revival* (Finney, 1988), aroused heated opposition while exerting a powerful influence upon the whole nineteenth century's movement in revivalist and perfectionist directions (McLoughlin, 1959, 1968, 1970).

Charles Finney represented the perfectionist and Lyman Beecher the romantic popularizer of the basic theological reorientation accomplished by Nathaniel Taylor's "New Divinity." The development of the New Divinity is the story of progressive modifications to Jonathan Edwards creative synthesis of revivalism and traditional Calvinism which had marked a new departure for theology in America (Kuklich,

1984; H. Smith, 1955). Taylor's fundamental modification of Edward's theology was to posit the will's power of contrary choice in order to guarantee human freedom and responsibility. Yet without rooting the will in the affections of man turned in upon himself, as Edwards had, Taylor offered a weak explanation for the universality of sin or the necessity of grace. But his categories rang true to the men of his age, an age in which democratic freedom and a revivalist call provided the driving forces.

Certainly there were other aspects to the story, for nineteenth century Evangelicalism had influential leaders other than Taylor, Finney and Beecher. Old School Presbyterianism continued its influence north and south, more traditional Congregationalists survived, calvinistic Baptists like Strong and Dagg resisted the arminian trends, and many ethnic conservatives remained relatively untouched (Holifield, 1978; G. Smith, 1985; Hood, 1980; Dever, 1987; Henry, 1951). But according to Timothy Smith's analysis of American Protestantism on the verge of the Civil War, "Revivalistic Calvinism," almost arminian in many of its manifestations, and "Evangelical Arminianism" dominated the Evangelical world. While Calvinism may not have been the "dying dogma" Smith suggests, certainly calvinist dominance was giving way under the pressure of Methodist expansion and internal modification (Smith, 1956, 31). Nineteenth century Evangelicalism had a consensus; but it was a theologically fluid and contested consensus undergoing broad shifts toward arminian and liberal orientations.

Social Pressures

These theological changes did not occur in a vacuum. During the latter half of the nineteenth century a new social situation was emerging, characterized by mushrooming complexity and the loss of time-honored and tradition-bound ordering principles (Boller, 1969; Wiebe, 1967; May, 1959; Marty, 969; Carter, 1971; Lippman, 1934). According to the dominant model of sociological interpretation, modern society was witnessing a progressive displacement of religious institutions from the centers of power, and the replacement of religious functions with nonreligious alternatives (Berger, 1967; Wilson, 1966, 1982; Martin, 1978). The separation of church and state had created a situation in which the economic forces of industrial capitalism could establish a social base capable of sustaining human interaction and providing services without reference to supernatural forces. As industrialization created the modern city, people were moved from societies characterized by communal relations and sacred traditions to ones defined by rational and material procedures. Furthermore, the professionalizing of academia relegated the study of theology to a faculty or separate divinity school, structurally eliminating the possibility of theology exercising intellectual control over the academy (Vesey, 1965; Noll,

1986, 32-61; Marsden, 1983; Carpenter, 1987). This "secularization" of the social system progressively pushed religion to the margins of society, outside the public arena and within the private world of individuals and subcultures. No longer did religion provide the rational justification for the exercise of social power or the cosmic explanation for the material universe. Increasingly the world was explained and evaluated in technical, empirical and natural terms.

The impact of these social changes upon a religious culture that had achieved social dominance and carried a strong custodial ideal is apparent. A new wedge is being driven between religion and culture. Religious leaders and groups are becoming socially and intellectually marginalized, experiencing a loss of the deep social base in institutions of education and government that had supported them. In so far as this social base provides a "plausibility structure," as Peter Berger maintains, giving intellectual credence to religious belief, this social dislocation would be experienced as an intellectual crisis. One way of interpreting the Modernist-Fundamentalist controversies, therefore, is to see them as conflicts between two alternative responses to this crisis—accommodation or reaction. While Modernists attempted to absorb the cultural shocks by reinterpreting the tradition, Fundamentalists responded by resisting such reinterpretations (Marty, 1986; Hunter, 1983, 1987; Carter, 1956).

The result was the creation of what Martin Marty labeled a "two-party" system within American Protestantism, the more pluralistic and culture affirming churches and denominations engaging directly in the public arena under the banner of the social gospel and ecumenical Council of Churches, and the marginalized Fundamentalist churches becoming a socially disengaged private party (Marty, 1971). But this two-party division should not be misunderstood. Conservative religion was never as marginalized and the culturally dominant denominations were never as secularized as this depiction implies, nor was the separation between parties precise or complete. All churches, denominations and ethnic traditions functioned as tradition-reinforcing communities. While Fundamentalist churches may have provided a greater degree of resistance, all religious communities filtered the acids of modernity, often enabling quite traditional belief and practice to continue on a local level. Therefore, decisions about how to respond to modern developments never reduced into simple choices between churches, denominations or even parties within denominations (Marty, 1986; Wuthnow, 1988; Handy, 1955).

Conservative Coalitions

Nevertheless, between the Civil War and World War I two parties did emerge in American religion. Competing coalitions began to form, progressively polarizing religious life and producing the institutional and ideological divisions that have defined the twentieth century situation. In the North, contested appointments, heresy trials and the publication of polemical literature in various denominations climaxed with acerbic controversies in the two groups with the strongest conservative contingents, Baptists and Presbyterians. These Fundamentalists, as they were labeled by the opposition, mobilized to gain control of the denominational and educational institutions they believed were tolerating unacceptable departures from historic Christianity (Cole, 1931; Marsden, 1980; Russel, 1976). In the South, or the more ethnically isolated denominations, these internal controversies were less pronounced, and the conflicts that arose were normally concerned with the infiltration of liberalism or evolutionary naturalism into the larger educational system (Gatewood, 1969). Among the Holiness and Pentecostal traditions, cultural separation generally preceded the period of acerbic controversies and took a more behavioral and less theological turn (Smith, 1962; Jones, 1974).

But whatever the form, the fundamentalist experience decisively shaped the Evangelical mosaic. Modern American Evangelicalism, consequently, is constituted by those traditions and communities whose family resemblances, born out of shared nineteenth century experiences, were maintained and modified by opposition to twentieth century developments. It was these culture-resisting traditions that achieved the notable Evangelical resurgence of the postwar years, and in particular the following four.

Four Dominant Traditions:
Northern Fundamentalist Evangelicalism

At least one conservative tradition has exerted a dominant influence upon twentieth century Fundamentalist and Evangelical developments. Associated in the present day with the names of Graham, Ockenga, and Henry, and the Bible colleges and seminaries that trace their heritage to Fundamentalist precedents, this tradition has provided core leadership and institutions for both the Fundamentalist movement and the postwar Evangelical resurgence. The tradition itself is composite, involving an array of churches, schools, publishing houses and organizations. But its history can be traced, in large part, to the coalition formed between millenarian Dispensationalists and Old School Presbyterians during, and prior to, the Fundamentalist controversies of the North (hence its name, Northern Fundamentalist Evangelicalism).

While the Princeton men provided the most influential scholarly defence of Fundamentalist opposition to liberalism, the dispensational Bible Conferences and Institutes provided much of its popular base. In fact, a direct line of historical continuity can be traced from the World Christian Fundamentals Association (W.F.C.A), which provided organizational leadership for Fundamentalist activities in the 1920s, to the Bible Conferences of Niagara and Northfield, founded by D.L. Moody. One influential Fundamentalist leader, William Bell Riley, maintained that the leaders of the W.C.F.A.

> were among the natural and recognized successors, both in doctrinal views and educational endeavors, of Moody, Morehead, Brooks, Gordon and that whole generation of believing Bible students and teachers who had given birth to the Conferences at Niagara and Northfield, and to the Bible Institutes at Boston and Chicago (Sandeen, 1970, 246).

These men and this movement endeavored to preserve, in a rapidly changing situation, the distinguishing characteristics of nineteenth century Evangelicalism. Theirs was, consequently, a *Bible movement*, spawning Bible institutes, Bible colleges, Bible churches, and Bible conferences which articulated and defended Bible doctrines for Bible believers (Hatch, 1984; Webber, 1987). It was also an *evangelistic movement*, centered around the activities of D. L. Moody and his associates and concerned to produced christian workers from its Bible Institutes who would proclaim the old fashioned gospel in the face of liberal defection (Marsden, 128, 43-48; Findlay, 1969; Pollock, 1983). And it was a *holiness movement*, introducing and disseminating the modified perfectionism associated with the Keswick Conventions in England (Marsden, 1980, 74-80; Pollock, 1964; Stevensen, 1963; Waldvogel, 1979). Finally, it was a *millenarian movement*, pioneering the shift from 19th century postmillennial optimism to the premillennialism that came to dominate conservative Evangelical theology (Webber, 1987; Marsden, 1980, 43-71).

While premillennial eschatology may have been this tradition's most distinguishing characteristic, it was by no means the most important. Popular leadership of a widespread movement that attracted the cooperation of an intellectual institution like Old School Princeton required an ability to form coalitions; and these coalitions, albeit forged in opposition to contemporary developments, were based upon a perceived unity in the preservation of an Evangelical heritage. Tensions between Reformed orthodoxy and the perfectionist and premillennial innovations of the Bible Conference movement eventually produced divisions among Northern Fundamentalists. But the coalition between Old School Presbyterians and popular premillenial revivalism was essential to the success of Fundamentalist concerns (Marsden, 1980; 1987, 31-32).

While the originality of nineteenth century Princeton in defining the Fundamentalist doctrine of Scripture has often been overrated (Noll, 1983, 34-45), the influence of Princeton as the intellectual center of emerging Fundamentalism can hardly be overemphasized. J. Gresham Machen resisted the novelties of popular Fundamentalism and B.

B. Warfield strenuously criticized the perfectionist drift of nineteenth century Evangelicalism (Stonehouse, 1954; Warfield, 1931, 1932; Russel, 1976). But Machen's *Christianity and Liberalism* (Machen,1923) provided a classic statement of the issues for Fundamentalist contenders and Warfield's articles on inspiration became the standard for generations of conservative Evangelicals (Warfield,1927). The subsequent development of American Evangelical history and theology, therefore, cannot be understood apart from the continuing influence of the Princeton men and their theological paradigm. The coalition formed between these conservative Presbyterians and participants in the Bible and Prophecy Conference movement (mostly Presbyterian and Baptist) provided an influential center for the Fundamentalist movement and subsequent Evangelical resurgence.

Holiness-Pentecostal Tradition

While the Northern Fundamentalist Evangelical tradition provided a leadership core for Fundamentalist engagement, it did not comprise the whole movement. The Holiness and Pentecostal traditions, for example, manifested a parallel continuation of Evangelical distinctives in opposition to an accommodating culture. From an inconspicuous beginning in the home of Sarah Lankford and Phoebe Worral Palmer, holiness teaching spread rapidly during the later half of the nineteenth century through the effective use of weekly meetings, holiness periodicals, revival camps and holiness conventions (Dieter,1980). Arising as a reforming movement within Methodism, it eventually resulted in divisions that produced the Church of the Nazarene, Pilgrim Holiness Church, The Wesleyan Church, Free Methodist Church, The Church of God (Anderson, Indiana), and others (Smith, 1962). It also provided the theological categories and historical context for American Pentecostalism, and influenced the spread of perfectionism throughout the entire popular Evangelical culture of the late nineteenth century (Smith,1956; Dayton,1987).

The effective use of class and camp meetings, as well as the persistent appeal to classic Wesleyan theology, mark the movement as a conservative reaction to the drift of enculturated Methodism. It provided a popular response to the modernist accommodations of late nineteenth century Methodism, just as biblicist, revivalist, and probably millenarian as the more calvinistic Northern Fundamentalism, but with a history and theology that made it a different tradition (Dieter, 1980, 129-30; Smith, 1962; Chiles, 1965).

In conserving traditional Wesleyan distinctives and extending them into the changing historical situation, however, the holiness movement also introduced innovations. Elevating holiness to the status of an institutional focus offers one striking example. But just as significant was Phoebe Palmer's modification of perfectionist doctrine itself.

Moving beyond tensions within Wesley's teaching, Mrs. Palmer unequivocally affirmed the possibility of immediate sanctification by faith. She applied the revivalist call for conversion to the experience of sanctification, replacing perfection as a distant end by perfection as an immediately available beginning to a new stage of Christian experience (Dieter, 1980, 18-31).

This two-stage theory also supplied the theological framework for Pentecostalism, another important conservative tradition emerging during the period of countermodern Fundamentalism (Hollenweger, 1972; Bruner, 1960). While both Wesleyan and Reformed strains of Pentecostalism can be traced, the movement emerged from a culture permeated with perfectionist teachings when the second stage of Christian experience was identified with the baptism of the Spirit and the sign of speaking in tongues. The Kansas Bible School of Charles Parham and the Azusa Street Revivals of Charles Seymor may have provided an historical beginning for American Pentecostalism (Nichol, 1966); but the rapid spread of Pentecostal experience through perfectionist circles reveals a close connection between the outbreak of glossolalia and the Holiness tradition. In his masterful analysis of the roots of Pentecostalism, Donald Dayton identifies this process with the emergence of a "fourfold pattern" of thought and practice. Encapsulated in Christian and Missionary Alliance founder A.B. Simpson's description of Jesus as "Saviour, Sanctifier, Healer and Coming King," the pentecostal pattern bears a striking resemblance to the distinguishing characteristics of broader nineteenth century Evangelicalism. Through an intense biblical literalism that derives its paradigm for Christian experience from the narrative passages of Acts, Pentecostals maintained and extended the biblicist, conversionist ("Saviour"), perfectionist ("Sanctifier, Healer") and millenarian ("Coming King") emphases of the Evangelical tradition (Dayton, 1987; Waldvogel, 1977; Hollenweger, 1972).

Pentecostalism also participated in the same countermodern orientation that characterized Northern Fundamentalism and the Holiness Churches. The behavioral boundaries established by the practice of glossolalia magnified this cultural separation, and even produced tensions between Pentecostalism and the Holiness tradition out of which it emerged (Anderson,1979; Quebedeaux,1983). Certainly its unique extension of nineteenth century distinctives has enabled it to form an historical tradition that has maintained its own identity while still associating with the twentieth century Fundamentalist and Evangelical mosaic.

Reformed Confessionalism

Two confessionalist communities of recent ethnic origin often identified with the Evangelical mosaic are the Missouri Synod Lutherans and the Christian Reformed Church of the American Midwest. While conservative Lutherans have maintained a cultural distance that has allowed only incidental participation in American Evangelical concerns (Rudnick, 1966), the influence of the Dutch Reformed upon the Evangelical mosaic has been much more significant. From the major Evangelical publishing houses of Eerdmans and Zondervan, to influential thinkers like Kuyper, Van Til, Berkhof and Berkouwer, the Dutch Reformed have exerted an influence well beyond their numbers.

Yet their history as an immigrant community with strict confessional boundaries has also produced a sense of cultural distance from American Evangelicalism. During the late nineteenth and early twentieth centuries—a period of large scale immigration and significant struggle over Americanization—ethnic identity and American culture were often in tension. And because of the fundamentally religious nature of community identity, public debates assumed theological form and occurred, for the most part, in religious periodicals. On the basis of an extensive study of these periodicals, James Bratt has identified three mentalities within the Christian Reformed Church of this period: the culturally engaging and optimistic "Positive Calvinists", the conservative and pietistic "Confessionalists" and the "Antithetical Calvinists," whose opposition to American culture and non-Reformed theology assumed a strident tone (Bratt,1978, 95-113).[8] But in spite of their differences, these Reformed Dutchmen shared a common history in the conservative Calvinist secessions of nineteenth century Netherlands and a common commitment to preserving their Reformed identity in America.

Therefore they shared, in varying degrees, two common enemies: American "Methodism"—the pragmatic and arminian tendencies that had come to dominate Evangelical religion, and American "Modernism"—the departures from Reformation orthodoxy infiltrating the Evangelical Protestant Church. While Dutch Reformed anti-Methodism separated them from American Evangelicals, their anti-Modernism drew them together.[9] In this regard they occupied a position similar to the Old School Presbyterians, who resisted the premillennial and perfectionist teachings of popular Fundamentalism while joining hands in opposition to liberal encroachment. It is not surprising, therefore, to find the 1918 Synod of the Christian Reformed Church condemning the dispensational premillennialism of Harry Bultema, while encouraging common action with erring brethren like him against modernism. Nor is it surprising to find the 1922 Synod engaged in a vociferous heresy trial of a Calvin Old Testament Professor on the ground of his higher critical views of Scripture. Nor, finally, is it surprising to find the primary points of cooperative engagement with Fundamentalist causes occurring through the Reformed connection with Princeton and the seceding Westminster.

Echoing the conclusion of James Bratt's extensive study, the

Christian Reformed Church of the American Midwest represents an "ethnically separate," theologically Reformed, "elaboration of the Fundamentalist program" (Bratt, 1978, 276). A parallel countermodernism, biblicism and confessional piety provided sufficient family resemblances to enable the Dutch Reformed to become an ethnically distinct member of the Evangelical Mosaic during the period of transition from nineteenth century heritage to twentieth century Fundamentalist experience.

Southern Evangelicalism

There also emerged during the later half of the nineteenth century a distinctive southern Evangelicalism, embedded in a conservative culture. In contrast to the North where social modernization and theological liberalism pushed conservatives into a defensive, marginalized position, the identification of southern region and conservative religion enabled nineteenth century religious distinctives to be preserved within a culturally dominant Evangelicalism. It created a geographical space in which Evangelical religion could thrive, somewhat isolated from the developments in northern culture. Besides the Southern Baptist Convention, now numbering more than fourteen million members, the southern states became a natural home for the mushrooming Holiness and Pentecostal tradition, dispensational Fundamentalism, and conservative Presbyterians and Methodists. It is no mere coincidence, therefore, that the postwar resurgence of Evangelical religion has paralleled the growth and expanding influence of the southern "Sun-Belt" (Marty, 1987; Wacker, 1986; Harrel, 1981).

Certainly the differences between regions that have led to differences in religion predate the Civil War. Even the impact of Awakening revivalism, while determinative in both cultures, was different. In the North a complex set of established institutions forced revivalism, in the course of its development, to infiltrate existing and often resistant structures. Revivalism revitalized Congregationalism, influenced and divided Presbyterianism, magnified Baptist and Methodist influences, and generally moved the whole culture in more conversionist and perfectionist directions. In the South, however, Baptist dominance was more rapidly and decisively achieved, resulting in a more homogenous and uncontested religious style. That religious style, in turn, was more pietistic than its northern counterpart, paralleling Evangelical religion on the frontier. Generally speaking, a more homogenous and less institutionally complex southern culture aided the spread of a revivalist religion that achieved an almost uncontested nineteenth century Evangelical hegemony (Hill, 1980; Matthews, 1977; Boles, 1972).

With the sacrifices and suffering of the Civil War a conservative identity was more deeply engraved in the religious South. Because the Evangelical church was at thecenter of southern culture it was called upon to defend the war between the States—including and especially the practice of slavery. In the process it became even more entrenched. It was defined and defended in opposition to a northern society where the inroads of liberalism and cultural decay were believed to abound (Matthews, 1977; Baily, 1964; Hill,1980).

The years following the Civil War witnessed increasing modernization in northern society, especially in its institutional centers of power. Southern culture and religion, on the other hand, were moving in almost opposite directions. Regional patriotism, a rural agrarian economy, the absence of serious foreign or heretical contingents, a pervasive religious style and a broad consensus on major values and concerns enabled the South to resist northern trends for many years. The result was a conservative southern Evangelicalism, culturally dominant, but separated from northern centers of power and therefore, adopting a countermodern orientation parallel to the other traditions within the Evangelical mosaic (Hill, 1980).

From Fundamentalist Experience to Evangelical Resurgence:
Fundamentalist Pattern, Fundamentalist Image

The twentieth century witnessed the emergence of a new religious situation. Within the context of an undergirding social base and overarching religious consensus, denominations had provided nineteenth century Americans with their primary means of religious identification. But with the loss of this social base and the consensus it supported, Evangelical identity was progressively relocated. It was relocated outside the northern mainline denominations and within those traditions and communities that maintained their conversionist heritage by means of a countermodern orientation. This relocation reshaped the Evangelical mosaic, introducing a fundamentalist pattern that constricted Evangelical identity.

The fundamentalist pattern, furthermore, corresponded to a fundamentalist image. Conservative Evangelicals were often construed as outmoded and obscurantist, clinging to ancient traditions or developing bizarre innovations in isolation from mainstream culture. Symbolizing this image were the much publicized denominational battles and the even more publicized evolution controversies, climaxing in the infamous "Monkey Trial" in Dayton, Tennessee—a media event that pitted three-time candidate for President and renowned Presbyterian layman,William Jennings Bryan, against the American Civil Liberties Union and its eminent lawyer, Clarence Darrow. "It would be difficult to overestimate the impact of 'the Monkey Trial'. . . in transforming Fundamentalism", argues the movement's historian, George Marsden. For "after the summer of 1925 the voices of ridicule were raised so loudly that many moderate Protestant conservatives quietly dropped support of the cause rather than be embarrassed by association" (Marsden,1980,

184, 191).
Certainly the image of Fundamentalism as outmoded and obscurantist, rooted in a rural and religious way of life that could not be maintained under the spotlight of modern scientific rationality, controlled interpretation of the movement for years (Cole, 1931; Furniss, 1954; Hofstadter, 1962). Many interpreters, therefore, failed to perceive the power of these conservative traditions, both the powerful following they represented and their power to maintain Evangelical belief in the modern world. As a result, the post World War II resurgence of an Evangelicalism rooted in turn-of-the-century Fundamentalism caught many by surprise.

In 1925 H. L. Mencken was nailing the lid on the coffin of southern Fundamentalism (Marsden, 1980, 184-195). Yet in 1976, after the election of a "born again" Southern Baptist to the Presidency, *Time Magazine* was proclaiming "The Year of the Evangelical". In that same year, Martin Marty was drawing a new religious map, one which recognized that "Evangelical," "Fundamentalist" and "Pentecostal" labels provide religious identity to a majority of Americans (Marty, 1976). Four years earlier Dean Kelley was pointing to what has become a commonplace observation: the astounding growth of disciplined and culture-resisting churches and the declining membership of the more inclusive mainline had altered the cultural balance of power (Kelley, 1972). Apparently the Fundamentalist coffin was prematurely shut. The fundamentalist image had produced a separation from centers of cultural power that distanced these traditions from sympathetic understanding. But the fundamentalist pattern of cultural resistance and relative separation had become a prelude to success.

Separation and Success, Relocation and Resurgence

Separation, however, does not designate only one relationship to culture. Several kinds and degrees of separation were represented in the Evangelical mosaic between the years of cultural defeat and cultural resurgence. Southern Evangelicalism, and the isolation of smaller ethnic communities like the Christian Reformed Church, represented a socially supported separation from external cultures, maintained by geographical distance and relatively uncontested internal cohesion. The separation of Northern Fundamentalism, on the other hand, was of a more internally contested kind. But even here, separation took several forms. Some Northern Fundamentalists, like the General Association of Regular Baptists (1932), the Independent Fundamental Churches of America (1930) or the Orthodox Presbyterian Church (1936), established a clear and decisive separation from inclusive denominational structures soon after it became evident their efforts for institutional control had been defeated. Others, like William Bell Riley, President of Northwestern Bible College and a powerful leader among Northern

Baptists in Minnesota, achieved regional separation by establishing control of a geographical area within an inclusive denomination. Many others maintained a de facto separation by pastoring a Fundamentalist church and participating in the non-denominational network of Northern Fundamentalism (Carpenter, 1984, 38-60; Marsden, 1987, 31-52).

Since the mainline denominations were inclusive, they contained within themselves a diversity of theological and cultural perspectives, allowing many conservative Evangelicals to remain within them, and even to establish institutions which voiced their concerns and served their constituencies. Northern Baptist Seminary in Chicago (1913) and Eastern Baptist in Philadelphia (1923), for example, were established to provide more conservative theological instruction within the Northern Baptist denomination several years before the separation of Conservative Baptists (in 1946) and the founding of Denver Conservative Baptist Seminary (in 1950) (Shelley, 1981). While the fundamentalist patterning of the Evangelical mosaic separated Evangelicals from centers of cultural power and relocated Evangelical identity within a conservative party of American Protestantism, the process of separation took many forms and occurred over an extended period.

But whatever the form, separation was often a means to success. While mainline Protestantism was experiencing a "Religious Depression"during the second and third decades of the twentieth century, marked by a loss of momentum and monetary investment, the constitutive traditions of the emerging Evangelical mosaic were experiencing unimpeded growth—a pattern that has continued throughout the century (Handy, 1984, 185).

> Nothing is more striking than the astonishing reversal in the position occupied by the churches and the role played by religion in American life which took place before the new century was well under way. By the 1920s, the contagious enthusiasm which had poured into the Student Volunteer Movement, the Sunday School Movement, the Men and Religion Forward Movement, the Layman's Missionary Movement, the Interchurch World Movement, and other organized activities of the churches had largely evaporated (Handy, 1984, 206).

But could it be, as Joel Carpenter suggests, that "the Evangelical fervor kindled in the Student Volunteer Movement had not died; it had only changed its institutional base from the old-line denominations to the myriad local, regional, and national organizations of the Fundamentalists and other Evangelicals"? (Carpenter, 1984, 32). Certainly the evidence would suggest this conclusion.

Between 1926 and 1940, for example, the Assemblies of God (in the Pentecostal tradition) grew from 47,950 to 98,834, the Church of the Nazarene (Holiness tradition) from 63,558 to 165,532, and the Southern Baptist Convention (Southern Evangelicalism) from one-and-one-half to nearly five million. The expansion of Northern Fundamentalism's network of Bible colleges, missionary organizations and publications was just as dramatic. While the number of missionaries supported by the American Baptists (508) remained unchanged between 1930 and 1940, the China Inland Mission, under Fundamentalist control, sent out 629 new missionaries from 1930 to 1936, to raise the total in the field to 1400. Many, if not most, of these missionaries were being sent by the expanding Bible Colleges of Northern Fundamentalism, with total enrollment in their 70 schools doubling between 1929 and 1940. Moody Bible Institute alone sent out 550 new missionaries during the thirties. Nor were these Bible Institutes training only missionaries. By the mid-1930s Gordon College had trained 100 of the pastors in greater Boston and 48 out of 96 Baptist clergymen in New Hampshire. W.B. Riley's Northwestern had placed 75 Baptist pastors in Minneapolis, a virtual monopoly, while R.A. Torrey's Bible Institute of Los Angeles had located 180 alumni in California. These schools, their alumni and supporters were sponsoring Bible conferences, radio programs and publications that reached thousands, providing a growing institutional network for a vigorous popular movement (Ibid.,16-34).

At the center of this resurgent Fundamentalism was an evangelistic impulse. The "Old Fashioned Revival Hour" of Charles Fuller, broadcasting to 456 stations and an estimated 20 million listeners by 1942, combined with a plethora of regional programs like Martin Dehaan's "Radio Bible Class", Donald Grey Barnhouse's "Bible Study Hour" and Moody Bible Institute's KWBI, to proclaim a conservative Evangelical message to a responsive popular culture. Charles Fuller also stood out as the most effective crusade evangelist of his day, drawing as many as 15,000 people to one 1937 Chicago Rally and 32,000 to meetings in the Boston Garden in 1941 (Fuller, 1972). But he was not alone. The New England Fellowship, for example, a group of more than 500 cooperating pastors who provided much of the leadership for the National Association of Evangelicals, sponsored 50 evangelistic campaigns and 700 conferences in 1935 alone (Carpenter, 1984, 1986).

During the forties Youth for Christ staged hundreds of Saturday night rallies that drew thousands of young people to hear contemporary music and captivating messages from evangelists like Percy Crawford, Torrey Johnson and the young Billy Graham (Shelley, 1986). Eventually these and other Youth for Christ evangelists would form the Billy Graham Evangelistic Association, Far East Gospel Crusade, Greater Europe Mission, Trans-World Radio, and World Vision International, and join with a broad range of emerging missionary organizations like Campus Crusade for Christ, Navigators, Wycliff Bible Translators, and the missionary outreaches of Southern Baptists, Assemblies of God, and the Church of the Nazarene to become the mainsprings of what one informed commentator has labeled "the 25 Unbelievable Years" of postwar Evangelical expansion (Winter, 1970).

A New "Evangelicalism"

Postwar America witnessed the emergence of a new phase of Fundamentalist history, distinguished by greater cultural engagement and signaled by the appearance of a new core of leadership and institutions. Billy Graham and his association provided a respected and successful evangelistic focus to the movement (Pollock, 1979); the launching of *Christianity Today* (1956), under the editorship of Carl Henry, created a forum for informed theological discussion and public communication; the founding of Fuller Theological Seminary (1947), with men like Ockenga, Carnell and Henry, and the formation of the Evangelical Theological Society (1949), introduced new intellectual centers for Evangelical reflection; and the formation of the National Association of Evangelicals (1942), representing 40 denominations and more than two million members by 1956, gave the movement its most comprehensive institutional framework. Within and around these leaders and organizations, generated by a resurgent Northern Fundamentalism, a broad range of conservatives began to achieve a new sense of cultural placement (Murch, 1956; Shelley, 1967; Marsden, 1987).

But at the heart of this movement was a tension, a turning in two directions. On the one hand, Billy Graham, the National Association of Evangelicals, *Christianity Today* and Fuller Seminary were expressions of Fundamentalism. As James Deforest Murch's official history of the National Association of Evangelicals contends, the N.A.E. was engaged in developing alternative power structures to represent the interests of its conservative constituency over against the Federal and World Council of Churches. Evangelical leaders were mobilizing constituencies and forming organizations to enable them to guard their use of the airwaves, accredit their schools, expand their evangelistic gains, and insure the fair and forceful representation of their point of view in the public arena—in other words, to resist and overcome social marginalization (Murch, 1956). These people and institutions were Fundamentalist.

But these leaders of resurgent Fundamentalism were also engaged in a criticism of Fundamentalism, a criticism that would eventually result in divisions within the movement. Possibly the classic statement of this position came from the pen of Harold Ockenga in a *Christianity Today* article entitled "Resurgent Evangelical Leadership" (Ockenga, 1960). Insisting upon the common historical origin and theological identity of resurgent Evangelicalism and turn-of-the-century Fundamentalism, both of which he equated with "orthodoxy," Ockenga indicted mid-century Fundamentalism for failure to impact its culture. In contrast to the Fundamentalist program of separation, which led to fragmentation and isolation, a "resurgent evangelical leadership" called for a strategy of Evangelical *cooperation* and denominational *infiltration* in an effort to bring "revival" and "reform" to church and society. In a series of earlier writings, Carl Henry shared with Ockenga in pioneering this redefinition and redirection of the movement. From *The Uneasy Conscience of Modern Fundamentalism* (1947a) to *Evangelical Responsibility in Contemporary Theology* (1957a), he charted a course for mid-century Evangelicalism between the "modernist revision" and the "fundamentalist reduction." Both the modernist denial of supernatural revelation and the separatist ecclesiology of postwar Fundamentalism came under heated fire (Henry, 1957a,b; 1947a,b).

This new Evangelicalism, therefore, was both an expression of resurgent Fundamentalism and a criticism from within aimed at redirecting the movement. Henry, Ockenga and other participatory interpreters attempted to resolve the tension between continuity and discontinuity by constructing a history of Evangelical development that affirmed its essential continuity with "classic" Fundamentalism—equated with orthodoxy and Evangelicalism—while distancing themselves from certain reductions or accretions in the early twentieth century development. The new Evangelicalism, therefore, was not really new, but rather a renewal of a broader, more culturally engaging conservatism that affirmed Evangelical cooperation without theological compromise (Nash, 1963; Carnell, 1959; Erickson, 1968; Ockenga, 1960; Grounds, 1956).

The problem with this historical interpretation, however, is that it fails to appreciate the *internal* and *unstable* nature of the Fundamentalist and Evangelical tensions. The American Evangelical mosaic of the early twentieth century had adopted a conserving, culture-resisting posture in response to specific pressures and had maintained its identity by means of separation. The fundamentalist pattern, therefore, influenced both institutional and theological development. To overcome separation through a positive policy of cooperative engagement was to strike a blow at the heart of Fundamentalist identity. Of course, Evangelicalism also contained—at its heart—a conversionist commitment to engage and transform culture.

What occurred in postwar Evangelicalism, apparently, was a shift in emphasis from the conservative to the conversionist impulse, or an attempt to integrate them, at a time when evangelistic success was building an expanding social base and inspiring new confidence. While this conservative-conversionist tension can be conceptually integrated through a philosophy of cooperative engagement *without compromise*, the practice of cooperation and engagement carries with it the risk of change. As astute observers have suggested, there is a "cognitive bargain" entailed in engagement, a risk that the attempt to transform culture will put one in a position to be transformed by it (Nelson, 1987; Hunter, 1983, 1987).

At least the separation-engagement tension as it existed within mid-century Fundamentalism proved historically unstable, resulting in divisions over the issues of cooperation and compromise. The first of these was the emerging Fundamentalist and Evangelical divide, described by one historian as "the dual alignment of modern Fundamentalism" (Gaspar, 1963). Probably a more accurate typology is provided by Richard Quebedeaux (1974), who identified a broad tripartite division within the resurgent movement: the separatist dispensational Fundamentalists, including but not limited to those aligned with the American Council of Christian Churches (Dollar, 1973; Woodbridge, 1969; McIntire, 1944; Rice, 1965); the more open dispensational Fundamentalists, many of whom have not aligned with the A.C.C.C. or the National Association of Evangelicals (Lightner, 1965, 1979; Walvoord, 1957; Dobson, 1985, 1986); and the cooperative Evangelicals of Fundamentalist origin aligned with the N.A.E (Murch, 1956; Marsden, 1987).

A New "New Evangelicalism"

Evangelical history did not stabilize, however, into Fundamentalist and Evangelical contingents. As resurgence brought greater cultural respectability, the more public and powerful Evangelicalism became larger and more internally diverse. In part, this internal differentiation resulted from developments within the Evangelical communities themselves—as a new generation continued to push the boundaries of theological identity outward. But it had other important sources as well. The strategy of denominational infiltration pursued by N.A.E. aligned Evangelicals converged with the rise of mainline renewal movements to produced new Evangelical streams, ones that joined the postwar resurgence without sharing its fundamentalist experience. Furthermore, the strategy of cooperative engagement brought together in the public arena an increasingly broad range of communities and traditions, demanding recognition of the internally diverse nature of even fundamentalist-patterned Evangelicalism.

As these constitutive traditions evolved, this diversity posed increasing problems for unified action and description. It was becoming evident that Evangelicalism was not a single entity passing through Fundamentalist, Evangelical and New Evangelical phases, but a complex set of communities and traditions passing through parallel stages, and joining in the public arena with denominational conservatives who had arrived at a similar place in different ways. This new situation required a new label, and since the "New Evangelicalism" of Ockenga, Henry and Graham had become established in public discourse as "Evangelicalism" plain and simple, Donald Bloesch (and Richard Quebedeaux after him) reappropriated the "New Evangelical" label, and this broad and internally complex Evangelicalism became the new "New

Evangelicalism" (Bloesch, 1973; Quebedeaux, 1974, 37-41).

Dwelling In and Breaking Out

This New Evangelicalism became the focus of heated controversy, however, for the generation of "young Evangelicals" (Quebedeaux, 1974) breaking out of traditional boundaries were perceived by many first generation Evangelicals, and those who continued to operate under the Fundamentalist banner, as calling into question commitments they considered fundamental. From the perspective of Ockenga and Henry, Evangelicalism differed from Fundamentalism in spirit and strategy, but not in basic theology. In fact, shared theological commitments forged and refined in opposition to modernism had provided the explicit theological basis for organizations of cooperative engagement like the N.A.E., *Christianity Today* and Fuller Seminary (March, 1956). Of particular sensitivity was the doctrine of Scripture, since it had been the primary source and symbol of conservative resistance to the inroads of liberal theology.

Therefore, when Harold Lindsell published his *Battle for the Bible* (1976), exposing conceptions of biblical authority which had developed within influential Evangelical institutions since the Second World War, it dropped like a bombshell upon the Evangelical world. He touched a sensitive nerve, and brought into focus a pattern of departure from previous perspectives of biblical authority occurring throughout the Evangelical mosaic. The departure consisted, according to Lindsell, in the denial of a creedally guarded commitment to the verbal, plenary inspiration and inerrancy of Scripture. Departure from this position was identified at Fuller Theological Seminary, once the educational flagship of postwar Evangelicalism, at seminaries and schools of higher education in the Southern Baptist Convention, especially Southern and Southwestern, and within the Christian Reformed Church. In his sequel, the list expanded to include, among others, The Church of the Nazarene, the Assemblies of God, and the N.A.E.. Certainly every dominant tradition within the American Evangelical mosaic was involved in Lindsell's battle (Lindsell, 1976, 1979).

Various attempts to analyze this battle have occurred, but the important point for the purpose of this study, is that American Evangelicalism in the seventies reached "an impasse" on the interpretation of biblical authority (Johnston, 1979).[10] Some institutions and denominations developed new doctrinal statements or position papers designed to include a range of opinion on the subject (Fuller Seminary, Christian Reformed Church, Wesleyan Theological Society). Others revised doctrinal statements to exclude broader interpretations (Assemblies of God), sponsored conferences to clarify and defend traditional doctrine (International Council on Biblical Inerrancy), or mobilized constituencies to gain control of educational institutions (Southern Baptist Convention). Neither the intensity of the debate, nor the employment of political structures of power, however, could reduce the diversity of opinion that had developed within the Evangelical mosaic. Inerrancy, and the concept of biblical authority it represented, had become a contested concept, and a symbolic boundary of modern Evangelicalism was being moved (Hunter, 1987, 157-213).

Other contested issues emerged on the boundary line of Evangelical identity as well, most notably the role of women in the church and appropriate strategies for social engagement. Because of the controlling role of Scriptural authority within Evangelicalism, these debates have been consistently argued in terms of biblical warrant, and the diversity of perspectives on biblical authority has been matched by a diversity of opinions on these issues. But it is not the mere fact of diversity that merits attention. Rather, it is what this diversity signifies: the loss of clearly defined distinctions between a conservative religious movement and modern culture.

The seventies and eighties, for example, witnessed a wave of conservative protest against the breakdown of traditional values within American society, centered around issues associated with the feminist movement—sexual roles, abortion, the Equal Rights Amendment. But a growing diversity of Evangelical opinion has also developed during this period (Johnston, 1979, 48-76; Hunter, 1987, 76-154). Some leaders and constituencies within Evangelical communities have come to espouse "feminist" positions, fostering internal debate at a point of heated external conflict. The inevitable result is boundary confusion.

The pattern is the same in Evangelical approaches to political action. Emerging from a turbulent period of social criticism, and impacted by the national crises of Viet Nam, Watergate and the Civil Rights movement, a new voice was raised during the seventies against the "establishment" Evangelicalism of Graham and Henry (Quebedeaux, 1974, 1976; Dayton, 1976; Peirard, 1970; Hatfield, 1971, 1976; Wallis, 1976). An important early statement was the 1973 "Chicago Declaration," in which Evangelical pioneers of social criticism "confessed" and "acknowledged" Evangelical complicity in America's sinful power structures and the injustices they have perpetuated (Sider, 1974). This declaration, however, represents a serious modification of the personal/structural polarities which had defined the political boundaries of the Fundamentalist-Liberal debate over the "social gospel" (Carter, 1954; Moberg, 1972). It also conflicted with the political agenda of the Evangelical Christian Right, a powerful force in post-sixties America (Jorstad, 1981, 1987; Streiker, 1972; Wuthnow, 1983). Once again, public debate exacerbated boundary confusion in a complex and changing Evangelical mosaic (Johnston, 1979, 77-112; Hunter, 1987, 116-54; Fowler, 1982).

Converging Conservatisms

As the Evangelical mosaic expanded from within, incorporating beliefs and practices which had been previously excluded or marginalized, events in the larger culture were producing converging movements of conservative and evangelically oriented faith and practice. The sixties and seventies witnessed the emergence of a striking array of grass roots conservative lobbies and renewal movements that cooperated, interacted and sometimes identified with the Evangelical movement: The Good News Movement, "A Forum for Scriptural Christianity within the United Methodist Church" (Mickey, 1980); Presbyterians United for Biblical Concern and the Presbyterian Lay Committee (Hutcheson, 1981); Biblical Witness caucus, the "Word-in-Deed" evangelism movement and the Mercersburg Society of the United Churches of Christ (Fackre, 1973, 1984a); and the Fellowship of Evangelical Lutheran Laity and Pastors, for example. Permeating some of these movements, and providing groups and organizations of their own, were the proponents of charismatic renewal arising within virtually every Protestant denomination, and the Catholic Church as well (Quebedeaux, 1983; Jorstad, 1973).

Of course, the complexion and causal forces of these various groups is truly diverse; but their parallel emergence within a shared social situation, America during the sixties, and their convergence with the expanding Evangelical movement justifies certain interpretive observations. One is that these movements constitute a reaction. The liberalization of theology and practice among educational and denominational elites during the student radicalism of the sixties—in the much publicized "death-of-God" theologies and liberal social activity— produced, according to many interpreters, a conservative backlash. As the dismantling of traditional authorities in the early sixties gave way to a pervasive sense of loss, even chaos, denominations that identified with the cultural trends and offered no authoritative message were discredited. Many Christians reacted by asserting traditional distinctives, which often meant reasserting conservative opinions and sometimes converting to new forms of belief and practice (Hutcheson, 1981; Sweet, 1984; Bloesch, 1975).

Paul Mickey's *Essentials of Wesleyan Theology* exemplifies the former, while the journey of United Church of Christ theologian, Gabriel Fackre, to the status of "evangelical ecumenical" is an instance of the latter (Fackre, 1984a, 15-16). Fackre's comments upon that journey are, in fact, quite instructive:

> The more the much-touted worldliness of theology had taken hold in mainstream churches (and I did my share of such touting. . .), the clearer became the importance to us of the biblical witness to Jesus Christ....The sounding of strong biblical notes and

> the contesting of the acculturation of faith brought us into contact and then collegiality with others long known for these emphases, "the Evangelicals" (Ibid.).

By speaking of a relationship of "collegiality" with "the Evangelicals" Fackre indicates the new situation represented by this convergence of Evangelical resurgence and conservative renewal. Although influenced by the constitutive traditions of the Evangelical mosaic, and sometimes led by historically connected participants, the renewal movements were not *located in* those traditions. For many, participation in a fundamentalist-patterned tradition was not part of their experience, or the experience of their forbears. The Evangelical tradition with which they identified, therefore, was either a resurgent New Evangelicalism or a distant nineteenth century Evangelicalism, neither of which were interpreted in strict theological terms. Consequently, these renewal movement Evangelicals bear more distant family resemblances to the Evangelicalism of Henry, Ockenga and Graham, and the relationship between the two is ambivalent.

Consider, for example, the most numerous and pervasive of the renewal movements. As a phenomenon in the mainline Protestant denominations of America, the charismatic movement emerged in the early sixties, often under the influence of classic Pentecostal leaders—men like David Du Plessis, David Wilkerson, Demos Shakarian and Oral Roberts. But as a phenomenon located outside Pentecostalism, the movement acquired a distinct identity. As an extension of the fundamentalist-patterned Holiness movement among the socially marginalized, Pentecostalism carries into the present situation separate institutions, doctrinal statements and practices forged during the early twentieth century. But the charismatic movement exists, for the most part, as a network of loosely connected renewal groups within a wide variety of churches. Some analysts argue that the tendency among charismatics is to move in a biblicist and conversionist direction; but the unifying characteristics among the diverse charismatic groups are primarily experiential. Certainly the more fundamentalist distinctives of classic Pentecostalism are peripheral to the later movement (Quebedeaux, 1983; Spittler, 1976).

Resurgent Pentecostalism decisively influenced the emergence of the charismatic renewal movement, joined in its leadership, but did not determine its direction or encompass its extent. Nevertheless, resurgent Pentecostalism and the charismatic movement have been converging in the present day, and in their convergence are creating a new religious situation: a broader, internally differentiated Pentecostal and Charismatic movement that transcends, or at least crosses over, the divisions of previous generations. When Oral Roberts, who for two decades had been one of the premier leaders within American Pentecostalism, left the Pentecostal Holiness Church to join the United Methodists, while continuing to function as a central leader in the charismatic movement, he symbolized the joining of these streams in the religious swell of the new "New Evangelicalism" (Harrel, 1985).

A Changing Evangelical Mosaic

Clearly the Evangelical mosaic has continued to change shape over the years. During the nineteenth century, when a revivalistic Evangelical Protestantism established cultural dominance, an undergirding social base and overarching theological consensus enabled diverse traditions to cohere in a broadly unified mosaic. Calvinistic and arminian tensions were present, among others, but contained within a denominationally differentiated Evangelical consensus.

The changing social situation between the Civil War and World War I, however, shattered that consensus and reshaped the Evangelical mosaic. Under social and theological pressures new divisions emerged within and between denominations, defined by their different responses to the changing situation. The communities and traditions destined to exert a dominant influence upon modern Evangelicalism sought to maintain their Evangelical heritage by adopting a conservative, culture-resisting posture, while the historic, mainline denominations internalized the cultural trends by adopting an inclusive, or broad church, strategy. Hence the fundamentalist-patterned Evangelical mosaic, comprised of culture resisting denominations and culture resisting parties within denominations, was born—and born, one should add, in controversy. From its beginning, however, this Fundamentalist Evangelical mosaic contained diverse traditions—Northern Fundamentalist, Holiness-Pentecostal, Ethnic Reformed and Southern Evangelical—and it overlapped the conservative parties within historic denominations. Nevertheless, the Evangelical mosaic before the second half of the twentieth century was characterized by a fundamentalist pattern that fostered a sense of identity and preserved, in diverse forms, continuity with a nineteenth century heritage.

But the Evangelical mosaic was destined to change shape again. As these conservative communities successfully pursued their conversionist objectives they developed growing constituencies and adopted strategies that overcame their social marginalization. When a younger generation of leaders began to create programs and organizations that enabled new levels of Evangelical cooperation and cultural engagement, the tension between strategies of separation and infiltration produced conflict and division within the Fundamentalist world. "Fundamentalist" and "Evangelical" labels emerged for the first time, designating parties within or separations between these conservative communities.

Nor was this two-fold division (superimposed upon already existing denominational distinctives) the end. As the constitutive traditions of the Evangelical mosaic continued along the trajectories set by these strategies, becoming a dominant public force in America, an even greater degree of boundary expansion and internal diversification occurred. A new generation of post-sixties Evangelicals, pushing beyond traditional boundaries of conservative identity, joined with converging renewal movements to forge even broader behavioral and conceptual spaces.

Resurgent American Evangelicalism seems to be entering a time similar, in some respects, to late nineteenth century Evangelicalism. The boundaries of Evangelical identity have been progressively expanded to include points of view and practices that had once separated Fundamentalist Evangelicals from non-Evangelicals. Each of the constitutive traditions now contains within itself Fundamentalist, Fundamentalist Evangelical and New Evangelical constituencies, having shed the fundamentalist pattern as comprehensively definitive. Because of this expansion, converging renewal movements have found relationships of collegiality and even identity with the latest phases of the Evangelical movement. Boundary definition itself has become problematic, and this New Evangelicalism, while centered on the distinguishing characteristic of historic Evangelicalism—a biblicist, conversionist faith and practice—contains within itself a significant plurality of theological conceptions.

In this context, Karl Barth, too, has found a place.

NOTES

1. Robert Webber (1978b) has suggested a fourteen category typology; Cullen Murphy (1981), with help from Timothy Smith, has proposed a twelve "ring" description; and Mark Ellingsen (1988) has identified eleven Evangelical groupings. For a detailed listing of the diverse forms of conservative Evangelicalism in America, see Peipkorn (1979).

2. Contained in this brief description are both the pietistic "renewal" and the fundamentalist "conserving" emphases of the movement. When James Hunter (1987, 3-4) defines Evangelicalism as "the North American expression of theologically conservative Protestantism" he captures one basis for cooperation among Evangelicals and therefore, one essential aspect of Evangelical identity. But Evangelicalism, even Fundamentalist Evangelicalism, is not just conservative; it is also conversionist.

3. Although evaluated differently, a similar theological reduction is common among American Evangelicals (Gerstner, 1975; Lindsell, 1976; Schaeffer, 1985; Ockenga, 1978; Kantzer, 1978).

4. Johnston (1991) has just recently employed the concept of "family resemblences" to explain the nature of American Evangelicalism. But he has not related these family resemblences to a shared narrative history comprised of an evangelical heritage, fundamentalist experience and postwar resurgence.

The Identity of American Evangelicalism

5. Hunter (1983, 145-6) identifies "four major religious and theological traditions" within American Evangelicalism: Baptist, Holiness-Pentecostal, Reformational-Confessional and Anabaptist. Dayton (1985, 121-6) suggests three historical paradigms—Reformation, Awakening/Wesleyan, and Fundamentalist. Timothy Smith (1986, 1987), in contrast, speaks of "four historical Evangelical movements"—Methodist Arminianism, Puritan Calvinism, Pietism and the "Peace Churches." My own categorization, while recognizing the differences between more distinctively Reformed-Confessional, (Northern) Fundamentalist and Wesleyan (Holiness-Pentecostal) traditions, also attempts to acknowledge the cultural impact of the War between the States, ie., Southern Evangelicalism (mostly Baptist). The Anabaptist "Peace Churches" would then be included as a fifth, less dominant, tradition. Black Evangelicals, numerically and culturally significant, have been excluded because their narrative history requires another, quite different, story.

6. For a doctrinal statement of the nineteenth century Evangelical consensus, see the statement of the Evangelical Alliance contained in Jordan, 1982. Although European, Americans did participate in this Alliance.

7. Mead (1954) lists six distinguishing characteristics: anti-historical biblicism, the voluntary principle, the missionary principle, revivalism, pietism, and competition between denominations. Stoeffler (1965) describes "Evangelical Pietism" in terms of the primacy of inward experience, perfectionism, a non-scholastic, sometimes antirationalist biblicism, and opposition to established orthodoxy. Bebbington (1988), whose list of characteristics is closest to mine, identifies conversionism, activism, biblicism and crucicentrism as the fourfold priorities of Anglo-Saxon Evangelicalism.

8. For a somewhat parallel analysis of postwar developments, see Stob, 1957a,b,c, 1961, and Boomsma, 1979. Bratt actually idenitifies four types; but the fourth is located, for the most part, outside the Christian Reformed Church.

9. The "principial" or "antithetical" thinking of Abraham Kuyper provided the predominant theological language for Dutch Reformed antimodernism. Combined with a confessional conservatism, and utilized in the context of a culturally separated religious community, this method of conceptual description became an effective means of maintaining theological and social identity (Bratt, 1978; Jellema, 1957).

10. Important analyses of the debate include Lindsell, 1976, 1979; Johnston, 1979, 15-47; Price, 1980; Hunter, 1987, 19-49; Coleman, 1980; Pinnock, 1976; and Sheppard, 1977. For representative examples of Evangelical views, see Geisler, 1980, which includes the "Chicago Statement on Biblical Inerrancy"; Rogers, 1977, 1979; Carson, 1983, 1986; Beegle, 1973; Bromiley, 1970; Pinnock, 1984; Bloesch, 1978b; and Bush, 1980.

2

FUNDAMENTALIST EVANGELICALISM

Barth Reception within a Dominant Paradigm

As the preceding chapter sought to demonstrate, the constitutive traditions of conservative Evangelicalism all manifested, in some form, a fundamentalist pattern of opposition to modern social and theological developments. They endeavored to preserve what they perceived as essential Christianity by diligently defending fundamental doctrines, and Scriptural authority occupied a particularly sensitive epistemological role. Changes in theology and practice during the postwar resurgence of Evangelical religion, consequently, have typically assumed the form of reaction to, and movement beyond, an established Fundamentalism, and have revolved around the symbolic issues of cultural separation and biblical authority.

The reception of Barth, not surprisingly, has followed a similar pattern. Within the Northern Fundamentalist and Orthodox Reformed communities, for example, there has emerged, between the cultural shocks of the twenties and sixties, *a characteristic form of reception rooted in a predominant theological paradigm.* Established by Cornelius Van Til and propounded by Carl Henry, this Fundamentalist Evangelical paradigm has been maintained, for example, by Louis Berkhof, Fred Klooster, Gordon Clark, John Gerstner, J. Oliver Buswell, Robert Reymond, R. Laird Harris, Francis Schaeffer, Charles Ryrie, Roger Nicole, R. C. Sproul, and John Warwick Montgomery—a veritable Who's Who in the Orthodox Reformed and Northern Fundamentalist traditions. From this reformed center, furthermore, Fundamentalist Evangelical theology has shaped and influenced the reception of Barth throughout the entire Evangelical mosaic.

What are the distinguishing characteristics of this Fundamentalist Evangelical reception of Barth? It is, in the first place, "frankly polemical" (Van Til, 1946, 3). The aim is predominantly critical, and criticism tends to focus upon the controlling philosophical presuppositions to which Barth is supposedly held captive. Departures from orthodox doctrine are interpreted as speculative distortions of biblical truth under the influence of post-Kantian philosophy. Barth's idea of history, represented by the distinction between *Historie* and *Geschichte*, and his concept of revelation, with its denial of direct identity between biblical words and divine communication, provide the most common examples. But the consequences of his philosophical captivity are manifold: denial of verbal inspiration, loss of general revelation, a distorted order of salvation, and an unbiblical understanding of election. For some interpreters, in fact, Barth's presuppositions radically distort his entire theology. But even those who resist this critical extreme share the basic Fundamentalist Evangelical standard of judgment: a system of doctrine in substantial continuity with Reformed Orthodoxy, supported by means of a well-developed theory of rationality. Barth's departures from this rational, orthodox system are characterized by such recurrent labels as subjective, irrational, dialectical and existential.

In a sentence, Fundamentalist Evangelical reception of Barth is self consciously *orthodox* and decidedly *apologetic*.

One of the most notable characteristics of conservative Evangelicalism between the twenties and sixties has been the attention given to apologetic and prolegomenal concerns.[1] Although important differences of opinion exist on the most appropriate apologetic method, producing considerable intramural debate, Fundamentalist Evangelical theologians manifest a shared commitment to the demonstrable truthfulness of Christian theism. As Dr. Kenneth Kantzer has claimed in his own descriptive overview of Evangelical theology, "all argue ...that one must believe if he chooses to act in an intellectually responsible way" (Kantzer, 1975, 46). Of course, behaving in an intellectually responsible way might mean acting like an empiricist, a rationalist, a presuppositionalist, or some combination thereof; or it may require regeneration by divine election. But whatever the case, there is an appropriate understanding of rationality by which an effective apologetic may be conducted so that any reasonable person could be persuaded of the truth of biblical Christianity.

Among these apologists there also persists an orthodox self perception, which James Barr disputes and many label repristination, but which Fundamentalist Evangelicals confidently defend (Barr, 1980, 168). A classic statement is Carnell's *Case for Orthodox Theology* (1959). But the tendency to identify conservative Evangelicalism with orthodoxy is pervasive, not just among Christian Reformed and Orthodox Presbyterian confessionalists, but also among influential Baptist and Free Church leaders (Carnell, 1959; Nash, 1963, 14; Henry, 1957a; Kantzer, 1975). Nor is the claim a weak one. Just as the the Fundamentalist movement in America enabled its participants to maintain substantial continuity with their Evangelical heritages, so the Fundamentalist Evangelical movement of the later twentieth century has enabled its participants to continue the preservation of those orthodox traditions. Of course, as chapter one argued, novelties and discontinuities were introduced along the way; but these modified rather than controverted the more basic continuity.

In the material that follows a diverse range of Fundamentalist Evangelical theologians will be analyzed as representatives of a characteristic type of Barth reception, rooted in a characteristic theology—theologians as apparently diverse as presuppositional Calvinist, Cornelius Van Til, reformed Baptist, Carl Henry, empiricist Lutheran, John Warwick Montgomery, and non-denominational Dispensationalist, Charles Ryrie. In chapters three and four, then, departures from this basic Fundamentalist Evangelical paradigm will be discussed.

Cornelius Van Til
Establishing an Interpretive Paradigm

Without a doubt the history of Barth's reception by American Evangelicals must begin with Dr. Cornelius Van Til, Professor of Apologetics for more than forty years at Westminster Theological Seminary. Not only was he one of the earliest, most prolific and well read of Fundamentalist Evangelical interpreters, Van Til was also the most influential.[2] He held an important post at an influential institution during a crucial period of time, and exerted a significant influence from this locus in the Evangelical matrix. Called to Princeton Seminary to teach apologetics just prior to the fateful reorganization of that institution's governing boards in 1929, Van Til joined J. Gresham Machen, Oswald Allis, and Robert Dick Wilson in the decision to resign their posts and found Westminster Theological Seminary. Because of the strong tradition of conservative scholarship represented by these men and their forebears at Old School Princeton, Westminster Seminary was uniquely positioned to exert a disproportionate intellectual influence upon Northern Fundamentalism.[3] And Cornelius Van Til was one of its most influential teachers. Among his students were Harold Ockenga, Carl McIntire, Francis Schaeffer, J. Edward Carnell, John Gerstner, Ned Stonehouse, Paul Jewett, and Edmund Clowney. Carl Henry, though not a student, dedicated an important early volume to him in recognition of his influence (Henry, 1946).

At Westminster, Van Til became a primary agent for a major intellectual shift in philosophy and apologetics within twentieth century American Evangelicalism, from the evidentialist apologetic of Butler, Hodge and Warfield, dependent upon some form of empiricist epistemology, to what has become known as presuppositionalism (Wells, 1989; Sproul, 1984; Van Til, 1948d).The essential insight of presuppositionalism is idealist: the manifold diversity of reality requires conceptual ordering to be meaningfully experienced, and the principles of order must logically precede that experience (Van Til, 1955b). This means that the "facts" of experience are unintelligible apart from their relation to an interpretive framework. And since one must "presuppose" an interpretive scheme, however basic, in order to experience reality in a meaningful way, Van Til argues for the rational validity of presupposing the Christian framework. By this he means the Reformed faith as revealed in Scripture and accurately interpreted by the Reformed creeds and classic Reformed theologians (Van Til, 1969a, 5; 1955a, 78-79).

Moreover, Van Til argues that true knowledge is possible only on the presupposition of divine revelation. If meaning is context dependent and context is infinite, then only God can determine ultimately what anything means. Only an infinite and omniscient Being, who sovereignly controls "whatsoever comes to pass," can know in an absolutely comprehensive way; and only if this God reveals what he knows is true knowledge possible. For Van Til, therefore, the mind of God, revealed in Scripture and creation, is the source and norm for all knowledge. Every fact is what it is by virtue of God's interpretation and control of it, and man's interpretation, if valid, must be a reinterpretation according to the divine plan—a thinking of God's thought after him. "To know truly," Van Til insists, "man's thought must be receptively reconstructive of the revelation of God" (Van Til, 1961, 5; 1955a,b).

Thus Van Til, following Herman Bavinck, endeavors to acknowledge God as the *Principium Essendi* of knowledge (1949, 9). He also considers this approach the only way to challenge the sinful assumption of human autonomy underlying all heterodox, or non-Reformed, thought. In this opinion he extends, in a particular direction, the "principial" thinking of Abraham Kuyper that has exerted such a dominant influence upon Dutch Calvinism.

For Van Til, principial thinking means that all human thought begins with one of two antithetical presuppositions: one either assumes the autonomy of man or his absolute dependence upon God. There is no middle ground. If one acknowledges the sovereignty of God as basic for all thought and life, then the method of knowing that results from this "starting point" is receptive reinterpretation of divine revelation. But if one does not consistently assume this presupposition, then some form of human autonomy must be introduced, undermining the very possibility of knowledge. Any man who constructs an edifice of knowledge without prior recognition of the foundation upon which all knowledge rests—namely, God's revelation—is building sand castles in the air. Van Til, therefore, insists upon the ultimate irrationality of all non-Christian and inconsistently Christian systems; and his own presuppositional apologetic is a rigorous attempt to apply the Tertullian dictum, "From this point onwards I shall contest the ground of my opponents appeal" (Van Til, 1971, 13).

There are, therefore, certain motifs that recur throughout the writings of Cornelius Van Til and determine his response to Karl Barth: the fundamental antithesis between consistent Reformed Christianity and all other forms of thought (since they assume, in one way or another, an autonomous knower); the normative validity of the Reformed theological system as defined by the confessional standards and classic theologians, including its metaphysical implications; the presuppositional nature of this commitment to Reformed orthodoxy; and the ultimate irrationality of all thinking that departs from these presuppositions. Consequently, few theologians escape Van Til's critical scrutiny (including American Evangelicals). But the most serious and sustained polemic is reserved for Karl Barth.

Barth Reception

One reason for this Barthian animus seems to be Barth's influence within the reformed circles in which Van Til moved, especially at Princeton and Amsterdam, but also within the American theological situation generally (Van Til 1936; 1938b; 1948b; 1954a; 1964a; 1974; 1975). Adding to this concern is the apparent similarity between Barth's theology and Reformed orthodoxy. By exposing the heterodoxy of the most orthodox of Neo-Orthodox theologians, and the one exerting the greatest influence, Van Til hopes to call the church back to the theology of the Bible and the Reformers (1969b, 107).

Most of Van Til's criticism of Barth came in two book length studies, *The New Modernism* (1946) and *Christianity and Barthianism* (1962). Between these he wrote three extended articles, "Has Karl Barth Become Orthodox?" (1954b), "Karl Barth on Chalcedon" (1960), and "Barth's Christology" (1962), and throughout his career he penned numerous book reviews, smaller articles and sections within larger works in which he interacted with Karl Barth and discussed his influence on modern theology (1931; 1936; 1937a,b,c; 1938a,b; 1948a,b,c;1950; 1951; 1954a,c; 1955c; 1958a,b; 1959a,b,c; 1964a; 1969c; 1974; 1975). Certainly Van Til sustained a lengthy and consistent polemic against the theology of Karl Barth, one that Bernard Ramm suggests became "the official Evangelical interpretation of neo-orthodoxy" (Ramm, 1983, 23).

The New Modernism

The basic thesis of Van Til's polemic is contained in the title of his first book. Barth's theology is, he claims, a new form of Modernism in essential continuity with the modern theology of Schleiermacher. Of course, this charge is made in the face of an overwhelming *prima facie* implausibility. It is contrary to Barth's professed intention, the apparent meaning of his statements and the predominant interpretation of him among contemporary theologians. Nevertheless, this is precisely the interpretation Van Til maintained throughout his career and which exerted such an influence upon Fundamentalist Evangelical thought. It is not by accident that the titles of his two major works on Barth, *The New Modernism* and *Christianity and Barthianism*, echo the title of Dr. Machen's classic statement of the Fundamentalist position, *Christianity and Liberalism.* Van Til's polemic was a conscious continuation of the Fundamentalist defense of the faith.

To demonstrate the essential continuity between modernist liberalism and Barthianism, however, Van Til must argue that Barth's objections to Protestant Orthodoxy are more basic than his opposition to Modernism. He calls attention, therefore, to the "arresting fact" that a common animus can be identified in Barth's criticism of the Catholic analogy of being, Modernism's "consciousness theology" and orthodoxy's doctrine of revelation. In each case the basic problem is the presence of a "theology of the *beati possidentes*," the claim to possess direct knowledge of God (Van Til, 1946, 1). In contrast, and as a solution, the crisis theologians propose a dialectical theology. But rather than free Barth and Brunner from the modernist path, this methodology locates them on a road that leads from Kant, through Hegel and Kierkegaard, to modern existentialism; and it demands they be clearly contrasted with the line of thought that extends from Calvin through Protestant Orthodoxy to the consistent Calvinism of the present day. As Van Til insists, careful examination of Barth's "system of theology in relation to its deepest philosophical bases" reveals a dependence upon modern philosophy not essentially different from the modernist theologians he so vigorously opposes (Ibid., viii).

Redrawing the "theological map" in terms of these two basic —and basically opposed—lines of thought, therefore, becomes the essential purpose of Van Til's book, *The New Modernism.*. While extensive ground is covered, Van Til's focus is singular. He sees a basic methodological orientation working itself out in all forms of post-Kantian theology. From the day when Kant introduced his infamous "Copernican revolution" modern philosophy and theology have been moving inevitably in a "subjective," "activist" and "antimetaphysical" direction (Ibid., xiii, 3). Kant's decision to explain knowledge in terms of the shaping influence of the mind allowed the human subject to define the limits of knowledge. What could be known became a product of the mind as it synthesized, according to the categories of understanding, objects received through the intuitions of time and space. What could not be known in this way, could only be affirmed "transcendentally," and could only function, therefore, as a regulative idea. Kant's epistemological revolution set philosophy on a course in which the activity of an autonomous self determined the limits of metaphysical affirmation.

As a result of this turn to the subject, inescapable dichotomies were introduced into the knowing situation—dualisms between the phenomenal and noumenal, between objects of knowledge and things-in-themselves, between reality as it falls within, and as it extends beyond, the limits of human understanding. The dialectical response to these dualisms, represented by Hegel and Kierkegaard, was to extend more completely the powers of the self. Of course, significant differences exist between Hegel's and Kierkegaard's form of extension, but neither departed from the post-Kantian path (Ibid., 62). For Hegel, Kant's dualisms are overcome by an ideal subject who incorporates within its own eternal movement all possible dichotomies. But "the System" of Hegel, Kierkegaard insists, identifies the absolute self with existing individuals by means of an illicit introduction of movement into logic—a criticism with which Van Til agrees. But Kierkegaard's own solution is equally inadequate. He absolutizes the post-Kantian dualisms—between time and eternity or logic and existence, for example—and then tries to overcome them by means of a radically subjective event. Both Hegel's absolute self and Kierkegaard's individual, therefore, attempt to overcome post-Kantian dilemmas by extending the powers of the self along "activist" lines, or so Van Til argues (Ibid., 1-80).

Van Til also finds a basic similarity in "general argument" between Kiekegaard's *Philosophical Fragments* and Barth's commentary on Romans, maintaining in fact, that Kierkegaard's "Individual" is "the main interpretive concept" in *Der Römerbrief* (Ibid., ix, 68). It is by means of the subjective individual that Kierkegaard and Barth are able to maintain both the "sweeping negations" and "sweeping affirmations" that mark their works as dialectical, first asserting the absolute incommensurability of God and man and then overcoming this infinite qualitative distinction in a moment of experience.

Corresponding to this Kierkegaardian "Individual" there is in Barth a new concept of history, borrowed from Franz Overbeck and equally indebted to post-Kantian dialectics. By it, Barth attempts to accomplish the same sweeping negations of human possibility and paradoxical affirmations of divine accomplishment. Acknowledging the inevitable "relativities and correlativities" of history, Barth negates any possibility of founding the knowledge of God upon direct revelation (Ibid., 89). Then he posits a realm of divine activity, indirectly revealed through the cross and resurrection, that stands before and beyond ordinary history. The important point for Van Til is that Barth's dialectical construction renders the relation between divine activity and ordinary history problematic, squeezing biblical affirmations about God's activity into an impossible Kantian framework.

Having thus analyzed *Der Römerbrief* in the first part of The New Modernism, Van Til then raises an important and obvious question: Does the later Barth manifest the same crippling captivity to post-Kantian dialectics? But in contrast to many contemporary interpreters, Van Til's answer is a resounding yes. As evidence he offers, first, the "civil war" with Emil Brunner and then, the theology of the first few volumes of *Kirchliche Dogmatik*.[4]

The division with Brunner occurs, from Van Til's perspective, because Brunner fails to purge theology of the last vestiges of blessed possession and Barth reacts to these "remnants of orthodoxy" (Ibid., 136). This is what is at stake in their dispute over an apologetic "point of contact." For Barth, the proposal constitutes an inadmissable reintroduction of natural theology into dogmatics. A psychologically, historically or philosophically definable point of contact between God and man opens the door to natural theology and its corollary, direct revelation. But since every form of natural theology must be resisted, the only path open to Barth is a consistent dialectic: he must maintain the radical discontinuity between God and man and the purely active, indirect and paradoxical nature of their unity.

This is precisely what he does in *Kirchliche Dogmatik* through the idea of the "Freedom of God." God's freedom is, according to Van Til, the "criterion of dogmatic construction" by which Barth "forms the doctrines of the trinity, the incarnation and...his conception of the attributes of God" (Ibid., 213). By means of this concept Barth maintains both the negations and affirmations of his theological dialectic, as well as the completely activist form a genuinely dialectical theology must take. Negatively, God's freedom means his **freedom from** any *a priori* definition of human possibility. By this Barth excludes Rome's analogy of being, Modernism's apologetic anthropologies, and Orthodoxy's doctrine of revelation. Not bound by the limits of human thought or being, God is free to be or become whatever He wills. This is the positive meaning of the freedom of God. His being is what He becomes in this freedom. This freedom from and freedom for constitutes, according to Barth, God's "Lordship," and as such is the "root" of the doctrine of the trinity and the key to understanding the incarnation (Ibid., 221-2).

In order to guard the divine freedom from any form of loss, Van Til continues to argue, Barth must "actualize" the being of God and the incarnation. His redefinition of trinity as three eternal modes of being and his radical identification of Christ's person and work are both aspects of this actualizing (Ibid., 221-7). Underlying these doctrinal reconstructions, furthermore, is a unique redefinition of time. Barth relocates divine being in an eternal act which allows temporal distinctions, but does not let those distinctions limit God's freedom. Of course, the only way to speak of this new time is dialectically: by negating any direct identity between ordinary history and divine action, and yet affirming that God, whose eternality includes temporality, reveals Himself in history. But for Van Til, all these "actualizations" are of a piece: they are the inevitable consequence of post-Kantian philosophical problems, the theological form of a dialectical response to unresolved dualisms. Because "Barth's concept of the freedom of God is constructed on [Kantian] critical lines" it results in a dialectical theology, and " a true dialectical theology must always be activist without residue" (Ibid., 217,219,225).[5]

Rather than a radical, or even relatively important, change in theology from *Römerbrief* to *Kirchliche Dogmatik*, Van Til sees a pervasive and predominant continuity, a unity produced by Barth's captivity to post-Kantian philosophy and manifested in his radical reconstruction of orthodox doctrine, especially the denial of direct revelation and the activist reinterpretation of divine being.

Christianity and Barthianism

Within the narrow circles of mid-century Fundamentalist Evangelical scholarship, *The New Modernism* was hailed as "a fine and scholarly work," its language echoed and its proposals appropriated (Walvoord, 1946; Kuhn, 1946; Stearns, 1948; Stonehouse, 1946, 100; Schaeffer, 1950; Harris, 1955; Henry, 1946, 301; 1948, 115-16, 149-50). But outside these communities Van Til's project received scathing criticism. Berkouwer accused him of "unsound" and "irresponsible" scholarship (1956, 386,9); Von Balthasar described the work as "vollig grotesque" (1971, 44); and Barth found it impossible to even recognize himself in Van Til's caricature. Some American Evangelicals concurred, for from the earliest days a minority report of a more appreciative kind was heard, and eventually these isolated voices became a broad interpretive tradition with numerous proponents in supportive Evangelical institutions, as the next chapter will show (Barnhouse, 1934; Riviere, 1934a,b; Robinson, 1928, 1935; Rolston, 1933; Stearns, 1949; Bromiley, 1940, 1947). Van Til's response to this growing appreciation of Barth, however, was to engage in consistent controversy, culminating in his second book on the subject, *Christianity and Barthianism* (1962).

This book, like the one before it, begins with an "Orientation" to Barth's location on the theological map. Fundamentally opposed to the "consciousness theology" of Schleiermacher, Barth adopts a position designed to sidestep the criticisms of Feuerbach and Strauss. Avoiding their criticisms, however, requires that he oppose all forms of direct revelation, whether Romanist, Modern or Reformed. He does this by means of a radical concentration upon and reinterpretation of Christ. As Van Til clearly states, "It is the purpose of this book to analyze Barth's basic position as it centers around his idea of Christ as *Geschichte*" (Ibid., 9).

For all the laudatory focus upon Jesus in later volumes of *Church Dogmatics*—which, at least, Van Til attempts to address—Van Til insists that what Barth means by Christ has not changed since 1946, and the key to that meaning is to be found in the category of *Geschichte*. *Geschichte* is the concept of history constructed by Barth to enable him to maintain his radically dialectical understanding of God and revelation, the same understanding that was conveyed by the concepts *Urgeschichte* and freedom in earlier works. By it, all forms of direct revelation are denied; and by it, all divine being is "actualized"(Ibid., 107).

Geschichte is the history of God's action. But as such it is also his form of being, for God's being is "*Actus Purus*," a trinity of eternal "procession" (Ibid., 17). Included within this *Geschichte* is what Van

Til calls the "Christ-Event," "the exhaustive Act of interrelationship between God and man" in which the radical discontinuity between them is overcome by an even more radical identification (Ibid., 90). This identification occurs in the intertrinitarian act in which the electing God becomes the elected Man by becoming the Son of the Father.

But this inclusion of becoming in being requires a conceptual redescription of the relationship between "Eternity and Time" (Ibid., chapter 6). This too is accomplished by the concept of *Geschichte*. While *Historie* and the human understanding of *Historie* is limited by temporal succession, *Geschichte*, as the locus of divine activity, is not. God's history contains both succession and contemporaneousness. It admits of temporal distinctions, but not in such a way that these distinctions limit it. They are distinctions of becoming within an eternal being. This enables Barth to reinterpret the humiliation and exaltation of Jesus as two aspects of a single event of atonement (Ibid., 97). It also enables him to assert that the events of salvation history—incarnation, resurrection, forty days, ascension, parousia—partake of temporal succession and yet participate in an eternal contemporaneousness. As Van Til interprets him, "The temporal togetherness of which Barth speaks, therefore, includes or envelops but for that very reason must not be directly identified with anything that takes place in *Historie*" (Ibid., 98).

A dialectical denial of direct identity and an activist reconstruction of orthodox doctrine—these are the distinguishing characteristics of the Barthian theology, and any theology incorporating dialectical forms of thought. Van Til's argument in *Christianity and Barthianism*, therefore, moves from an exposition of Barth's view of "Christ as *Geschichte*" in section one to a criticism of dialectical methodology itself. The root problem with all forms of dialectic, whether medieval or modern, is that they arise from an assumption of human autonomy. This is as true of Roman Catholicism, descending from Aquinas, as it is of post-Kantian philosophy. The forms of expression differ but the fundamental error remains the same. It comes as no surprise, therefore, that the final section of Van Til's book seeks to demonstrate parallels and convergences between Karl Barth and modern Catholic theology. As always, the basic division of theology is between a consistent Reformed orthodoxy and all other theological systems, which by definition presuppose some form of human autonomy and manifest some kind of dialecticism (Ibid., 319). All heterodoxy follows the same fundamental pattern.

And the pattern persists throughout Barth's theology. "The change from dialecticism to analogy" that Von Balthasar discerns in the later editions of *Church Dogmatics* "takes place," according to Van Til, "within the general overarching activist notion of revelation," formulated in dependence upon post-Kantian dialectical principles. And as long at it does there will be a more basic similarity between him and Catholicism (or Modernism) than between him and Reformation orthodoxy. As Dr. Van Til so clearly stated in the preface to his 1962 book,

> The present writer is of the opinion that, for all the verbal similarity to historic Protestantism, Barth's theology is, in effect, a denial of it....This was the writer's opinion in 1946 when he published *The New Modernism*. A careful consideration of Barth's more recent writings has only established him more firmly in this conviction (Ibid., vii).

Orthodox Reformed Theologians

Within the two streams of orthodox tradition to which Dr. Van Til belonged, Dutch Reformed and Old School Presbyterian, there were several influential thinkers who responded to Barth in a similar manner. Among these were Louis Berkhof, Fred Klooster, Francis Schaeffer and Gordon Clark. Beyond the confines of these conservative communities, in the broader streams of Evangelical thought and life, a Fundamentalist Evangelical response seemed to predominate as well, though sometimes in a less strident tone. This has certainly been the case within the Fundamentalist Evangelical communities represented by Carl Henry, Kenneth Kantzer, Charles Ryrie and the early Clark Pinnock. Of course, these leaders and their communities have been deeply influenced by the scholarship of Old School Princeton, Westminster, and the Continental Reformed; and men like Schaeffer and Clark were as much a part of Northern Fundamentalist Evangelicalism as the orthodox denominations to which they belonged.

But as one moves outside of these reformed traditions, into the more pietistic Baptist communities of Southern Evangelicalism, or the Holiness and Pentecostal movements, the situation becomes less clear. Interaction with Barth is less common, less important, and sometimes less critical. However, the basic structures of theological thought with which these populist traditions operate are much closer to the orthodoxy of Northern Fundamentalist Evangelicals than the Neo-Orthodox reformulations of Barth. So even here, Fundamentalist Evangelical Barth reception has predominated.

The Christian Reformed Church

According to the arguments proposed in chapter one, the Dutch Reformed community of the American Midwest represents an ethnically separate, theologically Reformed, Fundamentalist tradition within the Evangelical mosaic. Founded predominantly by confessionalist immigrants who seceded from the established church in the Netherlands, peopled by succeeding waves of immigrants who participated in Abraham Kuyper's "neo-Calvinist" resurgence, and drawn together by cultural and religious ties in a foreign country, the Dutch Reformed community has manifested a strong religious conservatism. This took the form of anti-modernism during the period of fundamentalist patterning in the Evangelical mosaic, namely, 1900 to 1950. Although diversity of opinion existed within this conservatism, Dr. James Bratt has persuasively argued that a pietistic confessionalism established itself as the predominant type during the middle third of this century. And "the intellectual monument of this era," according to him, is Professor Louis Berkhof's *Systematic Theology* (Bratt, 1978, 290).

Louis Berkhof

In its first edition, published in 1932, Berkhof's *Theology* contained no interaction with the work of Karl Barth. This could be attributed to its relatively early date or its purpose as a basic textbook. But when comment was added in the 1938 and subsequent editions, it became clear that the thinking of Dr. Barth was to have no substantive impact upon Berkhof. His theology had been formed and its standard of evaluation was the teaching of Scripture as interpreted by the Orthodox Reformed creeds and influential nineteenth century theologians, especially Bavinck. Compared with Van Til, his interpretation of Barth was both more positive and peripheral. But the same orthodox polemic characterized his work, and in his own way he further established a Fundamentalist Evangelical reception of Barth among the Orthodox Reformed.

Berkhof recognizes "elements of truth" in Barth's reaction to the "immanentism" of liberal theology, and he praises the way Barth has "raised his voice" in opposition to it (1949, 34, 30, 311). He also resists Van Til's tendency to interpret Barth's apparently orthodox affirmations as veiled heterodoxy, crediting Barth with a genuine defense of the virgin birth, orthodox two-nature christology, the transcendence and immanence of God, and a non-modalist doctrine of the trinity (Ibid., 336, 316, 33, 135, 83). Nevertheless, Berkhof's basic orientation is critical. There may be elements of truth in Barth's writing, but his idea of revelation is "foreign to Reformed theology," his doctrines of justification and sanctification represent an "unwarranted extreme," and his teaching on election is "not even distantly related to that of Augustine and Calvin" (Ibid., 34, 536-7, 111). Barth has reduced revelation to "mere flashes...coming to individuals," and he construes the creation and fall of mankind as "myths"—occurring in some "super-history" (Ibid., 39, 223). These interpretations are briefly stated, inadequately developed and based upon only Barth's earliest works. Barth plays the role in Berkhof's *Systematic Theology* of illustrating an influential modern movement of thought which merits commendation only in so far as it corresponds to Reformation Orthodoxy—which it seldom does.

Fred Klooster

Berkhof was eventually succeeded in his role as Calvin Seminary Professor of Systematic Theology by Dr. Fred Klooster, whose interaction with Barth was more sustained and significant, but whose orientation was similar. Between 1957 and 1962 Klooster published three articles and one book on Barth, and spent an academic year on sabbatical in Basel (1959-60). Then in 1975 he published a lecture series on the problem of history and faith in modern theology that included considerable interaction with Barth. Finally, in 1985 he penned an important critical review of Bernard Ramm's *After Fundamentalism*.

Over against Bernard Ramm's proposal that Evangelicalism, following Barth, should adopt a "dialectical" response to the Enlightenment, Klooster insists upon a strategy of "direct confrontation" (1985, 304). He does so because of the enduring validity of "Pre-Enlightenment Theology", represented by the "patristic dogma" of the early councils and the consensus of Reformed and Lutheran orthodoxy (1975, 24-26; 1977). He affirms a "strict confessionalism," believing that "the position of Calvin and Dort is in essential harmony with Scripture" and therefore, that any departure from that position is a departure from divine truth (1961, 66). Obviously, Klooster's orthodox self understanding provides the standard and motive for his apologetic confrontation with Barth.

Klooster focuses his criticism of Barth at what he considers the "heart and core" of his "massive, intricate... system": "the christological principle called 'Jesus Christ' " (1958, 180). Following a well trodden interpretive path, Klooster accuses Barth of a radical christocentrism, in which an idea of Christ, developed in partial dependence on philosophical concerns, functions as a "hermeneutical principle" that controls theological construction and distorts Scriptural interpretation (Polman, 1960). Dr. Klooster's published works, therefore, are devoted to explaining "Barth's view of Jesus Christ" and how it departs from the teaching of Scripture as represented by Reformed Orthodoxy (1961, 67,30,47). The doctrines of justification and sanctification receive some attention, but the primary focus is upon election and reconciliation, where Barth's distinctive departures and controlling principles are most clearly displayed (Ibid., 45-6,81).

The details of Klooster's analysis are manifold, corresponding to the complexity of both Barth and Reformed Orthodoxy. But there is a unifying thread: Barth's idea of Christ does not allow a genuinely biblical and historical understanding of revelation and salvation. According to the orthodox *ordo salutis*, creation, fall and redemption represent temporally distinct events in the historical enactment of God's eternal plan. There is a transition from divine judgement to grace in ordinary history by means of the incarnation, death and resurrection of Jesus Christ. But according to Klooster, Barth's soteriology undermines this genuinely historical accomplishment. By means of a christological reconstruction of the doctrine of election, the unity of God and man becomes an event in the being of God. In the eternal divine decision to give Himself in love to man as Jesus Christ, the entire "Christian dialectic of covenant, sin and reconciliation" occurs (Ibid., 81). Therefore the historical events of Christ's life loose their significance. Jesus' death is reduced to the status of manifesting the divine humiliation, and the resurrection to revealing the reality of human exaltation. Even the incarnation struggles to be more than a manifestation of eternal being. There is no transition from divine judgement to grace in and through history, Klooster argues.

This loss of historical significance is also manifested in Barth's distinction between *Historie* and *Geschichte*. This distinction, Klooster insists, denotes more than the difference between knowledge accessible to historical inquiry and knowledge that is not accessible. It designates, rather, two different kinds of happenings, possibly even located in different ontological realms. Although he recognizes Barth's claim that the divine *Geschichte* includes, overlaps or intersects human *Historie*, Klooster denies it any force. Barth's dialectical denials of direct revelation are rooted in a Kierkegaardian view of the relationship between God and man, and his attempts to overcome this dichotomy are judged a failure. "The Kierkegaardian problematic remains definitive throughout Barth's theology, even though in his later stages he attempts to distance himself from Kierkegaard" (1975, 47). In defense of this contention Klooster cites the work of Van Til (Ibid., 48).

In Klooster, Berkhof and Van Til one finds three different, but equally Fundamentalist criticisms of Barth within the Dutch Reformed subculture of American Evangelicalism. Van Til is the most philosophical and polemic; Berkhof, while more positive, remains fundamentally critical; Klooster, more polemical than Berkhof, is more theologically focused than Van Til. But the same orthodox and apologetic orientation marks each of their responses. Many other Dutch Reformed contemporaries manifested the same Fundamentalist Evangelical paradigm (Kuiper, 1959; Kromminga, 1941; Zerbe, 1930; Monsma, 1937; H. Hoeksema, 1966), and it continues to the present day as a well represented type (Hoekema, 1979; 1986, 49-58). But these examples should be sufficient to indicate the basic shape of this interpretive paradigm within Dutch Reformed orthodoxy.

Orthodox Presbyterianism

Van Til's other Reformed community was Orthodox Presbyterianism. This community, as the child of Old School Presbyterianism, fathered the earliest and most influential Fundamentalist criticism of Barth. Van Til remains the most important example. But J. Oliver Buswell, Francis Schaeffer, and Gordon Clark also played important roles in the early establishment and subsequent continuation of an orthodox and apologetic paradigm of Barth reception. And through them, a truly large and diverse group of Evangelical thinkers was affected, well beyond the small bounds of the denominations to which they belonged.[6]

An Early Encounter

Direct interaction between Barth and American Fundamentalist Evangelicals has been minimal, probably reflecting the degree of cultural and theological distance between them.[7] But in 1950, as recorded in the journals of The Bible Presbyterian Church and Faith Theological Seminary, a dialogue of sorts did occur. The occasion was the second plenary congress of the International Council of Christian Churches, held in Geneva to draw attention to the International Council's opposition to the World Council of Churches. An unofficial meeting between Barth and five International Council participants, including J. Oliver Buswell and Francis Schaeffer, was arranged at the Pestalozzi cottage where Barth spent much of his summer. According to Dr. Buswell's report of the interview the conversation was cordial, but confirmed opinions the interviewers had formed prior to the dialogue. These included the convictions that Barth espoused a sabellian modalism, an arian understanding of the divine Son as "produced" by the Father, a dialectical and therefore, unrealistic, view of time, and finally, theories of religious rationality that "reject logic, accept contradictions and resist historical factual verification" (Buswell, 1950c).[8]

Upon parting, Dr. Buswell offered to send Barth a copy of his recent review of *Dogmatics in Outline*, and Schaeffer, a paper he was writing on "The New Modernism" (Buswell, 1950b; Schaeffer, 1950). Barth responded to the reviews by penning a rather heated letter to Mr. Schaeffer in Switzerland, a copy of which was sent to Dr. Buswell in New York. He decried the treatment he received at their hands, suggesting that their theology resembled a "kind of criminology" in which self appointed "detective inspectors" set out to discover each and every departure from "views and statements" "not entirely (numerically!) identical with" their own. On the basis of a presumptuous identification of divine truth with the creed of their own "bible-believing" churches, Barth had been condemned as a "heretic" and "heathen." His theological work had been repudiated "as a whole." Consequently, Barth refused the invitation to future "conversations," insisting that genuine communication is "possible between *open*-minded people only" (Buswell, 1950c, 8 9).

Barth had been treated this way before. Therefore, he began the letter to Schaeffer and Buswell with the sentence, "I see: the things you think of me are approximately of the same kind as those I found in the book of van Til...." (Buswell, 1950c).[9] In fact, what Van Til argued at length and on the basis of extensive examination of primary sources (however distortive), Schaeffer and Buswell asserted briefly and with minimal investigation of Barth's written work. But their influence extended far beyond the limits of their scholarly expertise. This is especially the case with Francis Schaeffer.

Francis Schaeffer

Francis Schaeffer stands out as one of the most influential American Evangelicals in the latter half of the twentieth century. Labeled a "Guru of Fundamentalism" in *Newsweek*, a "leading spokesman" for Evangelicalism in *Christianity Today*, and identified by the Evangelical Theological Society as one of the four most influential thinkers in the lives of its members, his impact upon Evangelicalism during its cultural resurgence has been profound (Woodard, 1982, 88; Yancey, 1979; Noll, 1986, 209-14). During the seventies and early eighties he emerged as a central leader in conservative Evangelical reaction to developments in American culture. His 1979 book and film series, *Whatever Happened to the Human Race*, produced with Surgeon General C. Everett Koop, catalyzed Evangelical anti-abortion activity in the public arena (Dennis, 1986, 166- 9,182-S). His 1981 *A Christian Manifesto*, which advocated civil disobedience in turning the tide of moral disintegration in American society, was proclaimed by Reverend Jerry Falwell as one of the most important books of the decade. And an earlier book and film series, *How Should We Then Live?* (1976), provided a comprehensive interpretation of western civilization to justify the activism he and other conservatives were advocating.

By helping to found the International Council on Biblical Inerrancy, and by his own outspoken opposition to theological developments within American Evangelicalism, Schaeffer led the way in focusing public attention on the issue of biblical inerrancy (Dennis, 1986, 22,210). His last of twenty-three books, written (quite literally) from his death bed, decries with prophetic urgency *The Great Evangelical Disaster* of creeping accommodation to the spirit of the modern age. This has arisen, Dr. Schaeffer argues, because of Evangelicalism's failure to hold the line on biblical truthfulness, the "watershed" of its world view, and has issued ineluctably in moral compromise. The broadening boundaries of the American Evangelical mosaic were signs of compromising accommodation destined to undermine effective Evangelical witness (Schaeffer, 1984, 85; 1976b).

But Schaeffer was more than a popular proponent of Fundamentalist reaction. He was, in fact, a pioneer of Evangelical engagement, an early model of culturally aware and intellectually informed interaction with the modern world. During the decades of the fifties and sixties Schaeffer and his family lived in the relative obscurity of a Swiss mountain village. As a missionary to confused and disillusioned young adults, who flocked in large numbers to L'Abri, Schaeffer proclaimed "Bible-believing" Christianity in an intellectually credible and personally inviting way. As Clark Pinnock recollects, "He made orthodox Protestant theology live and have relevance in the twentieth century....he devastated liberal theology, not with the fiery rhetoric of the redneck preacher, but by means of intellectual analysis" (Pinnock, 1986b, 173).

The basic elements of this intellectual analysis were acquired by Schaeffer as a student of Machen and Van Til. But the unique form he gave it, distinguished above all by the ability to generalize, simplify and illustrate, was hammered out in dialogue with inquiring moderns. Most of his books, which began to roll off the press in 1968, were revised versions of lectures delivered at L'Abri, and they bear the marks of oral presentations to educated, popular audiences. They are not scholarly studies, with extensive documentation or precise analysis. They oversimplify, exaggerate and sometimes even misrepresent influential thinkers and cultural movements (E. Schaeffer, 1970, 227; Reugsegger, 1986, 274-5; Schaeffer, 1973). But for many Evangelicals, even Evangelical scholars, Francis Schaeffer provided a compelling account of the basic features of the modern predicament and a valid strategy for Evangelical engagement (Packer, 1986).

The distinguishing characteristics of the modern age, according to Schaeffer, are intellectual despair and moral disintegration. The pessimism of Sartre, Camus, and Gauguin exemplify the culturally aware modern man who has crossed over a "line of despair" and is no longer able to find secure meaning and purpose in life (Schaeffer, 1990, 8,233). The penultimate source of this despair is the modern shift in the nature of truth; its ultimate source, the assumption of human autonomy and the rejection of a biblical world view (Ibid., 210-11; Schaeffer, 1976, 84). Beginning with philosophy, and spreading through art, music, general culture and eventually theology, modern man has lost his confidence in the possibility of unified, comprehensive or absolute truth—what Schaeffer calls "true truth" (Ibid., 311). In its place has been substituted, sometimes unwittingly, a divided view of reality that is insufficient to halt the modern slide toward disintegration and despair (Ibid., 17).

Schaeffer traces the development of this dichotomous concept of truth from its introduction by Aquinas in Medieval philosophy through its progression in the Enlightenment figures of Rousseau and Kant to its fruition in the Hegel's dialectic and Kierkegaard's existentialism (Ibid., 13-25,209- 44,310-19; Schaeffer, 1976, 151-156). Philosophers before Hegel were what Schaeffer calls both rational and rationalistic: they affirmed the law of non-contradiction (rational) and believed in the possibility of a true and comprehensive interpretation of reality (rationalistic). But Hegel, attempting to overcome the irreconcilable dichotomies of Kant's philosophy, abandoned rationality for the sake of rationalism. He denied the law of non-contradiction, introducing a dynamic and dialectical method of reconciling contraries, in order to construct a system of thought that encompassed all reality. The ironic result, however, was a relativizing of truth, and man hovered on the edge of the line of despair.

In response to Hegel, Kierkegaard rejected the possibility of a comprehensive and unified knowledge of reality, and attempted to circumvent the Kantian dichotomies by a "leap of faith" (Ibid., 14, 237). But in that leap modern man stepped over the line of despair. Whether Kierkegaard intended it or not, his existentialism "gradually led to the absolute separation of the rational...from faith" (Ibid., 16, 43). As thinking men and women became more pessimistic about the possibility of rational explanation, they were forced by the sheer weight of their own need for meaning to leap into some "upper story" of irrational optimism (Ibid., 239). All that makes life meaningful—love, morality and purpose—became, in the hand of subsequent existentialists, the product of human action without rational foundation. Kant and Hegel, consequently, provided the "doorway" into modernity, and Kierkegaard, with his leap, was "the first man below" the infamous "line of despair" (Ibid., 14, 232).

When Schaeffer turns his attention to Karl Barth and twentieth century theology, he sees the same basic pattern emerging. Following Kant, Hegel and Kierkegaard—and in basic dependence upon them— Karl Barth was "the religious expression of the prevailing thought-forms," the extension into theology of the "titanic shifts" in philosophy and culture that produced the earthquakes of modernity. He is "the doorway in theology into the line of despair" (Ibid., 54, 240).

Acknowledging "a diversity within the unity of the New Theology," Schaeffer nevertheless insists, "if we miss the unity which binds together all expressions of modern theology, we have missed the essential point" (Ibid., 31). The essence of modern theology is its division of truth into a "lower story" of rationally verifiable truth-claims and an "upper story" of religious beliefs affirmed though a "leap of faith."

While admitting Barth's later attempts to distance himself from his Kierkegaardian point of departure, or "to get a toe back into history," Schaeffer thinks that Barth's basic methodological commitments make it logically impossible to do so (Ibid., 55). The "Death of God" theologians may be "a later phase" of modern theology, but they are the logically consistent result of walking through the doorway represented by Barth, concrete evidence of the despair produced by beginning with a dichotomous view of truth (Ibid., 83-6).

As evidence of this Kierkegaardian dichotomy in Barth, Schaeffer cites not only his resistance to rational verification of religious truth, but also, and especially, his admission of biblical error. For Schaeffer the logic is clear: either allow the conclusions of higher criticism to lead to theological agnosticism, and eventually to disbelief and despair, or return to "the historic view of Scripture" (Ibid., 54-5). Anything else is an attempt to hang theology "on a peg in mid-air" (Schaeffer, 1950, 4). Scripture contains, in Schaeffer's view, inerrant propositions that provide a comprehensive system of thought, a world and life view that can serve as a foundation and framework for rationality (Ibid., 100). And this propositional system, which he identifies with Reformed Orthodoxy (Schaeffer, 1976, 79-119), can be rationally verified in the arena of public argument.

Clearly Francis Schaeffer has continued the paradigm of Barth interpretation established by Cornelius Van Til. His stance is decidedly apologetic and self-consciously orthodox. Barth is interpreted as the primary representative of a heretical movement of thought that errs because it diverges from the orthodox Protestant system. Its departure from orthodoxy derives from the influence of modern philosophy, whose root problem is the assumption of human autonomy and the rejection of infallible biblical authority. The same analysis Van Til develops on the basis of extensive interaction with Barth and modern philosophy, Schaeffer proposes in a simpler and more memorable way, adding the important element of cultural interpretation. But his treatment of Barth lacks depth, both the depth of careful interaction with the Barthian corpus and the depth of a more accurate reflection of the dimensions of Barth's own thought.

Gordon Haddon Clark

Gordon Clark was another man who exerted a significant influence upon American Evangelical thought from within the relatively small circle of Orthodox Presbyterianism. Although a professional philosopher, with specialist expertise in early Greek thought, he lectured and published extensively on apologetics and theology. While a professor at Wheaton College Clark instructed, among others, Edward Carnell, Edmund Clowney, Paul Jewett, and Carl Henry. Henry, who would become one of the most influential scholars within modern Evangelicalism, relied heavily on the philosophical apologetics of Gordon Clark.[10]

A contemporary of Cornelius Van Til and for several years an ordained member of the Orthodox Presbyterian Church (the denomination of Machen and Van Til), Clark's perspective paralleled Van Til's. Criticizing all forms of empiricism as epistemologically untenable, he exerted a converging influence upon the shift from evidentialist apologetics to presuppositionalism within twentieth century Evangelicalism. Although Clark referred to his presuppositions as "axioms," and defined his position as "dogmatism," the basic theistic philosophy proposed is presuppositional (Clark, 1973). He championed the Reformed Orthodoxy of the Westminster divines as an accurate systematic restatement of Scriptural truth (Clark, 1963, 127; 1956b); he insisted upon the

Old School Princeton doctrine of Scripture as the Bible's self-description and the only rationally coherent understanding of revelation (Clark, 1982; 1957b); and he maintained the dependence of all true knowledge upon revelation, as well as the ultimate incoherence of non-Christian thought. However, there were definite differences between Van Til and Clark, differences in language, form of argument, and specific proposals. These led to heated intramural debate, and eventually, to the departure of Clark from the Orthodox Presbyterian Church (Klooster, 1951; Hakkenberg, 1986). But the Fundamentalist Evangelical family resemblances are strong.

As a Christian apologist Clark's published works are extensive. They include a history of philosophy (1957a), a comprehensive defense of theism (1952), a philosophy of science (1964), a philosophy of history (1971), several works on philosophy of religion (1962a; 1973) interpretations of Presbyterian doctrine (1956) and biblical books (1972), and a study of Karl Barth (1963). The two pillars of this apologetic edifice are his history of philosophy, *Thales to Dewey* (1957a) and his introductory theistic philosophy, *A Christian View of Men and Things* (1952). The former, published after thirty years of teaching, represents his mature analysis of the various attempts to construct an epistemologically adequate philosophical system through the course of western thought. This historical analysis provides the essential background and basic components of Clark's own apologetic proposals. *A Christian View of Men and Things*, written five years earlier, proposes that apologetic. His basic claim is that Christianity, understood as "a comprehensive system of philosophy" or "a comprehensive view of all things," provides the only logically consistent and meaningful explanation of reality (1952, 1).

Although Clark engages in detailed philosophical criticisms, his apologetic program can be fruitfully identified in terms of several basic principles. The first of these is the basicality of logic. Apart from the laws of identity, deduction, and contradiction there can be no meaningful assertions or intelligible ideas. Clark never tires of demonstrating the practical and logical impossibility of denying the validity of these laws, and insists upon their ontological status (1962a, 149; 1957a, 97-103). Another basic principle in Clark's apologetic program is the propositional and systematic nature of truth. The object of knowledge is the proposition, and truth is a "rational system" of logically consistent propositions that depict reality (1963, 130; 1952, 24-5). The concept of "nonpropositional truth" is for Clark, a meaningless term, not capable of clear and consistent definition (1982, 34); and the idea of unsystematic truth arises from the refusal to accept the implications of the basicality of logic.

Clark also insists upon the epistemological necessity of dogmatism. By this he means that all knowledge, or true assertion, depends upon first principles. No argument begins or justification ends outside the context of an implicit systematic whole, and therefore, without appeal to ultimately unjustifiable or self-authenticating premises. Clark's preferred word for these basic beliefs is "axioms." But he means more by dogmatism than simply the necessity of basic beliefs. He means the necessity of a revealed system of truth, a system whose basic axioms are revealed propositions (1973, 7). Clark argues for the necessity of this dogmatic starting point for knowledge on the grounds that all other proposed starting points—empiricist, rationalist and irrationalist (existentialism)—fail to provide a deductively valid explanation for the necessity and universality of truth (1962a, 68). In contrast to these failed attempts, Clark proposes the doctrine of verbal revelation as the epistemological axiom of a theistic system, and argues that the Westminster Confession is an accurate restatement of the propositions that constitute this revelation (1982, 34).

This basic epistemological axiom is combined in Clark's philosophy with an Augustinian "preformation" theory of truth. Following Plato, Augustine and Kant, Clark insists upon the basic idealist insight that knowledge requires a priori categories, intuitions or ideas. Universal ideas cannot be generated from, or justified by, particulars; nor can the manifold diversity of experience be selected, organized or analyzed apart from concepts and categories that attend, and logically precede experience. But in contrast to Kant, Clark maintains that the irresolvable dualisms created by the Kantian *Ding-an-sich* are overcome by asserting a created correspondence between human forms of thought and divinely created reality. Only this kind of preformation of mind and external reality according to divine plan will explain and justify the necessity and universality of truth (1957a; 1973).

Clearly Clark's apologetic program aims at a comprehensive philosophy and depends upon a specific theory of rationality. Furthermore, this theistic philosophy is constructed as an expression and defense of Reformed Orthodoxy. Like Van Til, and the other Fundamentalist Evangelical theologians discussed, Clark's theological paradigm is self-consciously orthodox and decidedly apologetic.

Barth Reception

Dr. Clark's interaction with Barth is contained, for the most part, in a single volume of moderate length, Karl Barth's *Theological Method*, published the year after the noted theologian's visit to America. There are incidental, though revealing, comments in books published before and after this work, as well as a few brief articles or book reviews (1961; 1962b,c,d; 1971). But this is the only extended study. Designated by *Christianity Today* as one of the "Best Evangelical Books" of 1963, and written by a scholar already influential within American Evangelicalism, the book established Clark as one of the more important interpreters of Barth within Evangelicalism during the

1960s.

The book is, as the title suggests, a focused study of Barth's theological method. Clark wants "to clarify the controlling concepts, to expose the underlying philosophy, and to evaluate his dogmatic method"—just what the reader would expect from someone with Clark's philosophical orientation (1963,4). Less predictable, however, is Clark's claim that "the present writer largely agrees with Barth on the matter of method, even if he also dares to suggest substantial alterations"(Ibid., 5). He praises Barth's vigorous opposition to the anthropological orientation of Protestant Modernism, and agrees with the soundness of his decision to grant priority to divine actuality over human possibility in the service of a theology of revelation. In marked constrast to Van Til, Clark insist that Barth's reorientation of theology to the Word as its source, center and norm is the fundamental distinguishing characteristc of his theological project (Ibid.,13). Nevertheless, Clark does propose "substantial alterations", and in the opinion of the present writer those alterations indicate that there is anything but "large agreement" between the two men.

To understand Dr. Clark's reception of Barth one must observe the strategy of intepretation he employs. Recognizing the changes in Barth's thinking, as well as the "prophetic," "oracular" and sometimes "ambiguous" nature of his language, Clark tries to construe him "sympathetically," that is, in sympathy with Barth's intention to be a Reformed theologian (Ibid.,7-8). But because of his own view of Reformed theology, Clark is driven into a hermeneutical corner. He can either interpret the "sweeping negations" of Barth's dialectic rhetorically—as showing "a singular felicity for saying what he cannot possibly mean"—or as genuine contradictions of Reformed theology. In the end, Clark opts for the latter course, attributing Barth's non-Reformed assertions to an "irrationalist strand of thought" produced by the persistent influence of post-Hegelian philosophy (Ibid., 10). Giving Barth the interpretive "benefit of the doubt," therefore, means construing one strand of his thought as an expression of Reformed Orthodoxy while arguing that the other is patently inconsistent, and then suggesting that the Reformed strand would be better maintained if supported by the kind of philosophy Clark espouses (Ibid., 6,76).

Throughout *Karl Barth's Theological Method* the pattern is the same. When discussing Barth's highly qualified definition of theology as a science, Clark affirms the necessity of resisting any definition that would subject theology to the control of *a priori* determinations of human possibility. But he criticizes Barth's manner of maintaining this independence. To reject Scholz's proposition postulate, which insists upon freedom from self-contradiction, or his axiomatization postulate, is to commit oneself to a "contemporary irrationalism" that is unnecessary and self-defeating (Ibid., 53-4). In contrast, Clark insists that Barth's legitimate intention can only be maintained by reaffirming theology as queen of the sciences and redefining science in the context of a comprehensive theistic view of reality—a move Barth clearly rejects.

Clark also affirms what he takes to be Barth's "main contention" in rejection of apologetic prolegomena, namely, the impossibility of a theologically neutral common ground (Ibid., 94-5, 99). But he criticizes the "extreme" to which Barth moves in his denial of apologetics, and offers instead a distinction between epistemological and ontological common ground. Clark categorically denies the possibility epistemological common ground between Christian and non-Christian systems of thought, since the meaning of any proposition within a system is determined by that system as a whole. But he maintains that an ontological common ground nevertheless exists between all men, since they do not operate within consistent systems of thought. By virtue of their creation all men possess some truth, and appeal can be made to that truth as a real point of contact (Ibid., 100, 103). This criticism is offered as a proposal "for improving and extending" Barth's apologetic method along a path consistent with his concern for the absolute priority of revelation (Ibid., 99). But one is hard pressed to understand how an extension of Barth's theology of the Word in Clark's apologetic direction can be construed as sympathetic interpretation.

In his analysis of Barth's so called "theory of knowledge" the fundamental nature of Clark's criticism is clearly revealed. After extensive quotation of passages in *Church Dogmatics* that affirm the rationality of revelation, and even its verbal character, Clark exposes what he considers an unreconciled strain of irrationalism He then attributes this irrationalism to a "theory of language and knowledge" which, "despite Barth's earnest protestations that man can really know God, make that knowledge impossible" (Ibid., 143). The theory Clark finds in Barth is a form of Aristotelian (or Kantian) empiricism, in which the meaning of human language is derived-from, and limited to, construction of concepts from human percepts (Ibid., 138). On the basis of this supposed linguistic theory, Barth rejects the knowledge of God as a human possibility. Then by means of a novel view of revelation, he attempts to reaffirm the possibility of this knowledge. But Clark insists that such a theory of language renders knowledge of God logically, not just humanly, impossible. And logical possibility is basic.[11]

Obviously the two men are operating with decidedly different views of the nature of revelation, and the success of Barth's opposition to orthodoxy depends upon his alternative account. At the center of this conceptual reformulation is the idea of a unitary Word in threefold form, undergirded by a concept of divine time that enables temporally distinct occurrences to participate in an eternal event. But according to Clark, "Barth has failed to provide an intelligible account of the unity of his three forms of the Word of God" (Ibid., 177). An event distinct in time, yet contemporaneous, which takes the form of incarnation, inscripturation and proclamation, and yet cannot be equated with these occurrences in any direct or finally specifiable way, is at best ambiguous, and more likely, unintelligible.

The basic problem is a separation of Scripture and revelation, the failure to identify the event of revelation with the verbal statements of the Bible. This limitation of identity to an event that cannot be conceptually "fixed", suggests to Clark that the identity, if any exists, is located "behind" the text or in a "subjective" encounter (Ibid., 162-5). Either way, the result is rationally unstable, tending toward skepticism. Clark's alternative, of course, is to offer the axiom of verbal inspiration as the first dogma of a comprehensive Christian system, and to argue that the Westminster Confession is an accurate restatement of the inerrant propositions contained in Scripture.

It becomes very clear, furthermore, in the final chapter of Karl Barth's *Theological Method* that the axiom of verbal revelation is incompatible with any assertion of biblical fallibility. "The logic of the Enlightenment is unimpeachable," argues Clark. "If the Bible is untrue, it cannot be the Word of God" (Ibid., 215). Specifically of Barth he asks, "Why is Barth unwilling to annul the results of the negative scholarship of the last century?" (Ibid., 216). Clark recognizes that his own apologetic proposals require such a repudiation. But anything less would entail the loss of the foundational principle of a valid religious epistemology.

Certainly Dr. Clark has located himself within a theological paradigm whose proponents received Barth in an apologetic manner, from an orthodox perspective, and with a philosophical focus. His appreciative comments must be noted, and his restrained tone is to be applauded. But it is difficult to conclude that the view of Barth's method he espoused and propagated differed significantly from that of Van Til, Klooster, or Schaeffer—especially since his positive comments depend upon the assumption of radical inconsistency. Clark also prepared the way, in a very important sense, for the next and possibly most influential Barth interpreter from within the American Evangelical mosaic.

Carl F. H. Henry: Evangelical Spokesman

The name of Carl Henry, like that of Billy Graham, has become synonymous with American Evangelicalism. Henry has occupied positions of influence in the centers of Evangelical power, and produced written statements of unquestioned significance from the earliest days of Evangelical resurgence. A founding member, president and first secretary of the Evangelical Theological Society, his book, *Fifty Years of Protestant Theology* (1950), was the society's inaugural lecture. He was also one of a handful of Fundamentalist scholars invited by Harold Ockenga and Charles Fuller to serve as founding professors at Fuller Theological Seminary, designed by its originators to be a model of scholarly engagement for the nascent movement. But most importantly, Henry was invited by the board of *Christianity Today*, which included Ockenga, Graham and Graham's father-in-law, L. Nelson Bell, to serve as its founding editor. In this position, which he occupied from 1956 until 1969, Henry became one of the most influential voices for Evangelicalism in America, even its "unofficial spokesmen" Patterson, 1983, 125).

In fact, one could almost chart the history of American Evangelicalism by Henry's books. In 1946 he published *Remaking the Modern Mind*, a postwar call for Evangelicals to seize the opportunity created by the demise of Modernist optimism to recapture the modern mind for Evangelical orthodoxy. In 1947, *The Uneasy Conscience of Modern Fundamentalism* issued a parallel call for Fundamentalist social engagement, and became an influential tract for the times. Then in 1957, with *Evangelical Responsibility in Contemporary Theology*, the new editor of *Christianity Today* produced another early statement of the self-understanding of an emerging "Evangelical" movement, determined to transform its culture while avoiding both the "modernist revision" and the "fundamentalist reduction" (1957).

But Henry's uncanny ability to function as Evangelical spokesman, capturing and portraying the ethos of the movement, continued. In 1967, after chairing the World Congress on Evangelism, Henry produced *Evangelicals at the Brink of a Crisis*, in which he indicated, early on, the theological and cultural crises which a growing Evangelicalism faced. This was followed, in 1975, by a series of *Christianity Today* articles published as *Evangelicals in Search of Identity* (1976). During "The Year of the Evangelical", when participants and observers alike were commenting on the emerging power of Evangelicalism come of age, Henry saw through its popularity to a basic problem: internal conflicts and identity confusion.

Henry has certainly been a leading spokesman for post World War II Evangelicalism, its frontier journalist and editor par excellence. But he has also been one of its most noted theologians, an honor due primarily to the publication, between 1976 and 1984, of his six volume magnum opus, *God, Revelation and Authority (GRA)*. In this work Henry sets out to do what he called for in his first book on theology, namely, provide an Evangelical engagement with the modern mind that defends the Christian world-view as the only adequate intellectual foundation for human life. The focus of the work, especially in the first four volumes, is the doctrine of revelation. It proposes and defends a theology of revelation in the context of a comprehensive theory of rationality, and it does so in the form of fifteen theses (volumes II-IV) and a volume of "preliminary considerations" (volume I). Volumes V and VI are then devoted to an exposition of a traditional orthodox doctrine of God in critical dialogue with contemporary currents of thought.

In spite of its linear presentation of numbered theses, *GRA* tends to spiral, that is, revolve around and repeatedly return to a set of fundamental convictions that provide the center, focus and thrust of the arguments (Fackre, 1984, 198). An impressively large and diverse array of issues is addressed from this center, ranging over the fields of philosophy, theology, biblical criticism, and the history of these disciplines. But the basic perspective, and the recurrent basis from which Henry criticizes all competing alternatives, is a theory of revelation and rationality learned at the feet of Gordon Clark (*GRA I*, 10). It is this theory, in turn, that informs, even defines, Henry's criticism of Barth.

In volume one the theory is introduced. It is identified as a "theological transcendent a priori" in the "Augustinian-Calvinistic tradition" that claims "divine revelation is the source of all truth...reason is the instrument for recognizing it...and the task of Christian theology is to exhibit the content of biblical revelation as an orderly whole" (*GRA I*, 215, 323, 330). It involves a doctrine of Scripture as infallible propositional revelation and a doctrine of Christ as the eternal Logos by which God reveals all truth, the truth of science as well as the truth of theology. It also involves a "pre-Kantian" affirmation of objective metaphysics by means of a "preformation" epistemology (Ibid., 282).

Nor are the doctrinal claims distinguished from apparently philosophical ones, for the biblical "world-and- life view" is presented as a comprehensive interpretation of reality which "not only champions its own metaphysics, but requires a distinctive knowledge-theory" (Ibid., 324). This theory of revelational rationality is proclaimed as the "biblical" and "Evangelical" solution to "the crisis of truth and word" besetting modern culture, and the only hope for a world mired in cultural relativism (Ibid., 17).

Revelation and rationality are thus inextricably linked in Henry's restorationist vision, and his fifteen theses are a condensed statement of the "Augustinian-Calvinistic" theory of revelational rationality he proposes. God revealing Himself becomes the basic presupposition of Henry's theological world view, the ontological and epistemological "axiom" that supports the entire "convictional framework" of Evangelical orthodoxy. "Evangelical theology dare harbor one and only one presupposition: The living and personal God intelligibly known in his revelation" (Ibid., 212). In this radical dependence upon revelation, Henry strikes a note reminiscent of Barth. But only a note. Henry is very clear in the development of this theme that he understands revelation differently; and that difference in understanding makes all the difference.

One striking feature of Henry's view of revelation is the extent to which it echoes the position of his most revered teacher, Gordon Clark. Henry's *God, Revelation and Authority* represents an advance upon Clark's work because it engages more broadly and deeply modern theology and biblical criticism; it also offers a more comprehensive statement, in one work, of the theory of revelational rationality the two men share. But the position being advanced is essentially, and in its most distinctive details, the same.

There is, most importantly, the same understanding of knowledge and truth. It is propositional, systematic and absolute. "There is but one system of truth, and that system involves the right axiom and its theorems and premises derived with complete logical consistency" (Ibid., 227). This system is a "system of propositions" (1957c, 159), for the "proposition, judgement or sentence" is "the minimal unit of meaningful expression" and "the irreducible unit of truth" (*GRA I*, 453, 449). Furthermore, this logically consistent propositional system is equated with the mind of God. Therefore, "Theological truth is...infallibly certain; all other claims for truth are subject to correction and at most are but probable" (Ibid., 228).

Two of Henry's most characteristic doctrinal concepts, and the most crucial ones in his reconstruction of rationality, are the "Logos of God" and "propositional revelation." By the first he identifies truth with the mind of God and by the second he identifies the words of the Bible with that Logos—and by means of both he mediates the communication of certain knowledge from God to man.

"The Logos is the eternal Reason or Mind of God" (*GRA III*, 205). It is also "the source of order and rationality in the universe" and "the mediating agent of all divine revelation" (Ibid., 195, 164). In these roles the Logos is identified with the eternal Christ: "In brief, the eternal and self-revealed Logos, incarnate in Jesus Christ, is the foundation of all meaning, and the transcendent personal source and support of the rational, moral and purposive order of created reality" (Ibid., 195). Therefore, all true knowledge is knowledge of what this Logos created, sustains and reveals. Furthermore, all of reality is rationally intelligible, for the human mind functions after the order God has created, apprehending the Logos of God. Not surprisingly, Henry considers the Logos "the crowning philosophical achievement of historic Christianity," and he believes its "loss...as an epistemic presupposition led Western philosophy to a ... skeptical predicament beyond which it has been unable to find passage" (Ibid., 194,167). Henry's recovery of the Christian revelation claim, therefore, requires a reinstatement of this Logos doctrine.

While the eternal Logos provides the ultimate source and foundation for created rationality in Henry's system, univocal propositional revelation guarantees its accessibility (Ibid., 196). Truth is revealed from the mind of God to the mind of man by means of revealed propositions, the meaning of which are univocally expressed in conceptual-verbal form (Ibid., 248, 456). Henry insists upon a "strict correlation" between divine revelation and written Scripture, explicitly following Warfield's construction of the doctrine of inspiration (*GRA IV*, 197, 69). "Inerrancy is implicitly taught, is logically deducible, and is a necessary correlate of Scripture as the inspired Word of God" (Ibid., 168). "How else," he asks, "can the truth of the language of the Bible be assured than by strictly correlating divine revelation with the written Scriptures?" (Ibid., 197).

Because identity between theological propositions and divine truth is so fundamental for Henry, he also resists anything that introduces ambiguity or distortion into religious knowledge. That which undermines identity produces skepticism. Analogical, symbolic and mythical construals of religious language are rejected (*GRA I*, 44-69). Hermeneutical theories that introduce irreducible subjectivity into the knowing situation are criticized (*GRA IV*, 83-96, 304-15). Ideas of revelation that oppose personal to propositional knowledge are resisted (*GRA II*, 151-66). And concepts of divine incomprehensibility that suggest God is irrational or even a-rational are critically engaged (Ibid., 47-57). Against these and other "unstable" positions, Henry consistently defends the "objective perspicuity" of an infallible, univocal, propositional revelation in Scripture (*GRA IV*, 279).

Barth Reception

There is little room in such a system for constructive appropriation of Barth. One would expect Henry, therefore, to follow in the tradition of Reformed Fundamentalist criticism established by Van Til, Klooster, and Clark, polemically engaging Barth's doctrine of revelation and the theory of rationality (or irrationality) that underlies it. And such is the case, as subsequent analysis will demonstrate.

But this is not the whole story. There is a dual aspect in Henry's reception of Barth, corresponding to his interpretation of the dual aspects of Barth's own theological construction. The leader of "Neo-Supernaturalism", as Henry designates the Neo-Orthodox movement, is both friend and foe: An ally in the warfare against Protestant liberalism and an enemy in the campaign for remaking the modern mind after the pattern of Evangelical orthodoxy. Therefore, alongside Henry's dominant polemic there are words of qualified praise. He does not designate Barth an "inconsistent Evangelical" as Carnell eventually did (Carnell, 1962). But he does acknowledge the presence of "surviving biblical elements" in Barth's thought, and aims his criticism at the inconsistency of affirming these sound insights on the basis of an alien philosophical framework (Henry, 1962). There is a change, therefore, from Van Til's uncompromising criticism. Henry represents the more positive posturing of postwar Evangelicalism—but still in the context of Fundamentalist Evangelical construals of the theological task.

This pattern of interpretation was established in his earliest works. In the immediate post war years, Henry produced four books that analyzed the mid-century theological situation and proposed a direction for Evangelical response (1946, 1947a, 1948, 1950). He issued a call for Evangelicals to recognize the perils and possibilities of the hour and to seize the opportunity created by the demise of modern liberalism (1946, 19-27). In analyzing this demise, Henry acknowledged the role of Neo-Orthodoxy and even relied upon its critique (1946, 31-

78). But when he turned his attention to the dominant "mid-twentieth century view" that had replaced the liberal consensus, commendation gave way to criticism. In the "Neo-Supernaturalist" attempt to reassert the transcendence of God, modern theology has reached an "impasse" (Henry, 1948). It cannot go back to the discredited immanentism of classic liberalism; yet it cannot go forward to occupy a supernatural "higher ground" without rejecting, in a more radical way, the fundamental assumptions of liberalism. The attempt to graft biblical truths into a dialectical theory of revelation only results in "inner contradictions" and inadequately supported claims (Ibid., 214). In the end, Henry indicts the whole movement for being little more than a "mid-century higher liberal mood" (Ibid., 217).

It should be noted, however, that Henry's interaction with Barth is, at this stage, limited. In *The Protestant Dilemma* (1948), which contains his most extensive treatment of Neo-Orthodoxy, it is Brunner, Niebuhr and Edwin Lewis who are center stage. Discussion of Barth is relegated, for the most part, to footnotes, and is dependent upon secondary interpretation. Van Til's *New Modernism* is cited with approval (Ibid., 83, 116); a Westminster Seminary symposium is quoted extensively (Ibid., 235-6, 114); an article in the journal of American Dispensationalism appears twice (Ibid., 100, 201); and well known commentators like Macintosh, Horton, and Pauck provide authoritative interpretations (Ibid., 201, 172, 200). Nevertheless, Barth is presented as the originator and prime exemplar of a theological movement proposing a return to biblical supernaturalism but failing to provide an adequate basis for such a return.

The same point of view recurs in the pages of *Christianity Today*. In the very first issue Henry defines the purpose of the magazine and the mont it represents by comparing Karl Barth to Billy Graham. He praises both as "symbols" of "a religious springtime after the long, cold winter of Liberalism." But then he accuses Barth of a "half- hearted confidence in the reliability and authority of Scripture," and declares that "whoever sees no essential difference between the views of the Bible represented by Barth and...the theology of the Evangelicals" needs "theological lenses" (Henry, 1956, 22-3).

Henry himself attempts to provide these lenses in a series of *Christianity Today* articles published in 1964 and 1965. In these pages he traces "the moving frontier of [European] theological debate" through three successive stages of dominance and collapse—Liberal, Barthian and Bultmannian—and argues that the leaders in all three phases shared a basic methodological error (Henry, 1965, 39, 9-29). Although Henry acknowledges differences between Barth and Bultmann, and the schools descending from them, Henry insists these differences occur within the context a common "dialectical-existential" method. Even the "objectifying elements" of Barth's *Dogmatics* are condemned as "too little and too late," for the distinction between *Historie* and *Ges-*

chichte and Barth's denial of general revelation ultimately undermine any claim to genuine objectivity (Ibid., 31, 61, 69). Henry does admit that Barth puts up a "defense" against Bultmann's radical existentialism; but the defense inevitably "deteriorated," he insists, because of inadequate epistemological foundations (Ibid., 30-40; see Henry, 1964).

But even at this stage in Henry's theological career, interaction with the Barthian corpus is limited, and his interpretive opinions are often defended by appeal to authoritative commentators (Ibid., 35, 36, 57, 71-2, 75-7). The content reveals the context: journalistic reporting in the pages of a popular magazine and lectures to theological students. One must turn, therefore, to the pages of *God, Revelation and Authority* to find Henry's mature academic interaction with the theology of Karl Barth.

God, Revelation and Authority

In these volumes Barth's role as foil becomes more prominent. Whereas Brunner, Niebuhr and even Edwin Lewis were primary exemplars of Neo-Protestant thought in *The Protestant Dilemma*, Barth is now center stage. No theologian, ancient or modern, is mentioned more often or discussed more extensively. Amidst this diversity, however, there is a unity of focus: Barth's doctrine of revelation and the theory of rationality it entails.

For Henry, "objective" revelation requires comprehensive and direct rationality, a revealing Logos and revealed propositions. Barth's reconstruction, however, entails a fatal two-fold reduction. The Word of God is restricted to the revelation in Jesus, and this revelation is further reduced to a "sporadic," "personal," even "internal" event only tenuously related to history and human rationality (*GRA II*, 127-8). "Barth is right," Henry claims, "in so far as he repudiates any second source of divine revelation outside of Jesus Christ." "But Barth wrongly interpreted the sense and scope of divine revelation" (*GRA III*, 208). He reduced it to a "Christ Event" divorced from the universal Logos, and therefore, incapable of direct revelation in history or consistent propositional definition. Barth has led the way in modern theology's loss of cognitive revelation. "Among twentieth century theologians, perhap none has been more influential than Karl Barth" in the "disavowal" of "propositional revelation" or the "reduction" of "comprehensive revelation" (*GRA III*, 466, 88).

Nor is Henry impressed with Barth's later "revisions." His proposals fall short of the kind of revelational rationality that Evangelicalism requires. "Dialectical-existential theology" remains the prominent descriptive label for Barth's method to the end, for it everywhere manifests the continuing influence of his denial of propositional revelation and a universal logos. For example, Henry follows Van Til, Klooster and Clark in their interpretation of *Geschichte* as a realm radically divorced from history, despite Barth's claims to the contrary (*GRA II*, 287). Likewise, Barth's attempt to both "disjoin and... correlate human concepts and knowledge of God" by a reconstructed doctrine of analogy is judged inadequate. "Barth struggles to overcome the subrational consequences of his early theory when, in the revision of his *Church Dogmatics*, he contends that by a miracle of grace our human concepts become adequate to the knowledge of God" (*GRA III*, 224). But quoting Clark, Henry argues that "it is irrational to ask omnipotence...to reveal knowledge in a situation which by definition excludes knowledge" (Ibid., 226).

This irrationality, in turn, is traced by Henry to the persistent influence of alien philosophical ideas. "Anti- intellectual" presuppositions, "handed down through Hermann" to Barth and Bultmann, have become an integral aspect of the dialectical-existential theology. They include, supposedly, the conviction that "God reveals only himself and not information, propositions or truths" and the belief that revelation is a "sporadic inner" event (*GRA II*, 159). But the ultimate source of these reductive denials is the critical epistemology of Immanuel Kant.

"Kant's denial of the universal cognitive validity of revelational knowledge became a [central] feature of the theological movement from Barth through Bultmann" (*GRA III*, 278). Bultmann's more radical denials of objectivity were simply consistent expressions of the basic methodological premises he and Barth shared. "Divine self revelation as Barth expounded it...could offer no persuasive resistance to this further existential reductionism" (*GRA II*, 160). In fact, "Bultmann unmasked a deforming weakness in Barth's theology: despite a theory of revelation and knowledge that in principle renounced objectifying metaphysical assertions, Barth had ventured to make quasi-objectifying statements about God-in-Himself" (Ibid., 161). But "in time, dialectical-existential theology with its nonobjectifying faith claims erupted into controversy over the reality or nonreality of God" (Ibid., 278).

In other words, Henry identifies a theological trajectory that moves logically from Kant through Herrmann (and Kierkegaard) to Barth, and from Barth through Bultmann to the death-of-God theologians. The common thread and driving force in this theological devolution is a critical epistemology that denies a revealing Logos and revealed propositions, the only sure guarantee of an objective revelation.

In these arguments the decisive influence of Gordon Clark upon Carl Henry is clear. Many are the times when *Karl Barth' Theological Method* provides the arguments by which Barth's position is criticized, and even the sections of *Church Dogmatics* that are quoted (*GRA I*, 202-12, 233, 242-3, 396-7; *GRA II*, 143-7, 287-8, 322-3; *GRA III*, 164, 225-29, 285-90, 466-9; *GRA IV*, 149-52, 156-8, 196-200, 266, 428-30). Many more are the times when Clark's solutions to the problem of rationality become the standard by which Henry judges Barth and the whole Neo-Supernaturalist movement. The lengthened shadow of Van Til, though less dominant, can also be perceived, especially in the persistent description of Barth's theology as "dialectical-existential".

From a position of significant visibility and influence, Carl Henry perpetuated the orthodox and apologetic paradigm and its polemic interpretation of Barth throughout the postwar Evangelical mosaic. As a Baptist, and a leading spokesman for the larger Evangelical movement, he represents the extension of reformed distinctives beyond the boundaries of Orthodox Presbyterianism into the broadening traditions of American Evangelicalism. Of course, the confluence of Reformation theology and revivalist pietism has always characterized the American Evangelical movement. Henry is just a particularly influential modern example of this reformed and revivalist mainstream within the tradition that has been designated Northern Fundamentalist Evangelicalism.

Other Fundamentalist Evangelical Interpreters

In the Van Til-Klooster-Schaeffer-Clark-Henry line of Barth interpretation a high degree of homogeneity has been observed. These men share a common orthodox self-understanding, with only slight variation in doctrinal detail; and they share a fundamentally polemic attitude toward Barth, although manifesting differences in the degree to which they voice qualified appreciation. For each of them apologetics has been a primary concern, and in order to defend the faith once delivered they have depended upon a similar theory of revelation and rationality. Their criticism of Barth, consequently, has focused upon his supposedly defective theory of revelation and its captivity to alien philosophical presuppositions.

The importance of this line should be recognized. In it are the earliest, the most prolific, and the most influential interpreters of Barth among American Evangelicals. To tell the story of Van Til, Schaeffer, Clark, Klooster and Henry, therefore, is to tell the most important part of the story of Barth reception within the Fundamentalist Evangelical paradigm. But to make the story complete, it is necessary to indicate how other leading thinkers have followed a similar pattern.

These other Fundamentalist Evangelicals are found throughout the Evangelical mosaic. The largest group comprises other self-consciously orthodox theologians who espouse a doctrine of revelation similar to Van Til and Henry, but who rely on a different theory of rationality to defend it. Among them are Missouri Synod Lutheran John Warwick Montgomery, Orthodox Presbyterians John Gerstner and R.C.Sproul, Baptist Clark Pinnock, Free Church theologian, Kenneth Kantzer, and Dispensationalist Charles Caldwell Ryrie. The apologetic position espoused is typically called evidentialist, empiricist, or even classical, and those who maintain it carry into the twentieth century the dominant philosophical tradition of nineteenth century Evangelicalism. Among Reformed Calvinists it has become the minority report because of the influence of Van Til, Clark, and Dooyeweerd (Wells, 1989; Dooyewerd, 1960). But outside the strictly Reformed communities, evidentialism in one form or another is common, preserving a connection between "common sense" rationality and theological scholarship that befits an intellectual tradition embedded in popular religious culture.

The fact that Evangelicalism is embedded in popular religious culture also demands that another group of Fundamentalist Evangelical theologians be recognized: those distinguished by the absence of interaction with Barth. The absence of interaction, combined with the presence of a Fundamentalist theological paradigm, is the most distinguishing characteristic of Barth reception among much of American Evangelical theology. It characterizes the Holiness and Pentecostal traditions, much of the dispensational Bible School movement, and most Southern Baptist theology before World War II. Therefore, some attention will be given to these traditions and their theological leaders in what follows.

Evidentialist Orthodox Apologists[12]
John Warwick Montgomery

Although the Missouri Synod Lutheran Church has not, strictly speaking, been a part of the American Evangelical mosaic, there has been at least one Lutheran scholar who has exerted a measurable influence upon the movement.[13] John Warwick Montgomery spent much of his academic career within the institutional structures of American Evangelicalism, especially Northern Fundamentalist Evangelicalism, and has been read widely by participating pastors and students. He has been a Professor at Trinity Evangelical Divinity School, an active member of the Evangelical Theological Society and a relatively frequent contributor to *Christianity Today*. As a visiting professor of theology at Concordia Seminary, a contributor to Lutheran periodicals, and author/editor of a two volume project on the *Crisis in Lutheran Theology* (1967), Dr. Montgomery has also participated deeply in the world of Missouri Synod Lutherans.

Dr. Montgomery presents himself as an unabashed "Confessional Protestant" in full agreement with the early ecumenical creeds and the confessions of the Lutheran Church (Campbell, 1968; Montgomery, 1970, 180). He also manifests unhesitating confidence in the rationality of this orthodox Christian faith. His understanding of rationality, however, differs in some respects from that affirmed by the presuppositionalist theologians. Like Clark and Henry, he insists upon the scientific nature of theology, arguing in his exposition of "The Theologian's Craft" that "theological theories whatever superscientific characteristics they may have, will most definitely display the full range of properties of scientific theories" (1970, 277). Like these men, Montgomery also insists that an inerrant and perspicuous Scripture provides the only absolutely authoritative source and norm for Christian theology.

But in contrast to Henry and Clark, he argues for empirical verification of theological proposals. Scripture makes historical claims and these claims can and must be verified by the same rational procedures applied to all historical argument. Orthodoxy depends upon an infallible Scriptural authority; but the authority of Scripture must be justified by historical and textual argument in the public arena. While the criteria of rationality has changed somewhat from Henry to Montgomery, the distinguishing characteristic of Fundamentalist Evangelical theology persists, namely, an apologetic defense of orthodoxy by means of a clearly defined doctrine of revelation and related theory of rationality.

When Dr. Montgomery turns his polemic attention to Barth a similar pattern emerges. There is the same focus upon Barth's failed doctrine of revelation and the theory of rationality that underlies it. But in Montgomery's case, the primary accent falls upon the removal of revelation from the objective realm of historical verifiability. The problem with Barth's dialectical response to "the collapse of modernism" is that he "reasserted the ancient Christian verities" while denying their "verifiability" (1970, 28). The resulting theology is characterized by laudatory "kerygmatic strength" and devastating "epistemological weakness" (Ibid., 191-3). Because of such "inherent instabilities" it did not, and logically could not, withstand the further erosion of biblical authority and doctrine that occurred in Bultmann, Tillich, and even the death-of-God theologians. In fact, Montgomery carefully traces the "Barthian" beginnings of the major figures in the death-of-God camp, and argues that the "movement takes its rise from the consistent appropriation and use of a central theme in Neo-Orthodoxy," namely the radical separation between God and human rationality (Ibid., 77).

Barth's method is perceived as an attempt to absorb the negative conclusions of historical criticism by removing theological assertions from realms accessible to scientific investigation. "One of the most central principles of Barth's theology" is "that theology is an autonomous realm in the sense that no bridge exists between it and other realms of human knowledge or experience" (1969, 109). This methodological dualism, furthermore, entails a metaphysical dualism— "between earth and heaven...history and theology...the Bible and Revelation." With these dualisms "inevitably comes a denial of incarnation, the Word actually made flesh" (Ibid., 110).

In this rather extreme conclusion Montgomery follows Van Til explicitly, positing a radical separation between the historical Jesus and Barth's "Christ-Event" because of the supposed import of his distinction between *Historie* and *Geschichte* (Ibid., 106-8). If the events of *Geschichte* cannot be directly identified with any events in *Historie*, and therefore investigated as historical events, then the two realms are ontologically distinct. The events in one cannot—logically cannot—be identified with the events in the other. Hence, a genuine incarnation cannot be maintained.

But Montgomery's criticism goes one step further. To the extent that Barth separates the actions of God from verifiable human experience his theological assertions become meaningless, for Montgomery unabashadly affirms the "Verifiability Criterion of Meaning" as espoused by A. J. Ayer. Acknowledging the validity of Flew's famous parable of the invisible gardener, he insists that meaningful assertions must be factually verifiable—subject to procedures of empirical investigation in the public arena by generally accepted standards of rationality. "Every theological 'truth,' to the extent of its isolation from empirical reality, becomes unverifiable and therefore meaningless" (1970, 337). By this criterion Barth's assertions about the *Geschichte* of Christ and a revelation never directly identified with Scripture become utterly meaningless.

Modern theology, according to Montgomery, finds itself in "crisis," the crisis of a loss of authority resulting from the denial of biblical infallibility (1967, 7, 15). "Contemporary theologians have destroyed themselves by their unnecessary and unwarranted destruction of biblical revelation, on which all sound theology is based" (1970, 37). It is a case of theological suicide that has been occurring since the rise of modern deism, and the infamous death-of-God theologians are its inevitable *terminus a quem*. Barth's dialectical theology, with its "closed circle of irrational commitment" and consequent metaphysical dualism, provides no more than an "inadequate first aid treatment" to a terminally wounded patient, despite his affirmation of creedal verities (Ibid., 29).

The only real hope for recovery is a return to Reformation orthodoxy by means of a confident reassertion of Biblical authority, in the context of a theory of rationality that guards the objectivity and clarity of that authority. Barth's theology has been judged inadequate, and in terms of its influence, positively damaging. Montgomery's solution, though differing in detail from Van Til, Clark and Henry, aims at the same Fundamentalist Evangelical objective.

John Gerstner and R. C. Sproul

Among Presbyterian Fundamentalists, the traditional evidentialist apologetics of Archibald Alexander and Charles Hodge was maintained by Machen, Warfield, Wilbur Smith and Buswell, and it has been recently defended by Evangelical theologians, John Gerstner and R. C. Sproul. In *Classical Apologetics* they offer "a rational defense of the Christian Faith" after the pattern of Edwards and Warfield (Gerstner, 1984). They maintain the rational validity of natural theology and propose updated defenses of the traditional theistic proofs, insisting that the existence of the Christian God is a rationally necessary conclusion for every "informed and honest person" (Ibid., 126).

The arch enemy of this approach, of course, is fideism, and "the common denominator" of all fideistic theologies "is the conviction that faith does not rest upon reason but functions prior to and independent of rational evidences" (Ibid., 34). In the Reformed and Evangelical world, the most common form of fideism goes by the name of presuppositionalism, and Cornelius Van Til is its most influential proponent. Half of Classical Apologetics, therefore, is dedicated to exposition and criticism of the presuppositional apologetics of Van Til.

The engagement with Barth is peripheral, but definite. "Theology found its grand master fideist in the person of Karl Barth," and "his *Epistle to the Romans*" contains "the magna carta of twentieth-century fideism" (Ibid., 33). Ironically, comment on Barth in *Classical Apologetics* serves the primary purpose of highlighting the irrational and heterodox nature of Van Til's position. Van Til is accused of beginning with the same self-authenticating circle of Scriptural authority that isolates Barth's theology from rational defense, of employing the same restriction of logic "to this side of the ontological boundary between God and the created order" and espousing the same "post-Kantian departure from classical Reformed apologetics" (Ibid., 75, 211). The conclusion is quite damaging for one who has condemned Barth's theology as the most dangerous form of "New Modernism" in theological existence today: "However orthodox Van Til's affirmations and convictions may be, the foundations on which he bases them are not a bit less paradoxical than those of Karl Barth" (Ibid., 263). In fact, "at bottom, presuppositionalism is a form of paradox theology" (Ibid., 287). The most positive thing Sproul and Gerstner say of Barth is that he is more consistent than Van Til in his irrational rejection of natural theology and a point of contact between created human consciousness and divine truth (Ibid., 226).

Clark Pinnock

The same antipathy to Barthian fideism in the name of an orthodox doctrine of revelation and an evidentialist theory of rationality is found in the early Clark Pinnock. Although both his doctrine of revelation and his view of Karl Barth were to change over time (Pinnock, 1984; 1986; Price, 1988; Mohler, 1989, 156-166), the perspective expressed in *Biblical Revelation* follows the Fundamentalist Evangelical pattern closely. Modern theology is diagnosed as suffering from "a crisis in valid authority" caused by a "defection" from "the historic Christian position on divine revelation" (Pinnock, 1971a, 10-13, 158-162). That position is the doctrine of verbal, plenary inspiration as articulated by B. B. Warfield, with inerrancy its necessary corollary (Ibid., 66-

106). Only such a doctrine of Scripture, which accurately represents apostolic teaching on the subject, provides the "epistemological base" Christian theology requires (Ibid., 11).

In defining and defending this epistemological base, however, Pinnock finds it necessary to articulate a theory of truth as well as a doctrine of revelation. In fact, modern departures from orthodoxy, whether Liberal or Neo-Orthodox, derive from a "divided field of knowledge" that removes theological assertions from the realm of empirical verifiability (Ibid., 164; 1971b, 9-15). Neo-orthodoxy, in particular, constructs "categories of evasion" by which it avoids submitting to an objective and infallible biblical authority. Foremost among these is its redefinition of revelation as "personal encounter" rather than "propositional truth." The result is a "transcendental, personalist view of revelation" that provides no fixed cognitive basis for theological understanding (Ibid.,162-6). Of this view, Karl Barth is designated "the primary spokesman" (Ibid., 166). Apparently following his early mentor, Francis Schaeffer, Pinnock construes Barth as the prime exemplar of a transcendental, "upper story" view of revelation that rests upon a shift in the concept of truth descending from Kant and Kierkegaard.

This divided field of knowledge manifests itself, of course, in Barth's fideism. "Barth is the great fideist of the twentieth century and allergic to Christian evidences, even as Kant and Kierkegaard, his mentors, were before him" (Ibid., 42). Pinnock regards the refusal to test religious truth claims by reason as a failure to provide an adequate foundation for Christian theology. Rationality requires that any assertion "be *criticizable* and subject to the constraints of the evidence," and Pinnock cites with approval the proposals of Hodge, Warfield, Gerstner, and Montgomery in the course of his argument for "revelational empiricism" (Ibid., 46-8). Like Montgomery, he argues that Barth's resistance to empirical verification undermines his claim to genuine historicity in revelation and the incarnation (Ibid., 46).

Although Pinnock's comment upon Barth in *Biblical Revelation* is brief, revealing a limited familiarity with the Barthian corpus and dependence upon the interpretation of others, it is sufficient to indicate his continuity in this early stage with the Fundamentalist Evangelical heritage out of which he came.[14]

Kenneth Kantzer

Another influential evidentialist within American Evangelicalism is Kenneth Kantzer. An elder statesman of the postwar movement, Kantzer has been an instructor at Wheaton College, Professor and Dean of Trinity Evangelical Divinity School, Editor of *Christianity Today*, a founding member of the Evangelical Theological Society, and a frequent contributor to Evangelical periodicals and edited publications. He also served as an early interpreter of Barth within Evangelicalism, having spent the sabbatical year of 1954-1955 studying in Basel, and being invited to deliver the 1957 W.H Griffith Thomas lectures at Dallas Theological Seminary on "Revelation and Inspiration in Neo-Orthodox Theology" (Kantzer, 1958a).

Before 1960 there were only a handful of Fundamentalist Evangelicals writing on Barth, and with Carl Henry, Dr. Kantzer was one of the first to strike a more positive note. He voiced "forthright appreciation" for Barth's effective opposition to Modernism, his affirmation of the centrality of Christ and his assertion of the authority of Scripture as witness (Ibid., 23-4.). Contrary to Van Til and Klooster, Kantzer interpreted Barth's affirmations of creedal Christianity as genuine, not subjecting them to comprehensive critique or reinterpretation (Kantzer, 1958b). Nevertheless, he insisted upon the necessity of opposition to Barth, and even argued at one point that the foe is more dangerous because less obvious (Kantzer, 1956b, 192).

Kantzer's basic assessment is that Barth's theology is an "illogical and uneasy" combination of "biblical insights" and a "nonbiblical philosophical framework." "At times his biblical exegesis is primary and his doctrine shines forth true to Evangelical faith. At other times the framework becomes basic and upon it he stretches and tortures the teaching of Scripture" (Ibid.). This distortion manifests itself most clearly on the level of epistemology. "The heart of the whole matter" and the "fundamental issue separating all Neo-Orthodox from the orthodox" is the doctrine of Scripture (Ibid.). Orthodoxy espouses direct identity between the words of Scripture and the Word of God in the form of an inspired and inerrant propositional revelation. Barth employs the category of witness, under the influence of Kierkegaard's infinite qualitative distinction, to undermine this direct identity. The inevitable result is subjectivity: human decision functions as a "sieve" for filtering what is authoritative Word among the biblical words (1958a, 29).

While Barth's doctrine of revelation is the fundamental error arising from his Kierkegaardian beginnings, Kantzer also claims that Barth's "dialectical method" embraces a basic irrationalism (1956b, 196). Thus we find the same two-fold emphasis in Kantzer as in other Fundamentalist Evangelicals: an unorthodox doctrine of Scripture and an inadequate theory of rationality produced by a controlling philosophy. Barth's dialectical negations indicate that "reason," exercised by the normal canons of rationality, leads to a denial of Christian truth. Nevertheless faith, or "divinely implanted intuition," enables one to acknowledge these truths. The result is a "paradoxical" affirmation of Christian verities without basis in reason—in other words, irrationalism (Ibid., 196). But the affirmation of Christianity's reasonableness is a distinguishing characteristic of Evangelical theology as Kantzer understands it (1975, 46; 1960a, 42).

"Barthianism," like all Neo-Orthodoxy, is "building a new theology on a new basis...just as much as did the modernists a generation ago" (1958a, 29). While Kantzer's interpretion of Barth as inconsistent enables him to be more positive than Van Til, the qualified praise is muffled by the sound of a dominant rejection.

Charles Caldwell Ryrie

In Charles Ryrie, Professor of Theology for more than thirty years at Dallas Theological Seminary, and one of American Dispensationalism's leading theologians, the note of muffled praise is hardly sounded. Rather, the uncompromising opposition of Cornelius Van Til is continued. Barthian theology "has been hailed as the new or neo-orthodoxy; in reality it is nothing but a false or pseudo orthodoxy" (Ryrie, 1956, 6). It is a "theological hoax," promising what it can never deliver: "a synthesis above and beyond the liberal-orthodox antithesis" (Ibid., 62). Even the orthodoxy of its terminology is deceptive, for "isolated statements" of apparently sound theology "seen in the context of the system take on an entirely different meaning" (Ibid., 7). To expose the fundamental antithesis between Evangelical orthodoxy and Neo-Orthodoxy by means of a brief critical exposition of the Barthian system is the purpose of Ryrie's early book, *Neo-Orthodoxy: An Evangelical Evaluation of Barthianism* (1956).

The brevity of the book, however, and its intended audience—"conservative pastors and laymen"—leave little room for serious and extended engagement. Nevertheless, Ryrie's position is clear.. The basic cause of the Neo-Orthodox deception is the attempt to proclaim orthodox truth while accepting liberal conclusions about the source and norm of theology. "It is both illogical and impossible to accept the 'findings' of destructive criticism and preach and speak in orthodox terms" (Ibid., 50). For Ryrie, and the dispensationalists he teaches and represents, either the Bible is a "verbally inspired authoritative external standard" and the destructive conclusions of higher criticism are to be denied, or one must affirm a liberal denial of biblical authority and reinterpretation of doctrine (Ibid., 59). The dialectical method of Neo-Orthodoxy, rather than providing analternative synthesis, simply shifts like an "unbalanced pendulum" between orthodoxy and liberalism, moving inevitably in the direction of subjective "mysticism" (Ibid., 63). Barth's "instrumental" and "dynamic" view of revelation, in which the words of Scripture become the Word of God, ultimately reduces to an "authority without actuality" (Ibid., 46, 63).

Ryrie also asserts that Barth's view of revelation and history "boils down" to a denial of actual occurrence in space and time (Ibid., 59). The significance of Jesus' historical life is inevitably denied and the cross and resurrection are redefined as mystical signs and pointers (Ibid., 24, 36). God, the "wholly other," "never passes over to the human side" (Ibid., 22). With this view of the import of the Barthian system, it comes as no surprise that Ryrie considers Barth's theology a "hoax".

Nor does Ryrie's position change over time, since the isolated and incidental comments on Barth in Ryrie's *Basic Theology* repeat the substance of statements made in *Neo-Orthodoxy* (1986, 21,75, 221, 310, 520). Nor is Ryrie unique among informed dispensationalists. In 1948, Dr. John F. Walvoord, Professor of Theology and President of Dallas Theological Seminary, assessed Van Til's *New Modernism* as fundamentally correct:

> Taking the argument as a whole, Dr. Van Til has assembled a massive argument against Barthianism. After allowing all due concessions of possible misrepresentation of Barth, the remaining material is not seriously weakened in its force or in its conclusions. Dr. Van Til has done a fine and scholarly piece of work and performed a real service to Evangelical Christianity... The book may well serve for some time as a scholarly warning to those who would embrace Barth and Brunner in the fold of traditional Protestantism (Walvoord, 1948).

Ryrie's book simply continues this tradition of warning, as have other dispensationalist statements (Aldrich, 1964, 1971; Rand, 1953; Lightner, 1986, 79; Walvoord, 1968, 196).

Pietistic Fundamentalist Evangelicalism

Fundamentalist Evangelicalism, as defined above, is marked by an apologetic orientation and orthodox self-understanding. The interpretation of Barth has been predominantly critical, and the polemic has focused upon his doctrine of revelation and the existential, dialectical or fideistic theory of rationality upon which it supposedly depends. The earliest and most influential interpreters, and typically the most sophisticated, were theologians who operated within orthodox Reformed communities or were directly influenced by them, namely, Van Til, Klooster, Clark, Henry and Montgomery. The influence of Reformed traditions within American Evangelical theology has a distinguished pedigree and the impact of Old School Princeton and Westminster Seminary upon Evangelical scholarship has continued in the history of Barth reception.

But to present this reformed theological tradition as if it were the entirety of American Evangelical theology, even Fundamentalist Evangelical theology, would be to misrepresent the situation. One of the strongest distinguishing characteristics of Evangelicalism as it developed in nineteenth century America, was the progressive predominance of more pietistic and arminian religious traditions. Therefore, some attention must be given to the reception of Barth among the Holiness tradition and Southern Evangelicalism.

Popular and pietistic traditions, culturally separated from Barth, tend to interact with him very little. But when the absence of interaction is combined with a fundamentalist pattern in theology, one often finds a basic opposition to modern theology.

This is obviously the case in various handbooks or volumes on systematic theology written by leading theologians in the dispensational Bible College movement (at the heart of Northern Fundamentalist Evangelicalism). The eight volumes of Lewis Sperry Chafer's *Systematic Theology*, written by the founder of Dallas Theological Seminary and published by that institution in 1947, proceed as if Karl Barth did not even exist (Chafer, 1947). Likewise, the very influential one volume *Lectures in Systematic Theology*, written by Henry Clarence Thiessen, Chairman of the Faculty of the Graduate School at Wheaton College until 1948, only mentions Barth once (Thiessen, 1949). This book has undergone multiple printings (18 by 1979) and functions as a standard reference work in many Evangelical seminaries and Bible colleges. In fact, it was the mimeographed edition of these lectures to which Carl Henry referred when he said, in comment upon his student days, "Apart from the fact that Neo-Orthodoxy held critical views of the Bible, we hardly knew that there was a Barth" (Henry, 1986, 65).

H. Orton Wiley

Beyond the Dispensationalist pale, within the Wesleyan Holiness tradition, the situation is similar. In the early 1920s, at the request of the Church of the Nazarene, H. Orton Wiley began "a work of systematic theology of sufficient scope and thoroughness" to "serve as a standard of doctrine" for that church and the movement it represented (Wiley, 1943, 5). The resulting *Christian Theology* was published in three volumes from 1940 to 1943, and was followed in 1947 by a condensed *Introduction to Christian Theology*. It is the only comprehensive systematic theology published from within the Holiness tradition during the twentieth century, and according to a recent survey of the Wesleyan Theological Society (a Wesleyan counterpart to the Evangelical Theological Society), it established its author as the most influential theologian among its members (Noll, 1986, 209-13).[15]

Denying any claim to originality, Wiley aimed at a concise presentation of "the great doctrines of the church" for those "entering the ministry," and he relied, for the most part, upon theological texts written before the twentieth century (1943, 3). Although he listed works by Barth in the "Contemporary Theology" section of recommendations for study, there is not a single reference in the three volume work, or its condensation, to Barth, Barthianism, or Neo-Orthodoxy. Apparently a concise and orderly restatement of the traditional Wesleyan position on doctrine provides appropriate and sufficient preparation for Christian ministry.

There are, however, certain emphases in Wiley's work that distinguish him from the reformed interpreters analyzed in the bulk of this chapter. Of course, a traditional Wesleyan doctrine of sanctification is affirmed and is the object of extended treatment. But there is also a slightly different idea of revelation proposed, in emphasis if not in substance. While Wiley understands Scripture "as the true and inerrant record of the Personal Word," he also denies the identity of revelation and the Bible apart from the continual activity of the living Spirit who makes the Word personal (Ibid., 125). The ultimate principle of religious authority for the Christian is not the church, reason, or the Bible, but the living Christ speaking in and through the Scriptures. "When, however, the living synthesis of the written Word and the personal Word is lost, the church thereby sunders the Bible from the spiritual communion in which it perpetually stands, and comes to view it as an independent book, apart from the living presence of the author". "This is the error of scholastic orthodoxy", and Wiley condemns it (Ibid., 141).

In its place he offers a doctrine of Scripture as "coincident" but not "identical" with the personal divine Word (Ibid., 125). It would be interesting to know, in light of this distinction, how Wiley would respond to Barth's three forms of the Word united in the event of revelation. But Wiley never discusses Barth. The most that can be said, therefore, is that certain emphases in Wiley seem to move more in Barth's direction than would be allowed by Van Til, Clark, and Henry.

Along with this emphasis on the priority of the personal Word, Wiley also gives experience a particularly sensitive role in Christian thought and life. In keeping with a Wesleyan orientation, he posits a continuity between generally human and christian experience secured by prevenient grace. Christianity is defined as a "religion" in which the effects of divine revelation are experienced in human consciousness. Indeed, it is "the distinctive and final religion" that satisfies the sense of human need and the awareness of divine holiness that lies at the origin of all religion (Ibid., 125). This whole orientation toward continuity between human religion and divine revelation stands in fundamental contradiction to Barth's strictures on natural theology and his understanding of religion. But again, Barth is not a conversation partner.

E. Y. Mullins and W. T. Connor

A similar dual emphasis on the personal nature of revelation and the importance of Christian experience is found in the two most influential Southern Baptist theologians before the Second World War, E. Y. Mullins and W. T. Connor. Like Wiley, they published their major works before 1945, and therefore, before most of the Barthian corpus was available in English. This is especially true of Mullins, whose systematic theology, *The Christian Religion in its Doctrinal Expression*, was published two years before Barth's *Römerbrief*. Nevertheless, it underwent multiple reprintings and from 1917 to 1947 and was the standard theological text at The Southern Baptist Theological Seminary. It was used by Mullins' successor between the wars, H. W. Tribble, and exerted a dominant influence upon Connor, another Mullins student, who taught for thirty-five years at Southwestern Seminary (George, 1985; Garret, 1990).

The published interaction with Barth by these three men—Mullins, Connor and Tribble—was negligible, and the absence of serious interaction was accompanied by doctrinal emphases that maintained substantial continuity with a conservative Evangelical past. Between Mullins' *Christian Religion in its Doctrinal Expression* (1947), or his condensed *Baptist Beliefs* (1925), and Connor's *Christian Doctrine* (1926), *Revelation and God* (1936) or *The Gospel of Redemption* (1945), there is little difference in doctrinal affirmation. Each of these works continues to operate within the parameters of the New Hampshire Declaration of Faith (Mullins, 1925, 5-6, 83-94; Garret, 1990a; Honeycutt, 1986). Dr. Mullins even published an important book at the height of the Modernist-Fundamentalist controversies, *Christianity at the Cross Roads* (1924), defending the Christian religion and its "irreducible Christ" against the "reductions" of "the modern spirit" (1924, vii).

There are, however, important differences between this Southern Baptist conservatism and the orthodoxy of Northern Fundamentalist Evangelicalism. While many of the doctrinal affirmations remain the same, the larger philosophical and theological context is different. Reformed Fundamentalist Evangelicalism focused primarily on modern theology's defective theories of revelation and rationality, causing its apologetic orientation to be decidedly philosophical. Consequently, the concept of propositional revelation, and the strict identity between Scripture and revelation, became a primary preoccupation. The approach of Mullins and Connor is not quite the same.

According to one historian of Southern Baptist theology, E. Y. Mullins was "a critical conservative who sought to restate the Christian faith in contemporary terms" (George, 1985, 38; 1985; Humphreys, 1990). This more mediating approach can be seen, for example, in the central role assigned to Christian experience in his theological constructions. The definition of Christianity as a religion, and theology as "simply the interpretation of the Christian religion," reveals a continuity between Mullins and the liberal tradition descending from Schleiermacher that would be objectionable to Van Til and Henry (Mullins, 1947, 24). Of course, it also reveals the influence of his more pietistic and revivalist heritage. But the conservative theological construction that he and Connor built on this methodological foundation manifests a deep confidence in the power of historical revelation and redemptive experience to reveal the biblical Christ and lead to traditional doctrinal affirmations.

The mediating approach of Mullins and Connor can be seen quite clearly in their doctrine of revelation, and the strategies they employ for reconciling potential conflicts between Scripture and science. Revelation is a personal transaction in which God gives himself to man in salvation. The experience of revelation is, therefore, an experience of redemption (Mullins, 1947, 141; Connor, 1945, 126). Quite naturally, the purpose of Scripture is to record and mediate these redemptive experiences, and its infallibility and authority are commensurate with its religious purpose (Mullins, 1947, 152-6; Connor, 1945, 87, 96).

W. T. Connor comments,

> The older view was that the Bible, as God's revelation, was a record of divine truth. Revelation was defined as the disclosure of new truth on the part of God to man. We are coming now to see that revelation is something more vital and per-sonal. It is a self disclosure on the part of God (1945, 90).

This self disclosure is identified, following P. T. Forsyth, with the speaking Christ: "as the revelation of the mind and will of Christ, the Bible is authoritative" (Ibid., 96). But it should be noted that both Mullins and Connor combine this correction of older views with continued affirmation of biblical infallibility.

Because of its nature and purpose as a religious book, Mullins and Connor also argue that the conflicts between science and Scripture are more apparent than real. In fact, one of the basic arguments of *Christianity at the Crossroads* (1924) is that philosophy, science and religion pursue different tasks by different methods, and therefore operate in fundamentally different "spheres" (or "levels"). The "reality" of redemption and communion with God in Christ is "religiously known" and "religiously evaluated" (Mullins, 1924, 40-54).

But when Mullins develops this concept of the independent "rights of religion" (or science), he does not maintain a radical separation. Reality as religiously known involves historical interpretation, the assertion of a Christian world view and rational reflection on the nature of Christian experience. Nevertheless, the concept of independence between science, philosophy and religion (based upon a particular understanding of the nature of biblical revelation) represents a very different approach from reformed Fundamentalist Evangelicalism as represented by Van Til, Henry and Schaeffer.

We are on the edge, therefore, of a different relation to the thought of Karl Barth, which can be seen in the incidental positive comments about the Barthians by Connor, as well as the progressive development of a more positive appropriation of Neo-Orthodox theology in post World War II Southern Baptist theology (Connor, 1945, 216; 1949, 2; Moody, 1950). Nevertheless, the absence of serious interaction with Barth and the continuing presence of a conservative, pietistic religion and theology, justifies inclusion of prewar Southern Baptist theology just within the line of Fundamentalist Evangelical Barth reception. But it does indicate the difficulty of drawing tight, narrow lines to encompass the entirety of even Fundamentalist Evangelicalism.[16]

In the following chapter it becomes increasingly clear that basic lines of Evangelical identity have been crossed. While the theologians analyzed belong in the Evangelical mosaic, by heritage and doctrinal beliefs, both their reception of Barth and the theological positions they espouse demand they be recognized as representatives of a kind of theology different from Fundamentalist Evangelicalism.

NOTES

1. Consider, for example, the predominant place apologetics has occupied in the work of these prominent Evangelical leaders: Machen (1921, 1923, 1925, 1930); Wilbur Smith (1946); Cornelius Van Til (1946, 1955a, 1964a, 1969a); J. Oliver Buswell (1950a, 1960), J. Edward Carnell (1948, 1952, 1957, 1959); Gordon Clark (1952, 1957a,b, 1962, 1964, 1973); Bernard Ramm (1953a,b, 1954, 1957a, 1961b, 1972); John Gerstner (1960, 1984); Carl Henry (1946, 1949, 1957a,d, 1976-84); Clark Pinnock (1967, 1971a,b); J. W. Montgomery (1962a, 1967, 1969, 1970); Francis Schaeffer (1950, 1968a,b, 1972, 1984); R. C. Sproul (1982, 1984); Robert Reymond (1968, 1969); Harold O. J. Brown (1969; 1984); Norman Geisler (1974).

2. In a recent survey of the Evangelical Theological Society, Van Til and his student, Francis Schaeffer, ranked third (behind John Calvin and George Ladd) in a list of scholars who "exerted the dominant influence" upon members' lives (Noll, 1986, 209); for other indications of Van Til's influence, see Clowney, 1984; Nicole, 1987; Ramm, 1983, 23; Pinnock, 1978; Kantzer, 1986; Gerstner, 1984.

3. When Westminster was established, with a mature faculty of accomplished scholars, Trinity, Fuller, Denver Conservative Baptist, Talbot, Covenant, Faith, and Grace Seminaries did not even exist. Wheaton College was a fledgling institution and Gordon-Conwell a Bible College. Dallas Seminary had been founded five years earlier, but its level of scholarship, judged by its journal, *Bibliotheca Sacra*, was comparable to the training offered in Bible Institutes. There were the relatively new Northern Baptist (1911) and Eastern Baptist (1923) seminaries—and of course, The Southern Baptist Theological Seminary—but the scholars at Westminster had no peers among Northern Fundamentalist scholastic institutions. According to the investigations of Mark Noll into the history of Evangelical biblical scholarship, "It is an exaggeration to say that conservative Evangelical Bible scholarship during the 1930s was confined to the faculty common room of Westminster Theological Seminary in Philadelphia. But not by much" (Noll, 1986, 93).

4. Van Til also discusses *Die christliche Dogmatik im Ent-wurf* and

certain lesser known articles that precede Barth's confrontation with Brunner, including *"Fate und Schicksal in der Theologie"* (Barth, 1929). Because of the signficance of this article for the question of Barth's relationship to idealist and dialectical philosophy, it is unfortunate Van Til did not offer a more serious analysis of its argument (see Rumscheidt, 1986; Sykes, 1986). Equally disappointing is Van Til's failure, even by 1962, to engage directly Barth's own interpretations of Kant and Hegel.

    5. For a sympathetic reading of Barth's conceptual redescription of divine being as being-in-act, see Jungel, 1976, and Gunton, 1978. Richard Roberts (1991), while manifesting a more responsible and sophisticated interpretation of Barth than Van Til, pursues a similar critical line: He traces Barth's reformulation of divine being to a herculean, but ultimately inadequate, attempt to overcome the idealist problematic by means of a radical redefinition of time.

    6. Other influential Orthodox Presbyterians who responded to Barth in the same way, but are not discussed below, include R. Laird Harris (1943; 1955; 1963a,b) and Robert Reymond (1968; 1969).

    7. Besides the dialogue reported below, other interactions include interviews by Donald Grey Barnhouse (1934) and Miner Stearns (1949), contact with Kenneth Kantzer (1954), Fred Klooster (1959) and Bernard Ramm (1957) during sabbaticals in Basel, questions posed by Carl Henry and Carnell at plenary sessions during Barth's visit to America, and a very brief correpondence with Van Til, via his student Robert Geehan (reported in Mohler, 1989, 105-6). Both Daniel Fuller and James Boice pursued doctoral studies in Basel during the fifties, but in New Testament (Fuller, 1965; Boice, 1970).

    8. Buswell, one-time President of Wheaton College, left his mark on Evangelical thought through the publication of a two volume systematic theology and a book on his empiricist theory of rationality, both of which are still used as texts in Evangelical schools (Buswell, 1960, 1962). Although recognizing the limitations of his scholarship, Kenneth Kantzer describes Buswell as one of the most influential Evangelical theologians during the middle third of the century (Kantzer, 1976).

    9. For other brief comments by Barth on his treatment by "these fundamentalists", see Barth, 1981, 7-8 and *CD* IV/2, xii.

    10. Henry extols him as "one of the profoundest Evangelical Protestant philosophers of our time," whose "analysis of secular philosophy has never been answered by professional philosophers," apparently because of "the validity of his views" (Nash, 1968, 20-21).

    11. It might indeed be true to say that some form of Aristotelian or Kantian "empiricism" characterizes Barth's "theory" of language when he discusses it as a human possibility apart from divine revelation. But as Eberhard Jüngel (1976) has demonstrated, Barth uses language in a decidely non-Aristotelian manner when depicting theological realities.

    12. Noteworthy examples of Fundamentalist Evangelical response to Barth that follow this evidentialist pattern, but which are not analyzed below, include Roger Nicole (1984), Gordon Lewis and Bruce Demarest (1987, 1990), Harold O. J. Brown (1968, 1969), William Fletcher (1962), and Harold Kuhn (1956).

    13. Although the arguments of Rudnick (1966) rest upon a restrictive definition of Fundamentalism, the Missouri Synod Lutherans have maintained a cultural distance from the American Evangelical Movement. The denomination's conservative tendency, however, and its development from a marginal-

ized immigrant community to a more culturally engaged denomination during the twentieth century have produced parallels with American Evangelical history and provided a basis for limited cooperation. For Missouri Synod criticisms of Barth which parallel Montgomery, see, R. D. Preus (1960a,b; 1962; 1967), Mayer (1949), Coates (1954; 1955), Scaer (1979) and T. Mueller (1934; 1963).

14. During the later seventies and eighties, Pinnock's theological paradigm shifted under the impact, primarily, of "empirical doubts" about the possibility of maintaining the doctrine of Scriptural inerrancy espoused by Warfield (Pinnock, 1984). He also adopted a more sympathetic interpretation of Barth's contribution to theology, and even to his teaching on apologetics and theological rationality (Pinnock, 1978; 1986a), although never becoming a significant Barth interpeter. For an account of Pinnock's development, see Price, 1988, and Mohler, 1989, 156-166.

15. *A Contemporary Wesleyan Theology* (1983), edited by Charles Carter and "produced by 23 theologians from 7 leading denominations of the Wesleyan persuasion" is a collection of essays on theological topics by contemporary Wesleyan leaders. Many contributions reveal theological language, structures and commitments very similar to Wiley (eg., Carter, Carpenter, Earl, Wilson and Agnew).

16. A similar pattern—experientially oriented, arminian theology that maintains extensive continuity with nineteenth century precedents while interacting minimally with twentieth century theologians—can be found in the major handbooks of Pentecostal theology (Pearlman, 1937; Williams, 1953; see Spittler, 1985) and prewar American Mennonite theology (Kaufman, 1914; Wenger, 1946).

3

BEYOND FUNDAMENTALIST

EVANGELICALISM

New Evangelical Reception in the Reformed Traditions

The orthodox apologetic reaction to Barth has occurred within a certain social context. It arose within communities that adopted a fundamentalist pattern of opposition to broader cultural and theological developments, namely, separated Orthodox Presbyterianism and the culturally isolated Dutch Reformed. It spread from this reformed center to the larger Evangelical mosaic primarily through the institutional network of Northern Fundamentalist Evangelicalism. During the postwar resurgence of Evangelical religion, when a new rhetoric of cooperative engagement was being voiced, a more positive tone was sounded by men like Carl Henry and Kenneth Kantzer. But the distinguishing characteristics of the Fundamentalist Evangelical paradigm were still present, and within those communities that maintained substantial continuity with Fundamentalist precedents, the orthodox and apologetic reaction to Barth has predominated.

For this reason New Evangelical departures in Barth reception have taken the form of reaction to, or movement beyond, the apologetic paradigm. The organization of the present study reflects this basic pattern. The theologians discussed below differ from the Fundamentalist Evangelicals of chapter two both in their perception of Karl Barth and their understanding of Evangelical theology. While the issues discussed and positions taken, as well as the historical context, justify their inclusion as American Evangelicals, they certainly occupy a different place in the mosaic. They also reflect the changing shape of that mosaic over time.

What are the distinguishing characteristics of this new paradigm of Barth reception? In the first place, it is diverse, at least more diverse than the Fundamentalist Evangelical paradigm. It is the nature of apologetic orthodoxy to possess well-defined boundaries. In fact, boundary definition is an important aspect of such a theology. But when a theologian moves beyond the boundaries of Fundamentalist Evangelicalism he can move in various directions. The kinds of theological positions that lie beyond Fundamentalist Evangelicalism and yet still claim to be within the Evangelical mosaic are, consequently, manifold.

Amidst this diversity, however, there are certain shared tendencies. First and foremost, there is a willingness to identify Barth as an Evangelical theologian. The notes of praise and appreciation among Fundamentalist Evangelicals, however strong, always fall short of this significant affirmation. With this basic judgment, therefore, a watershed in Barth interpretation is crossed. Secondly, there is a resistance to interpreting Barth as subject to controlling philosophical commitments. Barth's professed intention to orient theology to the Word is considered more decisive than any speculative commitments, and he is often judged successful in fulfilling this intention. In fact, Barth's own criticism of scholastic orthodoxy and rationalistic apologetics is often turned against Fundamentalist Evangelicals, and they are judged more philosophically controlled than Barth himself. In the third place, New Evangelical interpreters tend to appropriate dimensions of Barth's theology. Barth begins to function as a partner in genuine dialogue and even a model for theological reconstruction, a possibility never realized by Evangelicals whose orthodoxy is more resistant to reformulation. But finally, New Evangelical reception of Barth does have a critical dimension. Various aspects of Barth's theological project are criticized, and the basis of criticism is always the teaching of Scripture as interpreted within the Evangelical tradition. The combination of both constructive appropriation and historically rooted criticism is what makes this interpretive paradigm both "new" and "Evangelical."

Reception of Barth beyond the boundaries of Fundamentalist Evangelicalism, therefore, is *diverse*, but unified by an *affirmation of Barth's Evangelical identity* and by a *constructive, though* critical, *appropriation of his theology*.

As with Fundamentalist Evangelicalism, the New Evangelical reception of Barth reflects, and is rooted in, both a theological paradigm and a social situation. "New Evangelicalism" itself is a postwar phenomenon in America, produced as resurgent Fundamentalism, in the process of overcoming its marginalized status, adopted a strategy of cooperative engagement. Rejecting the separatist tendencies of their Fundamentalist forebears, Evangelical pioneers like Billy Graham, Harold Ockenga and Carl Henry forged networks between cooperating conservatives for the purpose of cultural engagement. One ironic consequence of this strategy was that it produced successive stages of division and boundary confusion. As the cooperative network expanded, diverse forms of conservative religion were brought within the growing Evangelical movement and the problem of pluralism emerged.

The theologians discussed in this chapter and the next participate in this New Evangelicalism, and they do so as representatives of modified Evangelical theologies. Through critical dialogue with broader streams of thought, including the writings of Barth, these men have adopted theological positions that mediate between contemporary currents and orthodox traditions. For most, if not all, these mediating positions have required movement beyond an earlier Fundamentalist Evangelicalism. Still self-consciously Evangelical, their understanding of Evangelicalism differs from the theologians discussed in chapter two, as do their strategies for maintaining continuity with a conservative heritage.

Not insignificantly, the social setting for this point of view corresponds to its more inclusive nature. Positive interpretation of Barth originated outside of the more separated conservative communities of American Evangelicalism and tends to thrive in institutions which pursue inclusive and progressive agendas. In fact, most of the New Evangelical interpreters are members of mainline denominations, and two of the earliest and most influential, Geoffrey Bromiley and G. C. Berkouwer, are not even American. A correlation exists, therefore, between positive reception of Barth and cultural distance from American Fundamentalism.

For the sake of accurate exposition, interaction with Barth among the more pietistic sectors of the Evangelical mosaic—Southern Baptist, Holiness-Pentecostal, and Anabaptist—will be separated from his reception within the more reformed traditions—Dutch Reformed and Northern Fundamentalist Evangelical. Not surprisingly, the reformed traditions have provided most of the interaction with the Swiss Reformed theologian.

Bromiley and Berkouwer: Early Influences, Enduring Models
Geoffrey Bromiley

If there is one person who has influenced the reception of Barth within the New Evangelical paradigm, it is Dr. Geoffrey W. Bromiley. Among English-speaking Evangelicals he is probably the only Barthian scholar of international reputation, earned by his skillful and prolific translation of Barth's writings. Because of this dual role as respected translator and practicing Evangelical, Bromiley has functioned as an interpretive expert for the Evangelical community. His "fundamental appreciation" for Barth's theology has also enabled him to become an influential advocate (Bromiley, 1979, xiii).

In America this role as expert interpreter and advocate was expressed in *Christianity Today* articles, essays in volumes published for Evangelical audiences, and his own introductions to historical theology and to the theology of Karl Barth. As a Professor of Historical Theology at Fuller Seminary for twenty-nine years (1958-1987), Dr. Bromiley exerted a sustained and significant influence upon the American Evangelical community of Barth interpreters.

It must be noted, however, that Bromiley came to Fuller as an established Anglican churchman and scholar. Educated at Emmanuel College, Cambridge and Tyndale Hall, Bristol, he was ordained in the Church of England, and served, among other charges, as Rector of St. Thomas in Edinburgh (1951-58) and as Lecturer and Vice-Principal at his theological alma mater, Tyndale Hall (1946-51).[1] During the forties he was granted a Ph.D. and D.Litt. by the University of Edinburgh for studies in eighteenth and nineteenth century German theology and Reformation sacramentalism (Bromiley, 1943; 1948). By the time he left the British Isles he had published numerous articles, written eight books, and become executive editor for the translation of *Kirchliche Dogmatik*, much of which he did himself. Dr. Bromiley's formative influences, therefore, were British, not American, and his "experience" of Karl Barth, as he once labeled it, was extensive long before he entered American Evangelicalism (Bromiley, 1986a).

It was also fundamentally positive. From his first encounter with Barth's writings, which occurred soon after his studies at theological college (in 1937), Bromiley was impressed. Their passion and penetrating insight aroused a vision for historical theology and dogmatics that shaped Bromiley's career. "Through Barth," he acknowledges, "theology became for me. . . an enthralling subject" (1986a, 67). Even before the "extensive and intensive immersion in *Church Dogmatics*" brought by years of translation, Bromiley claimed he "learned more real theology from [Barth] than from any other living teacher" (Ibid., 68).

But Bromiley was not a naive partisan of Barthian theology. From the beginning there was a critical side to his reception of Barth, arising from his own commitment to a self-consciously Reformed Evangelicalism. While deeply influenced by the great Swiss theologian, Bromiley's religious and theological community was still English-speaking Evangelicalism. He identified with the nineteenth century Anglican Evangelical party, comprised of people who saw "no reason for evasions, mental reservations, or fundamental tensions in their relation to the [Thirty-Nine] Articles." He believed, therefore, that these Articles should continue to provide the "dogmatic stratum" upon which the "hope of Evangelical renewal" is based (1963, 13).

This "reformed and therefore Evangelical" confessionalism, however, is of a different type than the apologetic orthodoxy of Van Til or Henry (Ibid.). It follows the more mediating path of Thomas Cranmer, who "made his articles of religion as comprehensive as possible within an Evangelical and scriptural framework" (1956b,c). It leaves many questions open, recognizes the necessity of diversity and development in theological expression, and eschews the distorting influence of philosophical apologetics (1978a, xxvi-vii, 452-5). Following Barth, Bromiley discerns the "inroads of rationalism" in seventeenth century orthodoxy and its descendants, including Fundamentalism, and suggests that "while biblical in its materials," it "is very far from biblical in its basis, structure and method" (1957, 5).

His was a conservative but mediating Evangelicalism in the Anglican tradition that sought to maintain continuity with the Reformed confessions, and through them, the apostolic testimony of the biblical witness. Obviously, when Bromiley came to America he brought this tradition with him, as well as a deep appreciation for, and knowledge of, Karl Barth.

Barth Reception

Bromiley's primary role within American Evangelicalism, besides translation, has been to provide expert interpretation of the expansive Barthian corpus, a function which grew quite naturally from his experience as translator. His major contributions, therefore, are mostly explanatory, and critical engagement is limited to brief sections at the conclusion of his exposition.[2] Nevertheless, there is embedded in his interpretive essays an obvious advocacy.

Bromiley focuses upon interpretation, in part, because "an enormous quantity of high-sounding and influential nonsense" has been produced by scholars who fail to read carefully and comprehensively in the Barthian corpus (1979, xi). Some of the common misunderstandings he challenges are the attempt to explain Barth's theology by means of a single controlling theme (Ibid.), the suggestion that his idea of revelation is ultimately subjectivist (Ibid., 77), irrational (Ibid., 10, 58, 248), or non-historical (Ibid., 14, 112), or finally, the assertion that he is a modalist (Ibid., 16) or christomonist (Ibid., xi, 51). Among others, Bromiley has specific American Evangelical interpreters in mind (Bromiley, 1962).

In a 1959 *Christianity Today* article Bromiley attributes these widespread misunderstandings to a failure to discern important changes that had occurred in Barth's thinking. He points in particular to "the decisive turn...taken by Barth in the early thirties...through his contact with Anselm," and then to the shift in emphasis "effected" during the fifties "by his decisive rejection of the new modernism associated with Bultmann" (1959a, 9). This turn and subsequent development produced "three underlying principles in Barth's work": "the historicity of God's saving action; the supremacy of the Bible; and the objectivity of God's work, particularly the atonement" (Ibid., 10). These principles, Bromiley insists, demand that Barth be viewed "in line with three of the great emphases of Evangelicalism" (Ibid., 10; 1961a). Not surprisingly, this affirmation of Evangelical continuity in the new Barth elicited a heated response from Van Til, and counterproposals from other influential Evangelicals (Van Til, 1959; Henry, 1966). Certainly Bromiley's fundamental appreciation of Barth was a lonely voice in the influential pages of *Christianity Today*.

Bromiley's advocacy of Barth, however, moves well beyond

correction of misunderstandings and affirmation of Evangelical identity; it involves extensive appropriation. In his own introduction to historical theology, for example, Barth's definition of the theological task shapes the entire work. Citing Barth, Bromiley defines theology as "the investigation of the church's word about God with the intent of testing and achieving its purity and faithfulness as the responsive transmission of God's Word in changing languages, vocabularies, and intellectual and cultural contexts" (1978a, xxvi). Bromiley then proceeds to make this task his task, selecting theologians and evaluating their work in light of the criterion of faithfulness to revelation. Not surprisingly, Barth receives more extensive discussion than any other theologian in the history of the church, and is one of only two twentieth century figures assigned considerable space (Thielicke, influenced by Barth, is the other).

Methodologically, Bromiley finds himself in fundamental agreement with Karl Barth. According to him, Barth displays a "healthy" (Ibid., 420), even "magnificent understanding of dogmatics and the dogmatic task" (1979, 248). "Few theologians have written so magisterially on the Scripture principle of the Reformation," carefully distinguishing the "direct, absolute and material" authority of the Word from the "indirect, relative and formal" authority of creeds, confessions and church (1978a, 420; 1979, 41-48). Even fewer have "undertaken so comprehensive a study of the Word of God in its various aspects" (1979, 248). While Dr. Bromiley insists that Barth's teaching on inspiration and infallibility needs "some rethinking"(1978a, 421), he believes "Barth points the way out of the incapacitating impasse between liberals and conservatives" by means of the basic lines and emphases of his doctrine of the Word (1986a, 70). The "rethinking" Bromiley suggests, therefore, takes the form of a more consistent consideration of the implications of Scriptural authority and a more careful interpretation of biblical teaching. This would lead to an affirmation of a past act of inspiration that insures the infallibility of biblical teaching (1986b, 291; 1970).[3]

With regard to other aspects of theological method, Bromiley finds himself in even more complete agreement with Barth. He applauds the concept of God's primary and secondary objectivity, Barth's careful development of the veiling, unveiling and self-impartation of God, and his reconstructed doctrine of analogy as "particularly helpful threads to guide us through the labyrinth of modern epistemological discussions" (1986a, 72; 1978a, 436, 427-8; 1979, 65-68). Reminiscent of Torrance, Bromiley repeatedly portrays Barth as modeling a genuinely scientific method for theology, following the absolutely unique way in which God makes Himself an object for knowledge. He also defends Barth's rejection of natural theology (although recognizing that he failed to distinguish this adequately from a rejection of natural revelation), and his consistent rethinking of creation and anthropology from a christological perspective (1986a, 72-3, 75). "Nowhere has the scriptural centrality of Christ found more convincing exposition," but not, Bromiley insists, in the form of a reductive christomonism, "since, as Barth constantly reminds us, all the persons are at work in all God's outward operations, so that to say Christ is to say God in all his fullness" (1979, 248, 179).

Beyond issues of method, which are of particular concern to American Evangelicals, Bromiley has also appropriated or applauded many of Barth's material insights. In an article on divine decrees in *Christianity Today*, he argues that "the decree of God must be strictly related to Jesus Christ" and construed as equally "pre-temporal," "post-temporal" and "co-temporal" in order to avoid an undesirable decretum absolutum—all insights gleaned from Barth (1961b). In an earlier symposium sponsored by the same magazine, Bromiley defends an approach to election that aims, with Barth, at avoiding both a scholastic determinism and an arminian freedom by taking election in Christ "absolutely seriously" (1959b, 16). He clearly sets off in Barth's direction while seeking to avoid his universalistic tendencies. Bromiley also finds Barth's discussion of the trinity masterful (1978a, 420), and his handling of the divine attributes of omniscience, omnipotence and omnipresence insightful (1986a, 72). "And richest of all in insights, perhaps, are the massive volumes on reconciliation" (Ibid., 73).

It must be acknowledged, however, that in much of this praise Bromiley only points to Barth's discussions, without developing his own dogmatic construction. Precisely how Bromiley would appropriate Barth, reconciling tensions between historical formulations and Barth's proposals, remains unknown. He does, however, see considerable convergence between Evangelical orthodoxy and Barth, especially in the doctrines praised, and tends to interpret Barth in conciliatory terms. Even in areas of definite disagreement, Bromiley places Barth in the most positive light possible. In the doctrine of Scripture, for example, his criticisms are highly qualified. While faulting Barth for not emphasizing the past act of apostolic inspiration, he insists that Barth does not intend to deny objective inspiration, and that the emphasis on the Spirit's continuing activity is a healthy corrective to some forms of orthodoxy (1986b, 291-293). With respect to infallibility, he criticizes Barth's failure to include it as an "implication" of Scriptural authority, but also notes that "he never specified actual errors" and that he "saw no place from which to decide the Bible is mistaken" (Ibid., 291-2, 284). While Barth's account of Scripture as witness can be used to serve weaker notions of inspiration and infallibility, it need not, and when correctly understood, Bromiley does not "see how the concept can legitimately be resisted" (1956a, 15).

While his advocacy of Barth does have a critical aspect, Bromiley's approach is extremely positive. Barth is construed as "the greatest of modern theologians" (1986a, 78), whose "secret of...greatness" is his "authentic" encounter with God in revelation and his determination to construct theology in obedient response to the sovereign self-revelation of that God (1979, 428). The consequent dogmatic construction manifests unparalleled beauty and passion, as well as penetrating insight.

A new and powerful voice for well-informed engagement and critical appropriation of Barth thus arose within American Evangelicalism, entering from the outside, but exerting a sustained and respected influence for many years. One of the keys to this influence was Bromiley's ability to affirm both a conservative Evangelical theology and positive reception of Barth. This was possible, in part, because he maintained a more mediating Evangelical paradigm and a more conciliatory view of Barth's theology. But most determinative of all may have been Bromiley's basic conviction that he, Barth and the Reformed Evangelical tradition share a fundamental methodological orientation—and that orientation is not primarily philosophic or apologetic.

G. C. Berkouwer

Another important outside influence within American Evangelical reception of Barth has been the Dutch Reformed theologian, Dr. Gerrit Cornelius Berkouwer. Raised as a member of the *Gereformeerde Kerken*, and educated in theology at the Free University of Amsterdam, Berkouwer was a true son of the Dutch Reformed Church. He served as a pastor of that Church from 1927 until 1945, and then was appointed to the prestigious chair of dogmatics at the Free University, held by Abraham Kuyper, Herman Bavinck and Valentinius Hepp before him. With this postwar appointment, claimed one American interpreter, a "fresh theological wind had begun to blow" in the Evangelical world (Smedes, 1966, 64).

The wind blew strongly for three decades at the Free University, and was felt well beyond the boundaries of the Dutch Reformed world. Of his many books the two most widely read were polemic studies, *The Conflict with Rome* (1958) and *The Triumph of Grace in the Theology of Karl Barth* (1956). The first earned him an invitation to the Second Vatican Council; the second received the praise of Barth himself. While acknowledging "all its reservations and criticisms," Barth called it "a great book on myself and the Church Dogmatics" (*CD IV/2*, xii), and paid it the supreme compliment of scholarly engagement in subsequent volumes (*CD IV/3*, 173-80; Busch, 1976, 381). Berkouwer also produced fourteen *Studies in Dogmatics*, which many conservatives consider one of the best Reformed and Evangelical theologies of the twentieth century. Certainly the quality and spirit of both his polemic and positive work have earned Berkouwer a position of respect and influence in the world of theological scholarship.

It has also enabled him to exert a decisive influence upon Evangelical theology in America. At first glance, this might seem surprising. But it is merely a continuation of the influence conservative Reformed theology has always had upon the American Evangelical tradition. Just as Van Til, Klooster, Schaeffer and Clark have shaped the Fundamentalist Evangelical paradigm, and Barth reception within it, so Berkouwer and his followers have helped create New Evangelical paradigms and change the reception of Barth within them.[4] Berkouwer's opposition to *The New Modernism*, and his own more constructive *Triumph of Grace*, provided the conservative Evangelical community in America its first and for several years only sophisticated scholarly alternative to Van Til's interpretative paradigm.[5]

Of course, Berkouwer's influence in America has a broader base than his response to Barth. Most of his works have been translated into English, and several important Evangelical theologians have studied under or near him at the Free University.[6] Some of these, like Lewis Smedes and Jack Rogers (both professors at Fuller and translators for Berkouwer), extol him as a primary model of how contemporary Evangelical theology should be practiced (Smedes, 1966, 92; Rogers, 1978; 1979, 9-10). Other scholars, like Cornelius Van Til and Henry Krabbendam, indict Berkouwer as a dangerous example of contemporary departure from the Reformed tradition (Krabbendam, 1980, 1984; Van Til, 1975; Bogue, 1984; Klooster, 1976; Schaeffer, 1970, 37-8). But friend and foe alike recognize him as one of the most influential proponents of "a new type of thinking in the Reformed and Evangelical world," a thinking that could be called New Evangelical (Krabbendam, 1980, 413).

A distinguishing characteristic of this New Evangelical theology is the combination of both continuity and discontinuity with the confessional tradition. Like Hepp, Bavinck and Kuyper before him, and like so many Fundamentalist Evangelicals in America, Berkouwer is a self-consciously orthodox theologian. Both his polemics and his positive theological *Studies* arise out of a commitment to the Reformed confessions and manifest a clear intention to maintain continuity with that tradition. Throughout his career he remained within the confessional boundaries of the *Gereformeerde Kerken*, and as Professor of Dogmatics in the denomination's university played an influential role in locating those boundaries in the modern situation. But in that process an important difference arose between him and Reformed Evangelicals like Van Til, Klooster and Clark. Berkouwer insisted that the confessions of the church require reinterpretation, and many of the interpretations he offered differed from traditional formulations. Of course, he was not alone. In fact, his survey of modern theology from 1920 to 1970 considered the loss of certainty created by confessional reinterpretation one of the predominant characteristics and most difficult problems of the period (1977, 8, 11-24, 215-263).

The need for reinterpretation arises, not primarily from the scientific criticisms of a secular age, but from the incomplete and inadequate nature of all time-bound utterance. "The reality" that church dogmatics endeavors to communicate "always transcends our words and thoughts and is never fixed within the grasp of human formulations" (Ibid., 243). Therefore, theological interpretation demands a "distinction between form and content, between the formulations of dogma and the truth that is expressed in those formulations"(Ibid., 218). Past confessions must be interpreted to determine the biblical insights they sought to express and then reformulated to express those truths in a different situation.

Unavoidably, this process "causes a certain amount of tension," "for the question always arises as to whether the new form has preserved the old message intact or whether the content itself has undergone transformation" (Ibid., 216). This tension is magnified when "new ways of interpreting old dogmas conflict with traditional ways" (Ibid.). If, as is sometimes the case, older dogmatic statements or confessional decisions must be corrected—not just reinterpreted—the tensions within the church can become severe (Ibid., 225; 1975, 181). Nevertheless, they "are inevitable," Berkouwer insists, whenever "a desire to maintain continuity with the church's confessions" exists alongside "a calling to cope with the development of human understanding in an honest manner" (Ibid.).

The fundamental "challenge" is to find a "criterion for judging between form and content" (Ibid., 220, 219). But Berkouwer offers no set of hermeneutical rules, only a principle, described by Lewis Smedes (and others) as the principle of correlation (Smedes, 1966, 65-71; Timner, 1969). Berkouwer asserts that man participates in the knowledge of God only in the concrete correlation of divine revelation and human faith. Therefore, theology must be "occupied in continuous and obedient listening to the Word", which, as divine self-witness, has the power to make its meaning known (Berkouwer, 1954, 9). This is the import of the Reformation principle, *sacra Scriptura sui ipsius interpres*, or as Berkouwer calls it, the "Reformation correlation" of Word and faith (1975, 120). The present day theologian must, in faith and dependence on the Spirit, hear what the fathers heard as they listened to what the apostles and prophets said. Only in this way can theology perceive and "preserve the deepest intentions of the church when it formulated its dogmas" (1977, 217).

As a model of this kind of hermeneutic, Berkouwer cites the "theological exegesis" of Karl Barth, which aims, "after all the [historical] research...has been done," to read the Bible "as the text itself invited us and to do that with a tested and critical naivete" (Ibid., 112, 120; Smend, 1972). In his earliest studies Berkouwer had followed much Dutch Reformed thinking and accused Barth of undermining the correlation between revelation and faith, introducing a radical discontinuity between divine Word and human dogma. But by the publication of his

Triumph of Grace (1954; 1956) it had become "clear" that this "earlier characterization...did not match the real state of affairs." Rather, "Barth was, with enormous emphasis, calling attention to the relation between faith and revelation," and he was doing so in a way that reaffirmed a properly strict submission to Scriptural authority (1977, 51). His radical opposition to every attempt "to grant an independent significance to the power of reason or to a 'pre-understanding' possessed by natural man" was a war waged in defense of the "sovereign power of the Word." "It was a product of his constant return to the Word of the Scriptures" and this constant returning is the essence of Berkouwer's principle of correlation (Ibid., 56).

This principle entails an important corollary: all speculation must be eschewed. Any a priori presupposition that determines theological outcomes, or any deduction that extends beyond the teaching of Scripture, involves stepping outside the concrete correlation of Word and faith. *Sola Scriptura* demands "a subjection to the Bible, free from *a priori* dogmas and free from predetermined categories in which Scripture must be understood" (Ibid., 107). In the hands of Berkouwer this anti-speculative principle performs many important services. It justifies his rejection of deterministic theories of election and providence (Berkouwer, 1960; 1952); it provides the standard by which he criticizes Van Til's "unreformed sanctioning of tradition" (1971b, 200); and it supplies the recurring criterion by which he judges Barth's theological errors—and praises his insights. In fact, this principle lies at the heart of Berkouwer's entire reception of Barth.

Barth Reception

Next to Bavinck and Calvin, there is no theologian to whom Berkouwer refers more often than Karl Barth. Not only has he written four books exclusively about Barth (1937; 1940; 1947; 1956), and a doctoral dissertation on late nineteenth and early twentieth century German theology (1934), but his *Studies in Dogmatics* reveal a continuous and significant dialogue with the Swiss thinker. The basic reason is that Barth's work has "dominated the theolgical debate of our century"—and with good reason, for he raises issues of genuine substance and enduring concern in a manner relevant to modern man. "In one way or another, the views of Barth in their exegetical, confessional and dogmatic expression, as they are set forth in his extensive dogmatic works, touch both the foundation and the superstructure of the whole of theology" (1956, 9).

It is not surprising, therefore, that a chapter in Berkouwer's survey of modern theology is devoted to "The Voice of Karl Barth" (the only chapter devoted to a single theologian). Nor is it insignificant that this chapter is placed like a hinge between "The Era of Apologetics" and the five chapters that address this century's major issues of theological discussion. It was Barth's voice that rang out most clearly against the apologetic orientation of nineteenth century theology (including the rationalistic apologetics dominant in conservative Reformed circles); and it was his writings that established the most influential and enduring trends in theological discussion. At least this is Berkouwer's point of view. Barth's thinking, therefore, plays an important and positive role in every chapter of *A Half Century of Theology* (1977).[7]

But such an attitude toward Barth has not always been the case. In the beginning of his theological career Berkouwer followed an interpretive path similar to Fundamentalist Evangelicals in America (and Reformed opinion in the Netherlands). In his 1932 dissertation and 1937 book, Berkouwer focused upon Barth's epistemology, accusing him of a nominalist view of revelation and the knowledge of God. The problem occurs, Berkouwer suggests, "as a logical consequence of Barth's doctrine of divine freedom" (1977, 44-6; 1956, 11). For the concept, as developed by Barth, introduces a radical separation between divine revelation and the knowledge of faith, undermining faith's certainty and the conceptual continuity upon which it depends. In time, however, Berkouwer judged that he had, in this criticism, "missed Barth's real intentions," and in the *Triumph of Grace* he endeavors to correct this misreading (Ibid., 45).

The Triumph of Grace

The most important aspect of Berkouwer's changed interpretation lies in his decision to construe Barth's intentions as Evangelical. Berkouwer argues, in stark contrast to Van Til, that the "central theme" and "basic motif" of Barth's theology, through all its stages of development, has been the triumph of God's grace in Jesus Christ (Ibid., 10).

> Throughout the whole of Barth's Dogmatics we hear at every significant point and in every polemic the words of the gospel . . . . These emphases determine the center of his theology with pronounced and ever increasing clarity (Ibid., 196).

Of course, Barth's intention to proclaim the gospel of grace in submission to the authority of Scripture provides "no guarantee of the validity of his dogmatics." "But it does mean that all criticism of his work must be governed by the same orientation if it is to be fruitful criticism"(Ibid., 70). It must acknowledge Barth's evangelical intention and evaluate him on the basis of it.

Berkouwer himself concludes that Barth's development of the evangelical triumph of grace falls short of biblical fidelity. But he objects to the "one sided" reaction that has characterized much conservative criticism:

> Even when it is felt that the elements that constitute Barth's conception of the triumph of grace clearly evidence the influence of certain presuppositions and peculiar tensions, it is not possible to avoid being impressed by the manner in which the gospel of God's grace breaks through (Ibid., 347-8).

It breaks through in Barth's opposition to the pelagian synergism required by Rome's *analogia entis* and Modernism's natural theologies (Ibid., 26-34, 166-95; 1955). It breaks through in his affirmation of sovereign election, his opposition to a hidden decree of reprobation, and even his resistance to the *apokatastasis* of a consistent universalism (Ibid., 90-7, 262-96). It breaks through in Barth's forceful proclamation of divine judgment and justification in Christ (Ibid.,135-47). And it breaks through in his sincere submission to the authority of Scripture.[8]

But it must, according to Berkouwer, break through a dogmatic structure that distends biblical truth. Although Berkouwer analyzes these distortions in detail (under the loci of creation, election, reconciliation and eschatology), the diagnosis is singular: Barth's innovative reformulations do not allow him to maintain the "serious kerygmatic significance of sin and unbelief" or a genuine "transition from wrath to grace in the historical sphere" (Ibid., 233-234). This can be seen most clearly in Barth's teaching on sin, election and reconciliation. Of course, Berkouwer contends that Barth's inadequately historical interpretation of the triumph of grace shapes his entire theological project, but in these doctrinal innovations the heart of Barth's theology and the essence of Berkouwer's criticism is revealed.

Sin, Election and Reconciliation

In any triumph of grace the nature of the victory is defined, in large part, by that over which grace triumphs. What is sin, and under what conditions does it originate? In Barth's answer to these questions, the words "chaos," "mystery," "enigma," and "shadow" permeate the narrative. But according to Berkouwer, the word "*impossibility*...explains all the others and forms the central category of his doctrine of sin and redemption" (Ibid., 234). He speaks not just of sin's incomprehensibility, which would be a familiar Reformed idea, but of it's "ontological impossibility" (Ibid., 228). In this "strange expression" lies "the heart of Barth's Doctrine" (Ibid., 226).[9]

What does it mean? That "sin is something *which in the very nature of the case cannot be*" (Ibid., 225). It cannot be because the being of man has been determined by his election in Jesus Christ. "Sin is ontologically *impossible* because sin means a falling away from grace and it is precisely *God's primordial will* that our unfaithfulness should not put to nought His faithfulness" (Ibid., 227). Barth does acknowledge "an incomprehensible and insane 'ability to sin' " (Ibid., 229). But it "exists" as an "absurdity" which has been rendered impossible for human being by the prior and overpowering election of God. Sin is, therefore, not "a choice between two possibilities but between man's own possibility (before God) and his *impossibility,* between being and not-being... " (Ibid., 228).

According to Berkouwer this definition of human being bears the marks of speculation: It "creates a peculiar tension which we find nowhere in the Bible" (Ibid., 233). "Once this conception becomes the basis of [Barth's] theological thinking, it is no longer possible to make the transition from the "impossibility" to the "reality" of sin. . . without being confronted by insoluble difficulties and antinomies" (Ibid., 253). The historical reality of sin can be affirmed only as that which *has been* rejected, and therefore, as that which cannot bear any decisive, or eternal, significance.

But the Bible, "while it speaks clearly about the dimension of 'from eternity'. . . never devaluates the decisive significance of the historical and the 'stepwise' character of creation and redemption..." (Ibid., 252). Following this biblical accent, Reformed confessions—and Berkouwer—speak "about reconciliation *only* in correlation with a *breach that took place in history"* (Ibid., 259). Barth, by replacing the Reformed order of salvation (creation-fall-redemption) with a christologically corrected supralapsarianism, creates a theological framework in which "the *decisiveness* of history can no longer be fully honored" (Ibid., 255).

The speculations that distort Barth's gospel triumph are rooted in his unique doctrine of election. As Barth himself says,

> Here, in this understanding of man's being as resting in God's election lies the basis and sense of our thesis of the ontological impossibility of sin... (Ibid., 226).

Barth contends that Reformed theology, while justly proclaiming the sovereignty of divine election, has erred profoundly in its formulation of that doctrine. It has erred by positing a separation between the gracious will revealed in Christ and the hidden (and possibly horrible) decree of the Father. In this separation between Father and Son, the joyous proclamation of elective grace is rendered futile. "There comes to stand behind the *revealed* will of God in Jesus Christ the *final,* deepest, and hidden will which constitutes the real decision" (Ibid., 95). In stark contrast, Barth proposes a doctrinal construction that relates election "exclusively" to Jesus Christ (Ibid., 96). He develops this christological concentration by declaring the incarnate Christ both electing God and elected Man, the comprehensive subject and object of divine election. There is no will of God beyond Christ, and there is no Man outside of Him. In Christ, furthermore, there is no reprobate, for Jesus himself has been predestined to rejection in man's place. The key to

Barth's doctrinal innovation is that he locates election to salvation within the "primal decision" of "divine self-determination" to be with man in Jesus Christ (Ibid., 90).

The apparent implication of this doctrine of election is universal salvation. But Barth resists this conclusion. In submission to the biblical witness, and in the name of divine freedom, he refuses to conclude that all men will or must be saved. For Berkouwer, however, this refusal is inconsistent. "There is no alternative to concluding that Barth's refusal to accept the *apokatastasis* cannot be harmonized with the fundamental structure of his doctrine of election" (Ibid., 116). At its base is "the already taken and no longer nullifiable decision" to be gracious to man in Jesus Christ (Ibid., 265). The appeal to divine freedom cannot perform the service Barth requires of it, for God's freedom, Barth has already insisted, is not hidden or arbitrary, but wholly revealed and wholly gracious in Jesus Christ.[10]

Nor does Barth's doctrine grant genuine significance to human decision. Barth may speak of "fatally dangerous unbelief and the open situation of proclamation" but his theology makes it supremely difficult to maintain these biblical motifs (Ibid., 279). Unbelief, like sin, is recognized but rendered powerless, and ultimately reduced to a form of ignorance. "The *difference* between belief and unbelief," Berkouwer contends, "lies exclusively in having or not-having knowledge of the factual happening of God's decision" (Ibid., 275).

This same tendency to create an inadequately historical and ultimately universal triumph is found by Berkouwer throughout Barth's theology. Most importantly, it is found at the heart of his exposition of reconciliation, in Barth's recasting of the traditional two-state Christology. The key to this "very decisive innovation" is, according to Berkouwer, a complete identification of Jesus' humiliation with his deity (Ibid., 299). "The decisive transition from humiliation to exaltation which took place at the resurrection" is replaced "with the idea of the *unveiling* of Christ's (already existing) glory" (Ibid., 315). Identification with man through suffering and death becomes the eternal and gracious mode of being God has chosen in Jesus Christ.

But the complete identification of God with the humiliation of Jesus suggests an extreme "Christological God-concept" that borders on "theopaschitism" (Ibid., 312, 299), or so Berkouwer contends. It "constitutes an attempt to comprehend the incarnation" and "violates the mystery of the trinity" (Ibid., 301, 297). Once again, Berkouwer claims to see signs of a biblically alien speculation about the being of God determining the nature of salvation's triumph and rendering the historical dimension of salvation insignificant. He does not accuse Barth of eliminating history or ignoring biblical motifs, but rather, of distorting biblical ideas and, as a result, producing peculiar and problematic tensions not found in the biblical narrative. His criticism can be severe, but it is not one-sided. Berkouwer affirms Barth's Evangelical intentions, identifies the triumph of gospel grace as his central theme, acknowledges his serious and laudable submission to biblical authority, and recognizes numerous biblical accents and ideas. But he is a serious critic nonetheless, and his Reformed Evangelicalism provides the standard by which Barth is criticized.

Cornelius Van Til

Based upon these criticisms, one might be inclined to locate Berkouwer near the Fundamentalist Evangelical paradigm of Barth reception. In fact, Van Til incorporated criticisms from *The Triumph of Grace* into his own polemic, and Clark praised Berkouwer's work as a model of theological scholarship (1956a).[11] By speaking of biblical insights that break through a speculative framework, Berkouwer also employs a rhetoric reminiscent of Carl Henry. Nevertheless, these family resemblances in criticism do not constitute an identical paradigm.

Berkouwer is as likely to criticize the Fundamentalist Evangelical as he is Barth, and for the same reason. Both are guilty of allowing speculative concepts to distort biblical witness (Berkouwer, 1975, 21-8, 157-69). This is especially true of Cornelius Van Til, a fellow Dutch Reformed theologian whom Berkouwer singles out for attention. Recognizing Van Til's influence upon the reception of Barth in America, Berkouwer appended to the English translation of *The Triumph of Grace* a brief essay on "The Problem of Interpretation" raised by the conflict between his book and Van Til's *The New Modernism*.

Berkouwer's criticism of Van Til in this essay is severe. He accuses him of an irresponsible and unsound analysis that misses "the deepest intents of Barth's theology" and has "neglected or distorted" many "essential statements," producing an interpretive caricature in which Barth cannot even recognize himself (1956, 386-9). The basic picture Van Til paints is of a theologian in complete captivity to controlling philosophical presuppositions and, therefore, in total opposition to historic Reformed orthodoxy.

But the relationship between theological proposal and philosophical presupposition is "too complicated" to admit of this kind of disjunctive analysis (Ibid., 389). All theologians—Barth, Berkouwer and Van Til included—utilize culturally conditioned concepts and are subject to philosophical influence. Discerning whether and in what way philosophy distorts the witness of the Word involves a "difficult...struggle" and even the "strong resistance" of Reformed theologians to philosophical intrusion is not "above suspicion, but...fraught with danger" (Ibid., 392, 389). To suggest, therefore, that the difference between Barth and orthodoxy is a difference between false and true presuppositions is to grossly oversimplify the situation. And to draw conclusions on the basis of these supposed presuppositions "which Barth himself . . . *has more than once and at great length opposed* " is simply unfair (Ibid., 386).

But Berkouwer does not stop with this criticism. Rather, he traces the differences in Barth reception to differences in theology. "More than once," Berkouwer claims, Van Til "has in his opposition to Barth drawn a picture of orthodoxy in which I cannot recognize the features of the real *Reformed* orthodoxy" (Ibid., 390). Specifically, he objects to Van Til's affirmation of the "equal ultimacy" of election and reprobation, to his definition of the trinity as "three centers of self-consciousness" and to his description of incarnation as the assumption of "an already existent human nature" (Ibid., 390-391). In each case Berkouwer sees the distorting influence of a philosophically determined concept of God.

Berkouwer also perceives "far reaching differences of opinion" between himself and Van Til concerning their "common confession of Holy Scripture as the authoritative and reliable Word of God" (1971b, 197). In place of a continual and concrete return to the Word that allows exegesis to "play a decisive role" in theology, Van Til has fallen back upon scholastic doctrines of God and a priori theories of inspiration and inerrancy. Berkouwer, therefore, concludes that "he must certainly be found on the way of an unreformed sanctioning of tradition" (Ibid., 200).

Clearly Berkouwer's opposition to Van Til's interpretation of Barth is intertwined with his criticism of Van Til's apologetic paradigm for orthodoxy, and related to his own interpretation of the Reformed tradition. Berkouwer is critical of Barth in many ways. But he is also critical of the Reformed orthodoxy represented by Van Til (and one might add, Berkhof, Klooster, Schaeffer and Clark). In his criticism of this "unreformed traditionalism" Berkouwer often sides with Barth against the so-called orthodox Evangelicals. A combination of criticism and convergence, in the context of an affirmation of Barth's basic Evangelical identity, therefore, is the distinguishing mark of Berkouwer's reception of Barth.

Fuller Seminary: Flagship of Evangelical Identity

Geoffrey Bromiley and G. C. Berkouwer exerted an early and enduring influence upon the Evangelical reception of Barth, pioneering a more positive interpretation during a time of important transition. In this postwar development, Fuller Seminary has also played a unique and leading role. Founded in 1947 by Charles Fuller and Harold Ockenga to be a flagship for scholarly engagement within the emerging Evangelical movement, the school attracted professors determined to lead the way in winning "modern minds" and souls for the Evangelical cause (Nelson, 1987; Marsden, 1987). But it also included scholars who would lead the way in forging new Evangelical coalitions and challenging symbolic boundaries of Evangelical definition. It became, therefore, a particularly visible microcosm of the tensions that surfaced as a resurgent Evangelical leadership sought to reform Fundamentalism from within.

Because of its unique position as both flagship (carrying acknowledged leaders of the Evangelical movement) and pioneer (exploring the expanding frontiers of Evangelical identity), it became a focal point of public controversy. There were battles with Fundamentalist luminaries over the cooperative evangelism of Billy Graham; battles with the Los Angeles Presbytery over ordination of professors and students; and battles with other Evangelicals over doctrines of biblical authority (Marsden, 1987, 197-229). These battles marked stages along the way as Fuller seminary and the Evangelicalism it represented "developed from a reform within Fundamentalism into a separate movement" (Ibid., 8).

While the Fundamentalist Evangelical leadership that founded the seminary intended the movement to operate within the boundaries of "classic" Fundamentalism, Fuller ultimately rejected those boundaries and fostered a more open and progressive New Evangelicalism. The crucial transition occurred during the sixties, and was marked by two seminal events: the revision of the school's doctrinal statement, particularly on the inerrancy of Scripture, and the appointment of a new President. Prior to these events, competing factions had been developing, and as a result of them, the Fundamentalist Evangelical contingent that had dominated the school's first decade eventually departed.

In the years that followed, Fuller Seminary became the largest independent seminary in the world and came to serve, in President Hubbard's words, an increasingly broad "cross section of the Evangelical movement," including a majority of conservatives from mainline denominations (Hubbard, 1979, 21; Marsden, 1987, 264-6). Because of the significance of this shift in social base away from Fundamentalist Evangelical churches, George Marsden has suggested that the 1965 decision of the L.A. Presbytery to finally accept Fuller students as candidates for ministry signaled, "as much as anything else...the end of the fundamentalist-evangelical era at Fuller" (Marsden, 1987, 255).

The Vassady Incident

During the first decade of Fuller's history an incident occurred that indicates the tensions Evangelical pioneers faced as they pursued a strategy of cooperative engagement from within a Fundamentalist Evangelical paradigm. It also reveals the ethos that characterized the institution at its inception. In the fall of 1948 Harold Ockenga proposed the Hungarian theologian, Bela Vassady, for a teaching post in theology at the fledgling institution. The suggestion itself was remarkable, since Vassady was at the time a visiting professor at Princeton, and had been brought to the United States under the auspices of the World Council and Federal Council of Churches. He was a visible member of the ecumenical movement and a respected churchman and theologian. He also held Karl Barth in high regard, and had served as "guide and interpreter" during Barth's 1936 visit to Hungary (Vassady, 1985, 61). But after interviewing him, Ockenga was convinced that Vassady's Reformed Calvinism was conservative enough for him to teach at Fuller. Besides, Vassady's academic credentials and ecumenical involvement could help gain respectability for Fuller and possibly even win acknowledgement of its professors and students within the L.A. Presbytery (Ibid., 130-2; Marsden, 1987, 102-7).

The faculty had some concerns, however, evidenced by letters from Henry and Carnell to Ockenga. But after conducting a formal interview on campus in December, 1948, both Carnell and Henry affirmed Vassady's orthodoxy and supported his nomination for the position. They did question his "refusal to indict Barthianism" and his openness to the dialectical language of paradox. But neither of these were deemed sufficient cause for disapproval, because, as Henry said, Vassady affirmed the Bible as "infallible" "inscripturated revelation" in marked contrast to "Neo-Supernaturalism" (Marsden, 1987, 102-3). Yet within a year of his appointment to the Professorship of Biblical Theology and Ecumenics, this very issue would force Vassady to resign. Apparently both the Fuller theologians and Vassady himself failed to appreciate the differences that separated them.

What became clear during the 1949-50 school year was that Vassady's form of Reformed and Evangelical Christianity did not fit within the Fundamentalist Evangelical paradigm predominant at Fuller during its first decade. He became, as it were, an early test case for, and indication of, the boundaries of Evangelical identity on the Fuller frontier. The specific issues of controversy were Vassady's outspoken support of the ecumenical movement, his supposed Barthianism, and most importantly, his refusal to affirm the inerrancy of Scripture. Vassady's ecumenism became a problem for the seminary when a fall, 1949 essay, "Through Ecumenical Glasses," elicited the heated opposition of Fundamentalist Carl McIntire and an alarmed reaction from Charles Fuller (McIntire, 1949; LaSor, 1976). In response, an emergency faculty meeting was held, a statement of non-endorsement for the World Council was drafted, and Vassady was asked to submit future publications for faculty review. Apparently his positive ecumenicity, a desirable characteristic when seeking approval from the L.A. Presbytery, became a liability when it put him in tension with the separatist heritage of Fundamentalist Evangelicalism (Vassady, 1985, Marsden, 1987, 107-15).

Vassady's "Barthianism" also became an issue at this time. The primary sources of this criticism were Chester Tulga, who represented a critical extreme within the Conservative Baptist movement (Shelley, 1971, 77), and Clarence Bouma, a Christian Reformed theologian who taught at Calvin Seminary. Both men corresponded with Ockenga during the fall of 1949 to express their concerns, Bouma claiming that he had letters from Hungarian theologians indicting Vassady as a leader of Barthianism in their homeland. Apparently concerned, Wilbur Smith, a Fuller faculty member and confidant of Charles Fuller, conducted an investigation of his own (Marsden, 1987, 110-11).

One of the problems in determining Vassady's position, of course, was the absence of textual data in English; another was the lack of any clear and consistent definition of Barthianism. But clearly Vassady was operating with a different view of Barth than either his Fundamentalist Evangelical critics or defenders. As subsequent English publications would demonstrate, his theological pilgrimage followed a path different from theirs, and one significantly influenced by Barth (Vassady, 1965; 1985). In his own interpretive reconstruction of that journey, contained in a 1985 autobiography, Vassady tells the story of his pilgrimage from an early "Theology of Synthesis" to a more mature and abiding "witnessing theology" (1985, 43, 145). In the former, the way of faith led *"through* the vestibule of the sciences of religion to the sanctuary of God's revelation," while in the latter, the order was reversed. Human science was "dethroned" and the "elements of truth" in it were "subordinated to the basic standards" of a theology "rooted and grounded in the Word of God" (Ibid., 51-2, 145).

The decisive transition in his theological development occurred in 1930-1931, when Vassady began an intensive reading of the dialectical theologians. He followed these men in their opposition to the anthropocentric theology of the nineteenth century, and in their return to the priority of the Word and the theology of the Reformers. But he also followed them in their distinctive interpretations of this theology of revelation. Paradox, for example, was considered "an integral element of theology," even "the blood cells in its arteries." In the "event" of revelation God "speaks and acts in a mysterious way, transcending our common sense" and remaining hidden even as He becomes revealed. The "faith experience" which corresponds to this revelation, paradoxically expressed in Christian doctrine, is therefore, *"an event* pointing beyond itself to him who initiated it" (Ibid., 51-2). That event occurs in response to the Spirit-enabled proclamation of the inspired Scriptures.

By inspiration, Vassady means the process by which "God speaks to us in and through the books of the Bible": "First he revealed himself through the Holy Spirit" to the biblical authors, then "prompted" them to "put God's revelation into writing," and now he "turns...the age-old Writ...into the dynamic of God's self-disclosure." This "dynamic" view of inspiration, in turn, requires a "pneumatic" concept of interpretation, parallel in its formulation to Barth's idea of theological exegesis. It also eliminates the need for a doctrine of inerrancy, since God "knows that through the internal testimony of the Spirit his eternal message can come through loud, clear, and flawless, even via human errors" (Ibid., 64-5).

While Vassady considered these ideas, all formed before 1948, legitimate expressions of Reformed Evangelicalism, and even consistent with "the basic principles of Calvin's theology," they were certainly not acceptable to those who adhered to a Fundamentalist Evangelical paradigm (Ibid., 59-61; Vassady, 1951). One wonders how Vassady's appointment was ever made. But the way it was unmade is no mystery. The faculty voted to adopt a statement of faith that Vassady could not sign, for it proposed a doctrine of autographical inerrancy in the Princeton tradition that he found objectionable. While the essential elements of the statement had been prepared by Carnell and presented to the faculty the preceding year, and therefore were not drafted in response to the Vassady incident, the decision to adopt the statement in 1950 was not coincidental. Vassady's departure resolved the crisis (Marsden, 1987, 113-4; Hubbard, 1979, 9).

But it did not resolve the issue of Evangelical identity at Fuller, or the relation of Evangelical theology to Barth. During the early sixties the question of biblical inerrancy was reopened, and by the end of that decade a revised statement of faith was adopted. According to Vassady, "The two paragraphs on revelation and Scripture in this second statement reflect the same ideas that I had represented in 1949" (1985, 139). By 1985, therefore, he was "more than happy" to note that "today's Fuller Seminary seems to be ready and willing to limp along with me on the evangelical and also on the ecumenical road" (Ibid., 141). Certainly the new Fuller tolerates a degree of theological diversity not possible in 1950. It also models a positive and diverse reception of Barth that corresponds to this New Evangelical pluralism. But before this period of New Evangelical openness could arrive, other experimental and contested overtures of appreciation toward Barth had to be tried.

Edward John Carnell: Evangelical Pioneer

Of course Bromiley's arrival in 1958 brought to Fuller its most important advocate and interpreter of Barth (and one whose commitment to inerrancy enabled his advocacy to be acceptable). But during the early years of his career in America other Evangelical scholars issued possibly more influential statements in support of the Swiss theologian. Of these, the most important was certainly Edward John Carnell, a founding faculty member and second President of Fuller Seminary.

Concerning his influence, President Hubbard has claimed,

> For those of us who sat under his teaching, he was far and away the most dominant influence on our life and thought during our seminary days...He left his stamp on generations of students at Fuller as no one has done since (Hubbard, 1979, 7, 10).

"His pilgrimage in rejecting the right...and seeking to understand the left...together with explorations away from rationalistic apologetics, presaged the directions of the seminary" (Ibid.,10). Along with Carl Henry, and a handful of young Fundamentalists earning doctorates in the postwar period, Carnell pioneered a pathway of scholarly engagement for the emerging Evangelical movement. But in his case, the process of engagement led to the very edge of, and possibly beyond, Fundamentalist Evangelicalism.

Like Carl Henry, Carnell studied under Gordon Clark at Wheaton and Edgar Brightman at Boston University (earning a Ph.D. in 1949). He also took a Th.B. and Th.M. under Van Til at Westminster, and another doctorate at Harvard. Like Clark, Van Til and Henry, he also devoted his best intellectual energies to developing an apologetic defense of "the Reformed faith" as "the most consistent expression of orthodoxy" and a true depiction of reality (Carnell, 1959, 13). Furthermore, he espoused a doctrine of verbal, plenary inspiration and biblical inerrancy in the Princeton tradition and was the author and consistent defender of Fuller Seminary's 1950 doctrinal statement (Marsden, 1987, 113-15, 211-5, 224). But Carnell manifested not only the influence of his Fundamentalist forbears. Brightman also left his impact, as did the subjects of his two dissertations, Kierkegaard and Niebuhr (1948b; 1949). The result was a series of apologetic books that not only shared a common commitment to the rationality of Evangelical orthodoxy, but also indicated growing appreciation for the subjective dimensions of knowledge and the problems and perils of maintaining a conservative faith in contemporary culture (Nelson, 1987).

In his first book, published while still a research student at Boston and Harvard, the influence of Clark and Van Til is obvious. Truth is defined as *"correspondence with the mind of God"* whose eternal decree provides the pattern of meaning for the "facts" of creation (1948a, 46-7). This purposeful pattern, while manifest everywhere, is clearly indicated in the "propositions" of Scripture (Ibid., 62, 174, 191). The Bible, therefore, reveals the mind of God on matters of importance, and Carnell considers Reformation orthodoxy the most accurate exposition of this divine interpretation of reality.

Following his presupposionalist mentors, Carnell also argues for the axiomatic character of ultimate beliefs, and proposes "the existence of the God Who has revealed Himself in Scripture" as the "logical starting point" of an orthodox "world view" (Ibid., 102, 89-90, 124). Only by assuming this beginning can one "solve [the] basic problems of epistemology and metaphysics" and adequately explain "the nature and destiny of man" (Ibid., 89-90).

Clark, Van Til and Henry would agree. But they would not agree with the procedure for rational verification Carnell proposes. In contrast to his mentors, Carnell insists that the basic "assumptions" of the Christian worldview be considered "hypotheses" that must be "tested" by the same "criteria of verification" applied to other rational assertions (Ibid., 89-111). Following Brightman, he defines this criterion as "systematic consistency," by which he means the ability of a system of assertions (and its assumptions) to manifest logical consistency and explain the entirety of human experience (Ibid., 56, 106-111).

Even the Bible must submit to this criteria. Scripture may be the propositional revelation of God's mind; but the decision whether to regard it as God's Word and the multitude of decisions concerning how to interpret it are based upon considerations of systematic consistency. Carnell's ultimate apologetic appeal, therefore, is to evidences that verify the biblical world view and its revelation claim, and his published works develop different aspects of this common evidential ground as "points of contact" between the Christian and unbeliever (Carnell, 1960, preface; Lewis, 1976).

Such a position hardly indicates a departure from the Fundamentalist Evangelical paradigm. All of the essential ingredients are present: an apologetic orthodoxy, a well-defined theory of rationality, even a doctrine of inerrant propositional revelation. Not surprisingly, therefore, Carnell's early reception of Barth was highly critical. With obvious dependence upon Van Til, he defined "Neo-orthodoxy" as a dialectical "revision" of the liberal tradition, not bearing any "essential" relation to "historic orthodoxy" (1950, 30, 36).[12] Rejecting orthodoxy's epistemic foundation in propositional revelation, Neo-orthodoxy sought to overcome liberalism's loss of the biblical God by means of a theological method learned at the feet of Soren Kierkegaard: dialectical discontinuity between God and man, mediated by existential experience.

Carnell considered Barth both the originator of this "New Theology" and its most consistent proponent (Ibid., 30). Again following Van Til, he argued that the basic difference between Barth, Brunner and Niebuhr was the degree of continuity allowed within their fundamentally "dialectical framework" (Ibid., 33). Brunner "conceded a *point* of contact," Niebuhr "whole *areas*," while Barth insisted upon "absolute discontinuity" (Ibid., 35-7). Barth's "absolute discontinuity," furthermore, constituted the clearest example of the existential and dialectical error: a "bifurcation in knowledge" that reduces religious faith to irrationalism (1952, 491). Such a "permanent split between theology and science" is "a fatal gesture" (1948a,76), for it renders rational verification of religious truth claims "impossible" (1950, 37).

These critical comments, contained in sections of Carnell's first three books, reveal minimal interaction with the Barthian corpus and an obvious affinity with Van Til and Clark. They also stand in marked contrast to comments he would make a decade later. Upon the occasion of Barth's lectures at the University of Chicago in 1962, Carnell was invited as a representative of the new generation of conservative Evangelicals to participate on a small panel of official questioners. As might be expected, he raised the question of inerrancy.

"How does Dr. Barth," he asked, "harmonize his appeal to Scripture, as the objective Word of God, with his admission that Scripture is, indeed sullied by errors, theological as well as factual?" Before allowing Barth to answer, however, Carnell made a surprising admission. He politely conceded, "This is a problem for me, too, I confess."

When Barth concluded his response, affirming both the reliability of Scripture as witness and its ultimate dependence upon God's freedom to reveal Himself, he added a personal comment: "Is that enough to encourage you to continue to cheerfully confess that here is a problem for you?" In the pause which followed, panel moderator, Jaroslav Pelikan, quipped, "That is just another way of saying 'Welcome to the Club'"(Criterion, 1963).

Carnell's fellow conservatives, however, did not appreciate this implication. Gordon Clark, in particular, penned a critical review of the interaction in *Christianity Today*, indicting Carnell for his failure to expose the weakness of Barth's position (Clark, 1962d). And of course, there were reactions in the Fundamentalist press (Lyons, 1963).[13] In response, Carnell publicly reaffirmed his commitment to the inerrancy of Scripture and wrote an article for *The Christian Century* clarifying his position on Barth. In that article he took care to identify "some disappointments" in his "encounter with Karl Barth," in particular, Barth's fondness for paradox and his radical christocentrism (Carnell, 1962, 713).

But to these rather predictable criticisms, Carnell added a significant qualification:

> If extreme Fundamentalists think I am going to join their "holy war" against Barth, they are sadly mistaken. I am convinced that Barth is an inconsistent Evangelical rather than an inconsistent liberal (Ibid., 714).

With this judgment a watershed in the interpretation of Barth was crossed. Contrary to his earlier written opinions, Carnell now chose to regard Barth's theological errors as lapses in consistency rather than evidence of a theological system "not *essentially* related to historic orthodoxy" (1950, 36). He even confessed feeling "actual physical pain" over Van Til's "irresponsible judgement" that "Barthianism is more hostile to the Reformers than is Roman Catholicism." And he gladly proclaimed that one of Barth's messages at Rockefeller Chapel "could have been given at Moody Bible Institute without offense, so rich was it in evangelical content" (Carnell, 1962, 714).

This article stands alone among Carnell's writings as a positive assessment of Barth, unaccompanied by any serious interaction with the Barthian corpus to indicate its interpretive basis. Most likely he had been influenced by Bromiley and Berkouwer. But more importantly, he had been prepared by his own changing view of Fundamentalism to adopt an open attitude to positions outside it. In 1948, when he published *Christian Apologetics*, the "Fundamentalism" of Machen, Van Til and Clark was equivalent to the "conservative Christianity" he endeavored to defend (1948, 10; 1950, 21-4). By 1959, however, with the publication of possibly his most important work, *The Case for Orthodox Theology*, Carnell's view had changed. He now considered these men guilty of a "cultic mentality" that undermined their claim to represent "classic" orthodoxy (1959, 113-41). This mentality is marked, above all, by "ideological thinking"—a "rigid, intolerant, and doctrinaire" identification of personal opinion with absolute truth (Ibid., 114). It manifests itself in sectarian separatism, resistance to self-criticism, preoccupation with intramural issues, and "a cultic refusal to enter into the wider Christian dialogue" (Ibid., 127, 92, 114-117, 120, 128-137, 141).

Of the issues which manifest these tendencies, the most symbolically significant is Fundamentalism's discussion of inspiration. Contrary to his mentors, Carnell in 1959 insists that the inerrancy issue was an unsettled one, and that Old School Princeton did not offer the only acceptable, or possibly even the best, Evangelical alternative (Ibid., 92-111).

Apparently his willingness to opt out of the "holy war" against Barth and to regard him as an inconsistent Evangelical was made possible by Carnell's changing view of Evangelical history and theology. His was a more open Evangelicalism and he opened the door for many to a broader interpretation of the Evangelical tradition and a more positive reception of Barth. In the years following 1962 many Evangelicals would walk through that door, especially at Fuller.[14]

New Evangelicalism At Fuller

By the early seventies a new situation had emerged at Fuller Seminary. The founding faculty had departed, a new President had been hired, the doctrinal statement had been revised, and Fuller graduates were now accepted as candidates for ordination by the Los Angeles Presbytery. The directions "presaged" by President Carnell and championed by a circle of young scholars were leading this flagship beyond the boundaries of Fundamentalist Evangelicalism. A shift was taking place, marked by changes in both social context and theological confession. Staff and student body began to reflect a broader cross-section of the Evangelical movement, with marked increases among mainline conservatives and charismatics. This broader social base, in turn, brought a new theological pluralism. Traditional signs and symbols of Evangelical identity were contested and statements of theological consensus had to be more broadly drawn. Fuller professors, therefore, often played conspicuous roles on the progressive side in intramural Evangelical debates.

Attitudes toward Barth had also changed. The apologetic orthodoxy of Henry and the early Carnell was replaced during the sixties and seventies by a new set of interpretive options, ranging from the critical appreciation of Colin Brown to the qualified appropriation of Paul Jewett, to the conservative advocacy of Geoffrey Bromiley, and even beyond, to the more radical views of Ray Anderson. Of course, not all the professors teaching theology manifested the kind of "fundamental appreciation" Bromiley or Anderson espoused. But even the more critical treatments during this later period manifest elements of affirmation missing from the most positive of Fundamentalist Evangelical evaluations.

Colin Brown

An important case in point is Colin Brown, currently Professor of Systematic Theology at the California school. Before assuming this post in 1977, Professor Brown had lived and studied in England, teaching at Trinity College, Bristol. So like Geoffrey Bromiley, Colin Brown entered the American Evangelical movement from the "outside," having already established himself as a Barth interpreter before emigrating. He had written an M.A. thesis on Barth's theological method (1960) and contributed several brief articles and book reviews to Evangelical publications (1961; 1962a,b,c). These were followed by an important book length study, *Karl Barth and the Christian Message,* published simultaneously in England and the United States, and hailed by *Christianity Today* as one of the "Choice Evangelical Books" of 1967. At the time of its publication it was one of the most informed and sympathetic treatments of Barth by an English-speaking Evangelical.

Brown proclaimed Barth "a theological Everest" "from whom more could be learnt" than any other modern theologian. His ability "to grapple with the really big questions" in "dialogue with the great thinkers of the past" and to "bring to bear on them a profound and penetrating understanding of the Bible" bestowed upon his theology a unique "breadth and depth" (1967, 10). It also made *Church Dogmatics* "the most impressive theological work of modern times" (Ibid., 27). But it did not protect Barth from serious overstatement, grave mistakes and even a "comprehensive" theological error (Ibid., 149). "The way forward," therefore, lies "neither in a wholesale acceptance nor in a wholesale rejection of what [Barth] has to say" (Ibid., 153).

The purpose of Brown's book, *Karl Barth and the Christian Message,* is two-fold: to identify the essential shape of Barth's theology and to provide a basic evaluation. In other words, "to bring into critical focus Barth's approach to the Christian message" (Ibid., 152,10). Brown's strategy, which determines the book's structure, is to analyze and evaluate Barth's position on three "main issues" that stand as "major road junctions" in theological method: revelation, natural theology and the role of Christ in doctrinal construction (Ibid., 10-11). The standard by which Brown judges is the one Barth himself proposes—the teaching of Scripture. But in order to identify Scriptural teaching Brown takes repeated soundings on "the older, classical Protestant and Catholic positions...to see which comes closer to the truth" (Ibid., 12). In almost every case where comparison suggests contrast, it is the older orthodoxy that provides the more biblical approach. So while Colin Brown tries to steer, and even pioneer, a course for Evangelical Barth reception between wholesale acceptance or rejection, it is still the Reformed Evangelical tradition that provides his interpretive standard.

In a manner reminiscent of the mainstream of conservative Reformed criticism, Brown argues that Barth's theology is ultimately shaped by a single "theme," "axiom," "principle" or "idea" (Ibid., 10, 12, 106, 116). This controlling principle is described most often as "the idea that all God's dealings with men are effected in and through the person of Jesus Christ" (Ibid., 102). As such, it is primarily methodological. But when Brown turns from Barth's discussion of revelation to his teaching on the Christian message, the description of this controlling idea changes. It becomes "the idea of a single, all-embracing covenant in Christ" (Ibid., 139).

The change is due, Brown would contend, to a "retrograde" development in Barth's theology. Beginning with his teaching on election in *CD II/2*, and continuing through the subsequent volumes on creation and reconciliation, Barth "works out" his "Christ-centered" method in a way that distorts the Christian message (Ibid., 99). He does this by "projecting" the "indissoluble bond" between God and man effected in the incarnation "back into the very being of God" and then "embracing all humanity" in "Christ's human nature" (Ibid.,109, 102). Barth locates "the election of man to be God's covenant partner" within the eternal trinity, and then defines this covenant to include all God's actions toward mankind (Ibid.,130). Moreover, this "radically different" idea of covenant election in Christ becomes "the key," Brown contends, to Barth's "understanding of God" and "every other doctrine" (Ibid., 124, 101). "Despite his protest that he is not concerned with a Christ-principle but with Christ Himself," Dr. Brown is "obliged to conclude that it is a Christ-idea that often gives Barth his characteristic emphases" (Ibid., 152). "The essence of Barthianism is to reshape all theology around this idea" and this reshaping "is the focal point of conflict between orthodoxy and Barthianism" (Ibid., 12, 139).

The similarity to Berkouwer, Klooster and even Van Til is marked.[15] But it is with the New Evangelicalism of Berkouwer rather than the Fundamentalist Evangelicalism of Van Til that Brown's study should be identified, for he affirms the basic thrust of Barth's method. "The central doctrine of Barth's teaching on revelation," Brown insists, "is the *biblical* one that revelation is none other than God revealing Himself" (Ibid., 144). While Barth's "christocentric approach" may lead him to "overstate" the case against general revelation, he "is surely right in the way he binds knowledge of God to the Word of God" and rejects natural theology as a "blind alley" (Ibid., 87,142,147). "Only God can reveal God," and only by operating within "the circle of self-asserting and self-attesting" revelation, as Barth demands, can theology maintain the strict orientation to its object that is the hallmark of "genuine science" (Ibid., 142-3, 36).

In theological method, therefore, Brown construes Barth in essential continuity with the "basic approach" of Anselm, Augustine and Calvin (Ibid., 90-93). He even aligns him, in a subsequent survey of philosophy, with Van Til and Schaeffer as a Reformed proponent of "the proper starting point for thinking about God" (1969, 245, 262). In response to the counterclaims of conservative critics, Brown cautions Evangelicals not to "saddle" "the Barth of today...with the Barth of 1920" (1967, 42). Certainly, "Barth, the Dialectical Theologian" undermined cognitive revelation; but the Barth of *Church Dogmatics*, under the increasing influence of Orthodox teachers and Scriptural truth, affirmed both the personal and propositional nature of revelation, defined faith as a form of knowledge and developed a doctrine of analogy that is both sound and suggestive (Ibid., 42-54). "In his doctrine of the Word of God," therefore, Barth has "more in common with traditional Protestantism...than is sometimes imagined" (Ibid., 139). Even his concept of the Word's three-fold form "can be helpful" (Ibid., 144).

Nevertheless, Brown does not propose wholesale acceptance. In spite of Barth's substantially successful "attempt to restate the position of the Reformers and of the Bible itself," his teaching on revelation "bears the marks" of its dialectical "parentage" (Ibid., 66). This is most clear in the doctrine of inspiration. By asserting both the verbal inspiration of Scripture and its capacity for error in every statement, Barth has placed the biblical student before an "intolerable dilemma" (Ibid., 146). By means of a dialectical "double-think" he must treat "the Bible as true and false at the same time—true in so far as it is the revealing Word of God, and false in so far as it is the erring word of man" (1969, 257). Fortunately Barth's practice is better than his theory, for he "does not take the question of error very seriously" (1967, 62). But indifference is not a solution, and Brown believes that Barth's "indifference to history" is the "Achilles' heel" of his doctrine of revelation and authority (1969, 257). For "it is impossible to maintain high doctrines of revelation and inspiration without at the same time being willing to defend in detail the veracity and historicity of the biblical writings" (1967, 62). Barth is not guilty, as Van Til and others have suggested, of taking revelatory events "out of history"; nor is an appropriate defense of historical veracity "incompatible with the main thrust of his teaching." But he certainly "neglects" to offer such a defense (Ibid., 65, 147). Brown, in contrast, has devoted a good portion of his scholarly career to developing just such a defense, and the philosophical underpinning for it

(Brown, 1976; 1984; 1985; 1990).

In the last analysis, Colin Brown can manage only a "cheer and a half" for Barth's theological contribution (1987). He is a dialogue partner of unparalleled depth and breadth. His insights are often penetrating and profound, and his basic approach to the doctrine of revelation is sound. Nevertheless, his radically christocentric theology has produced, especially in the latter half of the *Dogmatics*, a distorted picture of the Christian message. Even his fundamentally Evangelical doctrine of revelation bears the marks of a dialectical parentage and the distorting influence of Barth's radical christocentrism. While a pioneer for a more serious and sympathetic reception of Barth among English-speaking Evangelicals, Colin Brown must be considered one of the most conservative (and critical) examples of this New Evangelical type.[16]

Paul King Jewett

Another important New Evangelical pioneer at Fuller has been its Professor of Systematic Theology since 1955, Paul King Jewett. A close friend of Carnell since their student days at Wheaton, Westminster and Harvard, Jewett was called from Gordon Divinity School to Fuller when Carnell became President. Although beginning his career with a critical analysis of *Emil Brunner's Concept of Revelation* (dedicated to Gordon Clark), and maintaining a rather conservative Calvinism throughout his tenure at Fuller, Jewett became an influential proponent of theological change, and occasionally, a center of heated controversy. The reason lay primarily in his views on Scripture and the role of women, where Jewett was a definite progressive. Convinced (sometime during the later fifties) that certain historical errors in the biblical text were intractable, he became an early proponent for Fuller's revised statement of faith (Marsden, 1987, 201, 209). He also came to advocate a more personal and paradoxical understanding of revelation under the influence of Kierkegaard and Brunner (Jewett, 1961).

But not until the publication of his controversial book, *Man as Male and Female* (1975), did the extent of Jewett's departure from Fundamentalist Evangelicalism become manifest. In particular, Jewett suggested that Paul's teaching on the role of women needed correction because it was historically conditioned. He extended the category of error beyond issues of historical reporting and scientific assumption to matters of faith and practice, applying the principle of progressive revelation to apostolic teaching itself and claiming to find inadequacies and even errors in it. Jewett's position, not surprisingly, sent shock waves through the Evangelical community, for it pushed a symbolic boundary of Evangelical identity to the breaking point (Marsden, 1987, 280-2; Lindsell, 1976; Fuller Seminary, 1976).

That Jewett understood these developments as a movement beyond Fundamentalist Evangelicalism is implied in his decision to leave the separatist denomination in which he was raised and join, in 1956, the mainline American Baptists (he eventually became a Presbyterian). It is also suggested by the subtitle (and substance) of his final work, *God, Creation, and Revelation: A Neo-Evangelical Theology* (1991). In this magnum opus, Jewett defines his "theological approach" as "contextualized orthodoxy"—an Evangelicalism "rooted" in the "old catholic" and Reformation traditions and yet "impacted" by the "modern world" (1991, 16, 11). The result is a theology that manifests significant continuity with the Reformed and Baptist traditions of nineteenth century Evangelicalism, but has been self-consciously modified in conversation with contemporary thought, especially feminist theology, modern biblical theology and the writings of Brunner and Barth (Ibid., 11-16, 19-23; Meye, 1991).

As mentioned above, Jewett began his career with the publication of *Emil Brunner's Concept of Revelation* (1954), a revision of his 1951 thesis at Harvard. Prepared, in part, while studying in Switzerland, the book reflects an extensive knowledge of Brunner's writings and a formidable grasp of the decisive features of his doctrine of revelation. As such, it occupies a unique place among early Evangelical works on Neo-Orthodox theology.[17] It is not unique, however, in its critical conclusions. Brunner's attempt to transcend "the Orthodox-Liberal antithesis" by means of "a Kierkegaardian dialectic" and "Ebnerian Personalism" is judged a failure (1954, 76-7, 146, 158, 172). The problem of revelation's relation to history and faith cannot be solved, Jewett contends, on the basis of the Kantian "dualism" that informs this approach (Ibid.,175). Without an orthodox doctrine of verbal inspiration and a non-dialectical understanding of history, one cannot maintain a meaningful doctrine of Scriptural authority. Not surprisingly, Jewett's book became the first monograph published by the Evangelical Theological Society as an expression of its "endeavors to encourage true scholarship among those who have high regard for the integrity of Holy Writ" (Ibid., Forward).

This was Jewett's opinion of Brunner's epistemology in 1954, and though his book did not engage Barth seriously, it expressed a similarly critical opinion. In fact, Barth was construed as even more extreme in his affirmation of the Kierkegaardian dialectic, and therefore less balanced and biblical (Ibid., 13, 17-18, 139). But by the end of Jewett's career the situation changed. Extensive, though qualified, appropriation of both Barth and Brunner became one of the distinguishing characteristic of his *Neo-Evangelical Theology* (1991).

Theology is defined by Jewett, not as the systematic elaboration of inerrant biblical propositions, but "the self-reflection of the church on the content and meaning of the...gospel" (1990, xviii). It is "believing thought" that arises from, and reflects upon, the "divine-human encounter" established by God's personal disclosure in the midst of His people (Ibid., 19-23). It speaks of this encounter, and out of this encounter, by means of a Word it hears from God. While affirming general revelation, Jewett rejects natural theology and orients Christian dogmatics to God's revelation in His Word (Ibid., 54-8, 68-78). This revelation occurs in two "modes": God's self-disclosure in "salvation history" and in the "inspired witness to, and interpretation of, these events by apostles and prophets" (Ibid., 77-8).

To this must be added the illumination of the Scriptural witness in the ongoing proclamation of the church. Although Jewett does not define proclamation as a third mode of revelation, his understanding of it does converge with Barth's three-fold form of the Word. By means of a "Reformed and Evangelical hermeneutic" Jewett penetrates beyond the "surface meaning" of the text to its deeper dogmatic significance, "its meaning in salvation history" (Ibid., 161, 159, 151). That deeper meaning is found in its witness to Jesus Christ, who provides the "personal center" and ultimate "purpose" of all revelation, and therefore, the substance and focus of both dogmatics and preaching (Ibid., 143, 157). To perceive this meaning is the work of the Spirit, who brings the believer into a self-authenticating circle of revelation and faith where she hears the Spirit of Christ speaking in the Scriptures (Ibid., 155-7, 98).

The significance of the centrality of Christ should not be lost on the reader. By means of this idea Jewett defends the unity of revelation, distinguishes between the temporary and enduring aspects of it, and justifies the presence of erroneous biblical statements. It lies at the center of his appropriation of Barth and his rejection of Fundamentalist Evangelicalism. Criticizing the dictation theory of Protestant Scholasticism (and the related doctrine of inerrancy in contemporary Fundamentalism), Jewett proposes a "divine/human model" for Scripture (Ibid., 139). The Bible is verbally inspired in the sense that "the humanity of the authors...never expresses itself independently of the Spirit's guidance, which secures to the church the sure word of God"—but not in the sense that human form and divine message are identical (Ibid., 142). Divine Word and human words bear a "sacramental relation" of "indirect identity as "witness" and "medium" of revelation (Ibid., 137, 83).

The task of correctly "relating the divine revelation of Scripture to the human form in which it is given" is, consequently, an "ongoing challenge" for church and theologian, and Jewett finds Brunner's principle of "contiguity" a helpful guideline in pursuing that task: "The more the conclusions of science impact the personal center of revelation—the biblical witness to Jesus Christ—the more they concern faith," and therefore, must be reconciled with Scriptural statements. But "the less they impact that center the less they concern faith"(Ibid.,142-143).

Clearly a paradigm shift has occurred in Jewett's theological pilgrimage, and it reflects an undeniable movement in the direction of Brunner and Barth. Not only has he adopted a rather "Barthian" understanding of dogmatic method and the christological nature of revelation, but Jewett also uses Barth's doctrine of analogy and his concept of "Easter" time and space to portray the relationship between revelation and history (Ibid., 33-4, 36-7, 415-33). While affirming the reasonableness of theology, Jewett insists upon the inevitability of paradox when speaking of the divine Subject, who "always remains hidden even in his self disclosure (Ibid., 85).

In the doctrine of God, moreover, the impact of Barth is pervasive and pronounced. Jewett's "basic affirmations"—that YHWH is the "unique," "free" and "living God" who "names Himself"—are all defining elements in Barth's discussion (Ibid., 174-84; *CD II/1*, Section 28); and the comprehensive depiction of God as "A Trinity of Holy Love," while not necessarily derived from Barth, certainly parallels his approach. It is not surprising, therefore, to find Jewett's analysis of the divine attributes pursuing directions already taken by Barth (Ibid., 348-61, 396-412, 413-33). Karl Barth has become, by the publication of *God, Creation and Revelation* (1991), a primary dialogue partner and model for Jewett's "Neo-Evangelical" constructions.

But Jewett's use of Barth precedes this final work. It is, in fact, present in most of his theological monographs. In *The Lord's Day* (1971), for example, Jewett constructs a Christian theology of the Sabbath that manifests a careful and appreciative reading of Barth. While attempting to supply "a part of the theological task which Barth leaves undone"—namely, an explanation of the transition from the Jewish Sabbath to the Lord's Day—Jewett affirms Barth's understanding of what the Sabbath signifies, and sides with him in criticizing the Reformers (1971, 34, 92-100).

In *Infant Baptism and the Covenant of Grace* (1978) praise and appropriation are even more pervasive. Barth is clearly the great Reformed predecessor whose statements on baptism lie at the center of contemporary debate. Granted, "much of what he said had been said many times by Baptists," and at the critical point of "action" Barth lacked the "courage" to espouse rebaptism (1978, 211). Still, his arguments "anticipate" and support Jewett's at every major juncture (Ibid., 92, 11, 164, 196).

Jewett's most striking and fundamental appropriation of Barth, however, is contained in his theological anthropology, *Man as Male and Female* (1975).

> No one with a sense for theology can read Barth
> on the question of Man as male and female without
> admiration for his originality and his provocative
> insight into a subject too long in need of the grand
> treatment reserved to dogmatics (1975, 43).

There is "no more urgent task before the church today," Jewett believes, than framing an anthropology that assigns human sexuality its proper place (Ibid.). In his own efforts to construct such a theology Jewett builds upon the foundation Barth has laid in his *Church Dogmatics*. He attempts, however, to go beyond Barth by means of a more rigorous application of his fundamental insight: That "Man, as created in the divine image, is Man-in-Fellowship," and that "the primary form of that fellowship" and therefore, "the primal form of humanity," is "male and female" (Ibid., 49, 36).

Beginning his anthropology with a concise exposition of this Barthian insight, Jewett then proceeds to "examine" and "reject" the hierarchical view of male and female, offering in its place an ideal of full equality in partnership. In this context, Barth is discussed as the most formidable of contemporary advocates of female subordination. But in the end his position is judged untenable, because inconsistent:

> The theology of Man as male and female, which [Barth] himself has espoused, is inimical to a doctrine of sexual hierarchy. The basic thrust of that theology is rather one of a fellowship of equals under God (Ibid., 85).

Barth fails to follow through on the implications of his basic insight because he fails to distinguish between the historically conditioned patriarchalism of biblical culture and the divine ideal as revealed in Jesus Christ (Ibid., 134). This "drawing back" creates in his work a peculiar tension, affirmations of equality and subordination that "die the death of a thousand qualifications" (Ibid., 85, 82).

Ultimately Jewett attributes Barth's inconsistency in anthropology to a more basic theological flaw. Following the dominant tradition of conservative Reformed criticism, Jewett claims to discern in Barth a fundamental error that "permeates his whole theological vision" (1985, 85). It colors his doctrine of the Trinity, clouds his interpretive insight into anthropology, and radically distorts his teaching on election, "the first, last and central word" of dogmatics (Ibid., 107, 51; 1991, 296-7).

The problem is not Barth's idea of revelation and rationality, as most Fundamentalist Evangelicals would contend; but rather, his christocentric supralapsarianism. With rigorous consistency Barth reinterprets theology in terms of a universal and eternal covenant of election in Christ (Ibid., 85). The result is a doctrine of election that takes "more than a furtive glance in the direction of universalism" as it engages in some of the most "heady" and "quixotic theologizing" in the history of the church (Ibid., 51, 53; 1975, 47, n.34). This distortion also leads Barth to root subordination in the creation of male and female after the pattern of Christ and His Church (1975, 69-81).

Dr. Jewett, therefore, must be seen as both a serious student of

Barth and a conservative Reformed critic. Beginning his career under the influence of Clark and Van Til, he came to occupy a position quite similar to G. C. Berkouwer (or Emil Brunner). While criticizing Barth's christological and supralapsarian reconstruction of the doctrines of election and trinity, Jewett also appropriates Barth in his own New Evangelical theology, particularly in the doctrines of revelation, anthropology and theology proper. Certainly Jewett engaged in a degree of internal appropriation that exceeded Colin Brown's "cheer and a half," not to mention the apologetic opposition manifested by other students of Clark and Van Til. Paul King Jewett modeled a movement "beyond" Fundamentalist Evangelicalism from "within," and in particular, from within the Northern Fundamentalist tradition which had given birth to Fuller Seminary. His theological trajectory during almost four decades of change at this flagship of Evangelical identity provides an important example of the changing reception of Barth within the American Evangelical mosaic.

James Daane

Fuller Seminary and the Evangelicalism it represents were changing. Carnell, Ladd and Jewett exemplify this movement beyond Fundamentalist Evangelicalism from within the theological tradition dominated by Old School Princeton and Westminster. Brown and Bromiley, on the other hand, entered Fuller at a time when broadening boundaries made their influence possible. But whether from the "inside" or "outside," each professor participated in the transition to a more open Evangelicalism, and a more positive reception of Barth. A new pluralism had emerged and Fuller had become a more authentic microcosm of the large and complex New Evangelical mosaic—at least of those Evangelicals who had rejected a Fundamentalist Evangelical paradigm.

It must be acknowledged, however, that this microcosm had a reformed center. During the sixties and seventies Fuller's department of theology expanded to include, along with the original reformed Baptists (Carnell, Henry and Jewett), reformed Presbyterians (Rogers and Jewett), reformed Anglicans (Bromiley and Brown), and members of the Christian Reformed Church (Daane and Smedes). The theological consensus, therefore, while definitely New Evangelical, was still Reformed.[18] So it is altogether consistent to find the Dutch tradition exerting an important influence.

Dr. James Daane, Professor of Pastoral Theology at Fuller from 1966 until his retirement in 1979, was a founding editor and frequent contributor to the *Reformed Journal*, a monthly magazine that has provided, since 1951, a central forum for theological expression among progressives within the Christian Reformed Church. As such, he has played a visible role in the Dutch Reformed community as a critic of its cultural isolation and theological scholasticism.But not only in that community. As an associate editor for *Christianity Today* from 1961 to 1965, and then a Professor at Fuller Seminary, Daane has participated actively in the larger Evangelical world. In that role, he has been a vocal critic of the regnant Fundamentalist Evangelicalism and an advocate for a more authentically Reformed Evangelical theology.

In the first volume of the *Reformed Journal* Dr. Daane set the tone for both the magazine and his career with a call for "a progressive theology" in the name of "the Reformation Principle of self-examination in the light of Scripture" (1951a,b). "A genuine Reformed theology," he declared, "means constant enrichment through constant reformulation demanded by expanding insight" (1951b, 11). The greatest danger to such a theology is not the external "threats" of "liberalism" or "dialecticism," but the "pietistic" defense of a theological status quo" (Ibid., 10).

What Daane had in mind when he issued this call was made abundantly clear in a 1957 report on "The State of Theology in the [Christian Reformed] Church." While commending its "long-retained, over-all pattern of orthodoxy," he indicted the Church for its failure to make any meaningful contribution to contemporary thought and life (1957, 3-5). He traced this sterility to two sources. In the first place, its social status as a "small immigrant church" had produced a community more concerned to defend its denominational institutions than engage in missionary or theological advance (Ibid., 5). But even more importantly, Reformed theology had become divorced from a fresh reading of Scripture and had assumed the form of logical self-reflection upon an abstract system. Fascinated with scholastic definitions of divine sovereignty, the Christian Reformed Church had engaged in the kind of "theological hairsplitting" that produced "split churches," "but made no theological contributions...at least none that are taken seriously by anybody" (Ibid., 5, 6-14).

Behind this indictment lay his 1954 book, *A Theology of Grace*, which he prepared while on sabbatical at the University of Amsterdam. The book was written to provide a critical analysis of Cornelius Van Til's doctrine of common grace. But its significance extended beyond this confined scope, for in the Dutch Reformed debate over common grace Daane perceived a struggle over the very nature of Reformed theology. Van Til's redefinition of the doctrine comprised, according to Daane, a loss of genuine grace—as is the case, he contended, with every teaching rooted in a scholastic understanding of divine sovereignty (1954, 24-31; 1955). Therefore Daane pleaded for the Church's forthright rejection of decretal theology and its barren corollaries—a call he voiced repeatedly in the pages of the *Reformed Journal* (1956, 1960a-d; 1964a,c; 1965) and which reached a point of mature theological expression in his 1973 book, *The Freedom of God*.

In this book Daane drew a line of continuity between the Reformed Scholasticism of Van Til and the "Evangelical rationalism" of Clark and Henry, arguing that both operated on the basis of an abstract and unbiblical conception of God, revelation and truth (1973, 75). In fact, the theological rationalism of "America's most articulate Evangelicals" displaced the doctrine of abstract sovereignty as the primary focus of Daane's polemic during his last decade at the *Reformed Journal* (1980b, 24; 1968a; 1972; 1976; 1977a,b,c; 1979; 1980c,d). But whether criticizing a scholastic doctrine of divine decree or a rationalistic epistemology of propositional revelation, Daane consistently opposed any theological method that transgressed biblical boundaries in the name of reason. If not dependent upon Berkouwer's concept of concrete correlation between revelation and faith, he certainly maintained a similar methodological orientation (1973, 188; 1960a-d; 1968b).

In the late forties and early fifties Daane's articles in Dutch Reformed journals manifest a tendency to construe Barth as the proponent of a "Dialectical Theology" that struggles under a basic and pervasive methodological error (1949; 1952). But by 1960 the tone and substance of his published comments had changed. Although he knew "of no distinctive doctrinal formulation of Barth which Reformed theology ought to accept as a substitute for its own," he did believe that a study of the Swiss theologian could help the Reformed church "put an end" to its "long season of theological sterility" (1962).

In Barth one finds a renewed wrestling with the biblical texts and a refreshing rediscovery of Reformed insights. His rejection of an abstract decree in the name of a christological doctrine of election receives special attention by Daane. But he also affirms Barth's basic methodological orientation: "Barth built a theology on the objective, redemptive action of God in Christ, a theology of revelation, whose truth does not depend on man's discovery" (Ibid., 7). These are strong words of affirmation for an associate editor of *Christianity Today* in 1962.

In 1963 Daane provided a critical review of Van Til's *Christianity and Barthianism* that reveals an important affinity to Berkouwer. Distinguishing between Van Til's theological and philosophical critiques, Daane affirms those elements in the former that are dependent upon Berkouwer, and then rejects the latter. Barth may indeed construe "the over-arching character of grace" in such a way that it becomes difficult to retain "a genuine historical moment of transition from wrath to grace" or to avoid universalism. But "this difficulty...haunts every Reformed theology," Daane contends, and has little to do with philosophical presupposition. Rather than draw out "logical implications" from "alleged presuppositions" that run contrary to Barth's own intentions, therefore, Van Til should have learned to "accept Berkouwer's gentler and more restrained evaluation." Van Til's reading of Barth should also have confronted him with Reformed theology's failure to interpret election properly, and should have occasioned "further agonizing theological struggle," rather than a "militant" and "easy" appeal to "something called classical...Reformed orthodoxy" (Daane, 1963).

Daane's own constructive attempt to learn from Barth is given primary expression in *The Freedom of God*. Here he develops *in extensio* the thesis that the sterility of modern Reformed theology can be traced to the emergence of Reformed Scholasticism, and he attempts, by means of insights learned at the feet of Barth and Berkouwer, to outline an alternative approach. The primary sign of this sterility is the silence of the pulpit on the "sum and substance of the gospel" (1973, chapter 1). The doctrine of election as espoused by the church's most articulate theological spokesmen has become unpreachable, and in this ironic "gap" between the Reformed Church's central doctrine and its central task Daane places his critical finger (Ibid., chapter 2). The source of this problem, he contends, is the scholastic definition of sovereignty in terms of a single and simple divine decree that immutably determines "whatsoever comes to pass" (Ibid. chapters 3, 4).

Francis Turretin is Daane's prime exemplar of this ill-fated formulation; but he discerns the same basic structure in most Reformed theologies, and cites Warfield, Berkhof, Hoeksema, Boettner, Van Til and Clark as twentieth century representatives. There is an obvious convergence between Barth's assessment of scholastic orthodoxy and the argument of Daane's book. Both men discern in the doctrine of divine simplicity and the single decree, as developed in post-Reformation orthodoxy, an abstract and rationalistic interpretation of God's being that renders His action in creation and redemption problematic (Ibid., 45-74, 90-98; *CDII/1*, 261, 303-17, 519-22; *CD II/2*, 78-9).

The influence of Barth is even more obvious in Daane's construction of an alternative. Although he avoids the ideas that would lead to an implicit universalism, Daane borrows from Barth the basic concepts of his own exposition, namely, the freedom of God and election in Christ. Barth employed the idea of freedom to affirm the Lordship and aseity of the living God without falling into the Aristotelian trap of an impassable deity. In the same manner, Daane defines sovereignty as God's freedom to act. The freedom of God "means" that He is able

> to have time and space for man...free to will, as he in fact did from all eternity, his resolve to create man and his world, to be involved with man and his world even to the point of becoming man in order in this profound and amazing way to be for and with man (Ibid., 167).

The echoes of Barth are striking. But Daane, in contrast to Barth, does not identify this decision to redeem men in Christ with God's inner-trinitarian being.[19]

Daane does, however, insist that God's decree to redeem mankind is His only decree. As the introduction to his book states, "Our main concern is to demonstrate that God's only decree is the gracious and elective purpose that he in divine freedom purposed in Jesus Christ, and that this decree can be preached because it can be believed" (1973, 7). A major portion of Daane's book, therefore, is devoted to exposition of the "biblical" doctrine of election, as it moves from "the election of Israel," in whom "the meaning of Christ's election lies concealed," to "the election of Jesus Christ," in whom it is "revealed" and "fulfilled," and finally to the corporate and christological form this election takes in "the election of the Church" (Ibid., 100, 126). Although Daane's exposition does not follow Barth's in detail, it manifests notable resemblances.

While James Daane may not be "willing simply to swap doctrines with Barth," he is willing to follow him quite closely in forging a path out of the scholastic morass (1962, 9). He is also willing to rely on Barth's doctrine of the three-fold form of the Word. As an authentic "echo" of "the biblical idea of the nature of the divine Word," Barth's identification of sermon and Scripture with the personal communication of God Himself is just what the Evangelical church needs to overcome its pervasive loss of power in the pulpit. At least this is the first thesis of Daane's final book, *Preaching With Confidence* (1980).

The character of revelation as an "event" in which God both reveals himself and "creates hearing" has been lost by those Evangelicals who "reduce truth to mere propositional statements" (Ibid., 18, 20). Though Barth may "stand alone" in his statements on biblical fallibility, or his reduction of Scriptural revelation to an iterative "becoming" (1964, 33), he stands with Calvin and Luther "when he says, 'Through the activity of preaching, God himself speaks'" (1980, 15).

While always the Reformed critic, Dr. James Daane provides another example at Fuller of constructive appropriation of Barth's theology in the movement beyond a Fundamentalist heritage. As an influential editor and pastoral theologian within the Christian Reformed Church and the larger Evangelical community, he exemplifies theological development within the C.R.C. *and* the expanding influence of that community within other streams of American Evangelical history. Along with Lewis Smedes, who followed Daane to Fuller, and Jack Rogers, Daane served as an important proponent of a new and progressive Reformed theology in the postwar tradition of G. C. Berkouwer.

During his years as an editor of the *Reformed Journal*, Dr. Daane penned many positive reviews of books by and about Barth (1959; 1961b; 1963; 1964b; 1978; 1981). But his final one, published in the month of his death, entitled "Barth as Paradigm," merits comment. In it he called Bernard Ramm's *After Fundamentalism* "one of the most significant books to come out of the Evangelical community in quite some time" and predicted, with obvious pleasure, that it would "fall like a bombshell on the theological turf of American Evangelicals" (1983, 26). In his own way, Daane had been modeling the selective use of Barth as a theological paradigm for some time.

Ray Sherman Anderson

With the 1976 appointment of Ray Anderson to a teaching position in Theology and Ministry, Fuller acquired its most radical advocate of Barth. While Brown, Jewett and Daane, following the pattern established by Berkouwer, maintained a Reformed opposition to many of Barth's theological innovations, Professor Anderson manifests a degree and kind of appropriation that can only be described as operating *within* a Barthian paradigm. With Ray Anderson, "authentic Evangelical theology" becomes theology based upon the fundamental insights of Karl Barth, and criticism of Barth assumes the form of movement "beyond him" by means of a "trajectory" established by him (1986, 249, 261). Even Geoffrey Bromiley's advocacy is more reserved.

Anderson's primary model for this kind of radical appropriation is Professor Thomas Torrance, the "eminent Evangelical theologian" under whom he pursued his doctoral research (Anderson, 1979, v). The focus of Anderson's theological activity is more pastoral than Torrance's work, reflecting a primary concern for the "praxis" of Christian ministry (1992a; 1989a). But the "theological foundations" for this "christopraxis," as he calls it, are provided by theologians who "share a common assumption concerning the nature of theology and its methodology," and in the volume dedicated to giving those theologians and their "fundamental paradigm" voice, Barth and Torrance dominate the discussion (1979, v).

Such radical appropriation of Barth raises the question of Anderson's understanding of Evangelical identity. Although himself an ordained minister within the Evangelical Free Church (an indisputably conservative denomination in America), and a 1959 graduate of Fuller Seminary, Anderson manifests a rather broad and inclusive view of Evangelical identity. "No Christian theologian has a proprietary claim on the phrase Evangelical theology," for in a "fundamental sense" Evangelical theology is "Christian theology"—it proclaims "the gospel of God's act of saving grace through Jesus Christ" (1989b, 131; 1979, 4).

While Anderson recognizes a contemporary use of the term to designate self-consciously "orthodox," "conservative" "or even fundamentalistic" opposition to "modern or liberal" religion, he cautions that even here one must be careful to recognize the "dynamic" and "mosaic" character of the movement. Nevertheless, Anderson does identify three basic "concerns" which "set contemporary Protestant Evangelical theology apart" and create its "distinctive ethos": "a concern for orthodoxy, biblical authority...and a personal experience of salvation through Jesus Christ" (1989b,132 4). As important representatives of these concerns he cites G. C. Berkouwer, Helmut Thielicke, Carl Henry, Bernard Ramm, and Donald Bloesch.

But within this broad and diverse range of Evangelical theologians, Anderson discerns a basic divide. On one hand is Carl Henry, and all those who would defend an "Evangelical theism" on the basis of a "rational system of apologetics"; and on the other, are those who consider such apologetic orthodoxy a form of rationalism (Ibid., 143, 146). Following Thielicke, Anderson describes this basic division as a difference between Cartesian and non-Cartesian methods, that is, between those who allow a principle of human rationality to function as an ultimate criterion, and those who insist upon the absolute priority of Word and Spirit (Ibid., 139-40, 145-7; 1979, 59-110).

Anderson also objects to the inordinate concern for boundaries that characterizes apologetic Evangelicalism. "The Evangelical Christian" is a person whose life is "centered" on "the act of God in Jesus Christ," who has "received Jesus Christ as his Lord and Saviour through a direct response to the Word in the power of the Spirit" and is thereby "united" with him and "participates in his life" (1975, 266-8). While such faith has historic grounds and cognitive content, it does not have precise or static boundaries. In fact, "when Evangelical faith adopts a 'boundary mentality' it becomes fundamentalist, which is simply a variant form of the…attempt to seek the laws of truth and reality within boundaries which man can control" (Ibid., 271-2).

In *The Praxis of Pentecost*, Anderson's most recent book, he describes Fundamentalism as a form of "church theology" that attempts to locate authority exclusively in historical continuities and rationally verified propositions (1992a, 109-27). The problem with this approach, however, is that it fails to appreciate the hermeneutical implications of the resurrection. God's revelation is God's continuing act of self-disclosure in Jesus Christ and as such is a self-authenticating event in which God upholds both sides of the divine-human relation. In the Word and through the Spirit, the believer participates in an act of God that reveals his being, and theology exists as an attempt to speak of the reality revealed in this relation. The appropriate hermeneutic, therefore, is one that orients itself to the "praxis of God" and generates not an abstract "orthodoxy" but "an authentic orthopraxy"—defined as rightful participation in the life of the resurrected Christ (Ibid., 11-13, 126).

Clearly Professor Anderson operates with a vision of Evangelical theology that is open and dynamic, centered upon the continuing act of God in Christ and opposed to the boundaried and rule-governed theology of Fundamentalist Evangelicalism.

The essential contours of Anderson's theological vision, and his dependence upon both Torrance and Barth, are evident from his very first book, *Historical Transcendence and the Reality of God* (1975). This rather complicated and involved monograph begins with an imposing conceptual problem: how is it possible to affirm "the absolute difference of God," "the 'wholly other'," while "simultaneously" asserting his relation to the world (1975, 40)? In other words, how may we speak of a genuinely transcendent deity?

Convinced that most attempts to resolve this dilemma have

faultered because of an implicit dependence upon some form of cartesian dualism, in method or metaphysic, Anderson labors assiduously to avoid such an impasse. By means of a method learned at the feet of Thomas Torrance, and an understanding of divine being that reflects the influence of at least, John Macmurray, Dietrich Bonhoeffer and Karl Barth, Ray Anderson seeks to construct an account of transcendence that corresponds to the reality of God in His revelation. In the process, he also hopes to lay the foundation for an understanding of Christian life and ministry.

The understanding of rationality that Anderson learned from Torrance, and applies in *Historical Transcendence*, is a non-Cartesian "realism" that posits participation in reality as the source and norm of all knowledge. The personal act in which a subject encounters the object of knowledge precedes and makes thinking possible, and the purpose of thought, expressed in language, is to render the "intrinsic rationality" or "inner logic" of experienced reality transparent. To do so, it formulates "axiomatic statements" that correspond to this reality as it "imposes itself" upon the subject (Ibid., 105, 49-50; 1992b, 5-6). This is the method of both theological and physical science as Torrance defines it, and the form of theological thinking suggested by Barth's *Fides Quaerens Intellectum* (1960), as Anderson understands it.

Employing this method Anderson engages, through the course of *Historical Transcendence*, in an "axiomatic penetration" of God's revelation (Ibid., 107). Assuming "the intrinsic connection of divine Word to historical event" in the Incarnation, he procedes to explore the "inner logic" of this event—including its connections with Israel, the Church and world—and is led, step by step, to an understanding of the reality of God that bears remarkable resemblances to the thinking of Barth. God is understood as an "*intra*-active" being of trinitarian union and communion, who, in the "movement" "outside of Himself" to assume human flesh, enters into an "*inter*-active" union with "estranged humanity." Somehow, and we know not how, the "penetration of the Word into flesh," which occurs within the very being of God, enables men and women to participate, through "solidarity" with Jesus, in the history of God's actions in the world (Ibid., 178-9, 181-6). In the latter half of Anderson's book this trinitarian and incarnational understanding of God's being provides the basis for his vision of Christian life and ministry.

It also provides, Anderson contends, a new and more appropriate understanding of divine transcendence. Rather than equating transcendence with "that which lies beyond or at the furthest reach of finite reason," and contrasting it with God's immanence, Anderson presents a model for transcendence that corresponds to "the reality of God" in his incarnation" (Ibid., 151, 190). He thinks of transcendence not "in terms of" distance, but presence—as "the act by which a personal agent moves beyond his own self-existence to confront and interact with an

'Other'" (Ibid., 190). Divine transcendence is the personal presence of the "Eternal Spirit" who has placed himself through the history of Jesus in concrete relation. The "enfleshment of the divine Logos" is not, therefore, a "renunciation" or a "concealing" of divinity, as traditional concepts of transcendence would suggest, but "a particularly total revealing of it" (Ibid., 167, 149, 158). God has *become* present in man and his transcendence is manifest in history.

The contrast at this point between Anderson and more traditional forms of Reformed Orthodoxy is marked. The radical identification of God's being with his act, which was a focus of Van Til's criticism of Barth, has become for Anderson axiomatic; and the corresponding interpretation of divine humiliation as a complete manifestation of the reality of God, which Berkouwer labeled theopaschitism, has been made a central argument of Anderson's exposition. Where both Fundamentalist Evangelicals and many Reformed New Evangelicals demur, Professor Anderson boldly proceeds to adopt Barth's understanding of both trinity and "the hermeneutical horizon for the being of God" (1992b, 7).

Historical Transcendence, however, is not devoid of criticism for Barth. But in the opinion of the present author, this criticism is rooted in an understanding of Barth which Anderson sheds in time. Barth is construed, following the interpretation of Bonhoeffer, as the proponent of a "punctiliar" understanding of revelation, in which the action of God "recedes constantly from the sphere of the historical *(geschichtlich)* into non-objectivity" (Ibid., 216, 94, 97). This tendency, in turn, is rooted in a "dialectical" understanding of the relation between God and history that falls prey to dualism (Ibid., 150, 118). But this interpretation of Barth is difficult to maintain in light of Anderson's generous use of Barth's expositions of divine reality; and its absence in subsequent works strongly suggests that it was peripheral and passing.

What did not pass in subsequent writings was the use of Barth as a model for theology. In fact, it became more direct and extensive. In *Theological Foundations for Ministry* (1979), for instance, American Evangelicalism received one of its most radical statements of Barthian advocacy. Not satisfied with the predominant models for Evangelical theology available in the postwar years, Professor Anderson brings together in one volume a chorus of voices deeply influenced by Barth and offers them as a paradigm for theology.

Anderson's own vision for incarnational ministry, or christopraxis, is squarely placed in the context of Barth's theological method and his understanding of the reality of God. Selections from Barth not only "define" the nature of theology (1979, 4, 22-58) and the church (Ibid., 258f.), but also provide the original and paradigmatic statement of Anderson's "Christological foundation for ministry" (Ibid., 139f.). Appropriation of Barth in matters fundamental has become the distinguishing characteristic of Professor Anderson's work, and in subsequent writing, he is able to develop this Barthian paradigm in various ministry contexts, extending it to issues that arise in concrete pastoral ministry (eg., death and dying, marriage and family, pastoral counseling, sexual roles, even business management).

But this development and extension follows a certain order. It begins with the writing of a "Theological Anthropology" that serves as a bridge between the incarnational paradigm of his first two books and the proposals for practical ministry that characterizes Anderson's later volumes. The connection between them is found in the logic of the incarnation as expounded by Barth. "Pondering the significance of Karl Barth's remark that 'theology has become anthropology since God became man'" Anderson "began to see theological anthropology at the heart of the theological course of study," and since Karl Barth, "more than any other modern theologian, developed theological anthropology from this perspective" Anderson formulated his anthropology on the basis of *Church Dogmatics*, volume III (1982, viii).

Although one should recognize the creative contributions of Professor Anderson, especially in the integration of psychology and theology, the most striking characteristic of his *Essays in Theological Anthropology* (1982) is their appropriation of Barthian insights. Beginning with an indictment of all "non-theological anthropologies," which can "at best" indicate only "symptoms of real humanity, not real humanity itself," Anderson follows Barth in his fundamental decision to understand human nature through the person of Jesus Christ (Ibid., 14; *CD III/2*, 200). In Jesus the true nature of man is revealed: " 'Real Man', Barth says, 'is the being determined by God for life with God and existing in the history of the covenant which God has established with him' " (Ibid., 37-38; *CD III/2*, 204).

This is true not only because Jesus is Real Man—man as God intended and created him—but also, and especially, because all men are included in the humanity of Jesus and the covenant history enacted by him. As Anderson says, "Through the incarnation, Christ has taken to himself all humanity as the horizon of his own being. No person exists outside of this horizon." Because of this fundamental and comprehensive determination of human being, the history of Jesus Christ becomes "the hermeneutical horizon," or interpretive paradigm, "for authentic personhood" (Ibid., 201).

The implications of this christological orientation are profound and far-reaching. Beginning with Barth's method, Anderson proceeds to appropriate almost the entire substance of Barth's anthropology. He describes human being as an "embodied soul" whose essential "form" is "determined"—called into being and upheld—by the creative Word and Spirit (Ibid., 33-43, 210-14); he designates "humanity in its original form" as "co-humanity," man in the "encounter" and "relation" of "I and Thou," "male and female" (Ibid., 44-54, 69-87). Man, as Anderson and Barth understand him, is a being whose essential form is being-in-relationship, and whose ability to respond to the approach of another and in that free response to become aware of himself, is bestowed by God. It is given by God in his own creation of, and communication with, man; and it is given by God in the creation of man as male and female, as man in a community of relation. In these relationships mankind bears the image of God, and the bearing of this image in relationship constitutes his humanity.

By covenant election, which serves as the "inner ground" and gracious "goal" of creation, mankind shares in the humanity of Jesus (Ibid.,167-9, 223; 1992b, 1). In Jesus, God chooses to be "The God who is for Man" and "The Man who is for God," and even mankind's fall cannot undo this election. Certainly sin introduces a fundamental "disorder" into the human situation, a "contradiction" or "inversion" of the *imago Dei* (Ibid., 88-103). But even in contradiction there is "hope," for "God continues to address the person who has turned away from him." He continues to pursue him in the covenant history of Jesus, and therefore, does not let him slip into a state of mere creatureliness, but rather upholds him as an image bearer "even in" his "alienation" (Ibid., 78).

In fact, sin has the status for Anderson of an "ontological impossibility," something that "exists" in opposition to man's real being as determined by God's election (Ibid., 102). "The original human condition is that of belonging," and through the life, death and resurrection of Jesus all men are upheld, *de jure*, in that originally intended state (Ibid., 189). All that remains is the *de facto* restoration of humanity to its true and essential state by the Spirit—in and through the "rituals of reinforcement" that occur in Christian community (Ibid., 179-93). This brings us back to ministry, the subject with which Anderson's anthropology ends and around which his pastoral theology turns.

Professor Ray Anderson represents an extreme in the range of Barth reception found within the New Evangelicalism of Fuller Seminary. By his radical appropriation American Evangelical theology is being led into new waters, waters in which few other Evangelicals are sailing. But even apart from Anderson the Fuller flagship has been a conspicuous leader in exploring new frontiers of Evangelical identity; and one of these frontiers has been the positive reception of Barth. Not every theologian teaching at Fuller in the last four decades has allowed interaction with Barth to direct his pilgrimage or shape his theology. But several have. And these few have caused it to become a center for sophisticated and positive interpretation.

Of course, Fuller is not the only place where constructive appropriation of Barth has occurred. The Christian Reformed tradition, as influenced by Berkouwer, has more models of positive reception than James Daane—even if criticism has been common (Stob, 1962; Smedes, 1962, 1970; Palma, 1983, 1984). Beyond the predominantly reformed traditions—among Southern Baptists, Wesleyans, Pentecostals and Anabaptists—other examples of positive reception of Barth can be found as well.

Before analyzing these other responses, however, two important reformed interpreters must yet be recognized: Bernard Ramm and Donald Bloesch. Not only have these men been deeply influenced by serious engagement with Barth, but they have also been pioneers in reshaping Evangelical theology in postwar America. Along with Berkouwer and Bromiley, they are probably the most visible and influential interpreters of Barth among the New Evangelicals. They also represent, quite significantly, the convergence of broadening Fundamentalist Evangelicalism with movements of conservative renewal that has characterized postwar American Evangelicalism.

Bernard Ramm: Model of Fundamentalist Evangelical Transition

Dr. Bernard L. Ramm is the theologian with whom the story narrated in these pages began, for with the publication of *After Fundamentalism* (1983) the issue of Barth reception within the Evangelical community received unprecedented public attention. Although it merely brought to the surface a process that had been occurring for some time, the proposal of Barth as a primary paradigm for "the future of Evangelical theology" had never received such programmatic articulation. Widespread reaction from noted leaders revealed a sensitive nerve had been touched (Henry, 1983b; Lindsell, 1987, 169-212; Dobson, 1985, 84; Pinnock, 1990; Klooster, 1985; Daane, 1983; Bloesch, 1983b). It also testified to Ramm's status within the Evangelical community.

Dr. Ramm had emerged as a leader within resurgent Fundamentalism during the immediate postwar period, at a time when the distinction between Fundamentalist and Evangelical was just beginning to be articulated. While completing an M.A. and Ph.D. in philosophy of science at the University of Southern California (1947; 1950a), he taught at Los Angeles Baptist Seminary (1943-4) and the Bible Institute of Los Angeles (1944-50), both dispensational schools within the orbit of Northern Fundamentalist Evangelicalism. From there he moved to Bethel Baptist College and Seminary (1950-54), teaching hermeneutics, philosophy and apologetics at these conservative institutions (General Conference Baptist).

During these years he produced four books which established his reputation as a leading scholar within the emerging Evangelical movement: *Protestant Biblical Inter-pretation* (1950b), *Protestant Christian Evidences* (1953a), *Types of Apologetic Systems* (1953b), and *The Christian View of Science and Scripture* (1954). The first of these has seen three editions and numerous printings, been translated into Japanese, and continues to function as a standard textbook in conservative Evangelical schools (1956; 1970). The latter, hailed as a landmark in the Evangelical discussion of science and faith, evoked the same public attention in 1954 as *After Fundamentalism* did in 1984 (Butler, 1976, 109-16). Along with Carnell, Henry, Jewett, Kantzer and Ladd, therefore, Bernard Ramm became one of the recognized young leaders in the resurgence of Fundamentalist Evangelical scholarship (Smith, 1950).

Like these other men, Ramm's early scholarship had an apologetic focus and orthodox self-understanding. His first books were written with the express intention of defending "conservative Protestantism," "the historic Christian faith as reflected in the great creeds of the ancient Church..., the writings of the Reformers" and "the noble tradition of the closing years of the nineteenth century"(1950, 1; 1954, 9). Ramm is at home in the writings of nineteenth century conservatives, especially Warfield and Orr, and his own apologetic system shows the decided influence of contemporary heirs of that tradition. There is little if any difference, for example, between the apologetic proposed in *Protestant Christian Evidences* (1953a) and Carnell's *Introduction to Apologetics* (1948). Both defend a "theory of knowledge" that asserts the logical priority of revelation (all meaning is determined by God) and the validity of a modified rationalism (ideas and mental forms precede experience), while insisting upon openness to verification according to general standards of rationality (1953a, 30-38, 40-42; 1963b, 159-236). Their basic thesis is that Reformed Christianity is *"the most reasonable hypothesis to explain undoubted facts"* (1953a, 45); and the source of this hypothesis, or "network of hypotheses" is the Bible, a divinely inspired and infallible revelation of conceptual truth (Ibid., 36, 42-3, 48-51).

But Ramm, even during these early years, was no reactionary Fundamentalist. Rather, he was reaching back into the traditions of nineteenth century conservative scholarship in order to chart a course for mid-century Fundamentalism between the "obscurantism" of "hyper-orthodoxy" and the "Liberal" and "Neo-Orthodox" flight from Scriptural infallibility (1954, 15-31, 181). He proposed a "rapprochement," therefore, between conservative faith and critical science on the basis of a more sophisticated understanding of both science and Scripture.

His most notable contribution during the fifties to this mediating strategy is contained in *A Christian View of Science and Scripture* (1954). Distinguishing between science and "scientisms," Ramm argues that opponents of "biblical supernaturalism" typically "oversimplify" the nature of scientific rationality and illegitimately "reduce...the scope of reliable knowledge" (Ibid., 38-42). They also tend to underestimate the provisional nature of scientific theories. But this does not mean that Christians can ignore scientific conclusions, especially those established by an "overwhelming" convergence of evidence (Ibid., 123, 128-30, 165-7, 220). Such "obscurantism" is surely an unnecessary and "suicidal" strategy (Ibid., 26).

It arises, Ramm contends, from a failure to discern the "pre-scientific" and basically theological nature of Scripture. Although using culturally "embedded" language as the "vehicle" for communicating truths of revelation, "the Bible is singularly lacking in any definite [scientific] *theorizing"* (Ibid., 48-9). References to nature are "popular" and "phenomenal," and the Genesis account of creation and fall is, with respect to science, a "non-postulational literary vehicle for conveying the revelation of God" (Ibid., 223). Evangelical hermeneutics, therefore, must distinguish between cultural form and "trans-cultural" substance, though Ramm admits that *"no simple rule can be devised to divide one from the other"* (Ibid., 53).

While such proposals seem far from radical, and possibly even anachronistic, they elicited significant reaction among American Evangelicals during the fifties. They also revealed the basic problem complex that was destined to shape the course of Bernard Ramm's career. In an effort to maintain continuity with a conservative heritage in an intellectually responsible manner he felt compelled to reconcile his dual commitment to modern science and Reformed Orthodoxy. It is not surprising, therefore, that his 1953 book, *Types of Apologetic Systems*, defines the purpose of apologetics as "mediating" the "intellectual tensions" that have arisen because of "modern knowledge" (1953b, 2-3). Of course this problem is not unique to Ramm. But under the pressure of this problem, Dr. Ramm became a pioneer in the development of a New Evangelical paradigm for theology, and interaction with Karl Barth came to play an impotant role in his pilgrimage.

The Reception of Barth and the Reappraisal of Evangelical Theology

During the first decade of his academic career Ramm's reception of Barth can justly be described as uninformed. References to him occur exclusively in the context of general comments about "Barthianism," "Barthian theology" or "Neo-Orthodoxy," and Ramm's interpretation depends upon the opinion of others. He is construed, following Van Til, as the proponent of an "existential" and "paradoxical" doctrine of revelation, produced by his acceptance of Kant's "metaphysical agnosticism" and evidenced in the rejection of verbal inspiration and infallibility (1953a, 43; 1950, 42-47). He is guilty of an "extremely faulty and anti-Biblical" view of natural revelation, a "high handed dismissal of Christian philosophy" and an understanding of Christ that "is not the Christ of the historical documents" (1954, 57; 1953b, 82; 1953a, 180). In no case are these claims supported by specific references or detailed exegetical argument. In partial defense, however, it must be acknowledged that Ramm recognized the mediating intention of Neo-Orthodoxy, Barth included, praised its influence upon the biblical theology movement and expressed hope "that it might be the harbinger of a great revival of Evangelical theology" (1954, 223; 1950, 42-7; 1953a, 79). He also manifested a serious and appreciative reading of Brunner (1949, 31-52; 1953b, 62-84; 1954, 222-4).

By the publication of *A Christian View of Science and Scripture*, however, Dr. Ramm gave no evidence of serious interaction with Barth. This conclusion corresponds to his own historical account, for it was not until 1956, when the English translations of *Church Dogmatics* began to roll off the press, that Ramm started a systematic reading of Barth's work. Before this, in 1945, he had read Thompson's translation of I/1 but found it difficult to assimilate. He had also tried to learn something of Barth during his seminary days at Eastern Baptist (1938-41), but could not find anyone to provide helpful interpretation (Ramm, 1986a; 1983, 8-9). The reading of *Church Dogmatics* during the later fifties bore fruit. It led Ramm to spend the sabbatical year of 1957-1958 in Basel, and together with this personal exposure to Barth began a process of constructive and critical interaction that played a decisive role in Ramm's theological development.

According to Ramm's own testimony, this early turning to Barth followed in the wake of a life-changing personal experience. While lecturing in a public forum sometime during the fifties (probably 1954-56), he was unnerved by a request to define his version of American Evangelical theology. "Like a drowning man who sees parts of his life pass before him at great speed," Dr. Ramm reports, "so my theology passed before my eyes." What he saw was a disordered collection of conservative doctrines "warped" by a half century of "orthodox-liberal" debate (1983, 1, 8-9).

Sensing the need to find a more coherent and historically informed understanding of Evangelical theology, he turned not only to Barth, but also to the writings of Abraham Kuyper, John Calvin, and to a lesser extent, P. T. Forsyth. The result of these reflections is contained in a trilogy of books on the doctrine of revelation produced between 1957 and 1961 *The Pattern of Authority* (1957a), *The Witness of the Spirit* (1960) and *Special Revelation and the Word of God* (1961a). In these books one finds the firstfruits of Ramm's interaction with Barth as he develops a doctrine of revelation that pushes beyond his Fundamentalist Evangelical heritage.

While acknowledging the valid apologetic intention of the Fundamentalist fight with Liberalism, Ramm indicts the movement as "a serious narrowing of the Christian faith" (1960, 127). In the heat of the battle over doctrinal truth it developed a "formalistic and scholastic doctrine of inspiration" that became the focus of its apologetic defense, and it lost sight of the Reformers' "more comprehensive" understanding of revelation (Ibid., 123-7). It lost sight of, for example, the essential role of the Spirit in enabling the mind to receive divine truth (Ramm, 1960); or the inseparable connection between revelation and redemption, between the divine speaking in all its modes and the person of Jesus Christ (Ramm, 1961a, 106-110, 101-3, 58-9, 147); or the inescapably "accommodating," "mediated" and therefore "analogical" nature of divine communication (Ibid., 31-44); or even, the interpenetration of divine and human that demands a distinction, but allows no clean separation between revelatory substance and cultural form (Ibid., 34-5, 63-9, 76, 153). All these dimensions of the doctrine must be given their due, and if they are, "rationalistic" views of inspiration and inerrancy that "abstract" revelation from its soteric and spiritual context cannot legitimately be maintained (Ibid., 90, 118, 147; 1960, 124-7).

The primary sources for this shift in Ramm's thinking were Calvin and Kuyper (Ramm, 1961, 140-1; 1960, 26). But one of the distinguishing characteristics of *Special Revelation and the Word of God* (1961a) is Ramm's new freedom—and ability—to cite Barth in support of his positions. "Time and time again," he professed twenty years later, "I found parallels between Barth's thought and Kuyper's" (Ramm, 1983, 9). He found parallels in their discussions of divine incomprehensibility (1961a, 22); in their doctrines of accommodation and analogy (Ibid., 33); in their christological understanding of Scripture (Ibid., 111); in their insistence upon the unity of word and event in the divine act (Ibid., 73, 81); and in their teaching on the testimony of the Spirit (1960, 26-7). Ramm also cited with approval Barth's discussions of revelation and history (1961a, 92-6; 1963) and his seminal effort to define the *special* nature of theological science (Ibid., 141, 144; 1961b, 18). By 1961 Barth had become, rather quickly, a primary and influential dialogue partner in Ramm's theology.

But Barth had *not* become a paradigm. Ramm still discerned basic errors in the Neo-Orthodox program, centering in its doctrine of revelation. Whether expressed as a denial of direct revelation, a reduction of Scripture to the status of witness, or a refusal to affirm biblical infallibility, the problem is essentially the same: Barth introduces a "cleavage" between the Word of God and the modes of revelation that keep the speech of God from becoming "an abiding deposit" with enduring conceptual content (1961a, 36, 163, 143; 1966b, 111-13, 89-91). Because of this, he undermines, at least in part, the ability of Scripture to function as the source and norm for theology (1965).

Of course Barth continues to write theology, copiously citing Scripture in the process; but this only indicates "an undigested something" in his methodology (1957a, 97). Or to employ another metaphor, in "The Continental Divide in Contemporary Theology" between those who affirm "the historic doctrine of revelation" and those who reject it, Barth and Brunner "have a theology of the cracks!" (1966a, 14-5). In 1983, Ramm will refer to the difficulty he experienced getting Barth's mediating theology "into focus" (1983, 16, 108, 119). But in the decade of the sixties, and even the early seventies, Ramm seems to think the problem is primarily Barth's.

In 1973 Dr. Ramm published *The Evangelical Heritage*, an

important book for at least two reasons. It provided a public statement of Ramm's understanding of Evangelical identity nearly twenty years after the unnamed inquirer had called it into question; and he incorporated into this statement a recommendation about how Evangelicals should respond to Neo-Orthodoxy. The book represents, therefore, a landmark in Ramm's reflection upon the twin issues of Evangelical identity and Karl Barth, and an important trailmark on the path toward his 1983 recommendation of Barth as an Evangelical paradigm.

Distancing himself from the two "Evangelical" extremes of Van Til's indictment of Barth as heretical and Torrance's affirmation of him as orthodox, Ramm proposes a "dialectical" reading. "This means being very hard on Barth when he clearly drifts away from historical Evangelical positions but applauding him when he scores a point" (1973, 109-110). The implications of this approach are that Barth is both right and wrong, and that something called "historic Evangelicalism" is the standard of judgment.

But what is historic Evangelicalism? It is that version of the Christian faith which has maintained "the essential affirmations" of the ancient creeds, the Protestant Reformers and the orthodox divines (1973, 56). While acknowledging the limitations of human comprehension, the necessary development of doctrine and the inevitable diversity of theological formulation (Ibid., 61-2, 129, 42-47), Ramm nevertheless insists "there is a core of Christian doctrines which if surrendered is the surrender of the Christian faith" (Ibid., 101). He sympathizes, therefore, with the Fundamentalist opposition to Liberalism and locates the "Evangelical Heritage" on a line that extends from the Reformation through Protestant Orthodoxy and into the modern Fundamentalist movement.

But Ramm combines this concern for essential Christianity with an equally strong opposition to the Fundamentalist strategy of ignoring the post-Enlightenment gains in scientific knowledge. In fact, the basic distinction between Evangelicalism and its Orthodox and Fundamentalist forebears is, for Ramm, a more positive appropriation of Enlightenment knowledge (Ibid., 70-73).

On the basis of this commitment to an updated Evangelical Orthodoxy, Dr. Ramm both criticizes and commends Barth. He commends him for his "strong" affirmation of Scripture as the Church's "direct, absolute, and material" authority, and for his powerful opposition to both Liberalism and Roman Catholicism in defense of this authority (Ibid., 111-113, 117). He also applauds Barth's deep and serious interaction with the whole history of theology, especially the Reformers (Ibid., 115-118). As Ramm marveled in 1957, Barth has "almost single handedly" "laid the death blow" to liberalism and "restored theology to its proper place of dignity in the Church" (1957c, 4, 33: 1957b); and he has done so in the name of a theology of the Word that affirms historic Evangelical doctrine.

But Ramm also criticizes Barth. He thinks Evangelicals have a right to be "unhappy" with Barth's denial of direct revelation, objective inspiration and biblical infallibility (1973, 114-115). Ramm also claims that "Barth is a Christomonist," someone whose attempt to interpret Scripture christologically has been carried to an extreme. The result is a "monism" of grace that denies a proper distinction between creation and redemption, distorts the doctrine of atonement and does not allow room for a biblical understanding of divine wrath (Ibid., 119; 1966, 16). He even wonders whether many more of Barth's doctrinal reformulations might be distortions of biblical data, as Van Til has suggested (Ibid., 118-119).

As examples of the kind of "dialectical" response to Barth that Ramm is proposing, he cites Clark, Runia, Bromiley and Berkouwer. While Clark only "grants Barth the minimum," the other men manifest a degree of appreciation that parallels Ramm's own. In fact, he describes Berkouwer's *Triumph of Grace* as "a calm, accurate, fair, and positive appraisal of the theology of Karl Barth" (Ibid., 110). It would not be far from the truth, therefore, to identify Ramm's dialectical response to Barth during the sixties and seventies with the spirit and substance of Berkouwer's position in the fifties. Certainly Ramm's commitment to historic Reformed orthodoxy did not allow him to propose Barth as a model for the future of Evangelical theology.

After Fundamentalism: The Future of Evangelical Theology

With the publication of *After Fundamentalism*, however, the situation seems to have changed. At least, criticism of Barth has receded into the background and the proposal that he function as a model for Evangelical theology has become Ramm's central theme. Nor is it simply a matter of shifting emphases, for Ramm affirms in 1983 positions he denied a decade earlier. But there is also continuity between 1980 and the preceding three decades, a continuity of concerns and directions that culminate in this apparently radical proposal.

The basic thesis of Ramm's book is straightforward. He argues that both Liberal and Fundamentalist theologies have failed to develop an adequate response to the "crisis" of the Enlightenment, the "great cultural watershed" that gave birth to the modern world and inflicted a "mortal wound" upon Protestant Orthodoxy (1983, 8; 1973, chapter 5). Absorbing the Enlightenment to excess, Liberals "capitulate" to the "modern mentality" and thereby fail to maintain the "substance" of historic Christianity (1983, 14, 37-43). Fundamentalists, on the other hand, create a theology that cannot incorporate even the valid gains of modern science and history (Ibid., 26-27, 44-47). According to Ramm, this route "commits them to the strategy of obscurantism," and he includes in the list of offending Fundamentalists not only Cornelius Van Til, but also Schaeffer, Clark and Henry (Ibid., 26-

27).

The only "workable solution" to the Enlightenment challenge, therefore, is to adopt a mediating strategy. While Ramm recognizes the fruitful work of other theologians, he believes that "Barth's method of coming to terms with modern learning and historical Reformed theology" provides the best paradigm for this strategy (Ibid., 18). The purpose of *After Fundamentalism*, therefore, is to provide a sympathetic interpretation of Barth in order to illustrate how he might serve as a model for a mediating response to post-Enlightenment rationality.

Ramm is careful to insist, however, that his focus is methodological. He even claims (three times) that "one may be a five-point Calvinist, a five-point Arminian, or a seven-point dispensationalist and still learn to write theology from the paradigm of Barth" (Ibid., 28). Of course as Ramm admits, "it is not always possible to draw a clear distinction between Barth's methodology and his conclusions" (Ibid.). But by aiming at this distinction, Dr. Ramm does limit his advocacy and leave room for a "dialectical" response. While some interpreters have minimized the significance of the "Reservations About Barth's Theology" outlined in "Appendix One" of *After Fundamentalism* (Mohler, 1990b; 1989, 266-72), I would insist they must be taken seriously. Otherwise, the contrast between the early and later Ramm may be overdrawn, and his real intentions for Evangelical theology missed. Would-be interpreters must be able to absorb Ramm's 1986 "warning": "If it were on a line-by-line basis, I would be in far more agreement with G. C. Berkouwer than Karl Barth" (1986a, 5).

What has occurred between *The Evangelical Heritage* (1973) and *After Fundamentalism* (1983) is a "progressive spiral" in sympathetic interpretation (Jones, 1985), leading to the new conclusion that Barth's theology provides, in fundamental matters, the best paradigm for Evangelicalism. Aiding Ramm to reach this conclusion was his perception that a crisis had engulfed the American Evangelical community, producing fruitless battles over biblical inerrancy and a persistent failure to incorporate the insights of modern criticism (1983, 25-27; 1974; 1977b).

"The central problem" raised for Christianity by the Enlightenment is "the authority in a scientific age of a book (the Bible) written in a prescientific age" (1983, 38). Therefore, Barth's primary contribution to Evangelical theology is his doctrine of the Word, and most of Ramm's 1983 book is dedicated to this subject. The twin issues of revelation and modern rationality had drawn Ramm's attention from the beginning of his career, and he engaged in pioneering efforts to recover a comprehensive doctrine of revelation (1960; 1961a), and to chart a course between Modernism and Fundamentalism (1954; 1973). But Ramm had always stopped short of the Neo-Orthodox reconstruction, resisting Barth's concept of witness and the loss of identity between revelation and Scripture it implied (1973, 114; 1966b, 111-112). In *Af-*

ter Fundamentalism, however, Ramm now argues that it is precisely the Hodge-Warfield identification of divine Word and biblical words that has kept Fundamentalism from absorbing the valid insights of biblical criticism (1983, 44-45, 105, 113).

Barth, in contrast, is able to "touch bottom" on "the humanity of Scripture." He can take the cultural and linguistic phenomena of the biblical text "in stride" because he acknowledges a "diastasis" between the Word of God and its temporal form that can be bridged only by a divine action. The Word must be "sought" through Spirit enabled exegesis and may be found in the "theological witness" the texts bear (Ibid., 89-92, 109-111). Yet in contrast to the liberal revision, Ramm insists that Barth does not compromise historic Evangelical theology. The "identity" between Word and words achieved in revelation, though "diffracted" and "indirect," still enables Scripture to serve him as a "direct, absolute, and material authority" (Ibid., 91-97).

Obviously Ramm has rejected (or updated) his previous interpretation of Barth. But he has also revised his own doctrine of Scripture: incorporating a more radical recognition of the historically conditioned nature of the biblical texts, he now espouses rather completely Barth's doctrine of the Word of God. [20]

Ramm also approves of Barth's apologetic. As early as 1953 Ramm had declared himself in support of the priority of revelation over reason (1953b). But he had combined this with an emphasis on the rational verifiability of revealed truths that included a rather traditional appeal to christian evidences (1953a). Over the next three decades, however, under the influence of first Kuyper, Calvin, and then Barth, Ramm forged a somewhat different understanding of faith and reason. He came to emphasize more completely, revelation's priority and reason's dependence, and in the end argued that Barth's statement of the "Anselmic program" provided the best paradigm for the proper "ordering" and "functioning" of human reason (Ibid., 70). Ramm declared "traditional apologetics" defeated by Hume and Kant, and decried the fact "that this message has not been heard very clearly in Evangelical circles" (Ibid., 59). He insisted that Christianity was no "scientific theory" or "metaphysical system" established by "philosophical" or "empirical test" (Ibid., 61-2), but rather a revelation from God, objectively present in salvation history and subjectively known through the testimony of the Spirit (1972, 38-45).

There is indeed a place for reason, and Ramm considers absurd the interpretation of Barth as an irrational fideist. But reason's place is "ministerial": it attends to the transcendent Subject and seeks to "clarify," within the limits of revelation, what can be known of Him (1983, 61-65). It aims at a "synoptic" restatement of biblical revelation (1972, 58-70). The best apologetic, therefore, is a coherent and beautiful dogmatics. In the construction of that dogmatic edifice the theologian may use his reason to the full; but he must be open, radically open, to following revelation wherever it leads. From *"Carlos Magnus"*, therefore, Ramm learned not to fear reason but to use it "Christianly," and thereby to avoid both Fundamentalism's "sacrifice of the intellect" and Liberalism's "tragic loss of historic Christian substance" (1977a; 1983, 67, 60, 43). In fact, Ramm cited this new freedom as one of three great "helps" he received from Barth in his own journey beyond Fundamentalism (1986b, 121).

After penning his 1983 manifesto on Barth, Ramm published two other books: *Offense to Reason: The Theology of Sin* (1985b) and *An Evangelical Christology* (1985a). In these he offers his mature position on the fundamental issues of soteriology, and indirectly illustrates what it means for him to write Evangelical theology after the pattern of Karl Barth.

Both books pursue a similar strategy: They articulate and defend an updated version of "historic" doctrine in the face of post-Enlightenment denials (1985a, 15; 1985b, 8). They also manifest serious and constructive engagement with the work of Barth (and others). But this does not mean Ramm offers the Evangelical public a restatement or even revision of Barth's position. In fact, his own proposals converge with Berkouwer more often than they do Barth (1985a, 23, 59; 1985b, ix). Nevertheless, Ramm does regard Barth as an important ally in the defense of historic theology and relies at crucial junctures on his work.

On the doctrine of sin, for example, Barth's approach to Genesis provides the hermeneutic by which Ramm attempts to "maintain...with some adjustment" the traditional teaching (1985b, 76). By interpreting the creation narrative as "saga" Ramm is able to affirm the Augustinian doctrine of original sin while leaving room for the conclusions of modern science about the origin of man and the history of the biblical documents.

Ramm is also able to affirm the best insights of the "typological interpretation"—which construes the Fall as an "existential cross-section" of human experience—without abandoning the historicity of Adam (Ibid., 62-75; 1983, 82-87). The Fall, according to Ramm, is a divinely inspired story that portrays, in a non-literal form, the origin of sin and its eternal nature. This is not, of course, the position of Barth, who with Kierkegaard rejects the idea of a fall from original righteousness at the headwaters of the human race. So while affirming Barth's concept of saga, and praising his "strong Augustinian doctrine" of depravity, Ramm criticizes his rejection of the traditional three phase order of salvation (Ibid., 140, 120).

This same dialectical response characterizes Ramm's *Evangelical Christology* (1985a). The purpose of the book is to provide a restatement and defence of the "historic" position of the ecumenical and reformed creeds in the context of contemporary debate (1985a, 3-15). As in the earliest days of his career, Ramm defines that debate antithetically. He discerns a basic "dividing line" between those who maintain the confessional tradition and those who do not, and he believes the battle between these "two camps" concerns the very life of the church (Ibid., 119, 108).

The location of the battle line, however, has changed since the fifties: Barth and Bultmann have now become prime exemplars of the two sides of contemporary debate (contra 1966a). The real nemesis of Evangelical theology is the "extreme historical skepticism" of "the Bultmannian program" and the "christological reductions" it has inspired (1985a, 3, 196-7). The solution, in the tradition of Martin Kähler and Karl Barth, is to defend Scripture as an historically authentic "theological witness" to the person and work of Christ (Ibid., 134-9, 162-6). "Fundamentalist views" of inspiration and inerrancy need not, and cannot, be maintained (Ibid., 138).

Thus Ramm proclaims Barth an Evangelical paradigm. But he is also selective in his use of the Swiss theologian. While affirming his view of the virgin birth and bodily resurrection (including the distinction between *Historie* and *Geschichte*), Ramm criticizes Barth's understanding of the divine incognito (Ibid., 68-9, 95-7). But more importantly, he repeatedly sidesteps many of Barth's characteristic reinterpretations of christology (election, humiliation and exaltation, for example). Apparently what it means for Barth to serve as a model for Evangelical theology can be quite restricted, and in specific doctrinal proposals Ramm follows Berkouwer much more often than Barth. He also interprets Barth in a manner that highlights his continuity with historic Evangelical theology.

Nevertheless, Bernard Ramm has become possibly the most visible example of an American Evangelical theologian whose pilgrimage beyond Fundamentalist Evangelicalism was decisively shaped by interaction with Karl Barth. He is, therefore, an important model of transition for New Evangelicals who find themselves on a similar path.[21] Ramm's journey, it should be noted, involved a change in social context as well as theological position. He left Bethel College and Seminary in 1954, after writing *A Christian View of Science and Scripture*, and spent the next four years (excluding the sabbatical in Basel) at Baylor University, a Southern Baptist institution in Texas. But then from 1959 until his retirement in 1986 (excluding 1974-77) he worked in the pluralistic context of American Baptist Seminary of the West, and participated as a professor in Berkeley's very diverse Graduate Theological Union. Like many other models of New Evangelical transition, an altered social setting provided the space in which theological change occurred.

Donald Bloesch: Converging Mainline Evangelical

As Bernard Ramm and other members of conservative Evangelical communities were pushing beyond the boundaries of Fundamentalist Evangelicalism, movements of reform and renewal which advocated similar concerns were emerging within traditional mainline denominations. The convergence of these two currents in the broadening stream of resurgent Evangelicalism tended to produce, during and after the sixties, an increasingly complex and diverse American Evangelical river.

Even though these renewal movements were sometimes led and often influenced by denominational conservatives who identified with the Fundamentalist Evangelicalism of Ockenga, Henry and Graham, they were not located in, or limited to, this institutional matrix. They had a life of their own, and in many cases drew into the Evangelical orbit people whose theology and practice did not fit within the boundaries of "classic" Fundamentalism, or even an early resurgent Evangelicalism. In fact, an important leadership element has been provided by theologians "nurtured on Neo-Orthodoxy," who in their recovery of an Evangelical heritage kept many things learned at the feet of Barth and Niebuhr (Bloesch, 1968a, 19). Their sense of Evangelical identity, therefore, is ecumenical and mediating; and the Evangelicals with whom they are most likely to identify are those who have pressed for revisions of the Fundamentalist heritage.

A pioneer in this vision for Protestant renewal under an inclusive Evangelical banner has been President Emeritus of Princeton Seminary, John Mackay, whose call for an "Evangelical renaissance" to unite Pentecostal, Neo-Evangelical and mainline Protestants in a truly ecumenical movement reached the pages of *Christianity Today* (Mackay, 1972a,b; Bloesch, 1970, 186; 1973, 78). Of course, this vision of an Evangelical center between Modernism and Fundamentalism had been championed much earlier (Richards, 1934; Lewis, 1934; Homrighausen, 1934, 1935, 1936). But the perceived "collapse" of a Neo-Orthodox "middle ground" among mainline conservatives (Allen, 1974), combined with the emergence of a culturally engaged Evangelicalism and grassroot renewal movements, had created a unique opportunity for Evangelical resurgence during the sixties. As contemporary proponents of this ecumenical and evangelical center, one could cite Bela Vassady (1965), Paul Mickey (1980), Richard Lovelace (1979, 1983), Gabriel Fackre (1973, 1984a), Elton Trueblood (1948, 1952, 1961), Kenneth Hamilton (1965, 1971a,b) and of course, numerous New Evangelical theologians discussed earlier in this chapter. But probably the most important spokesman and model for this New Evangelicalism in the current day is United Church of Christ theologian, Donald G. Bloesch. Not coincidentally, he is also an important advocate and interpreter of Barth.

For thirty five years a teacher at the University of Dubuque Theological Seminary (Presbyterian Church, U.S.A.), Dr. Bloesch has been a leading advocate of reformation and renewal within America's mainline denominations (Lovelace, 1983; Bloesch, 1991, x). He has also participated actively in the Evangelical movement: a member of the Evangelical Theology Group in the American Academy of Religion (Bloesch, 1985); a participant in the "Chicago Call," a 1977 appeal by noted Evangelicals for the recovery of an historically rooted and catholic Evangeli-calism (Bloesch, 1978a); and the author of numerous widely read books on Evangelical identity and theology (1970, 1973, 1978a, 1979, 1984). In fact, a recent survey of Evangelical theologians by *Moody Monthly*, a publication of the Moody Bible Institute, identified Dr. Bloesch as "the most brilliant, creative Evangelical working in systematic theology" today. In response, this Fundamentalist Evangelical magazine produced a brief, approving article introducing him to its conservative readership (Keylock, 1988).

But as the article acknowledged, Donald Bloesch's background is not typically Evangelical—at least not twentieth century American Evangelical. The son of a German Reformed pastor and the grandson of Swiss missionaries to America, Bloesch was raised in the same Evangelical and Reformed Church in which the Niebuhr brothers grew up, and attended the same denominational college. In fact, the Niebuhr's and Bloesch's were family friends (Bloesch, 1991, ix-x). He was "nurtured," therefore, "on Neo-Orthodoxy," and did not for many years "consider any of the leading conservative Evangelical theologians in America as viable options" (Bloesch, 1968a, 19; Keylock, 1988, 62).

But there were other forces present in Bloesch's early life that moved him in an Evangelical direction. Devotional literature from his pietist grandmother deeply influenced his development, as did confirmation training in the *Evangelical Catechism*. Then during graduate school at the University of Chicago he "participated actively" in Inter-Varsity Christian Fellowship, finding "a spiritual bond" with these Evangelicals he did not sense at the Divinity School (Keylock, 1988, 623). Even his affirmation of what he called a "Barthian" theology during graduate school had a conservative purpose: to combat the "extreme liberal theology" of the reigning "Neo-naturalists" at Chicago (Keylock, 1988, 62; Bloesch, 1991, 56). An early reformed and pietistic heritage, therefore, nurtured an Evangelical impulse that found its first intellectual form in the Neo-Orthodoxy of Niebuhr and Barth (Bloesch, 1956; 1986b, 126).

Bloesch's "deepest affinities," however, are with movements of spiritual reformation and renewal—Catholic monasticism, the Reformation, Pietism, Puritanism and Awakening Evangelicalism—and the recovery of these traditions provided the real shaping force for his "theological development" (1968a, 31, 9). Following doctoral studies, Bloesch spent the 1956-1957 school year in Oxford exploring monastic movements. Then in 1964 he produced a study of eight Protestant communities whose form of life made them models and *Centers of Christian Renewal*. This book, his first, was followed in the later sixties and early seventies by four other descriptive analyses of renewal movements (1968c, 1971b, 1973, 1974a) and several proposals on how to best facilitate evangelical reformation within Christ's church (1968a, 1970, 1973, 1983a). As early as 1964 Bloesch identified the "basic concern" of his theological "vocation" as "the renewal and reformation of the church in a secular society" (1991, 3), and by the early seventies he had emerged at the forefront of interpreters and advocates of renewal within American Protestantism.

Like Bela Vassady and John Mackay before him, Bloesch flew this flag of renewal under an Evangelical banner. And like these men, the Evangelicalism he advocates is decidedly ecumenical. "Evangelicalism may take the form of a particular party within the church," he acknowledged. But ideally "it seeks to confess not a party line, but the holy catholic faith" and "to serve as a catalyst that unifies the whole church under the gospel." It "is best understood," therefore, "as a movement of spiritual renewal within the wider church" distinguished by its fidelity to biblical Christianity (1983a, 15-16, 5).

Present throughout Catholic history, "Evangelical Christianity" was decisively articulated in the Protestant Reformation, renewed and extended in the spiritual movements of Pietism, Puritanism and the Anglo-Saxon Awakenings, and has been manifested, at least partially, in twentieth century Fundamentalism, Neo-Orthodoxy and Neo-Evangelicalism (1973, 48-50; 1978b, 1-23). None of these movements, however, have achieved the Evangelical ideal. That ideal, as envisioned by the Reformers, is a genuinely "catholic Evangelicalism" that clearly proclaims the gospel of free grace while maintaining essential continuity with the historic Catholic tradition (1968, 33; 1970, 186; 1978b, 15; 1979, 283; 1983a, 48, 151). Bloesch's own statement of this reformed and catholic Evangelicalism is contained, among other places, in his two volume *Essentials of Evangelical Theology* (1978b, 1979).

The purpose of these volumes is "to enunciate the salient features of the Evangelical faith," and in so doing, to help Evangelicalism "rediscover its identity" and "present a united witness to the church and the world" (1978b, ix, 1). Bloesch is aware of the difficulty of this project; he knows that diverse forms of Evangelical religion have always existed and that these traditions have interpreted essential doctrine in different ways. But he also believes Evangelical Christianity "has an inner theological unity" that can be identified, however imperfectly, in the midst of its obvious diversity (1983a, vii). He believes, moreover, that the present religious situation demands a fresh statement of these "fundamental tenets of the faith" (1978b, x).

Not only has "a new modernism" arisen within the contemporary church, threatening "to engulf mainline Christianity" and "bury the gospel," but an older Fundamentalism continues to fragment Evangelicals by its twin strategies of cultural separation and theological repristination (1978b, 1; 1975, 37; 1983a, 84-96). By carefully defining *The*

Essentials of Evangelical Theology, Bloesch hopes "to build bridges" between divergent Evangelical traditions while at the same time draw clear "lines of distinction" between Evangelical Christianity and all forms of liberal defection (1979, 235; 1978a, 15). He endeavors, therefore, to push beyond the polarities present in diverse formulations of "Evangelical essentials" and to reach "a synthesis that negates the misconceptions of both sides, but at the same time fulfills their legitimate hopes and concerns" (1978b, x; 1992, chapter 2). As a result, he often finds himself battling on two fronts: opposing the repristination of "a narrowly conservative Evangelicalism," on one hand, and the radical redefinition of an accommodating liberalism on the other (1973, 29).

This centrist position demands both recovery and achievement. Bloesch is self-consciously trying to recover the vision of a vital, apostolic orthodoxy that animated both the Reformers and the post-Reformation Pietist movements, including the Anglo-Saxon Awakenings (Bloesch, 1973). In its best representatives and better moments this ecumenical tradition practiced and proclaimed a "Biblical faith" that affirmed "Evangelical distinctives" without denying essential "Catholic substance" (1979, 265-289; 1973, 41). It maintained the "sovereignty of God" without denying the significance of human decision. It proclaimed "justification by faith" as well as "scriptural holiness." It affirmed "the primacy of Scripture" while recognizing the relative authority of church traditions and the necessity of spiritual illumination. It pursued "the church's spiritual mission" and yet demonstrated concrete social concern (1978b, 24, 51, 227; 1979, 31, 167). In other words, it sought a genuinely catholic—comprehensive and historically continuous—Evangelicalism.

But Bloesch's articulation of this reformed and catholic Evangelicalism involves more than recovery. It is also an achievement. He does not seek a simple restoration of Reformed and Pietist teaching, or even an amalgamation of these and other Evangelical traditions (whatever that might be). Rather, Bloesch engages in a contemporary and creative restatement of Evangelical theology "that stands in continuity with the Protestant Reformation and the Evangelical Awakenings" but also moves beyond them in some important ways—or at least diverges from them (1978b, ix).

The direction of this divergence, quite significantly, is often influenced by Dr. Bloesch's interaction with the theology of Karl Barth.

Barth Reception

Although "not wishing to be known as Barthian or neo-Barthian," Donald Bloesch has repeatedly expressed admiration for and indebtedness to Barth's "monumental theological achievement" (1973, 80; 1986a, 8; 1986b, 128). As "the most profound and influential Christian theologian of our age" he "must be taken with the utmost seriousness" (1973, 80). But he should not be slavishly imitated, for many of his theological proposals are "problematic," reflecting interpretive "imbalances" and even "nonbiblical" and "philosophical" influences (1973, 84; 1986b, 130; 1992, chapter 9). The discerning Evangelical theologian, therefore, while having "much to learn" from Barth, "cannot simply remain with him but must strive to go through him and beyond him" (1971, 13; 1986b, 130). This is, after all, "what he would have wanted" (1986b, 130; 1986a, 8).

It is also an apt description of Donald Bloesch's own theological journey. As a graduate student at the University of Chicago he had turned to Barth in search of "solid answers" to the process thought of Wieman, Meland and Daniel Williams, and had assumed a "Barthian" approach to theology (1986b, 126; 1991, 56). But by the 1960s Bloesch had shed the Barthian label and moved in more traditionally Reformed and Evangelical directions. He had also published two books that articulated in preliminary fashion what would become his primary criticism of Barth—that Barth's "objectivist slant" undermined the significance of human decision in salvation (1976, 32; 1967, 60, 64, 130, 142; 1968b).

These developments, however, should not be misunderstood. Bloesch had not rejected Barth, but carefully criticized certain elements of his theology from what he considered a more biblical perspective. As a result, the "paradoxical" and "dialectical" understanding of *The Christian Life* Bloesch penned in 1967—and maintained throughout his career—reflects the continuing impact of Barth as much as the growing influence of Luther, Calvin or the Evangelical Pietists (1967, 19-32). Bloesch had moved "beyond" Barth under the influence of reformed and pietistic Evangelicalism, but he had also carried with him many of the insights he learned from the Neo-Orthodox theologian.

"While openly questioning much of what Barth says," Bloesch insists that Barth is a genuine "Evangelical theologian" whose "novel and daring formulations" sometimes provide uniquely clear insights into biblical truth. American Evangelicals, consequently, need to "reassess" their attitudes toward Barth and begin to recognize him as an important and powerful theological ally—a thesis Bloesch develops at length in his award-winning analysis of *The Evangelical Renaissance* (1973, 80-100).[22] Bloesch even expresses the hope, in this and other volumes, that the "convergence" between a chastened "Neo-Orthodoxy" and a resurgent "New Evangelicalism" may provide the cutting edge of theological and spiritual renewal in the latter half of the twentieth century, especially if a catholic concern for sanctification and the sacraments can be recovered as well (1973, 44-5; 1971, 18; 1968a, 19-20).

Bloesch himself has become an important model of a theologian who, in pursuit of this Evangelical ideal, has relied in significant measure upon the guidance of Barth. But he has also engaged in serious criticism of the Swiss theologian from his own "New Evangelical" perspective. While this critical appropriation pervades Bloesch's entire theological project, its essential features are displayed in his engagement with Barth's methodology and soteriology.

Methodology

In matters of method Bloesch's affirmation of Barth is fundamental and far-reaching. With some reservation—and several clarifications—he follows Barth in his understanding of the nature of theology, the role of philosophy, the doctrine of Scripture, and even his approach to hermeneutics. As Bloesch declares in the final pages of his most recent manuscript,

> I am not urging a repristination of Barthian theology...but I believe we need to take his way of doing theology over that of Tillich, Küng and Pannenberg (and I might add Carnell, Francis Schaeffer and Carl Henry) (1992, chapter 9).

In light of the central role issues of method have played in conservative Evangelical scholarship, this declaration is significant. By it Bloesch distinguishes himself from the "revisionist" theologies of the academic establishment, which he believes lead ineluctably to "modernist" reconstruction, and the "restorationist" strategies of Fundamentalist Evangelicalism (Ibid.; 1983, 84-110). But Bloesch also believes his "theological approach is strikingly similar to that of the magisterial Reformers, especially Luther and Calvin" (1992, forward). So in affirming Barth's method (with some qualifications) Bloesch believes he is reaffirming the essential insights of the Protestant Reformation and charting a course for contemporary Christianity that is biblical and Evangelical (1992, chapter 1).

"Where I have been helped most by Barth," Bloesch declares, "is in his fresh interpretation of biblical authority" (1986b, 127). By positing a "paradoxical" relation of "indirect identity" between the Word of God and its "threefold form"—achieved "by the action of the Spirit"—Barth has made it possible to acknowledge a distinction between revelation and Scriptural "witness" while still affirming "their indissoluble unity" (1978b, 52-3; 1986b, 127). In continuity with the fundamental insight of the Reformers he has designated "the voice of the living God" speaking through the Spirit-illumined Scripture the believer's ultimate authority (1978b, 60-5). But he has done so without falling prey to a Fundamentalist Evangelical "rationalism" that identifies the Word of God with biblical propositions "directly available to human reason" (Ibid., 75-6). The union of divine Word and human words, undeniably achieved in revelation, remains a divine event of self-revelation that can never be controlled from the human side.

The theological implications of this "dynamic" and "paradoxical" doctrine of revelation are manifold (1978b, 60). For example, it allows a redefinition—some would say denial—of biblical infallibility. The guarantee of truthfulness that attends God's self-revelation applies only to the Bible's "inspired meaning," and that meaning cannot be precisely identified with the expressed intentions of the biblical writers (Ibid., 68). Bloesch espouses the inerrancy of Scripture "in all that it *affirms*," following the Lausanne Covenant of the World Evangelical Fellowship. But he identifies what Scripture "affirms" with the salvific message intended by the *Spirit*, and distinguishes this from its culturally conditioned form and even the limited "theological and ethical ideas" of its human authors. (Ibid., 65, 68).

In order to determine this "inspired meaning" Bloesch engages in what he calls a "christological hermeneutic": He seeks the meaning of the words in the witness they bear to the one Word of God, Jesus Christ (1985, 81-83). Only when "related to and refined by" the personal "center and culmination of sacred history" does the biblical witness bear "infallible authority" (1978b, 68). But if so interpreted—a possibility only realized by the illumination of God's Spirit—the teaching thus discerned is infallibly true, regardless of the limited and imperfect form in which it is conveyed. While acknowledging his debt to Barth in this matter, Bloesch believes his view of Scripture and hermeneutics is "in accord with the deepest insights of both Luther and Calvin" (1985, 84).

Bloesch also believes that Barth's doctrine of revelation provides a paradigmatic statement of the Reformed and Evangelical view of the relation between faith and reason. Objecting to the "rationalism" of men like Clark, Montgomery, Schaeffer and Henry—which seeks a comprehensive synthesis between philosophy and theology—Bloesch opts for a "dialectical" approach.

While affirming the cognitivity of revelation, he insists upon an understanding of rationality that honors the unique and independent nature of theology. Theology is "the faithful explication of the Word of God," a "systematic reflection...on the self-revelation of God in Jesus Christ as attested in Holy Scripture" (1978b, 19; 1992, chapter 5). Its cognitive source and epistemological ground, therefore, is a divine act of personal communication, objectively present in sacred history and Scripture, and subjectively known through the internal testimony of the Spirit. It arises out of, and reflects upon, this "self-authenticating" event, and the words it uses and concepts it employs derive their meaning by reference to this event. There is, consequently, an inevitable "circularity" in theological reflection.

But not only that. Because the "object" of knowledge is God Himself—in the "secondary objectivity" of His revelation—there is an inescapably "mysterious" and "paradoxical" dimension to theology.

Human concepts, "pressed into the service" of divine revelation, convey "analogical" knowledge and manifest "paradoxical intelligibility." What we know of God, although true, cannot be finally systematized or fully comprehended (1971, 71-77; 1978b, 76-78; 1992, chapter 4). Dr. Bloesch describes this view of theological rationality in his first book on the subject as an "Evangelical" and "biblical...fideism" in the tradition of Luther, Anselm and Barth (1971, 178, 187), and throughout his writings he contrasts it with the apologetic rationalism of contemporary Evangelicalism.

As stated before, Bloesch's appropriation of Barth's theological method is fundamental and far-reaching. But it is not completely uncritical. "In contradistinction to Barth," for example, Bloesch thinks "the doctrine of inspiration is preeminently concerned with the written product" and that it guarantees theological infallibility (1978b, 56). Even more importantly, he argues that Barth has been "unable to maintain his understanding of the three-fold unity of the Word" because of an inordinate "stress on the transcendence of the Word over the words" (Ibid., 53). This tendency to separate divine revelation and historical medium, though always present, became more prevalent in Barth's later writings, according to Bloesch. In fact, he claims to discern a change in Barth's theology between the publication of *CD* I, which he designates Barth's "neo-Calvinist" phase, and subsequent works.

Bloesch's own position reflects an attempt to maintain more effectively Barth's original intention, and to demonstrate how a dialectical doctrine of indirect identity between the three forms of God's Word provides a genuinely Evangelical approach. Ironically—at least from the perspective of many conservative Evangelical interpreters—Bloesch's primary criticism of Barth on matters methodological seems to be that his doctrine of the Word becomes less paradoxical and dialectical over time.

Soteriology

While Dr. Bloesch's response to Barth's theological method involves fundamental affirmation, his reaction to Barth's views on salvation and the Christian life have been much more critical. In the tradition of men like G. C. Berkouwer and Colin Brown, Bloesch locates the primary tension between Reformation Evangelicalism and Karl Barth, not in doctrines of revelation or theories of rationality, but in their divergent interpretations of the biblical teaching on salvation. This indictment surfaced quite early in Bloesch's career, with the publication of *The Christian Life and Salvation* (1967), and it received focused treatment in his 1976 monograph, *Jesus is Victor! Karl Barth's Doctrine of Salvation*. Bloesch's "principle criticism" in both works is that Barth "fails to hold together the objective and subjective poles of salvation," introducing instead an "objectivist slant" that distorts biblical teaching

(1976, 10, 32).

But even here Bloesch's orientation is not completely negative. "On occasion" Barth "does succeed in maintaining" the "delicate balance" between objective accomplishment and subjective appropriation, between the divine and human dimensions of salvation, and sometimes Barth's views even represent an advance upon Reformation orthodoxy (Ibid., 10). So while assuming the posture of a serious Evangelical critic, Bloesch also sits as a "student" at the feet of "a theological master" with whom he shares "the same basic presuppositions of faith" (Ibid., 104).[23]

Barth's creative "synthesis" of the classic and Latin theories of the atonement, for example, constitutes "a rediscovery of patristic themes" and a "deepening" of traditional satisfaction motifs. Barth places the doctrine of penal redemption in the context of a cosmic "triumph of Christ" that radically transforms the human situation (Ibid., 43-48, 104). Furthermore, he construes this redemption, in some contrast to Anselm, as "a divine self-sacrifice" arising from God's eternal and gracious election (Ibid., 46). Satisfaction for sin is "rendered by God rather than [simply] to God," for on the cross "the holy God makes himself the object of his own wrath in the person of his Son" (1986a, 6; 1978b, 160). With this view Bloesch is in fundamental agreement, and he declares that "Thanks to Barth, the atonement has once again become a credible doctrine" (1986a, 6).

Bloesch also believes that "Barth has made it possible to speak again of hell...and predestination" (1986a, 6). While he objects to "one strand" in Barth's teaching that "virtually rules out the possibility" of eschatological judgment, implying a universal salvation, Bloesch claims to discern another strand in which the ideas of universal atonement and particular salvation are held in biblical balance (1978b, 168). In this second strand Barth rightly affirms a single covenant of elective grace that encompasses all men, a universal atonement, and even the *de jure* reconciliation of mankind in Christ. But Barth recognizes as well that some men refuse to acknowledge this election, and therefore exist, *de facto*, in a state of sinful unbelief and "under the dire threat of God's judgement" (1986a, 6-7; 1976, 60-66, 118).

Barth's refusal to posit universal salvation, furthermore, leaves open the possibility that some will continue in this state and experience the judgment of resurrected existence under the wrath of God. But Barth also leaves open the possibility of ultimate reconciliation—even after death—an attitude Bloesch labels his "universalism of hope," and which he himself affirms (1978b, 168). Thus Bloesch is "remarkably close to Karl Barth" in his doctrines of election and judgment—with the qualification that the comments in Barth which undermine the decisiveness of personal faith must be rejected (Ibid.).

This is an important qualification, however, for in the final analysis Bloesch "agrees with Emil Brunner...that Barth does not succeed in doing justice to the subjective dimension of salvation" (1976, 110). He tends toward a "pronounced objectivism" that breaks the paradoxical "correlation" between divine action and human response by regarding every dimension of reconciliation completely accomplished in Christ (1986a, 8). Not only does this undermine the delicate biblical balance between universal atonement and particular salvation, but it blurs the distinction between the saved and the lost and leads Barth to underestimate the seriousness of the battle between the kingdom of God and the kingdom of Evil (1976, 110, 123-126). Sometimes Barth even denies the dramatic and eternal significance of gospel proclamation and personal conversion, and tends, in his devaluation of the subjective side of salvation, to "downplay personal sanctification" (1986a, 8-9). All of these imbalances are of particular concern for Evangelicals like Bloesch who desire to maintain the distinctives of the post-Reformation movements of Pietism, Puritanism and the Evangelical Awakenings.

Bloesch's critical appropriation of Barth extends well beyond the issues of theological method and soteriology, into theology proper (1978b, 24-50), ethics (1987), preaching (1978b, 71-103), the sacraments and more. But what has been written is sufficient to indicate the decisive impact Barth's theology has had upon Bloesch's work. Without a doubt, Barth has been one of Bloesch's "principle mentors," and along with Luther and Calvin, the most influential (1986b, 126; 1978b, 4). As the author of a widely read statement on the *Essentials of Evangelical Theology*, and an influential interpreter of Evangelical renewal, Donald Bloesch has himself exerted an important influence upon the reception of Barth among American Evangelicals.

Concluding Comment

Bromiley, Berkouwer, Ramm and Bloesch have been the four most visible and influential interpreters of Barth among postwar New Evangelicals in America, and Fuller Seminary has provided a unique institutional focus for changes in both the reception of Barth and the interpretation of American Evangelical theology. By means of these men and this school, therefore, we have been able to discern in this chapter basic contours and essential features of Barth reception within the American Evangelical mosaic.

We have seen, for example, a correlation between theological paradigm and response to Barth. Every theologian discussed in this chapter has been distinguished from the Evangelicals in chapter two by a more progressive theology and a more open attitude toward Barth. The doctrine of inerrancy, which has played such an important role in Fundamentalist Evangelical theology, simply is not a defining characteristic among New Evangelicals. Nor do traditional interpretations of theology exert the same kind of control. More room is left for a positive appropriation of Barth's arguments and emphases.

We have also discerned a correlation between theological position and social setting. Just as the apologetic reaction to Barth arose within traditions decisively shaped by Reformed Fundamentalism—namely, Northern Fundamentalist Evangelicalism and the Orthodox Reformed—so the more positive reception of the Swiss theologian has originated outside these contexts. It was brought into American Evangelical discussion from the outside, by an influential Dutch theologian and an Anglican historian—G. C. Berkouwer and Geoffrey Bromiley—both of whom were world-class Barth scholars. This positive reception was then fostered at institutions and among theologians who pioneered in the development of New Evangelical paradigms, most notably, Fuller Seminary and the members of its theological faculty. But it was Bernard Ramm whose forty year career provided the most notable model of transition beyond a Fundamentalist Evangelical paradigm under the influence of Karl Barth.

Donald Bloesch has provided a valuable window into the reception of Barth within the Evangelical mosaic, too. Not only has he become an influential interpreter of theology and history for the American movement; he is also the most obvious spokesman for mainline renewal under the Evangelical banner, and a notable example of the convergence of conservative renewal movements and the expanding Evangelical frontiers of contemporary Evangelicalism. Bringing to this leadership role a perspective deeply influenced by Karl Barth, he has served as a model for the convergence of Neo-Orthodox and Evangelical themes that both he and Bernard Ramm hope will provide the cutting edge for theological renewal in years ahead.

Through the consideration of Bromiley, Berkouwer, Ramm and Bloesch, along with the men at Fuller Seminary, a coherent story about the changing reception of Barth among American New Evangelicals has emerged. But it is a story about theological reception within predominantly reformed traditions—Northern Fundamentalist Evangelical and Orthodox Reformed—and those movements of renewal which have been shaped by reformed influences. Certainly it is the case that American Evangelical Barth reception—both Fundamentalist Evangelical and New Evangelical—has had a reformed center, as one would expect in light of Barth's own Reformed orientation and the pervasive influence of reformed scholarship upon American Evangelicalism. But there are other dimensions to the story, some of which were discussed at the end of chapter two, and the rest of which will be addressed in the chapter that follows.

NOTES

1. When Bromiley attended as a student, Tyndale Hall (now Trinity College) was the Bible Churchman's Missionary and Theological College (B.C.M.S.). This theological school has been the workplace of many conservative Evangelical Anglicans, e.g., Philip Hughes, J. I. Packer, Colin Brown, and Alec Motyer.

2. It is difficult to overestimate the importance of translation in the reception of Barth among English-speaking Evangelicals. The translation and publication of important secondary studies, many by Eerdmans, should also be recognized.

3. In contrast to most other New Evangelical theologians discussed in this chapter, Bromiley (along with Carnell) defended the inerrancy clause in the 1950 Fuller Seminary doctrinal statement (Marsden, 1987, 214-5). He did so, however, on a basis different from Evangelicals like Carl Henry. He also authored the revised articles on Scripture in the 1972 Fuller Statement of Faith.

4. In 1952 Berkouwer was invited by the Christian Reformed Church to teach theology at Calvin Seminary. In that year he also delivered the Calvin Foundation Lectures, published as *Modern Uncertainty and the Christian Faith* (1953). Ironically, Van Til was a guest professor at Calvin during the second semester of the 1951-1952 school year, and had himself been invited to assume a lifetime post at Calvin. Apparently, the divergent streams of Reformed Evangelicalism represented by these men had not become manifest by 1952.

5. Bromiley's contributions during the fifties and early sixties were limited to translation, brief articles and popular advocacy.

6. These include James Daane, Lewis Smedes, Jack Rogers, Robert Knudsen, R. C. Sproul and Klaas Runia. Although not an American Evangelical, Runia's study, *Karl Barth's Doctrine of Holy Scripture* (1962), published by Eerdmans, has exerted an influence within the English-speaking Evangelical world. For an exposition of his argument, see Mohler, 1989, 142-9. Runia, a Dutch Reformed churchman who spent much of his teaching career at Reformed Theological College in Geelong, Victoria, Australia, has also written appreciative though critical articles on Barth for Australian (1958, 1959), British (1965, 1967, 1982) and American (1969) Evangelical publications.

7. Of all his works, *Half Century* contains the most positive affirmation of Barth's theological contribution. Quite probably it indicates a degree of appreciation exceeding that found in *Triumph* and the earlier *Studies in Dogmatics*.

8. Although this affirmation of Barth's hermeneutic did not receive comment in *The Triumph of Grace*, both *Holy Scripture* and *Half Century* focus on it.

9. Berkouwer's own development of the noetic incomprehensibility of sin, which follows Bavinck and Calvin, converges with some aspects of Barth's analysis (Berkouwer, 1971a, 11-148).

10. For a more sympathetic interpretation of Barth's supposed universalism, see Bettis, 1967.

11. According to Van Til, Dutch Reformed criticism of Barth points consistently in two directions: he is accused of an extreme "nominalism" that denies direct revelation and renders God's relation to the world problematic, or he is indicted for an overreaching "realism" in which the identification between God and man in salvation is universal and triumphalist. Van Til uses Berkouw-

er's earlier work to illustrate the nominalist criticism and his later work to exemplify the realist, and then argues that both the sweeping negations of Barth's nominalism and the extreme affirmations of his realism are predictable consequences of his more basic dialecticism. In defending this thesis, one wishes Dr. Van Til would have engaged more directly Barth's own discussion of the relation of idealist, realist and dialectical philosophy to the theological task (Barth, 1929; 1968; Sykes, 1986).

12. He even suggested that Machen's criticisms of Modernism in *Christianity and Liberalism* "apply, *mutatis mutandis*, to neo-orthodoxy" (1948, 22).

13. For an earlier Fundamentalist criticism of Carnell's *Case for Orthodox Theology*, see Rice, 1959.

14. George Eldon Ladd, another Fuller Professor during the postwar years (1950-1982), wrote a brief article in 1962 defending Barth's distinction between *Historie* and *Geschichte* as the most viable "method" for interpreting the "supra-historical events" of biblical history (1962, 56), a distinction he used later in his own study of the resurrection (1975). Because of Ladd's stature within the world of Evangelical scholarship—second only to Calvin in a survey of most influential scholars among the Evangelical Theological Society (Noll, 1986, 209-14)—this article, and the attitude toward Barth it suggested, elicited heated critical response (Montgomery, 1963; Harris, 1963a,b). It also revealed that important theological changes were taking place at Fuller and within the wider Evangelical community, changes in which Barth was playing a visible role.

15. Brown considered Berkouwer's *Triumph* one of "the two best general introductions to Barth," containing "a full and fair critique written from a conservative evangelical perspective" (1967, 154, 155). In an early book review, when the ideas for his own study were still developing, Brown argued that Klooster's criticism of Barth's covenant idea correctly identified the central Barthian weakness (1962b). While he maintained a critical distance from Van Til's work, Brown affirmed elements of its "sometimes penetrating" critique, as well (1967, 155).

16. In some ways Brown lives on the border between the two types, along with men like Klaas Runia (1958; 1959; 1962; 1969; 1982) and J. I. Packer (1988; 1986), both non-American Evangelicals. Packer, however, would best be described as a Fundamentalist Evangelical after the pattern of Kenneth Kantzer (Packer, 1957; 1958; 1961; Manwaring, 1985).

17. Dale Moody of The Southern Baptist Theological Seminary demonstrated a comparable grasp of Brunner's writing (1947a,b; 1962).

18. For a defense of this Reformed consensus under pressure from the Pentecostal "third wave," see Smedes, 1987.

19. The fundamental difference between Daane and Barth on the doctrine of election would seem to lie here. Barth correlates the being of God *ad extra* with His Being *ad intra* in such a way that election to save mankind in Jesus Christ and election to be the Son of the Father become the same divine action (or at least become united in such a way that salvation history becomes necessary). Daane, on the other hand, and Berkouwer before him, resist such an identification of God's being and election on the ground that it undermines the genuine significance of history and leads, ineluctably, to universalism (Berkouwer, 1956).

20. including the distinction between *Historie* and *Geschichte* (1983,

75-87), the doctrine of the Word's three-fold form (1983, 50-56), and the interpretation of revelation as trinitarian in structure and christological in substance (1983, 127-134; 1973, 118).

21. Jack Rogers and Clark Pinnock have been equally visible models of transition (Rogers, 1974; Price, 1988), but interaction with Barth has not played an important role in their development. Instead, they have been American Evangelicalism's two most influential advocates for new views of Scriptural authority (Rogers, 1967, 1977, 1979; Pinnock, 1976, 1984). Both men have however, come to a more positive appreciation of Barth as a genuinely Evangelical theologian (Rogers, 1979; Pinnock, 1978), and Pinnock has clearly modified his earlier interpretation of the Swiss Doctor as an irrational fideist (Pinnock, 1986a).

22. *The Evangelical Renaissance* was named Book of the Year by the Evangelical Book Club.

23. As a result of continuing research between his first studies of Barth's soteriology (1967, 1973) and his later ones (1975, 1978b; 1979), Bloesch "became more positively disposed" to "Barth's doctrine of salvation," and even manifested significant appropriation (1976, 12).

4

NEW EVANGELICAL RECEPTION

IN THE PIETISTIC TRADITIONS

Distinguishing between traditions within the Evangelical mosaic by means of the labels "reformed" and "pietist" is, to say the least, a hazardous venture. Not only are the labels themselves rather broad, especially when used to cover a diverse range of Evangelical traditions; but even more importantly, the labels are not mutually exclusive. A distinguishing feature of the American Evangelical movement as it developed in the nineteenth century has been the influence, and even predominance, of pietistic revivalism. Separating the so-called Pietist traditions out of the Evangelical mosaic, therefore, is like dividing the currents and cross-currents of a moving river. Pietism is present in every Evangelical tradition, and Donald Bloesch's vision of an Evangelicalism that integrates the pietistic movements of renewal with the theology of the Reformers has grown quite naturally from the soil of American religious history.

Nevertheless, the basic distinction between "reformed" and "pietistic" does communicate something, both about Evangelicalism and the reception of Barth within Evangelical traditions. Put as simply as possible, the Evangelicals of chapter three (and the largest part of chapter two) have been decisively and self-consciously influenced by classic Reformed theology. They are located in traditions where Calvinist Orthodoxy, mediated by Hodge, Bavinck, Edwards, or Strong, has provided the basic theological framework, reinforced by a fundamentalist experience. Of course, many within these traditions have moved beyond and modified their inherited frameworks; hence the New Evangelical designation. But their categories and conversation partners have still been predominantly Reformed and Calvinist.

The same is not true within the traditions being labeled pietistic. Southern Baptists, Wesleyans and Pentecostals—even Anabaptists—have been influenced by Protestant Orthodoxy and the Fundamentalist movement. But their most decisive theological voices have been more Arminian than Calvinist, and their distinctive emphases have been more "pietistic" than "reformed." Through the course of historical development these traditions have manifested, for example, a more definite concern for vital, personal experience and the ministry of the Holy Spirit, placed a higher priority on the ethical over the intellectual dimensions of faith, expressed suspicion of advanced scholarship in the name of a simpler and more accessible Christianity, and have often been quite critical of established hierarchies, orthodox creeds, or other forms of institutional power.

As a result of these distinctive emphases, or what one historian has described as "a different axis of thought" (Dayton, 1985, 132), the reception of Barth within the more pietistic traditions has taken a somewhat different course. The issues with which Wesleyan, Pentecostal and Anabaptist theologians are concerned, for example, have provided a different focus to their study of Barth. His ethics, his pneumatology and his teaching on sanctification have become more central to the discussion than questions of epistemology and election. In fact, one of the signal contributions which the Wesleyan, Donald Dayton, and the Anabaptist, John Yoder, have made to American Evangelicalism is to introduce Barth as a model for "radical" social ethics—in the face of a visible absence of Reformed Evangelical discussion of Barth's ethic.[1] One will also find the more pietistic interpreters of Barth concerned about his "objectivism" (which does not allow human experience a decisive role in salvation), and his epistemological exclusivity (which denies the apologetic value of general human experience). Of course these complaints are not unique to Evangelicals within the pietistic traditions; but they are characteristic.

Another general characteristic of the reception of Barth within the non-Reformed traditions is the more peripheral nature of the interaction. The interpretation of Barth does not play a central role in theological discussion within these traditions, and the number of scholars who interact with him in a serious manner remains quite small. Among Pentecostals, for example, dialogue with Barth is almost non-existent; among Wesleyans, only two theologians of note engage in serious interpretation; and even among Southern Baptists, where examples of interaction are more common, Barth's thought has not decisively influenced many. This may be due, in part, to the relative absence of well-established scholarly institutions within these traditions (The Southern Baptist Theological Seminary being an exception). But it also results from the vast differences in culture and theology separating them from Barth.

There have been, however, important interpreters of Barth within these traditions. And like their counterparts in chapter three, the theologians analyzed in this chapter are proponents of a more positive, New Evangelical attitude toward the Swiss theologian. In contrast to the orthodox apologetic of Fundamentalist Evangelicals—also found within these traditions—Barth is regarded as an Evangelical theologian whose commitment to the authority of the Word is more decisive than any supposed philosophical captivity. He is a genuine partner in dialogue, a source for theological innovation, and in some cases, a dominant theological model. Positive interaction with Karl Barth has also been a bridge for some of these Evangelical theologians in their own journey beyond a Fundamentalist Evangelical heritage.

Southern Baptist Evangelicalism

Chapter one of this study identified southern Evangelicalism as one of the four dominant traditions within the twentieth century Evangelical mosaic. Included within this cultural and geographical designation are not only the fourteen million members of the Southern Baptist Convention, but also, at least, a plethora of independent Baptist and Bible Churches that espouse the Dispensationalism of Dallas Theological Seminary and Bob Jones University, many Holiness and Pentecostal groups spread throughout the southern United States, and even the Presbyterian and Methodist Evangelicals who have maintained conservative commitments in the context of a more supportive southern culture. The Holiness, Pentecostal, and conservative Methodists, however, comprise a distinctive tradition, while the conservative Presbyterians are Reformed Evangelicals with strong intellectual ties to Old School Princeton (Wells, 1985). Most of the independent Baptist and Bible Church Dispensationalist, furthermore, have been decisively shaped by the Fundamentalist Evangelical paradigm analyzed in chapter one. This leaves the Southern Baptist Convention, which by virtue of number and influence is the dominant Evangelical presence in the South.

But Southern Baptists, while certainly a cohesive religious group, are by no means a monolithic movement (Rosenberg, 1989; Hill, 1981). Cultural homogeneity and social dominance enabled southern Evangelicals to withstand many of the liberal influences that divided the northern religious culture during the first half of the twentieth century. But it did not protect Southern Baptists from the social and theological stresses that attended the Evangelical movement during the postwar period. They, too, have experienced battles over biblical inerrancy as traumatic as anything known within other Evangelical traditions (Bush, 1980; Lindsell, 1976, 1979; Proceedings, 1987).

In fact, some of the most influential leaders within Northern Fundamentalist Evangelicalism (on both sides of the battle for the Bible) hold membership in the Southern Baptist Convention and have taught at Southern Baptist institutions. The most well-known of these men who dwell in the crosscurrents of Northern and Southern Evangelicalism is, of course, Billy Graham. But Harold Lindsell and Carl Henry are Southern Baptists by church affiliation (though not by upbringing or education), and Clark Pinnock and Bernard Ramm taught at Southern Baptist schools during the early years of their careers.

So when northern and southern Evangelicals are singled out for separate analysis, the extent of interaction, influence, and convergence (especially among Baptists) must also be acknowledged. The kind of Fundamentalist Evangelicalism represented by Carl Henry and the early Pinnock, Ramm, Carnell and Jewett (all Baptists) is certainly an influential paradigm among Southern Baptists (Patterson, 1983). The Dispensationalism of Charles Ryrie and Lewis Sperry Chafer has exerted a pervasive influence, too. And one might well claim that the positions being espoused by progressive Southern Baptists like Moody, Rust, and Mueller differ little from the theological opinions expressed by New Evangelicals Pinnock, Jewett and Ramm.

The Southern Baptist Theological Seminary

Parallels between Northern Fundamentalist and Southern Baptist traditions also extend to the decisive influence of progressive institutions of theological instruction. Premier among these are Fuller Theological Seminary in Pasadena, California and The Southern Baptist Theological Seminary of Louisville, Kentucky. As the only Southern Baptist seminary in existence since the nineteenth century, and the alma mater of almost every influential Southern Baptist theologian since that time, its significance as an intellectual center is unparalleled. It has also become, since the second World War, the largest Protestant seminary in the world.

Nineteenth century home of James P. Boyce, a leader of southern theology during its most calvinistic period (Dever, 1987), Southern Seminary was also the place where E. Y. Mullins, the most influential of all twentieth century Southern Baptist churchmen, taught theology and served as President (Ellis, 1985; Humphreys, 1990). Through his own leadership and the influence of his students, especially H. W. Tribble and W. T. Connor, Dr. Mullins' theological perspective dominated Baptist thought and life for the first half of the twentieth century. Not until 1947, when Dale Moody replaced Tribble as Professor of Systematic Theology at Southern, did Mullins' 1917 work, *The Christian Religion in its Doctrinal Expression*, cease to serve as the standard textbook at that institution; and not until Moody's own *Summary of Christian Doctrine Based on Biblical Revelation* (1981) did Southern Baptists have an alternative text produced from within their own tradition.[2]

As Timothy George has recently suggested, the history of theology at Southern Baptist "divides into three distinct periods of roughly forty years each," corresponding to the "three major theologians" who occupied "the Joseph Emerson Brown chair" and wrote "an influential textbook on systematic theology" (George, 1985, 31-32). Under Boyce, the regnant theology was a Baptist variation of the orthodox Calvinism he had learned as a student of Hodge at Princeton. But when Mullins replaced Boyce's *Abstract of Theology* with his own systematic text, he gave Southern Baptists a different paradigm—one that assigned a determinative role to Christian experience, construed revelation in more personal terms, and sought a positive, though cautious, openness to modern science and biblical criticism (see chapter two).

Mullins' critically conservative "theology of experience," as Timothy George labeled it, was then followed in the postwar period by a theological orientation—under the leadership of Dale Moody—that reflected the growing impact of contemporary biblical theology and its Neo-Orthodox background (George, 1985).

If this historical analysis is correct, then in its evolution under the leadership of Boyce, Mullins and Moody, Southern Seminary has served as an influential flagship sailing the frontiers of Southern Baptist Evangelical identity, somewhat like Fuller has done within the Northern Fundamentalist Evangelical tradition. And like Fuller it has become embroiled in sometimes heated theological controversy along the way (Hinson, 1971; Honeycutt, 1986). It has also been the place within Southern Baptist Evangelicalism where the most interaction with Karl Barth has occurred.

Eric Rust

When asked in 1981 to identify the significant trends and distinctive theological emphases at Southern Baptist during the three postwar decades, Eric Rust, who had been a Professor there since 1953, focused upon the changing views of Scripture, tradition and hermeneutics. He discerned a greater willingness, and ability, to become involved in ecumenical dialogue. He also perceived a concern for critical hermeneutics. But most significant of all was the "creative" and "liberating" view of revelation that had come to the fore during these years (Rust, 1981).

In marked contrast to the scholastic doctrine of inspired propositions, professors of theology at Southern Seminary understood revelation in personal and historical terms: as "divine self-disclosure" in the form of "salvation history" and "revelatory events" interpreted in the "inspired testimony" of Holy Scripture. They construed Scripture, after the model of Forsyth, Brunner and Barth, as a theological "witness." It is the Word of God because it witnesses to the Living Word, and infallibility is a quality which pertains to that salvific witness, not to its every statement (Ibid.).

These were certainly the theological convictions Rust expressed in his own writings, beginning with his first two books, *The Christian Understanding of History* (1947) and *Nature and Man in Biblical Thought* (1953). But since both books were written before Rust assumed a teaching post at Southern, it was a point of view he developed as a student, minister and teacher among Baptists in England, his homeland, and one he brought to the Southern Baptist world from the outside. It was also a perspective that had been forged, in part, through critical interaction with the Neo-orthodoxy of Barth and Brunner (Rust, 1946, preface). At least, these first two works show the fruit of such interaction.

In particular, Rust employs the concept of *Geschichte* to explain the unique nature of salvation history (1946, 48, 65-83), utilizes the category of "inspired witness" to define how the Bible functions as the Word of God (1953, 1-7), insists upon the "veiled" and "paradoxical" form of revelation and religious language (1946, 52, 258), asserts the "mythical" nature of the Biblical Fall (1946, 209-14), and appeals to Brunner's "law of closeness of relation" to Christ in an effort to distinguish between biblical ideas which carry binding force and those that merely reflect the historically conditioned thinking of its authors (1953, 19). Rust also follows Barth and Brunner in rejecting natural theology and insisting upon the priority of revelation and faith in religious knowledge, although distancing himself from Barth's more radical denial of any point of contact in general revelation (1946, 47; 1953, 245-249). In Rust's discussion of God at the conclusion of *Nature and Man in Biblical Thought,* the language of the two Swiss theologians echoes through the text, providing the basic insights by which he explains the nature and activity of "the triune God of creation"—the "wholly Other" who reveals Himself as a trinity of "holy love" (1953, 245-303).

By 1953, therefore, when Eric Rust began his teaching career at The Southern Baptist Theological Seminary, positive appropriation of Karl Barth had already played a visible role in his theological development. But upon closer examination, the extent of influence must be questioned. As Glenn Hinson has observed, Rust "is interpreted most accurately as a representative of the 'salvation history' school who has spiraled out from this traditional base" in directions determined by his fundamental interest in the dialogue between contemporary science and Christian faith (Hinson, 1979, 19). During Rust's career at Southern, he has labored energetically to develop a "theological understanding" of nature and history that would integrate the teaching of biblical revelation with the valid insights of modern science and historical-critical scholarship (Patterson, 1979).

In pursuit of this basic task, however, the theology of Barth has played a peripheral role. More important by far have been the writings of H. Wheeler Robinson, his revered Professor at Regents' Park College, Oxford (Polley, 1979), and the training he received at the Royal College of Science where he served as instructor of mathematics before deciding to pursue a career in theology. As Rust indicated in the 1981 essay cited above, it was the views of Barth as "modified" by Brunner, Baillie, Tillich and Temple that shaped his idea of revelation (1981, 260). Along with the positive citations of Barth in his first two books, therefore, one finds qualifications and criticisms that indicate serious reserve (1946, 47, 49; 1953, 291, 295, 299). So when Rust came to express his mature understanding of nature and history during the decade of the sixties, it is not surprising to find little interaction with the writings of Barth (Rust, 1962; 1963; 1967).

While appropriating Barthian insights in his pioneering efforts to reconcile theology and science, and modeling a positive reception of both Barth and Brunner as Evangelical theologians, Eric Rust did not engage in serious and sustained dialogue with the Swiss theologian over the course of his career. His primary concerns and influences lay elsewhere, and his basic orientation was much too inclusive to find significant help in Barth.[3]

Dale Moody

Eric Rust, for nearly thirty years Professor of Christian Philosophy at Southern Seminary, did much to shape the distinctive emphases of theological instruction at Southern. But pride of place in the competition over influence must be given to Dale Moody, a 1941 graduate of the institution and for thirty-eight years a teacher of theology in its faculty (1945-1983).

Unlike Rust, Moody is a native son. Deeply impacted by an uneducated but powerful preacher in a small Baptist church in Texas, Moody was called by God to the gospel ministry during his teens, and served as the pastor of his family's church while a senior in high school. After three years at Baylor in the mid-thirties, he attended, for one year, Dallas Theological Seminary, before finding his way to Southern in 1937 (Hinson, 1979, 5-7). Southern Evangelical revivalism and Dallas Seminary dispensationalism were both, therefore, a part of Moody's early years, and continued to be conversation partners throughout his career.

But Dale Moody is no parochial American Fundamentalist (although his systematic theology is filled with local color). More than any twentieth century Southern Baptist, he has been a model for the kind of positive ecumenicity that Rust described as a distinctive emphasis of postwar Southern Seminary. In 1944-45, just before assuming a post at Southern, he served as a teaching fellow for Paul Tillich at Union Seminary. Then in the summer of 1948, after completing his Th.D. dissertation on Emil Brunner's doctrine of revelation, Moody studied with Brunner in Zürich (and met Barth as well). In 1961-63 he was a Fellow of Regents' Park College, Oxford, and in 1966 he completed a treatise on baptism that earned him an invitation to lecture at The Gregorian University in Rome—only the second Protestant and the first Baptist ever to receive such an invitation. Moody also served as a member of the Faith and Order Commission of the World Council of Churches, and in numerous other ways sought to foster ecumenical dialogue between Baptists and the wider church (Hinson, 1979).

In a way unique among American Evangelicals, Moody considered the luminaries of twentieth century Neo-orthodoxy—Barth,

Brunner and Tillich—his "friends" (Moody, 1988, 13-14). As Glenn Hinson once proclaimed, "If Southern Baptists have had a world-class Bible teacher and preacher, it [is] Moody" (Hinson, 1979, 17).

As a "world-class" teacher Dale Moody has interacted significantly with the writings of both Brunner and Barth, and he began to do so at a period in American Evangelical history when this kind of sophisticated interpretation was relatively unknown. For example, his dissertation on Brunner was completed in 1947, seven years before the Evangelical Theological Society published Paul Jewett's study on the subject (Moody, 1947a,b; Jewett, 1954). And concerning Moody, Brunner himself claimed, "I think I would not be in error if I call him the theologian best informed on my theological works" (Brunner, 1962, 346).

While Moody's familiarity with Barth probably never equaled his knowledge of Brunner, he did manifest an early and appreciative reading of the Basel theologian. In a 1950 article in the Southern Baptist journal, *Review and Expositor*, for example, Moody confidently claimed that "Barth's *The Doctrine of the Word of God* is no doubt the greatest treatise on the doctrine of the Trinity that has ever been written," and added that his discussion of "The Reality of God" in volume II of *Kirchliche Dogmatik* "is no less powerful" (Moody, 1950, 17). Though Moody found it "impossible to agree with" some of Barth's "extreme views" on revelation, predestination and the image of God in man, just as Brunner had, he still suggested that Barth "is perhaps the most important Protestant theologian since Calvin" (Ibid., 19).

"A generation ago," Moody contended, theology found itself languishing between "a petrified forest" of scholastic Fundamentalism and "the scorching winds of a limitless criticism." But with the emergence of the movement known as "biblical realism," "the serious study of systematic theology" under the authority of the Word had been revived (Ibid., 3, 9-10). Though the people and positions contained within this label were quite broad—from Niebuhr and Aulen to Brunner and Baillie—"it must ever be said," Moody insisted, "that Barth was the peak of the range" in the mountain of protest that went up against nineteenth century liberalism and forever altered the modern theological landscape.

This last comment is contained not in Moody's 1950 article on "Present Theological Trends" but in the introductory section of his 1981 magnum opus, *The Word of Truth*. It suggests, therefore, an important continuity in Dale Moody's view of Karl Barth and Evangelical theology. From the beginning of his career Moody had placed himself on a path that passed between Modernism and Fundamentalism, and though his journey as a conservative Southern Baptist had not taken him from Liberalism to Neo-Orthodoxy, as it had Barth or Brunner, he did find himself in basic sympathy and creative dialogue with the "biblical realism" that marked their work.

Thirty years later, in his concluding contribution to theological discussion, he would describe his method as a "critical conservatism" that maintained both the radical authority of Scripture and a serious openness to modern science, historical criticism and doctrinal reformulation. Of course, many postwar Evangelicals would claim a similar openness; but as Moody expounds it, his "critical conservatism" converges more with the school of thought he labels "Neo-Orthodoxy" than it does with "the pre-critical and pre-scientific" opinions of "Protestant Fundamentalism"—a "current of modern theology" that includes not only the "old conservatism" of Hodge and Warfield but also the "conservative Evangelicalism" of Carl Henry (Moody, 1981, 21-30).

This basic sympathy with Barthian Neo-orthodoxy, however, should not be misunderstood, either in the early or the later Moody. As he himself said, "It is true that my earliest days in theology took Karl Barth and Emil Brunner seriously," but "my former colleague David Mueller and my friend Bernard Ramm revel more in Barth than I do" (Moody, 1988, 13, 11). For Moody, Barth was a theologian of great historical significance, the "highest peak" and therefore, "the great watershed" that separated nineteenth from twentieth century theology. "But Brunner was the theologian who helped a generation to get over the mountain through the Brunner pass," and Moody himself was always closer to the critically conservative formulations of Brunner, Aulen, or the Baillie brothers than he was to the more radical doctrinal reformulations of Karl Barth (Ibid., 28, 179; 1967, 341-2).

But even this observation may leave the wrong impression, for the most obvious distinguishing characteristic of Moody's theological writing is not its similarity to Brunner, Baillie, or any other systematic theologian. It is, rather, his extensive engagement in historical exegesis. As he claimed in the very first sentence of the preface to his systematic theology, "The publication of *The Word of Truth* is meant to issue a clarion call to the reformation and revival of theology on the basis of the historical exegesis which is so prominent a feature of recent biblical scholarship" (Ibid., xi).

The form of writing that results from this intention is what one student has described as "a biblical theology on the way to a systematic theology" (Stiver, 546-7). In the context of a simple outline of nine theological loci, Moody's 1981 systematic theology discusses the doctrines of God, creation, man, sin, salvation, Christ, the church and consummation, providing innovative and alliterative outlines to order his conceptual re-description of the biblical teaching. In the process, he manifests great confidence in the ability of biblical doctrine to order contemporary theological discussion and considerable freedom to both affirm and criticize a wide range of contemporary theologians, including Karl Barth (see Moody, 1964; 1968). He also reflects, I would suggest, the biblicist and revivalist tradition from which he comes.

The Word of Truth

The most positive and extensive appropriation of Barth in Moody's mature theology occurs in the doctrine of God, although even here there is freedom to criticize and go his own way. Following Barth he divides the discussion of God's attributes into those that pertain to the "perfection" and "properties" of His holiness and those that depict His love (Moody, 1981, 94f., 104f.). Throughout the biblically controlled description of the "Mystery" and "Majesty" of God's nature as "the Eternal Being who acts in freedom" Moody cites Barth's discussions in CD II/1 with approval (Ibid., 95-115).

He also credits Barth with placing the doctrine of the Trinity at the center of theological discussion after years of "eclipse" (Ibid., 124). But in his exposition of "the modes of God's Being" Moody suggests that Barth's distinction between Father, Son and Spirit as Creator, Reconciler and Redeemer, or as Revealer, Revelation and Revealedness tends toward modalism (Ibid., 121-128; 1967, 351-2).

Moody also ventures a "reconsideration of the classical arguments for belief in God," a theological project for which Barth would have no patience (Ibid., 78f.). But Moody is of the opinion that Barth's whole approach to the relationship between revelation and philosophy suffers from a tragic exclusivity. By constricting revelation to the covenant relation in Christ, Barth collapses the two biblical covenants, denies the reality of general revelation and places Christian theology in a "strait-jacket" that "is too narrow for biblical support and the missionary task of the church" (Ibid., 41, 65-66, 57-61).

Moody, in contrast, argues for the salvific significance of "a general revelation. . . outside the covenant and prior to Christ," a position that moves well beyond the objections of Brunner in its opposition to Barth. Dale Moody desires to right the "pyramid" of religious epistemology Barth has turned "topside down," and thus to provide a "broader base" for Christian theology (1967, 341; 1981, 80, 179). In light of this, his claim to be "nearer to Pannenberg and Moltmann than any other German [speaking] theologian" can be more easily understood (Moody, 1988, 14).

Not only does Moody object to Barth's "christomonism" in the name of a more inclusive and biblical theology, but he also takes serious exception to Barth's "neo-Calvinism" (Moody, 1981, 107). While praising *CD II/2* as "he most Christ-centered view of election yet formulated," Moody complains that Barth "ruins a good idea...by coming to the very brink of universalism" (Ibid., 25). He does so, however, because he remains bound to the Augustinian tradition that construes original sin and divine election "in such a way that the real freedom of man to reject or receive the grace of God is removed." "As long as this Calvinist-Barthian theology is followed," Moody insists, "there is no way to do justice to all the New Testament teachings and to human responsibility" (Ibid., 337).

In stark contrast, but in partial dependence upon Barth's work, Moody combines a strictly christological doctrine of election (Ibid., 337-48) with an account of salvation that, in his own words, places "human experience at the center" (Ibid., 367). He also disputes every one of the "five points" of Calvinist doctrine affirmed at the Synod of Dort, including the eternal security of the believer (Ibid., 348-365). Moody elevates the significance of human experience in keeping with his Southern Evangelical heritage, and he defends it by an appeal to the authority of Scripture over all ecclesiastical tradition, even the revered tradition of Augustine and Calvin.

Needless to say, such a stance places him at a distance from Barth. But he does find in Barth an ally in the debate over infant baptism, claiming, with obvious approval, that "here, more than any other place, Barth sounds like a Baptist" (Ibid., 26; Moody, 1967, 57f.). Therefore Moody has engaged in careful exposition of Barth's teaching on the subject, as well as the responses of Cullman, Jeremias and Aland, and as a result has made a widely recognized contribution to ecumenical dialogue on this sensitive issue (Moody, 1967).

There are other dimensions to Moody's interaction with the theology of Karl Barth—the most important of which may be his qualified appropriation of Barth's typological interpretation of Adam and Christ (1981, 198, 291), or his affirmation of similar views of atonement and divine suffering (although objecting to what he calls Barth's "Hegelian" doctrine of divine *kenosis*) (Ibid.,104-14, 371, 423; 1949). But enough has been written to indicate the contours of this important Southern Baptist response to the Swiss Reformed theologian.

Dale Moody engaged in an early and appreciative reading of Barth's work, praised his salutary influence upon the renewal of biblical theology in the twentieth century, and even affirmed many of the basic insights of this "great watershed" of modern thought. But he also maintained a critical distance that could at times be quite pronounced. In the end, it would seem, Barth was one dialogue partner among many in Moody's critically conservative construction of a contemporary biblical and Baptist theology. Certainly one would have to look elsewhere to find a Southern Baptist theologian who would enthusiastically support the distinctive elements and primary thrust of Barth's Reformed theology. But one would not need to look far.

David L. Mueller

In David Mueller, a Professor of historical theology at Southern Seminary since 1961, and therefore a younger colleague of both Rust and Moody, Southern Baptists have found their most convinced advocate of Karl Barth's theology. He is also one of the most well-informed and sophisticated interpreters of the Swiss theologian within the postwar Evangelical movement.

By his own testimony, he was introduced to Barth by his father and first "theological mentor," William A. Mueller, who wrote a dissertation on dialectical theology during the early thirties and who preceded his son as a teacher of historical theology at Southern (W. Mueller, 1954). The elder Mueller also raised his son in a bilingual home, providing the young scholar not only an early acquaintance with Barth, but also an essential tool for serious study of German-speaking theology. This introduction and preparation led David Mueller, in time, to pursue his own study, completing a doctoral dissertation at Duke University on Barth's theological method in 1958, and then in 1959-60 taking a leave of absence from Baylor University, where he was teaching, to spend an "unforgettable" year of post-graduate studies in Basel (Mueller, 1972, 12).

As a result of this early and sustained interaction, Karl Barth became, by Mueller's own testimony, "the single most decisive influence on my thought" (1974, 165). Though his scholarly endeavors included significant (and somewhat appreciative) studies of Protestant Liberalism—especially Ritschl (1969) and Bultmann (1988, 1990)—Karl Barth remained Mueller's dominant theological model and the focus of his written work. In 1972 Mueller provided an introduction to the theology of Barth for the *Makers of the Modern Theological Mind* series (Mueller, 1972). This was followed by three essays in Baptist journals (1974, 1988, 1989), and an important paper on Karl Barth's doctrine of Scripture presented at a Southern Baptist Conference on Biblical Inerrancy (1987). Mueller's most significant contribution to Barthian studies, however, appeared in 1990, with the publication of his monograph on the *Foundation of Karl Barth's Doctrine of Reconciliation*.

As a consequence of these books and articles, and his more than thirty years of teaching at Southern Seminary, David Mueller has exerted a definite influence upon the positive reception of Barth within the Southern Baptist Convention. He has become its official interpreter and probably the one example of a Southern Baptist scholar whose own theology has been decisively shaped by Barth (as, for example, one might say of Bromiley, Anderson, Ramm, Vassady or Bloesch). He has also supervised several doctoral studies on the Swiss theologian, including Richard Mohler's recent investigation of "Representative models of [Evangelical] response" (Mohler, 1989).

Mueller's most important writing, from the perspective of his influence upon the reception of Barth within the Evangelical movement, is his 1972 book, *Karl Barth*. Reprinted six times before the publication of Bromiley's more specialized *Introduction* to Barth's *Dogmatics* (in 1979), Mueller's book is possibly the most widely read introduction to Barth among American Evangelical students. And rightfully so. In less than 150 pages of text it provides a very readable, surprisingly comprehensive and insightful introduction to both the development and salient features of Barth's theology. It also indicates the essential elements of Dr. Mueller's response.

The book itself is comprised of four parts: an historical survey of Barth's development up to the year when he began to write the *Dogmatics*, two chapters designed to indicate the essential features of his mature theology and a final, brief evaluation of Barth's contribution. In tracing "the main lines of Barth's theological development" from his "early years" through his "transition" "to Dialectical theology" and then "to Dogmatics," Mueller's concern is to indicate both a progression of thought and a basic continuity of direction (1972, 14, 17, 30, 49).

The progression is revealed in at least two ways: First, Barth develops, through intensive study of both Reformed theology and Anselm, a theological method that enables him to shed his reliance upon Kierkegaard's dialectic and to make positive, analogical statements about the being of God (Ibid., 30-41); and secondly, he engages through the course of the *Dogmatics* in a progressive "intensification" of his christological orientation to theology, producing quite novel reinterpretations of election, creation and the doctrine of man (Ibid., 96, 49f.).

Recognizing these changes in Barth's thinking, however, should not be allowed to obscure the "basic continuity" that has characterized Barth's work (Ibid., 142). From the very first page of *Der Römerbrief*, which sounded the bell that led a "revolution" in modern theology, to the final form of the massive doctrine of reconciliation in *CD IV*, Barth has endeavored to bear witness to the Word of God revealed in Holy Scripture in such a way that the Word really is, and remains, *God's* Word (Ibid., 28, 36, 61-3, 143). This has required a consistent, and some would say, extreme opposition to every form of theology that denies or qualifies God's sovereign freedom and grace in the act of revelation, for "through God alone may God be known" (Ibid., 62). It has also led to Barth's rigorous concentration upon the revelation of God in Jesus Christ as the single source and norm for Christian theology. The result is a theology whose "basic direction" is determined by Barth's desire "to be a theologian obedient to the Word of God" and whose "decisive mark" is its radical "christocentricity" (Ibid., 49-50).

Corresponding to this basic direction and distinguishing mark, Mueller devotes the heart of his book (pp. 49-139) to an exposition of the essential features of Barth's "Doctrine of Revelation" in *CD I* and his "Christocentric Theology" as developed in *CD II, III* and *IV*. Although the details of exposition lie beyond the scope of this study, it will be important to indicate elements of Mueller's response.

Although raising "some critical questions" that reflect concerns similar to those of Rust, Moody and other Evangelical interpreters, Mueller's primary accent is positive. First and foremost, he commends Barth for the veritable "revolution" he has effected in modern theology, "stem[ing] the tide" of nineteenth century anthropocentrism by means of a "creative" and powerful "reassertion" of the sovereignty of God and the authority of His Word. He has precipitated, Mueller claims, a twentieth century "renaissance of exegesis and biblical theology" and "reestablished the significance of [systematic] theology in the life of the church" (Ibid., 143-6). Not only that, but the specific way in which Barth articulated the doctrine of the Word and the task of biblical interpretation constitutes a much needed recovery of the position of the Reformers after years of liberal and orthodox accretion (Ibid., 144-5).

Mueller also praises Barth for recovering the biblical idea of "the triune God who reveals himself actively as Father, Son, and Holy Spirit," and even claims that all modern attempts to avoid "static and timeless" conceptions of divine being are indebted at some level to Barth (Ibid.,146-7). But Barth's "most significant contribution" to the future of theology, Mueller suggests, is the way he has faithfully pursued his primary task. "No theologian in the history of the church has interpreted the nature of God and all of his relationships to man and the universe in terms of his self-revelation in Jesus Christ as rigorously as has Barth." His theology manifests, therefore, an "objectivity" and "comprehensiveness" that "is hardly surpassed in Christian history" (Ibid., 147-8, 41).

In light of these commendations it is difficult to regard Mueller's criticisms as much more than footnotes to a fundamental affirmation. But he does raise areas of critical concern that reflect not only his own questions, but also the complaints of fellow Evangelicals. The most "fundamental" of these criticisms has to do with the doctrine of election:

> The basic question is whether Barth's depiction of creation, history, human existence, and all things pertaining to the relationship between God and man can be derived so strictly and logically from the conception of God's eternal election and predestination (Ibid., 151).

It appears that in this particular doctrine Barth may have "succumbed to metaphysical speculation" and produced "an all-encompassing system" that leaves little room for human appropriation—or rejection. At least, "certain ambiguities remain in Barth's thought" at this point (Ibid., 152-3).

Dr. Mueller also finds Barth's denial of general revelation "more restrictive than...the Scriptures" and maybe even unnecessary in light of his teaching on creation in *CD III* (Ibid., 150). This particular complaint is one that Mueller picks up in an article on christian experience, written two years later, suggesting that Langdon Gilkey "may be more helpful [than Barth] in addressing the issue of how modern man in a post-christian society may experience transcendence" (1974, 193-4). However one may judge that suggestion, it is at least clear that Mueller is looking for ways to modify the consequences of Barth's radical christocentricity.

But it is also clear that Mueller does not desire to forfeit the gains made by Barth. In his latest book, for example, Mueller engages in careful and extensive exposition of Barth's doctrine of reconciliation, including his understanding of history, election, atonement, divine suffering, incarnation and resurrection—to name an important few— and assumes a position of fundamental advocacy (1990, 243-6, 320-1, 424).

He also engages Barth's most sophisticated Evangelical critic, Berkouwer, at two important places. To Berkouwer's claim that Barth's reinterpretation of traditional two-states christology undermines the historical significance of the transition from humiliation to exaltation, Mueller counters with a more careful and complex articulation of Barth's position (Ibid., 413f.); and to Berkouwer's contention that Barth is guilty of an a priori and therefore un-historical idea of Christ's triumph, Mueller cites Barth's own response in *CD IV/3,1*. In spite of Mueller's questions and concerns, he still prefers Barth's reinterpretations of reformed doctrine on election, atonement and incarnation to Berkouwer's contemporary defense. This fact alone places him on the extreme end of Evangelical appropriation of Barth's theology.

Mueller's location on the Evangelical map of Barth reception was clearly indicated in his paper on "The Contributions and Weaknesses of Karl Barth's View of The Bible" presented at the Southern Baptist Conference on Biblical Inerrancy in 1987. After providing a concise exposition of Barth's doctrine of Scripture, including its threefold form, its nature as inspired witness and its capacity for revelation, Mueller summarizes typical "Evangelical Criticisms," using Henry (1976-83), Runia (1962) and Bromiley (1986b) as sources. Mueller then concludes by restating Barth's "dominant emphases" and declaring himself "in agreement with the conclusion of Bernard Ramm...that Barth's doctrine of Scripture and his mode of exegesis provides the best model for Evangelical theology today" (Ibid., 435-7). He also appended to this article an exposition of Barth's analysis of the historical development of the orthodox doctrine of verbal inspiration—declaring himself in essential agreement here, too.

Certainly in the person of David Mueller both Southern Baptists and the wider Evangelical movement have found a convinced advocate for the theology of Karl Barth. But he also stands alone among Southern Baptists, not as a New Evangelical voice for changing views of Scripture, ecumenicity and tradition, but as someone who thinks Barth's Reformed paradigm provides the most helpful model for the future of Evangelical theology.

The Holiness-Pentecostal Tradition

While interaction with Karl Barth among Southern Baptists has been limited, it has at least been substantial among a few influential teachers. With the Holiness and Pentecostal tradition, however, the sense of cultural and theological distance from Barth becomes even greater, and the interaction quite limited. [4]

Among Pentecostals, for example, the most widely used handbooks of theology, both older and newer, do not even engage Karl Barth (Pearlman, 1937; Williams, 1953; Pruitt, 1981; Sauls, 1979); and according to informed participants the study of theology in Pentecostal schools during most of the postwar period has been done with the aid of texts bearing the names of Finney, Hodge, Shedd, Strong and Torrey (Spittler, 1985, 57; Nichols, 1984, 57).

Even among the more progressive members of the recently established Society for Pentecostal Studies, meaningful interaction with Barth's thought is almost non-existent. One article in the society's journal, *Pneuma*, does suggest "that the work of Barth can be a starting point for Pentecostal theologians" who are ready to move beyond their reliance upon nineteenth century models and develop a "Pentecostal Structure" for systematic theology (Nichols, 1984, 57). But the article itself is quite disappointing in its execution, manifesting a limited and at points questionable understanding of Barth.

J. Rodman Williams

One exception to this dearth of informed interaction with Barth is Dr. J. Rodman Williams, whose training as a southern Presbyterian before experiencing a pentecostal baptism of the Spirit in 1965 provided significant and positive exposure to contemporary thought, including that of Karl Barth (Williams, 1965).

In his first book written after that experience, *The Era of the Spirit* (1971), Williams devotes the entire second part to a consideration of what contemporary theologians—namely, Barth, Brunner, Tillich and Bultmann—said concerning the renewal of the Church and the ministry of the Holy Spirit. His purpose in this book is to demonstrate, as far as possible, a convergence or compatibility between these leaders of mainline theology and the distinctive teachings of the charismatic renewal movement.

With respect to Barth, Williams expresses "enthusiastic endorsement" for the distinction he makes between Easter, Pentecost and the Final Advent as "different forms or stages" of Christ's one coming (1971, 73, 67). If properly developed this exegetical distinction could provide the foundation for Pentecostalism's separation between the coming of Christ's Spirit to indwell (Easter) and His subsequent coming to empower believers to bear witness (Pentecost).[5] Williams acknowledges that Barth, unfortunately, does not draw such a conclusion, opting instead for the view that the Spirit's coming in the life of the believer is a single event "with two aspects" (Ibid., 71). But in spite of this weakness, Williams insists that Barth needs to be praised—and imitated—for never "losing sight" in his dogmatic work of the Spirit's role in enabling the believer to participate in Christ (Ibid.).

Williams also finds Barth's views on extraordinary spiritual manifestations similar to his own, although again, Barth does not go all the way with Pentecostalism in identifying glossolalia as the essential evidence of the outpouring of the Spirit. But he does express an expectation that the Christian community will be "the scene of...new and supremely astonishing" events, and raises the critical question whether the absence of these events might not indicate "a nominal and not a real relationship" between the community and its Lord (Ibid., 73, 75). For as Barth says, with words which Williams chooses to quote twice, "only where the Spirit is sighed, cried, and prayed for does He become present and newly active" (Ibid., 77).

With a keen eye focused upon Barth's pneumatology Williams has found possibilities for fruitful dialogue between the movement of charismatic renewal and Karl Barth. One might expect, therefore, to find him engaged in a continuing interaction with the Swiss theologian. But such is not the case; at least, not in his recent two volume systematic theology (1988, 1990). There are occasional citations of Barth in the footnotes, and possibly echoes of his language and ideas at selective points, but whatever study has occurred is very much in the background.[6] As Williams himself acknowledges in the preface, there is "little difference" between his text and "what may be found in many books of theology" that "follow traditional patterns"—except for his "charismatic perspective" (1988, 12).

The Wesleyan Theological Society

Presently one must look outside the Pentecostal movement to find significant and sustained interaction with the theology of Karl Barth among members of the American Holiness tradition. One must look to the Wesleyan Theological Society, which is "the theological commission of the Christian Holiness Association," and has provided, since 1965, the central forum for theological discussion among conservative Wesleyan scholars (Morrit, 1986, 185). This society has also been, not surprisingly, the primary place where theological tensions between an older and newer Wesleyan Evangelicalism have been expressed and debated.[7]

But even in this society, interaction with Barth has been limited: one article in its journal (Spross, 1985) and two scholars in its membership who manifest a serious engagement with the Barthian corpus. In contrast, therefore, with the more reformed American Evangelical traditions, and even in distinction from The Southern Baptist Theological Seminary, Karl Barth has played a very peripheral role in conservative Wesleyan theological development. There are, however, two important exceptions.

Laurence Wood

Dr. Laurence W. Wood, has been Professor of Systematic Theology and Philosophy of Religion at Asbury Theological Seminary, editor of the seminary's theological journal, and President of the Wesleyan Theological Society. He also studied for his Ph.D. in theology at Edinburgh, where he gained inevitable exposure to the theology of Karl Barth. The fruit of this exposure and subsequent study is revealed in two written works, a 1980 book entitled *Pentecostal Grace*, and a 1986 article in *The Asbury Theological Journal* on the concept of revelation in Barth and Pannenberg (Wood, 1986).

In the book, the more significant contribution of the two, Wood follows a line of Barth interpretation similar to the one suggested by Neo-Pentecostal, J. Rodman Williams. In an effort to demonstrate "the biblical-theological foundation for the Wesleyan doctrine of Christian perfection," Dr. Wood turns to the distinction between Resurrection and Pentecost and argues that "this two-fold sequence within salvation history is also normative for the believer's individual history of salvation" (1980, 13). In the process of his argument Wood interacts quite fully with Barth's exegesis of the Pentecostal outpouring and baptism of the Spirit in *CD IV/4*, and concludes that Barth's separation between baptism with water and the Spirit, and his correlation of the latter with the "fullness" or "totality of sanctifying grace," are "compatible with Wesley's emphasis that Pentecost signifies the fullness of the Christian life" (Ibid., 52-4). Of course, Barth does not develop his exegetical insights in Wesleyan directions. But Wood attributes this to his "theologically disappointing" objectivism that tends to make the "totality of the Christian life" an "exclusively...divine event" occurring "positionally and formally *in Christ*" (Ibid., 52).

While acknowledging that Wood has identified, in Barth's objectivism, a basic difference between the Wesleyan tradition and Barth, one might have hoped for a more penetrating discussion. As Wood himself argues in chapter four of *Pentecostal Grace*, Barth's doctrine of time and the trinity provide a conceptual "framework" that enables Christian theology to affirm the believer's "real participation in the events of Easter and Pentecost" (Ibid., 102f.). "More specifically," as Wood so clearly states, the temporal events of Easter and Pentecost have saving significance today...since those events are not simply past and done with. Rather, Jesus Christ is the transcendent unity of all time and he mediates grace into the present through allowing us to participate in his resurrected life and his Spirit of power (Ibid., 105).

A basic difference remains between Calvinist and Wesleyan over the possibility of "entire sanctification" prior to the eschaton; but whether Calvinist or Wesleyan, Wood has argued deftly for a doctrine of time, trinity and covenant history that converges with Karl Barth. With the fourth chapter in *Pentecostal Grace*, therefore, interaction with Barth among conservative Wesleyan scholars has reached one of its highest points.

Unfortunately the same cannot be said for Dr. Wood's 1986 article on revelation. Although sub-titled, "Toward a Synthesis of Barth and Pannenberg," it reveals an understanding of Barth's idea of revelation that differs little from Carl Henry. Barth is construed as the proponent of a radical "redefinition" of doctrine that restricts revelation to God's personal "*self*-disclosure" in Jesus Christ and does not allow it to refer, in any consistent sense, to the communication of information *about* God.

In contrast, and in partial dependence upon Pannenberg, Wood proposes that revelation be construed as God's "indirect self-communication" in biblical history that reaches "proleptic culmination in the Christ event" (Ibid., 91, 96). While one may question Wood's interpretation of Barth, it should be acknowledged that he has expressed a recurrent point of tension between American Wesleyans and Barth, namely, the adequacy of Barth's doctrine of Scripture.

Laurence Wood and J. Rodman Williams, both of whom were exposed to Barth through educational experiences outside of the Holiness-Pentecostal tradition, exemplify the beginning of a dialogue between their tradition and the theology of Karl Barth. But their limited and critical appropriation also indicates the cultural and theological distance that still separates them from the Swiss Reformed leader of Neo-Orthodoxy. There is one member of the Wesleyan Theological Society, however, whose appreciation for Barth is as great as any American Evangelical's.

Donald W. Dayton

Donald Dayton, Professor of Theology and Ethics at Northern Baptist Theological Seminary, is an important person in any study of the reception of Barth among American Evangelicals, for he lies near the center of several significant developments in postwar Evangelicalism. He was, for example, one of the early and influential members of the movement of Evangelical self-criticism that produced the *PostAmerican/Sojourners* magazine and the Chicago "Declaration of Evangelical Social Concern" (Sider, 1974; Dayton, 1974a, 26). As a contributing editor to this influential magazine, and the author of a widely read study on nineteenth century Evangelical activism (*Discovering an Evangelical Heritage*), Dayton became a recognized spokesman for "young Evangelical" criticism of the Graham-Henry-*Christianity Today* "establishment" (PostAmerican, 1975; Dayton, 1976). As an historian of American religion, and especially the Wesleyan holiness tradition, Dayton has continued to make creative and influential contributions to Evangelical definition and redefinition (Merrit, 1986, 198; Dayton, 1985a,b, 1987, 1990). Dr. Dayton has also been a visible advocate for Evangelical appropriation of Karl Barth.

The December, 1978 issue of *Sojourners* magazine was an important one from the perspective of Evangelical reception of Barth, for it chose as its advent focus two rather unexpected "saints," Thomas Merton and Karl Barth (*PostAmerican*, 1978). Among the comments on Barth were not only a glowing testimony by Clark Pinnock to his newfound appreciation for this "great theologian and Christian," but also an autobiographical article by Donald Dayton (Pinnock, 1978; Dayton, 1978a, 25).

Having rejected as a teen an Evangelical heritage that he describes as a mixture of "experientially oriented revivalism" and "rationalistic fundamentalism," Dayton became a Christian in his early twenties through reading Soren Kierkegaard. While a divinity student at Yale during the sixties, he then encountered Karl Barth. He reports:

> I can still sense the excitement with which I devoured Church Dogmatics in my dorm room. I often had to pace around the room or take long walks around New Haven to dissipate the spiritual energy that had built up. (Yes, from reading the Church Dogmatics!) (Ibid., 25).

Thus began, in an almost conversion-like experience, Dayton's study of the theologian who would exert a "determinative influence" upon his life, "breaking down the barriers to faith that had been erected" in reaction to the Evangelicalism of his youth (Ibid.). He found in Barth the means to recover an Evangelical heritage that had been distorted by generations of Fundamentalist experience. "I can remember still," Dayton proclaims, "the exhilarating liberation of realizing that Fundamentalist Evangelicalism had mislead me by elevating the Scriptures to the place of Christ" (Ibid.).

Even more important than helping him find "a way beyond" a Fundamentalist doctrine of Scripture, however, was the way Barth helped him to understand Christ:

> Barth unfolded for me a cosmic vision of the universe, centered in Christ, that radically relativized my own little struggles with faith.... Barth taught me the meaning of the incarnation and, in so doing, radically transformed my inherited theological categories (Ibid.).

Barth also played a crucial role in Dayton's recovery of an Evangelical social vision. The incarnation and death of Christ became "pregnant with meaning and guidance" as he learned that "the divine condescension in grace and mercy" must be lived out in concern for the poor and oppressed (Ibid.).

In light of these declarations of personal influence, it is not surprising to find Dayton becoming an advocate for Barth within the American Evangelical movement. By means of this testimony, and numerous review articles in Evangelical magazines (Dayton, 1971; 1974a; 1975; 1976b; 1978), as well as two brief analyses of the reception of Barth (1974a,b; 1985a), Professor Dayton endeavored to keep the study of Barth before the American Evangelical public. But more than this, he sought to encourage renewed engagement with the famous Swiss theologian, believing that "a revival of the study of Barth," if it should occur, "could be one of the most powerful forces possible for the renewal of biblical and Evangelical theology in America" (1974a, 26).

Dayton was encouraged by the emergence of a new cultural and religious situation in America to think that such a fruitful engagement might be possible. Vietnam, Watergate and the social turmoil of the sixties, not to mention the ill-fated "Death of God" theologies, had given birth to a new spirit of opposition to American Civil Religion and the bankruptcy of an established mainline Protestantism. Some were even speaking of the need for "an American Barmen Declaration." In fact, Dayton declared, the "'Thanksgiving Workshop,' which produced the [Chicago] 'Declaration on Evangelical Social Concern,' was aware of the 'Barmen Declaration' as an antecedent" (Ibid., 24-26).

Certainly Dayton himself, as a member of that workshop, believed that serious study of Barth's theological ethics, in a manner modeled by Joseph Bettis and George Hunsinger (Hunsinger, 1976), could provide a foundation for the revival of a radical and Evangelical social criticism (Dayton, 1976b). As he said in the conclusion to his review of Hunsinger's *Karl Barth and Radical Politics*,

> In Barth I find important elements of the theological, historical and biblical analysis that forced me toward the vision of *Sojourners* as the most pertinent and the most biblical response to the current cultural situation (Ibid., 35).

Donald Dayton's advocacy of Barth as a model for social criticism is an important event in the history of American Evangelical interpretation. In distinction from the more common Evangelical focus upon Barth's doctrines of revelation, election, soteriology or even anthropology, Dayton has brought the issue of his ethics into consideration—and he has done so in a way that is highly relevant to the post-Vietnam struggle of certain "young Evangelicals" against an "established" Evangelical theology and practice.

An important question remains, however, in our consideration of Dayton's reception of Barth: How does his advocacy relate to his identity as a Wesleyan scholar? In order to answer this question, one must turn to Dayton's typology of Evangelical identity, in which he distinguishes between predominantly "Reformed," "Pietist," and "Fundamentalist" paradigms of Evangelical experience and self-understanding (1985a,b).

While acknowledging overlap and influence between these traditions, Dayton argues for an essential and irreducible diversity between their basic approaches to theology and life. Of particular importance are the differences Dayton sees between Fundamentalist and Pietist Evangelicalism. In contrast to the Fundamentalist preoccupation with an intellectual and apologetic defense of orthodoxy, the Pietist Evangelical tradition, which includes the Wesleyan "Awakening," has a more practical and ethical focus. It is oriented primarily to the present experience of the Holy Spirit and the need for sanctification or holiness of life. Further, its mode of thinking is more "conjunctive" than "disjunctive," especially in its Wesleyan form, and therefore, is not essentially apologetic. While admitting that the early Wesleyan tradition affirmed doctrines very similar to Fundamentalist Evangelicalism, Dayton insists that Wesleyan theologians have also demonstrated a greater ability to incorporate modern intellectual developments (1985b).

With respect to the reception of Barth, these general characteristics speak well for the possibility of fruitful dialogue. Not only is there a converging concern for social action, as Dayton has sought to demonstrate, but Pietistic Evangelicalism ought to be able to absorb Barth's post-critical hermeneutic and his accent upon the present activity of the Spirit in revelation. Opportunities for theological convergence can also be found in Barth's appreciation for Zinzendorf and the Blumhardts (1985a, 21-22).

Nevertheless, Dayton does acknowledge the striking absence of interpretive interaction in the American situation, and the existence of tensions and contrasting emphases between Barth's "objectivism" and the Pietist concern for personal experience. But even here Dayton argues the differences are reconcilable (Ibid.). An issue Dayton does not raise, however, is one that is central to both William's and Wood's interaction with Barth, namely, the relation between Barth's soteriology and the holiness doctrines of entire sanctification and Spirit baptism. In light of their status as symbolic boundaries of Holiness-Pentecostal identity, a failure to engage these issues is a significant ommission.

Donald Dayton stands alone as an important advocate for Barth within the American Wesleyan tradition. He points to fruitful opportunities for dialogue, and personally engages in such dialogue. But he still waits for partners to arise within the Wesleyan current of the Evangelical stream.

The Anabaptist Evangelical Tradition

The American Anabaptist tradition is comprised predominantly of Mennonites and Brethren in Christ whose churches trace their historical roots back to sixteenth century European Anabaptism and eighteenth and nineteenth century immigrations to North America. For most of their history they have maintained a strong ethnic identity, reinforced by participation in close-knit agrarian communities, continued use of a distinctive language, and pacifist commitments that separate them from the larger culture (Dyck, 1981; Loewen, 1988). They have not, therefore, been a dominant tradition within the American Evangelical mosaic, and some interpreters even question the appropriateness of including them within the movement (Kraus, 1979).

There are, however, good reasons to do so. As immigrant religious communities the Anabaptists maintained continuity with an early Reformation heritage by separating from a secularizing culture. This caused them to adopt a posture that paralleled, in some sense, the countermodernism of other American Evangelical traditions, and it has produced family resemblances that have enabled Anabaptists to identify with and become involved in Evangelical developments.

They have, for example, been influenced by both nineteenth century revivalism and twentieth century Fundamentalism, although not without conflict and tension (Wenger, 1981; 1979; Dyck, 1981, 410f.); and during the postwar period of resurgence in Evangelical religion Mennonite colleges have chosen to participate in Evangelical associations and their scholars in Evangelical publications and events (Yoder, 1985; Sider, 1974, 1979; PostAmerican, 1975). It is not surprising, therefore, to find representative theological statements and surveys of member opinion showing that Anabaptist beliefs have converged through the years with conservative Evangelical convictions (Kauffman, 1914; Wenger, 1946, 1979; Loewen, 1985; Dyck, 1981, 414-8).

As long as due allowance is made for the differences between traditions within the Evangelical mosaic, it would seem appropriate to consider Mennonite Anabaptism an American Evangelical tradition. Certainly one Anabaptist scholar, John Howard Yoder, has exerted an important influence upon contemporary Evangelical thought. He also happens to be one of the only Anabaptist Evangelicals who has interacted seriously with Karl Barth's theology.[8]

John Howard Yoder

John Howard Yoder, Professor of theology at the University of Notre Dame, was for most of his scholarly career associated with Goshen Biblical Seminary, where he served as Professor of theology and eventually President. In the tradition of Harold Bender, who led a mid-century revival in Mennonite historical studies as Dean at Goshen College and Seminary (Dyck, 1981, 223-8, 402, 413), much of Dr. Yoder's scholarship has been devoted to sixteenth century Swiss Anabaptism, including his doctoral research at Basel (1962, 1968, 1973, 1977, 1981, 1989).[9] But his work has not been limited to this focus. While anchored in and nourished by "the Anabaptist Vision" of his Swiss heritage, Yoder has made substantial and pioneering contributions to theological ethics. He has become, since the publication of *The Politics of Jesus* (1972b), probably the most influential spokesman within the English-speaking world for a non-violent, free church social ethic (1972a,b; 1982, 136-145; 1984).

Professor Yoder's place in the Evangelical mosaic, is not only Anabaptist; it is also, to use the language of this study, New Evangelical. Although a member of a small, ethnic denomination, John Yoder has been engaged from the beginning of his career in sophisticated dialogue with the wider Christian tradition—as a representative to the World Council of Churches, a member of the Faith and Order Colloquium, a contributor to ecumenical periodicals and conferences, and an internationally respected scholar (1957; 1958; 1968c; 1975; 1980; 1984, 1-2, 105ff.) Yoder's universe of discourse has been more ecumenical than most Evangelicals.

But it has included participation in Evangelical publications and associations. As a participant in the Evangelical Theology Group of the American Academy of Religion, for example, Yoder contributed an essay on "The Use of the Bible in Theology." While presenting one "Evangelical Option" among many, he clearly distinguished himself from the "apologetic rationalism" and "scholastic orthodoxy" of men like Clark and Van Til (Yoder, 1985, 115). In their "naively precritical" attempt to construct a "stable and closed" system of thought they have, he argues, failed to appreciate the radically historical nature of both Scripture and theological reflection (Ibid., 115-116).

The Bible, Yoder claims, is the testimony of qualified witnesses to the saving acts of God, centering in Christ; and its general structure is that of historical narrative. Theology is the process by which teachers within the believing community—gathered around and living by this Word—test whether their words and actions are faithful to the person revealed in the narrative. But the process of testing is an irreducibly complex one; it involves the reading of an historical text in the context of historical traditions, and also the reading of a current situation in light of the text. We can never, therefore, as Protestant Orthodoxy did, equate "our systematic restructuring of [the Bible's] contents" with the Word of God (Ibid., 116; Yoder, 1968, 285).

Professor Yoder identifies this "post-critical" hermeneutic with the "Biblical Realism" of Kraemer, Minear and Barth (both Karl and Markus), and maintains that his own *Politics of Jesus* represents "a late ripening, in the field of ethics, of the biblical realist revolution" (Ibid., 113, 116; 1972b, 5).

Barth Reception

As indicated by this identification with biblical realism, the influence of Barth lies deep within the structure of John Yoder's thought. The focus of his published interaction with Barth, however, is more limited: one thirty page booklet on *The Pacifism of Karl Barth* (1964a) and a more extensive book on *Karl Barth and the Problem of War* (1970). Although published later, Yoder's 1970 study is a revised version of essays prepared during the course of his doctoral studies under Professor Barth, and a "substantially similar" text was presented to his Swiss mentor in the summer of 1957 (1970, 17).

The book indicates not only the substance of Yoder's interpretation of Barth on the problem of war, but also the mature nature of Yoder's interaction at the beginning of his career. What strikes the interpreter of American Evangelicalism is that Yoder was engaged in a sympathetic and sophisticated reading of Barth's ethic, making an original contribution to Barthian scholarship, when serious interpretation by American Evangelicals had hardly begun, and when Van Til's *The New Modernism* dominated Fundamentalist reception. One is also struck by the respect which Yoder expresses for Barth's theology and the convergence he discerns between the Anabaptist position and certain developments in Barth's own thinking.

The professed purpose of *Karl Barth and the Problem of War* is to provide a "rigorous yet respectful critique" that exposes Barth's justification of war as internally incoherent—based upon a confused concept of the "limiting case" in which war may be justified, and in tension with Barth's own best insights about the nature of theology. Most damaging of all, if sustained, is Yoder's claim that Barth's actual justification of war depends, in the last analysis, upon a form of natural theology (Ibid., 17, 64-74, 83, 99).

But criticism is not Dr. Yoder's final or even dominant word. Rather, he begins by praising Barth for "faithfully [filling] the office of teacher in the church" and leading a generation of European pastors "to rethink [their] faith in light of the Word of God" (Ibid., 7). Barth has constructed, Yoder proclaims, "the most monumental body of theologically integrated Protestant ethical thought which our century has seen," and he has done so by pursuing, with rigorous consistency, a radically theocentric and christological orientation (Ibid., 15, 17-26).

Because of this orientation, Barth rejected the Church's traditional just-war theories as mired in natural theology, and exposed them to "a merciless critique" "unique in the history of mainstream European Protestant theology" (Ibid., 37-8). Yoder, therefore, considers his engagement with Barth "a debate...within the pacifist camp," and the gist of his criticism is to expose the remnants of non-theological and non-christological thinking that yet remain in Barth's social ethic (Ibid., 52).

To do this, Yoder identifies "a line" or "movement" of thought in Barth that leads, if consistently pursued, to a pacifist and even Anabaptist ethic. While acknowledging that Barth himself did not fully take this step, Yoder argues that his radically christological orientation, his emerging position on baptism, and his development of the doctrine of sanctification as obedient imitation of the life of Christ definitely tend in this direction (1964a, 21-3, 28-30; 1970, 111-118, 129-131). Certainly Yoder consider's *The Politics of Jesus* an explicit development of this line of thought and an extension of the "biblical realist revolution" instituted by Karl Barth (1970, 5).

As a student of Barth, John Howard Yoder is fairly unique among Anabaptists—one of few significant commentators and the only one to make a widely read original contribution to Barthian studies. Yoder is also unique among American Evangelicals. In the decade of the sixties, long before the emergence of *Sojourners* magazine, Dr. Yoder was discovering in Barth a model for radical social ethics. A decade later Donald Dayton would join with Yoder in this engagement and together they would make a signal contribution to American Evangelical reception of Barth. But Yoder's contribution remains original.

Concluding Comment

In spite of the significant contributions of Yoder, Dayton, and Mueller, it must be acknowledged that interaction with Barth has remained peripheral within the more pietistic sectors of American Evangelicalism. While it may be true that the pietistic "axis of thought," as Dayton labels it, has enabled some theologians to adopt a positive and open attitude toward Barth, it is also true that a great cultural and theological distance remains between Barth and Pietistic Evangelicalism.

Barth has served as a bridge for some between a Fundamentalist Evangelical heritage and a more New Evangelical future; and a handful of Southern Baptist, Wesleyan and Anabaptist Evangelicals have found in Barth a model for the future of Evangelical theology. This handful, furthermore, has definitely impacted public discussion. But in the final analysis, the reception and influence of Barth within American Evangelicalism has had a reformed center.

NOTES

1. Donald Bloesch is an important exception to this omission. Not only does he engage in a significant and supportive discussion of Barth's ethic in his recent *Freedom for Obedience* (1987); he has also utilized Barth's critique of ideology as the basis for his own criticism of aberrant forms of Evangelical faith (Bloesch, 1983a). Of course, Bloesch has been deeply influenced by Pietist traditions.

2. William McClendon, Jr., a theologian on the very edges of the Southern Baptist community, published the first volume of an intended three volume Systematics in 1986, entitled *Ethics*, and James Leo Garret, a student and successor of W. T. Connor at Southwestern, has just recently published a one volume *Systematic Theology* (1990b). Neither man interacts significantly with Barth.

3. Rust's final book on preaching, however, did bring some basic insights from Barth to bear on the church's homiletic task (Rust, 1982).

4. Because of substantial Reformed influences among Southern Baptists, they exist in the confluence of Pietistic and Reformed traditions more than the Holiness-Pentecostal tradition does. But as always, the Pietist and Reformed labels represent more a continuum among Evangelicals than discreet categories.

5. Williams associates the Baptism of the Spirit with power to witness rather than sanctification, which is typical of Pentecostals influenced by reformed rather than Wesleyan currents of the holiness movement (Dayton, 1987; Waldvogel, 1977).

6. Selective appropriation of Barth is most visible in Williams' discussion of "The Reality of God" (1988, 47f.), the nature of man (Ibid., 198f.), and the doctrine of the atonement (Ibid., 370-7). But even here Barth's discussions do not determine the basic direction and shape of Williams' proposals.

7. This theological "ferment," as analyzed in Merrit, 1986, has centered around the issues of inerrancy and the relation of the baptism of the Spirit to the Wesleyan distinctive of entire sanctification. See Thompson, 1984, for the description of this tension as the result of a "paradigm shift."

8. There are others, however: Howard John Loewen, discussed earlier (pp. 10-11), and Vernard Eller (1980, 1983a), though he would resist being considered an American Evangelical (1983b).

9. Harold Bender served as the central leader of a mid-century movement within the Mennonite tradition beyond a fundamentalist patterned Evangelicalism, not by appeal to classic nineteenth century theology (as with Carnell, Ramm and Henry), but by a return to sixteenth century Anabaptist sources (Dyck, 1981, 402, 413).

Goshen Biblical Seminary, which became associated with the Mennonite Biblical Seminary in 1958, began as a theological course within Goshen College in 1933.

5

CONCLUSION

There are many ways to conclude a study such as this. What I intend is a brief retrospective survey, a backward glance at the terrain already traversed in order to discern the essential contours and notable landmarks of the reception of Barth in the place called American Evangeli-calism. Most of what will be said can be found in the introductions, conclusions and transitions of the preceding four chapters. Fruitful purposes are served, however, by interpretive summary.

Probably the most important pattern that has been discerned, and one that provides the basic structure for this monograph, is the correspondence between social history and theological development. Not intending to deny the independent validity of theological argument, this study has sought to explain Evangelical reception of Barth by reference to the religious history in which it is embedded. The distinguishing marks of this history—shared by every tradition within the Evangelical mosaic—have been three-fold: a formative heritage in nineteenth century Evangelical Protestantism, a countermodern orientation during the twentieth century Fundamentalist movement, and positive identification with the postwar resurgence of conservative religion that has appropriated the name Evangelical. Many of the dynamics of Evangelical debate and development, including those revealed in the reception of Barth, can be explained by reference to this historical framework.

A Basic Historical Pattern
A Fundamentalist Evangelical Paradigm

One of the most visible consequences of this history is the pervasive and persistent influence of a fundamentalist pattern in theology. By "fundamentalist pattern" is meant the attempt to maintain continuity with an Evangelical heritage by defining and defending boundaries that protect, and hence, separate one's tradition from modern cultural developments. That this pattern pervaded the American Evangelical mosaic during the first half of the twentieth century has been argued in chapter one; that it led to the early predominance of a Fundamentalist Evangelical paradigm in theology was claimed in chapter two.

Because of this pattern an orthodox and apologetic approach came to dominate the early reception of Barth within American Evangelicalism. Established by conservative Reformed theologians whose traditions and training brought them into early dialogue with Barth—especially Cornelius Van Til—this polemic paradigm spread to the larger Evangelical mosaic through scholars active within the institutions of Northern Fundamentalist Evangelicalism—men like Clark, Henry, Schaeffer, Montgomery and Ryrie.

Although a more positive note was sounded by some of these men, the distinguishing characteristics of the Fundamentalist Evangelical paradigm remained: Barth was judged—as the proponent of a dialectical theory of revelation and consequent distortions of doctrine—to lie outside the boundaries of Evangelical faith. In fact, opposition to Barth's Neo-Orthodox innovations became a defining boundary for Evangelical identity within the Fundamentalist Evangelical paradigm.

Beyond Fundamentalist Evangelicalism

During the later fifties and early sixties, however, things began to change. While the Fundamentalist Evangelical paradigm continued to prevail, especially within communities and institutions that maintained continuity with Fundamentalist precedents, new views of Barth emerged. Originating with theologians who entered American Evangelical scholarship from the outside, namely Berkouwer, Bromiley and Rust, these more positive interpretations developed among scholars who rejected the Fundamentalist Evangelical model for theology and worked within institutions that pursued progressive and open Evangelical agendas.

In fact, constructive appropriation of Barth became one source and sign of the changes taking place in postwar American Evangelicalism as it shed its fundamentalist pattern and entered a more pluralistic and less clearly defined social and theological situation. The histories of Fuller and The Southern Baptist Theological Seminary have provided, in chapters three and four, key examples of institutions that sailed as flagships on this expanding frontier of Evangelical identity. Many of their professors led the way both in forging new Evangelical boundaries and in modeling more positive engagement with Barth—men like Carnell, Jewett, Anderson, Moody and Mueller.

As these Evangelicals, and many more like them, were pushing beyond the boundaries of a previously predominant Fundamentalist Evangelicalism, conservative movements of reform and renewal were emerging within traditional mainline denominations. The convergence of these two currents in the broadening stream of resurgent Evangelicalism tended to produce, during and after the sixties, an increasingly large and complex American Evangelical river. Within this broadening river sailed a growing number of theologians who regarded Barth as a fellow Evangelical and who had been deeply influenced by him— men like Berkouwer, Bloesch, Bromiley, Moody, Ramm, Dayton and Yoder.

Conclusion

A General Pattern and a Basic Divide

The preceding analysis would suggest, at least, two conclusions. In the first place, *the most basic general pattern to be discerned in American Evangelical reception of Barth is the correspondence between a progressive expansion of the religious tradition and an increasingly positive response to Barth.* Quite obviously, as the tradition grew to include more diverse theological positions and to define itself less apologetically, it was able to incorporate a more positive view of Karl Barth. While this new respect for Barth is due, in part, to the growing familiarity that recent translations and more adequate secondary studies facilitated, it results primarily from social and theological changes within American Evangelicalism itself.

The second conclusion to be drawn from the observations of this study is that American Evangelical *boundary expansion has produced a basic division within the movement, a division between those who maintain a Fundamentalist Evangelical paradigm and those who have moved beyond such an orthodox and apologetic pattern.* The tensions produced by these competing visions of Evangelical theology and life have been reflected in numerous battles and debates over the years, and have also surfaced in divergent opinions about the person and work of Karl Barth. These tensions and differences, however, have proven resistant to resolution, for they exist *within* Evangelical institutions and communities, rather than *between* Evangelicals and non-Evangelicals. Every dominant tradition within the Evangelical mosaic now contains within itself Fundamentalist-Evangelical and New Evangelical participants and perspectives.

Other Patterns

Although partially accurate, it would be simplistic to interpret the history of Evangelical Barth reception by means of a two-fold pattern of progressive expansion and internal division, or to explain every difference between Evangelical interpreters in terms of two basic paradigms. These patterns exist, but they are not the only patterns, nor do they explain all the data. In one sense, every Evangelical theologian's response to Barth has been shaped by the specific dimensions of his own theological position, as well as the particular way he has interpreted Barth's complex and evolving corpus. But for the sake of interpretive analysis, and in the search for a usable past, at least two more patterns should be recognized.

Differences Between Traditions

From the very beginning of this study American Evangelicalism has been defined as *a mosaic of traditions whose parallel histories have produced important family resemblances*. The value of this definition is that it enables one to recognize, and interpret, both the similarities and differences between the major currents of Evangelical thought and life. Every Evangelical subculture has experienced a similar broadening of its boundaries in the postwar period. But each of them has passed through this development in a manner that reflects its unique heritage. Distinctive differences have always existed between the traditions that comprise the Evangelical mosaic, and they have been manifest in the history of interaction with Barth.

From the beginning, for example, it has been the orthodox Reformed communities that have demonstrated the greatest interest in and ability to interpret Barth. Whether Fundamentalist Evangelical or New Evangelical, the reception of Barth within American Evangelicalism has had a *reformed center*. The most prolific and influential commentators—Van Til, Klooster, Henry, Berkouwer, Bromiley, Bloesch and Ramm—have been decisively influenced by classic Reformed traditions.

The reception of Barth within the more pietistic Evangelical traditions—those further removed from the influences and emphases of Reformed Orthodoxy—has, in contrast, been more limited and peripheral. This may be due, in part, to the relative absence, or newness, of academic institutions within these more populist and pragmatic traditions. But it also stems from the vast cultural and theological distance that separates Barth and the American Pietists.

There is another side of the story, however. The Wesleyan theologian, Donald Dayton, has suggested that the different "axis of thought" (1985, 132) upon which the pietistic traditions turn enables them to be more open to theological innovation. Because Protestant Orthodoxy has exerted less influence upon the Pietists, their boundaries of belief are not as tightly defined, or at least not defined in a way that erects barriers to Barth's theology. Barth's Christological and dynamic doctrine of revelation, for example, or his reliance upon the continual work of the Holy Spirit, should provide fruitful points of contact between him and the Pietistic traditions.

Certainly some theologians within these traditions have found Barth's theological orientation helpful, and have manifested an openness to his thought quite different from the Fundamentalist Evangelicalism of Henry or Van Til, most notably, Dale Moody, David Mueller, Donald Dayton and John Howard Yoder. It is also true that certain emphases in their Southern Baptist, Wesleyan or Anabaptist heritages have made it possible for them to respond to Barth in this more positive manner. Nevertheless, beyond these few examples interaction with Barth has remained peripheral among Pietists.

One's tradition within the Evangelical mosaic, therefore, makes a difference. Next to the Fundamentalist Evangelical and New Evangelical divide—which crosses through every subculture—

differences between traditions are the most basic and influential factors in determining how an Evangelical theologian is likely to respond to Barth. Of course, specific interpretive arguments may never be discounted; but one must also recognize that those arguments have been shaped by tradition. And the recognition of differences between traditions within the Evangelical mosaic is essential if one hopes to interpret the contours of theological argument in this place called American Evangelicalism.

Shifting Issues and Growing Sophistication

Progressive boundary expansion, internal division and diversity between traditions—these are the basic contours of the reception of Barth among twentieth century American Evangelicals. But there have also been certain key issues around which that interaction has occurred, and these issues reflect, as much as anything else, the nature of Evangelicalism and its relation to the theology of Barth.

Among Fundamentalist Evangelicals, for instance, the issue of primary concern is epistemological: What is Barth's doctrine of revelation and what rational support does it provide for the theological truth claims he makes? As chapter two endeavored to demonstrate this epistemological focus is not arbitrary, but reflects the foundational role doctrines of revelation and rationality have played in Fundamentalist Evangelical visions of theological identity. Not surprisingly, therefore, the Fundamentalist Evangelical interaction with Barth has concentrated upon his earlier writings, where issues of revelation and rationality are in the forefront, and has tended to construe Barth's supposed dialecticism as a fundamental and enduring characteristic of his theology. While acknowledging some measure of development, Fundamentalist Evangelicals argue that Barth's methodological consistency is more basic than any changes, and that his method is the ultimate source of his doctrinal errors.

With the emergence of New Evangelical interpreters like Berkouwer, Bromiley and Bloesch, however, the theological focus changed. Unwilling to construe Barth as subject to a controlling philosophy, and even affirming many aspects of his methodology, these theologians turned their attention to other parts of the Barthian corpus. Following the seminal work of Berkouwer, *The Triumph of Grace in the Theology of Karl Barth*, many New Evangelical interpreters have focused upon Barth's soteriology rather than his method. While some have been highly critical of Barth's innovative doctrines of election and reconciliation (Berkouwer, Brown, Moody and Jewett), others have taken a position of fundamental affirmation (Anderson, Bromiley, Mueller, Dayton). But whatever position has been taken in soteriology, these New Evangelicals have been united in their more sympathetic interpretation of Barth and in their more extensive engagement with the later volumes of *Church Dogmatics*. An influential few have also argued that Barth's theological method may provide Evangelicalism its finest model for future development (Ramm, Mueller, Dayton).

New Evangelicals have engaged in serious study of Barth's anthropology and his ethics, as well, subjects that have received little attention among Fundamentalist Evangelicals. Jewett's publication of *Man as Male and Female* (1975) not only ignited heated debate within the American Evangelical community, but also offered Barth as, at least, a partial model for a doctrine of sexuality; and Ray Anderson's *Essays in Theological Anthropology* (1982) were written self-consciously and extensively on the basis of Barth's work. One of the signal contributions of pietist Evangelicals, furthermore, has been to introduce Barth as a model for social ethics. The work of Donald Dayton, John Howard Yoder, and more recently, Donald Bloesch, are examples of this often neglected focus of study among American Evangelicals.

It is certainly the case that theological attention has shifted for many New Evangelicals. As some Evangelicals have come to adopt a more positive attitude toward Barth, and to regard him as both a genuine partner in dialogue and even, at points, a theological model, they have become more interested in extensive engagement with various aspects of the Barthian corpus—with soteriology, anthropology, ethics and theology proper. With few exceptions, however, the Fundamentalist Evangelical interpretation of Barth has remained focused upon issues of method.

This shift in interest among New Evangelicals also corresponds to a growing interpretive sophistication. Even the most affirmative interpreters have filtered Barth through the grid of their own English-speaking and Evangelical grid; but the posture of sympathetic appreciation which characterizes the approach of many New Evangelicals has enabled them to enter more deeply and deftly into the Barthian corpus. If one hopes to find an Evangelical work that makes a significant contribution to Barthian studies, one must look to the writings of New Evangelicals. But even here the primary contributions have been made by theologians who entered the American movement from the outside—Berkouwer and Bromiley. Among native members of constitutive American Evangelical traditions, the primary use of Barth has been to modify or develop an inherited Evangelical theology, and significant contributions to the study of Barth are difficult to find (perhaps Mueller, 1990; Yoder, 1970; Palma, 1983; Bloesch, 1976). But in contrast to much of the theological reflection being carried on outside of the Evangelical tradition, interaction with Barth has come to play an increasingly important role in American Evangelical theology.

Whither Evangelicalism?

The question naturally arises, where will this growing appreci-

Conclusion

ation for the theology of Karl Barth lead within the American Evangelical movement? Will it lead, as Bernard Ramm hopes, to an even greater appreciation and appropriation of Barthian methods and conclusions? Or will it produce a greater polarization between Evangelical theologians? Will it lead to more sophisticated and penetrating scholarly analysis? Or will it be lost in the pursuit of other theological concerns and resources? To hazard a guess—even an educated one—is certainly to step beyond the boundaries of scholarly caution.

But if anything has become clear from the preceding chapters it is the expectation that Evangelical diversity is here to stay. Evangelicalism has always been comprised of a diverse mosaic of traditions and perspectives, and postwar developments have produced a situation in which the social and theological boundaries of American Evangelicalism have become even less clearly defined. Lines that may have defined the difference between Evangelical and Liberal during the first half of the twentieth century now cut within communities and institutions that label themselves Evangelical.

A new pluralism has emerged within the American Evangelical mosaic, marked by new levels of diversity and mirrored by diverse and developing responses to the theology of Karl Barth. For some, Barth has become a bridge between their Fundamentalist Evangelical past and a New Evangelical future. For others, he has remained a defining boundary, lying at the limit of legitimate Evangelical identity. Many are not sure where they stand.

But one thing is sure: the extent to which American Evangelicals are influenced by the theological voices of Berkouwer, Bromiley, Bloesch, Ramm, Moody, Mueller, Dayton and Yoder will define the extent to which Barth may exert an increasingly constructive and determinative influence upon the future of Evangelical theology. It is also clear that men like Henry, Sproul, Ryrie, Klooster and Van Til remain the dominant models for an Evangelicalism that chooses to regard Barth as more foe than friend. Sometimes it appears that Evangelical identity is stretched beyond the limits when both groups and both paradigms dwell in the same household of faith. But they do. And barring an institutional and theological division parallel to the Fundamentalist-Modernist controversies that separated the likes of Warfield and Briggs, these two theological paradigms—and the various constitutive traditions of Evangelicalism—will continue to exist within the ever flowing American Evangelical river.

What upon the surface would seem to be a surprising conclusion, has proven true: Whether friend or foe—or some combination thereof—Karl Barth has exerted, and will probably continue to exert, a profound and persistent influence upon the theological development of American Evangelicalism. Men like Warfield, Henry, Van Til, Berkouwer or Bloesch will most likely be the dominant theological voices within American Evangelicalism's future, since they maintain substantial continuity with an Evangelical past and speak with an American accent. But the ideas of Barth will never be far removed from Evangelical discussion. Bernard Ramm has, I think, overstated the ability of Barth to function as a model for the future of Evangelical theology—even Ramm's own version of that theology. But as one particularly important voice among many, Karl Barth is destined to remain an influential partner in American Evangelical dialogue—especially for those who believe, with Berkouwer, Bromiley, Bloesch and Ramm, that Barth has identified and engaged some of the most enduring concerns for the future of a theology that seeks to maintain continuity, in the modern age, with a genuinely Evangelical heritage.

BIBLIOGRAPHY

ABRAHAM, William
    1981   *The Divine Inspiration of Holy Scripture.* San Francisco: Harper and Row.

AHLSTROM, Sidney
    1955   "Scottish Philosophy and American Theology." *Church History* 24 (10/55): 257-72.
    1975   "From Puritanism to Evangelicalism." *The Evangelicals: What They Believe, Who They Are, Where They Are Changing.* Edited by David Wells and John Woodbridge. Nashville: Abingdon Press.

ALDRICH, Roy
    1964   "Obscurity of Barthianism." *BibliothecaSacra* 121 (July 5): 253-257.
    1971   "The Sign of Pompous Obscurity." *BibliothecaSacra* 128: 3-15.

ALLEN, Diogenes
    1974   "What's the Big Idea?" *Theology Today* 30:4 (January): 333.

ANDERSON, Robert Mapes
    1979   *Vision of the Disinherited: The Making of American Pentecostalism.* New York: Oxford University Press.

ANDERSON, Ray Sherman
    1975   *Historical Transcendence and the Reality of God.* Grand Rapids: Eerdmans Publishing Company.
    1979   *Theological Foundations for Ministry.* Grand Rapids: Eerdmans Publishing Company.
    1982   *On Being Human: Essays in Theological Anthropology.* Grand Rapids: Eerdmans Publishing Company.
    1985   *Theology, Death and Dying.* Oxford: Basil Blackwell.
    1986   "A New Direction for Natural Theology." *Theology Beyond Christendom: Essays on the Centenary of the Birth of Karl Barth. May 10, 1986.* Edited by John Thompson. Allison Park, Pennsylvania: Pickwick Publications.
    1989a   "Christopraxis: The Ministry and Humanity of Christ for the World." *Christ in Our Place: Essays in Honor of James B. Torrance.* Edited by T. Hart and D. Thimell. Exeter: Pa-

ternoster Press and Allison Park, PA: Pickwick Publications.
1989b   "Evangelical Theologians." *The Modern Theologians*, Volume 2. Edited by David Ford. Oxford: Basil Blackwell.
1991   *The Gospel According to Judas*. Colorado Springs: Helmer and Howard.
1992a   *The Praxis of Pentecost*. Pasadena: Fuller Theological Seminary.
1992b   "Theological Anthropology." Expanded Course Syllabus: ST512. Fuller Theological Seminary.
1992c   "Reconciliation and the Healing of Persons." Expanded Course Syllabus: ST514. Fuller Theological Seminary.

BAILEY, Kenneth
1964   *Southern White Protestantism in the 20th Century*. New York: Harper and Row.

BARNHOUSE, Donald Grey
1934   "An Interview With Karl Barth." *Revelation* 4:1 (January): 5, 30-33.

BARR, James
1980   *Fundamentalism*. Second Edition. London: S.C.M. Press.

BARTH, Karl
1928   *The Word of God and The Word of Man*. Translated by Douglas Horton.
1957   Harper Torchback Edition. New York: Harper and Row Publishers.
1929   "Fate and Idea in Theology." Translated by George Hunsinger. *The Way of Theology in Karl Barth: Essays and Comments*. Edited by H. Martin Rumscheidt. Allison Park, Pennsylvania: Pickwick Publications.
1933   *The Epistle to the Romans*. Translated from the Sixth Edition by Edwyn C. Hoskyns. New York: Oxford University Press.
1934   *Come Holy Spirit: Sermons by Karl Barth and Eduard Thurneysen*. Translated by George W. Richards, Elmer G. Homrighausen, and Karl J. Ernst. New York: Round Table Press.
1935   *God's Search for Man: Sermons by Karl Barth and Eduard Thurneysen*. Translated by George W. Richards, Elmer G. Homrighausen, and Karl J. Ernst. Edinburgh: T. and T. Clark.
1936-69   *Church Dogmatics*. Thirteen Volumes. Translated by Geoffrey Bromiley, et. al. Edinburgh: T. and T. Clark.
1949   *Dogmatics in Outline*. Translated by G. T. Thompson. London: S.C.M. Press.
1960   *Anselm: Fides Quaerens Intellectum*. Translated by Ian Roberts. Richmond: John Knox Press. Allison Park, PA: Pickwick Publications, 1985.

1963   *Evangelical Theology: An Introduction*. Translated by Grover Foley. Grand Rapids: Eerdmans Publishing Company.
1968   *Protestant Theology in the Nineteenth Century*. Translated by B. Cozens and H. H. Hartwell. Valley Forge, Pennsylvania: Judson Press.
1981   *Karl Barth: Letters*. Translated and Edited by Geoffrey Bromiley. Grand Rapids: Eerdmans Publishing Company.

BEBBINGTON, David W.
1988   *Evangelicalism in Modern Britain: A History from the 1730s to the 1980s*. London: Unwin Hyman.

BEEGLE, Dewey M.
1973   *Scripture, Tradition. and Infallibility*. Grand Rapids: Eerdmans Publishing Company.

BERGER, Peter
1967   *The Sacred Canopy: Elements of a Social Theory of Religion*. New York: Doubleday.

BERKHOF, Louis
1934   *Systematic Theology*. Two Volumes. Grand Rapids: Eerdmans Publishing Company.
1949   *Systematic Theology*. Fourth Revised and Enlarged Edition. Grand Rapids: Eerdmans Publishing Company.

BERKOUWER, Gerrit Cornelius
1937   *Karl Barth*. Kampen: V.H. Kok.
1940   *Barthianisme en Katholicisme*. Kampen: V. H. Kok.
1947   *Karl Barth en de Kinderdoop*. Kampen: V. H. Kok.
1952   *The Providence of God. Studies in Dogmatics*. Translated by John Vriend. Grand Rapids: Eerdmans Publishing Company. Original Dutch Edition, 1950.
1953   *Modern Uncertainty and the Christian Faith*. Grand Rapids: Eerdmans Publishing Company.
1954   *Faith and Justification. Studies in Dogmatics*. Translated by Lewis B. Smedes. Grand Rapids: Eerdmans Publishing Company. Dutch Edition, 1949.
1955   *General Revelation. Studies in Dogmatics*. Grand Rapids: Eerdmans Publishing Company.
1956   *The Triumph of Grace in the Theology of Karl Barth*. Translated by Harry R. Boer. Grand Rapids: Eerdmans Publishing Company.
1958   *The Conflict With Rome*. Philadelphia: Presbyterian and Reformed Publishing.
1960   *Divine Election. Studies in Dogmatics*. Translated by Hugo Bekker. Grand Rapids: Eerdmans Publishing Company. Original Dutch Edition, 1955.
1971a   *Sin. Studies in Dogmatics*. Translated by Philip Holtrup. Grand Rapids: Eerdmans Publishing Company. Original Dutch Edition, 2 Volumes, 1959, 1960.

	1971b	"The Authority of Scripture (A Responsible Confession)." *Jerusalem and Athens: Critical Discussions on the Philosophy and Apologetics of Cornelius Van Til.* Edited by E. R. Geehan. Nutley, New Jersey: Presbyterian and Reformed Publishing Company.

1975   *Holy Scripture. Studies in Dogmatics.* Translated and Edited by Jack Rogers. Grand Rapids: Eerdmans Publishing Company. Original Dutch Edition, 2 Volumes, 1966,1967.

1977   *A Half Century of Theology.* Translated and Edited by Lewis B. Smedes. Grand Rapids: Eerdmans Publishing Company. Original Dutch Edition, 1974.

BETTIS, Joseph
 1967   "Is Karl Barth a Universalist?" *Scottish Journal of Theology* 20: 423-436.

BLOESCH, Donald
 1956   "Reinhold Niebuhr's Re-evaluation of the Apologetic Task." Ph.D., University of Chicago.
 1964   *Centers of Christian Renewal.* Philadelphia: United Church Press.
 1967   *The Christian Life and Salvation.* Grand Rapids: Eerdmans Publishing Company.
 1968a   *The Crisis of Piety.* Grand Rapids: Eerdmans Publishing Company.
 1968b   *The Christian Witness in a Secular Age.* Minneapolis: Augsburg Publishing House.
 1968c   *Christian Spirituality East and West.* Co-author. Chicago: Priory Press.
 1970   *The Reform of the Church.* Grand Rapids: Eerdmans Publishing Company.
 1971a   *The Ground of Certainty: Toward an Evangelical Theology of Revelation.* Grand Rapids: Eerdmans Publishing Company.
 1971b   *Servants of Christ: Deaconesses in Renewal.* Minneapolis: Bethany Fellowship.
 1973   *The Evangelical Renaissance.* Grand Rapids: Eerdmans Publishing Company.
 1974   *Wellsprings of Renewal: Promise in Christian Communal Life.* Grand Rapids: Eerdmans Publishing Company.
 1975   *The Invaded Church.* Waco, Texas: Word Book, Publishers.
 1976   *Jesus is Victor! Karl Barth's Doctrine of Salvation.* Nashville: Abingdon Press.
 1978a   *The Orthodox Evangelicals.* Edited with Robert Webber. Nashville: Thomas Nelson Publishers.
 1978b   *Essentials of Evangelical Theology.* Volume 1. *God, Revelation and Authority.* San Francisco: Harper and Row.
 1979   *Essentials of Evangelical Theology.* Volume 2. *Life, Ministry and Hope.* San Francisco: Harper and Row.

	1983a	*The Future of Evangelical Christianity*. New York: Doubleday.
	1983b	Review of Bernard Ramm, *After Fundamentalism*. *Christianity Today* 27: 19 (December 16): 55-56.
	1985	"A Christological Hermeneutic: Crisis and Conflict in Hermeneutics." *The Use of the Bible in Theology: Evangelical Options*. Edited by Robert K. Johnston. Atlanta: John Knox Press.
	1986a	"The Legacy of Karl Barth." *TSF Bulletin* 9:5 (June): 6-9.
	1986b	"Karl Barth: Appreciation and Reservations." *How Karl Barth Changed My Mind*. Edited by Donald McKim. Grand Rapids: Eerdmans Publishing Company.
	1987	*Freedom for Obedience: Evangelical Ethics for Contemporary Times*. San Francisco: Harper and Row.
	1991	*Theological Notebook: The Spiritual Journals of Donald G. Bloesch, Volume II: 1964-1968*. Colorado Springs: Helmer and Howard.
	1992	*A Theology of the Word and Spirit: Authority and Method in Theology*.

BOGUE, Carl
  1984   "Berkouwer and the Battle for the Bible." *Inerrancy and the Church*. Edited by John Hannah. Chicago: Moody Press.

BOICE, James Montgomery
  1970   *Witness and Revelation in the Gospel of John*. Exeter: Paternoster Press.

BOLES, John B.
  1972   *The Great Revival, 1787-1805: The Origins of the Southern Evangelical Mind*. Lexington: University Press of Kentucky.

BOLICH, Gregory
  1980   *Karl Barth and Evangelicalism*. Downers Grove: Inter Varsity Press.

BOLLER, Paul
  1969   *American Thought in Transition: The Impact of Evolutionary Naturalism, 1865-1900*. Chicago: University of Chicago Press.

BOOMSMA, Clarence
  1984   "What has happened theologically to the Christian Reformed Church since World War II?" *Calvin Theological Journal* 19:1 (April): 32-49.

BOZEMAN, Theodore Dwight
    1977   *Protestants in an Age of Science: The Baconian Ideal and Antebellum Religious Thought*. Chapel Hill: University of North Carolina Press.

BRATT, James D.
    1978   "Dutch Calvinism in Modern America: The History of a Conservative Subculture." Ph.D., Yale University.

    1984   *Dutch Calvinism in Modern America: A History of a Conservative Subculture*. Grand Rapids: Eerdmans Publishing Company.

BROMILEY, Geoffrey
    1940   "The Biblical Concept of Revelation." *Evangelical Quarterly* 12: 312.
    1943   "Herder's Contribution to the Romantic Philosophy of History." Ph.D., University of Edinburgh.
    1947   "The Authority of the Bible: The Attitude of Modern Theologians." *Evangelical Quarterly* 19:127-35.
    1948   "The Anglican Reformers and Baptism." D.Litt., University of Edinburgh. Published as *Baptism and the Anglican Reformers* (1953).
    1956a   "Barth's Doctrine of the Bible." *Christianity Today* 1 (December 24): 14-16.
    1956b   "Cranmer's Message to Our Time." *Christianity Today* 1:3 (November 12): 12.
    1956c   *Thomas Cranmer, Theologian*. London: Oxford University Press.
    1957   "Fundamentalism-Modernism: A First Step in the Controversy." *Christianity Today* 2:3 (November 11): 5.
    1959a   "Barth: A Contemporary Appraisal." *Christianity Today* 3 (February 2): 9-10.
    1959b   "The Debate Over Divine Election." *Christianity Today* 4:1 (October 12): 3-6, 14-18.
    1961a   "Dare We Follow Bultmann?" *Christianity Today* 5 (March 27): 6-8.
    1961b   "Decrees of God." *Christianity Today* 5 (April 10): 8-19. Reprinted in *Basic Christian Doctrines*. Edited by Carl Henry.
    1962   "More Questions on Barth's Views." *Christianity Today* 6:7, 14-17.
    1963   "Evangelicals and the Anglican Articles, 1563-1963." *Christianity Today* 7: 12 (March 15): 18.
    1966   "Karl Barth." *Creative Minds in Contemporary Theology*. Edited by Philip E. Hughes. Grand Rapids: Eerdmans Publishing Company.
    1970   "The Inspiration and Authority of Scripture." *Eternity* (August): 12-20.
    1978a   *Historical Theology: An Introduction*. Grand Rapids: Eerdmans Publishing Company.

1978b	"Authority and Scripture." *Scripture, Tradition and Interpretation: Essays Presented to Everett Harrison.* Edited by Ward Gasque and William Sanford LaSor. Grand Rapids: Eerdmans Publishing Company.
1979	*An Introduction to the Theology of Karl Barth.* Grand Rapids: Eerdmans Publishing Company.
1986a	"The Karl Barth Experience." *How Karl Barth Changed My Mind.* Edited by Donald McKim. Grand Rapids: Eerdmans Publishing Company.
1986b	"The Authority of Scripture in Karl Barth." *Hermeneutics, Authority and Canon.* Edited by Donald Carson and John Woodbridge. Grand Rapids: Zondervan Publishing House.
1988	"The Influence of Barth after World War II." *Reckoning With Barth: Essays in Commemoration of the Centenary of Karl Barth's Birth.* Edited by Nigel Biggar. London: A.R. Mowbray and Company, Ltd.

BROWN, Colin

1960	"A Critical Examination of Karl Barth's Theological Method with Special Reference to the Doctrine of the Word of God." M.A., Nottingham University.
1961	"Barth on Creation, Part Three." Review of CD III/3. *Christianity Today* 5 (July 31): 949-50.
1962a	"Christ's Prophetic Office." Review of *CD IV/3. Christianity Today* 6 (June 22): 949.
1962b	"Two Studies of Barth." Review of *Karl Barth's Doctrine of Holy Scripture* by Klaas Runia and *The Significance of Barth's Theology* by Fred Klooster. *TSF Bulletin* 35:14-16.
1962c	"Barth's Free Man in Christ." Review of *CD III/4. Christianity Today* 6 (March 16): 598.
1967	*Karl Barth and the Christian Message.* Downers Grove: InterVarsity Press.
1969	*Philosophy and the Christian Faith.* Downers Grove: InterVarsity Press.
1976	*History, Criticism and Faith.* Editor. Leicester: InterVarsity Press.
1984	*Miracles and the Critical Mind.* Grand Rapids: Eerdmans Publishing Company.
1985	*Jesus in European Protestant Thought, 1778-1860.* Durham, North Carolina: Labyrinth Press.
1987	"A Cheer and a Half for Barth." *Reformed Journal* 37 (March): 18-20.
1990	*Christianity and Western Thought*, Volume 1. Downers Grove: Inter Varsity Press.

BROWN, Harold O. J.

1968	"The Bizarre Courage of the Modern Theologian." *Christianity Today* 12: 20 (July 5): 8-11.
1969	*The Protest of a Troubled Protestant.* Grand Rapids: Zondervan Publishing Company.

1984 *Heresies: The Image of Christ and the Mirror of Heresy and Orthodoxy from the Apostles to the Present.* Garden City, New York: Doubleday Publishing.

BROWN, William Adams
1902 *The Essence of Christianity: A Study in the History of Definition.* New York: Charles Scribner's Sons.
1906 *Christian Theology in Outline.* New York: Charles Scribner's Sons.

BRUNNER, Emil
1962 "Reply to Interpretation and Criticism." *The Theology of Emil Brunner.* Edited by Charles W. Kegley. New York: The Macmillan Company.

BRUNNER, Frederick Dale
1960 *A Theology of the Holy Spirit: The Pentecostal Experience and the New Testament Witness.* Grand Rapids: Eerdmans Publishing Company.

BUSCH, Eberhard
1976 *Karl Barth: His Life from Letters and Autobiographical Texts.* Second Revised Edition. Translated by John Bowden. Philadelphia: Fortress Press.

BUSH, Russ
1980 *Baptists and the Bible.* Edited with Tom Nettles. Chicago: Moody Press.

BUSWELL, J. Oliver
1950a *The Philosophy of F. R. Tennant.* New York: The Philosophical Library.
1950b "Karl Barth's Theology." Review of *Dogmatics in Outline. The Bible Today* 44: 261-271.
1950c "Geneva for the Faith: Karl Barth Questions the Truth." *The Bible Today* 45 (October): 3-9.
1960 *A Christian View of Being and Knowing.* Grand Rapids: Zondervan Publishing House.
1962 *A Systematic Theology of the Christian Religion*, 2 Volumes. Grand Rapids: Zondervan Publishing House.

BUTLER, Farley P., Jr.
1976 "Billy Graham and the End of Evangelical Unity." Ph.D. Dissertation, University of Florida.

CAMPBELL, Robert
1968 *Spectrum of Protestant Beliefs.* Editor. Milwaukee: Bruce Publishing Company.

Bibliography

CARNELL, Edward John
- 1948a   *An Introduction to Christian Apologetics.* Grand Rapids: Eerdmans Publishing Company.
- 1948b   "The Concept of Dialectic in the Theology of Reinhold Niebuhr." Th.D., Harvard University.
- 1949   "The Problem of Verification in Soren Kierkegaard." Ph.D., Boston University.
- 1950   *The Theology of Reinhold Niebuhr.* Grand Rapids: Eerdmans Publishing Company. Revised Edition, 1960.
- 1952   *A Philosophy of the Christian Religion.* Grand Rapids: Eerdmans Publishing Company.
- 1957   *Christian Commitment: An Apologetic.* New York: The Macmillan Company.
- 1959   *The Case for Orthodox Theology.* Philadelphia: The Westminster Press.
- 1960   *The Kingdom of Love and the Pride of Life.* Grand Rapids: Eerdmans Publishing Company.
- 1962   "Barth as Inconsistent Evangelical." *Christian Century* 79 (June 6): 713-714.
- 1965   *The Burden of Soren Kierkegaard.* Grand Rapids: Eerdmans Publishing Company.

CARPENTER, Joel A.
- 1980   "Fundamentalist Institutions and the Rise of Evangelical Protestantism, 1929-1942." *Church History* 49 (March): 62-75.
- 1984   "The Renewal of American Fundamentalism." Ph.D., Johns Hopkins University.
- 1986   "From Fundamentalism to the New Evangelical Coalition." *Evangelicalism and Modern America.* Edited by George Marsden. Grand Rapids: Eerdmans Publishing Company.
- 1987   *Making Higher Education Christian: The History, Purpose and Agenda of Evangelical Colleges in America.* Edited with Kenneth Shipps. Grand Rapids: Eerdmans Publishing Company.

CARSON, Donald A.
- 1983   *Scripture and Truth.* Edited with John D. Woodbridge. Grand Rapids: Zondervan Publishing House.
- 1986   *Hermeneutics, Authority, and Canon.* Edited with John D. Woodbridge. Grand Rapids: Zondervan Publishing House, Academia Books.

CARTER, Charles
- 1983   *A Contemporary Wesleyan Theology: Biblical, Systematic and Practical,* Two Volumes. Grand Rapids: Zondervan Publishing House.

CARTER, Paul A.
- 1956 *The Decline and Revival of the Social Gospel: Social and Political Liberalism in American Protestant Churches, 1920-40.* Ithaca, New York: Cornell University Press.
- 1968 "The Fundamentalist Defense of the Faith." *Change and Continuity in 20th Century America: the 1920s.* Edited by John Braeman, et. al. Columbus: Ohio State University Press.
- 1971 *The Spiritual Crisis of the Gilded Age.* DeKalb: Northern Illinois University Press.

CARWARDINE, Richard
- 1978 *Trans-atlantic Revivalism: Popular Evangelism in Britain and America, 1790-1865.* Westport, Connecticut: Greenwood Press.

CAUTHEN, Kenneth
- 1962 *The Impact of American Religious Liberalism.* San Francisco: Harper and Row.

CHAFER, Lewis Sperry
- 1947 *Systematic Theology*, 8 Volumes. Dallas, Texas: Dallas Theological Seminary.

CHILES, Robert E.
- 1965 *Theological Transition in American Methodism, 1790-1935.* New York: University Press of America.

CLARK, Gordon H.
- 1952 *A Christian View of Man and Things.* Grand Rapids: Eerdmans Publishing Company.
- 1956a "Honest Criticism." Review of *The Triumph of Grace* in *The Theology of Karl Barth* by G.C. Berkouwer. *Christianity Today* 1 (October 29).
- 1956b *What Presbyterians Believe.* Philadelphia: Presbyterian and Reformed Publishing Company.
- 1957a *Thales to Dewey: A History of Philosophy.* Boston: Houghton Mifflin Company.
- 1957b "The Bible As Truth." *BibliothecaSacra* 114:157-70.
- 1958 "Special Revelation as Rational." *Revelation and The Bible.* Edited by Carl F.H. Henry. Grand Rapids: Baker Book House.
- 1961 "Karl Barth: Teacher and Preacher." *Christianity Today* 5 (June 5): 784.
- 1962a *Religion, Reason and Revelation.* Philadelphia: Presbyterian and Reformed Publishing Company.
- 1962b "Barth's Critique of Modernism." *Christianity Today* 6 (January 1): 11-13.
- 1962c "More Questions on Barth's Views." *Christianity Today* 6 (January 5): 318-321.

	1962d	"Special Report: Encountering Barth in Chicago." *Christianity Today* 6 (May 11):35-6.
	1963	*Karl Barth's Theological Method.* Philadelphia: Presbyterian and Reformed Publishing Company.
	1964	*The Philosophy of Science and Belief in God.* Philadelphia: The Craig Press.
	1971	*Historiography: Secular and Religious.* Nutley, New Jersey: The Craig Press.
	1972	*The Johanine Logos.* Nutley, New Jersey: Presbyterian and Reformed Publishing Company.
	1973	*Three Types of Religious Philosophy.* Nutley, New Jersey: The Craig Press
	1982	*God's Hammer.* Trinity Foundation. Nutley, New Jersey: The Craig Press.

CLARKE, William Newton
  1898 *An Outline of Christian Theology.* New York: Charles Scribner's Sons.

CLOWNEY, Edmund
  1984 "Preaching the Word of the Lord: Cornelius Van Til, V.D.M. (Verbum Dei Ministerium)." *Westminster Theological Journal* 46:2 (Fall): 233-253.

COATES, Thomas
  1954 "Barth's Conception of the Authority of the Bible." *Concordia Theological Monthly* 25 (August): 595.
  1955 "Barthian Inversion: Gospel and Law." *Concordia Theological Monthly* 26 (July): 481-491.

COLE, Stewart
  1931 *The History of Fundamentalism.* New York: Richard Smith.

COLEMAN, Richard
  1980 *Issues of Theological Conflict: Evangelicals and Liberals.* Grand Rapids: Eerdmans Publishing Company.

CONNOR, Walter Thomas
  1926 *A System of Christian Doctrine.* Nashville: Broadman Press.
  1936 *Revelation and God: An Introduction to Christian Doctrine.* Nashville: Broadman Press.
  1945 *The Gospel of Redemption.* Nashville: Broadman Press.
  1949 *The Work of the Holy Spirit.* Nashville: Broadman Press.

CRITERION
  1963 "Questions to and Discussion with Dr. Karl Barth." *Criterion* (Winter): 11-18.

DAANE, James
- 1949 — Review of *The New Modernism* by Cornelius Van Til. *The Calvin Forum*
- 1951a — "Self Examination Expanded." *The Reformed Journal* 1: (March): 3-4, 12.
- 1951b — "A Progressive Theology." *The Reformed Journal* 1:7 (September): 10-12.
- 1952 — "Theological Dialecticism." *The Reformed Journal* 2:11 (November): 10-12; 2:12 (December): 9-12.
- 1954 — *A Theology of Grace: An Inquiry into and Evaluation of Dr. Cornelius Van Til's Doctrine of Common Grace.* Grand Rapids: Eerdmans Publishing Company
- 1955 — "A Theology of Grace."*The Reformed Journal* 5:3(March): 10-12; 5:4 (April).
- 1956 — "The Free Offer of the Gospel." *The Reformed Journal* 6:8 (September): 6-7.
- 1957 — "The State of Theology in the Church." *The Reformed Journal* 7:8 (September): 3-17.
- 1959 — "The Faith of the Church." Review of *The Faith of the Church*, by Karl Barth. *The Reformed Journal* 9:3 (March): 21-22.
- 1960a — "The Sovereignty of God." *The Reformed Journal* 10:3 (March): 13-15; 10:6 (June): 18-22.
- 1960b — "Divine Election Re-Examined." *The Reformed Journal* 10:9 (October): 9-11.
- 1960c — "Election and Arbitrariness." *The Reformed Journal* 10:10 (November): 15-17.
- 1960d — "Election: Concealed or Revealed?" *The Reformed Journal* 10:11 (December): 10-12.
- 1961a — "The Great Misconception." *The Reformed Journal* 11:1 (January): 13-15.
- 1961b — "Karl Barth on Chalcedon." Review of "Karl Barth on Chalcedon," by Cornelius Van Til. *The Reformed Journal* 11:9 (October): 21.
- 1962 — "Can We Learn From Karl Barth?" *The Reformed Journal* 12:4 (April): 7-9.
- 1963 — "Christianity and Barthianism." Review of *Christianity and Barthianism*, by Cornelius Van Til. *The Reformed Journal* 13:1 (January): 27-29.
- 1964a — "A Case of Rationalism." Review of *Predestination*, by Lorraine Boettner. *The Reformed Journal* 14:2 (February): 11-14.
- 1964b — "A Clear Overview." Review of *God Here and Now*, by Karl Barth. *Christianity Today* 8:18: 33-34.
- 1964c — "What Doctrine of Limited Atonement?" *The Reformed Journal* 14:10 (December): 13-16.
- 1965 — "What is Grace?" *The Reformed Journal* 15:9 (November): 20-23.
- 1968a — "In the Beginning Was Logic." *The Reformed Journal* 18 (August): 21-23.

1968b	"Accent on History." Review of *Accent on History*, by H.M. Kuitert. *The Reformed Journal* 18:12 (December): 11-14.
1972	"Faith or Fideism: What Authenticates the Bible?" *The Reformed Journal* 22 (September): 24-26.
1973	*The Freedom of God: A Study of Election and Pulpit.* Grand Rapids: Eerdmans Publishing Company.
1976	"The Odds on Inerrancy." *The Reformed Journal* 26: 10 (December): 5-6.
1977a	"Impoverished Evangelicals." *The Reformed Journal* 27:2 (February): 27-28.
1977b	"The Lust for Certitude." *The Reformed Journal* 27:3 (March): 26-27.
1977c	"Knowledge, Faith and Reason." Review of *God, Revelation and Authority*. Volume I, by Carl Henry. *The Reformed Journal* 27:4 (April): 26-27.
1978	"Dutch Treat." Review of *A Half Century of Theology*, by G.C. Berkower. *The Reformed Journal* 28:1 (January): 24-25.
1979	"Battling On." Review of *The Bible in the Balances*, by Harold Lindsell. *The Reformed Journal* 29:9 (September): 24-26.
1980a	*Preaching With Confidence*. Grand Rapids: Eerdmans Publishing Company.
1980b	"Looking for Jesus." *The Reformed Journal* 30:1 (January): 24.
1980c	"What is Truth?" Review of *God, Revelation and Authority*, Volume II, by Carl Henry. *The Reformed Journal* 30:5 (May): 27-29. Responses in 30:8 (August): 5-7 and 30:9 (September): 8-9.
1980d	"When More is Less." Review of *God, Revelation and Authority*, Volume IV, by Carl Henry. *The Reformed Journal* 30:10 (October): 27-8.
1981	"Bromiley's Introduction." Review of *Introduction to the Theology of Karl Barth*, by Geoffrey Bromiley. *The Reformed Journal* 31:10 (October): 28-29.
1983	"Barth as Paradigm." Review of *After Fundamentalism*, by Bernard Ramm. *The Reformed Journal* 33:5 (May): 26-7.

DAYTON, Donald

1971	Review of *The Theology of Karl Barth*, by Hans Urs Von Balthassar. *Christianity Today* 15 (February 12): 40.
1974a	"An American Revival of Karl Barth." *Reformed Journal* 24: 8 (October): 17-20; 24:9 (November): 24-26.
1974	Review of *Footnotes to a Theology*, Edited by H. Martin Rumscheidt. *Christianity Today* 19 (November 8).
1975	Review of *Theologie und Sozialismus: Das Beispiel Karl Barths*, by Friedrich-Wilhelm Marquardt. PostAmerican 4:1 (January): 30-31.
1976a	*Discovering an Evangelical Heritage*. San Francisco: Harper & Row.

	1976b	"Karl Barth and Radical Politics." A Review of *Karl Barth and Radical Politics*, by George Hunsinger. *Sojourners* 15 (December): 32-35.
	1978a	"Breaking Down the Barriers to Faith: Karl Barth's Determinative Influence on My Life." *Sojourners* 7:12 (December): 25-26.
	1978b	"Bibliographic Look at Barth." *Sojourners* 7 (December): 32-34.
	1985a	"Karl Barth and Evangelicalism: The Varieties of Sibling Rivalry." *TSF Bulletin* (May-June): 18-23.
	1985b	"The Use of Scripture in the Wesleyan Tradition." *The Use of the Bible in Theology: Evangelical Options*. Edited by Robert K. Johnston. Atlanta: John Knox Press.
	1987	*Theological Roots of Pentecostalism*. Grand Rapids: Zondervan Publishing Company.
	1991	"Some Doubts about the Usefulness of the Category 'Evangelical'." *The Variety of American Evangelicalism*. Edited by Donald Dayton and Robert K. Johnston. Knoxville: The University of Tennessee Press.

DENNIS, Lane
    1986   Francis A. Schaeffer: *Portraits of the Man and His Work*. Editor. Westchester, Illinois: Crossway Books.

DEVER, Mark
    1987   "Representative Aspects of the Theologies of John L. Dagg and James P. Boyce: Reformed Theology and Southern Baptists." Th.M. Thesis, The Southern Baptist Theological Seminary.

DIETER, Melvin
    1980   *The Holiness Revival of the Nineteenth Century*. Studies in Evangelicalism. Number 1. Metuchen, New Jersey: Scarecrow Press.

DOBSON, Edward.
    1985   *In Search of Unity: An Appeal to Fundamentalist and Evangelicals*. Nashville: Thomas Nelson Publishers.
    1986   The Fundamentalist Phenomenon: The Resurgence of Conservative Christianity. Second Edition. With Ed Hindson and Jerry Falwell. Grand Rapids: Baker Book House.

DOLLAR, George
    1973   *A History of Fundamentalism in America*. Greenville, South Carolina: Bob Jones University Press.

DOOYEWEERD, Herman
    1960   *In The Twilight of Western Thought*. University Series, Philosophical Studies. Nutley, New Jersey: Craig Press.

DYCK, Cornelius J.
    1981   *An Introduction to Mennonite History: A Popular History of the Anabaptists and the Mennonites.* Editor. Scottdale, Pennsylvania: Herald Press.

ELLER, Vernard
    1980   *Thy Kingdom Come: A Blumhardt Reader.* Editor. Grand Rapids: Eerdmans Publishing Company.
    1983a   *Towering Babble: God's People Without God's Word.* Elgin, Illinois: The Brethren Press.
    1983b   " 'Evangelical': Integral to Christian Identity?" *TSF Bulletin* (November December): 5-10.

ELLINGSON, Mark
    1988   *The Evangelical Movement: Growth, Impact, Controversy, Dialogue.* Minneapolis: Augsburg Publishing House.

ELLIS, William E.
    1985   *A Man of Books and A Man of the People: E.Y. Mullins and the Crisis of Moderate Southern Baptist Leadership.* Macon, Georgia: Mercer University Press.

ERICKSON, Millard
    1968   *The New Evangelical Theology.* Old Tappen, New Jersey: Revell.

FACKRE, Gabriel
    1973   *Do and Tell: Engagement Evangelism in the "70s."* Grand Rapids: Eerdmans Publishing Company.
    1983   "Narrative Theology: An Overview." *Interpretation* 37:4 (Fall): 340-52.
    1984a   *The Christian Story: A Narrative Interpretation of Basic Christian Doctrine.* Grand Rapids: Eerdmans Publishing Company.
    1984b   "Carl Henry's Reasoned Apologetic." *Theology Today* 41 (July): 198.

FEINBERG, Charles L.
    1958   *The Fundamentals for Today.* 2 Volumes. Editor. Grand Rapids: Kregel Publications. Third Publication of *The Fundamentals.*

FINDLAY, James
    1969   *Dwight L. Moody: American Evangelist, 1837-1899.* Chicago: University of Chicago Press.

FINNEY, Charles G.
    1988   *Lectures on Revival.* Minneapolis, Minnesota: Bethany House Publishers.

FLETCHER, William C.
　　1962　　*The Moderns*. Grand Rapids: Zondervan Publishing House.

FOSTER, Charles
　　1960　　*An Errand of Mercy: The Evangelical United Front, 1790-1837*. Chapel Hill, North Carolina: University of North Carolina Press.

FOWLER, Robert Booth
　　1982　　*A New Engagement: Evangelical Political Thought, 1966-76*. Grand Rapids: Eerdmans Publishing Company.

FULLER, Daniel P.
　　1965　　*Easter Faith and History*. Grand Rapids: Eerdmans Publishing Company.
　　1972　　*Give the Winds a Mighty Voice: The Story of Charles E. Fuller*. Waco, Texas: Word Books, Publishers.

FULLER SEMINARY
　　1976　　"The Authority of Scripture at Fuller." *Theology, News and Notes* (Special Issue)

FURNISS, Norman
　　1954　　*The Fundamentalist Controversy, 1918-1931*. New Haven: Yale University Press.

GARRET, James Leo
　　1983　　*Are Southern Baptists Evangelicals?* With E. Glenn Hinson and James E. Tull. Macon, Georgia: Mercer University Press.
　　1990a　　"Walter Thomas Connor." *Baptist Theologians*. Edited by Timothy George and David Dockery. Nashville: Broadman Press.
　　1990b　　*Systematic Theology*, Volume 1. Grand Rapids: Eerdmans Publishing Company.

GASPAR, Louis
　　1963　　*The Fundamentalist Movement*. Paris: Mouton and Company.

GATEWOOD, Willard B. Jr.
　　1969　　*Controversy in the 20's: Fundamentalism, Modernism, and Evolution: A Sourcebook with Introductions*. Nashville: Vanderbilt University Press.

GEISLER, Norman L.
　　1974　　*Philosophy of Religion*. Grand Rapids: Zondervan Publishing House.
　　1980　　*Inerrancy*. Editor. Grand Rapids: Zondervan Publishing House, Academia Books.

GEORGE, Timothy
  1985   "Systematic Theology at Southern Seminary." *Review and Expositor.* 82: 31f.
  1990   *Baptist Theologians.* Edited with David Dockery. Nashville: Broadman Press.

GERSTNER, John
  1960   *Reasons for Faith.* New York: Harper and Row.
  1975   "The Theological Boundaries of Evangelical Faith." *The Evangelicals: What They Believe, Who They Are, Where They Are Changing.* Nashville: Abingdon Press.

  1984   *Classical Apologetics: A Rational Defense of the Christian Faith and a Critique of Presuppositional Apologetics.* With R.C. Sproul and F. Duane Lindsey. Grand Rapids: Zondervan Publishing House. Academia Books.

GROUNDS, Vernon
  1956   "The Nature of Evangelicalism." *Eternity* (December): 21-29.

GUNTON, Colin E.
  1978   *Becoming and Being: The Doctrine of God in Hartshorne and Barth.* London: Oxford University Press.

HAKKENBERG, Michael
  1986   "The Battle Over the Ordination of Gordon H. Clark, 1943-1948." *Pressing Toward the Mark: Essays Commemorating Fifty Years of the Orthodox Presbyterian Church. 1936-1986.* Edited by Charles Dennison and Richard Gamble. Philadelphia: Committee for the Historian of the Orthodox Presbyterian Church.

HAMILTON, Kenneth
  1965   *Revolt Against Heaven: An Inquiry into Anti-Supernaturalism.* Grand Rapids: Eerdmans Publishing Company.
  1971a   *Words and the Word.* Grand Rapids: Eerdmans Publishing Company. Originally delivered as the Payton Lectures at Fuller Theological Seminary, Pasadena, California.
  1971b   "The New Evangelism." *Christianity Today* 15:9 (January 29): 4-7.

HANDY, Robert
  1955   "Fundamentalism and Modernism in Perspective." *Religion in Life* (Summer, 1955): 381-94
  1984   *A Christian America: Protestant Hopes and Historical Realities.* New York: Oxford University Press.

HARREL, David
1981 *Varieties of Southern Evangelicalism.* Editor. Macon, Georgia: Mercer University Press.
1985 *Oral Roberts: An American Life.* San Francisco: Harper and Row.

HARRIS, R. Laird
1943 "More Barthian Books: A Brief Discussion...." *Sunday School Times* 85 September): 746. Reprinted in *Christian Beacon* 9 (March, 1944):2.
1955 "Barthian Theology Today." *Reformation Review* 2 (April): 129-142.
1956 Review of *A Christian View of Science & Scripture,* by Bernard Ramm. *Bible Presbyterian Reporter* 1 (October): 7-8.
1963a "Barth and Eschatology." *Bulletin of the Evangelical Theological Society* 6:114-23.
1963b "The Evangelical Theological Society and Karl Barth." *The Evangelical Presbyterian Reporter* 8 (March): 6-7.

HATCH, Nathan
1984 *The Bible in America: Essays in Cultural History.* Edited with Mark Noll. New York: Oxford University Press.

HATFIELD, Mark O.
1971 *Conflict and Conscience.* Waco, Texas: Word Books, Publisher.
1976 *Between a Rock and a Hard Place.* Waco, Texas: Word Books, Publisher.

HENRY, Carl F. H.
1946 *Remaking the Modern Mind.* Grand Rapids: Eerdmans Publishing Company.
1947a *The Uneasy Conscience of Modern Fundamentalism.* Grand Rapids: Eerdmans Publishing Company.
1947b "The New Evangelicalism." *Christian Life and Times* 2:6: 13-15.
1949 *The Protestant Dilemma: An Analysis of the Current Impasse in Theology.* Grand Rapids: Eerdmans Publishing Company.
1950 *Fifty Years of Protestant Theology.* Boston: W.A. Wilde Company.
1951 *Personal Idealism and Strong's Theology.* Wheaton, Illinois: Von Kampen Press.
1956 "Why Christianity Today?" *Christianity Today* 1:1 (October 15): 20-23.
1957a *Evangelical Responsibility in Contemporary Theology.* Grand Rapids: Eerdmans Publishing Company.
1957b "Dare We Renew the Controversy?" *Christianity Today* 1 (June 24): 23f.

1957c	*Christian Personal Ethics*. Grand Rapids: Eerdmans Publishing Company.
1957d	*Contemporary Evangelical Thought*. Editor. Great Neck, New York: Channel Press.
1958	*Revelation and the Bible: Contemporary Evangelical Thought*. Editor. Grand Rapids: Baker Book House.
1960a	*Jesus of Nazareth: Savior and Lord*. Editor. London: Oxford University Press.
1960b	"Barth Among the Mind Changers: Some Unresolved Issues." *Christianity Today* 4 (February 15): 410.
1962	"Barth in the Balances." Review of *Christianity and Barthianism*, by Cornelius Van Til. *Christianity Today* 7 (December 21): 43.
1964	"The Deterioration of Barth's Defenses." *Christianity Today* (October 9): 16-19.
1966	*Frontiers in Modern Theology*. Chicago: Moody Press.
1967	*Evangelical at the Brink of a Crisis: Significance of the World Congress on Evangelism*. Waco, Texas: Word Books, Publisher.
1976	*Evangelicals In Search of Identity*. Waco, Texas: Word Books, Publisher.
1976-1983	*God, Revelation, and Authority*. Six Volumes. Waco, Texas: Word Books, Publisher.
1983	Review of *After Fundamentalism*, by Bernard Ramm. *TSF Bulletin* (May-June): 16.
1986a	*Confessions of a Theologian: an Autobiography*. Waco, Texas: Word Books, Publisher.
1986b	*Conversations with Carl F.H. Henry*. Lewiston, New York: Edwin Mellon Press.
1986c	"My Encounter with Karl Barth." *TSF Bulletin* 9:5 (May-June): 10.

HILL, Samuel Jr.
1980	*The South and North in American Religion*. Athens, Georgia: University of Georgia Press.
1981	"The Shape and Shapes of Popular Southern Piety." *Varieties of Southern Evangelicalism*. Edited by David Harrel. Macon, Georgia: Mercer University Press.

HINSON, E. Glenn
1971	"Southern Baptist Theological Seminary." *Encyclopedia of Southern Baptists*. Nashville: Broadman Press.
1979	"Eric Charles Rust: Apostle to an Age of Science and Technology." *Science, Faith and Revelation: An Approach to Christian Philosophy. Festschrift for Eric Charles Rust*. Edited by Robert E. Patterson. Nashville: Broadman Press.
1983	*Are Southern Baptists Evangelicals?* With James Leo Gareet and James E. Tull. Macon, Georgia: Mercer University Press.
1987	"Dale Moody: Bible Teacher Extraordinaire." *Perspective in Religious Studies* 14:4 (Winter): 3-18.

HOEKEMA, Anthony A.
  1979   Review of *Essentials of Evangelical Theology*, by Donald Bloesch. *Calvin Theological Journal* 14: 84-87.
  1986   *Created in God's Image*. Grand Rapids: Eerdmans Publishing Company.

HOEKSEMA, Herman
  1966   *Reformed Dogmatics*. Grand Rapids: Reformed Free Publishing Company.

HOFSTADTER, Richard
  1963   *Anti-Intellectualism in American Life*. New York: Knopf Publishing.

HOLIFIELD, E. Brookes
  1978   *The Gentleman Theologians: American Theology in Southern Culture, 1795-1860*. Durham, North Carolina: Duke University Press.

HOLLENWEGER, Walter
  1972   *The Pentecostals: The Charismat Movement in the Churches*. Minneapolis: Bethany Publishing House.

HOMRIGHAUSEN, Elmer George
  1934   *Come Holy Spirit: Sermons* by Karl Barth and Eduard Thurneysen. Translated by E.G. Homrighausen, G.W. Richards, and K.J. Ernst. New York: Round Table Press, Inc.
  1935   *God's Search for Man: Sermons* by Karl Barth and Eduard Thurneysen. Translated by E.G. Homrighausen, G.W. Richards and K.J. Ernst. Edinburgh: T. and T. Clark.
  1936   *Christianity in America: A Crisis*. New York: The Abingdon Press.

HONEYCUTT, Roy L.
  1986   "Biblical Authority: A Treasured Heritage." *Review and Expositor* 83: 605-622.

HOOD, Fred J.
  1980   *Reformed America: The Middle and Southern States, 1783-1837*. University of Alabama Press.

HUBBARD, David Allen
  1979   "Destined to Boldness: A Biography of an Evangelical Institution." The Ezra Squire Tipple Lectures, The Theological School, Drew University. Madison, New Jersey: Drew University.

HUGHES, Philip Edgecombe
  1966   *Creative Minds in Contemporary Theology*. Grand Rapids: Eerdmans Publishing Company.

HUMPHREYS, Fisher
　1990　　　"E.Y. Mullins." *Baptist Theologians*. Nashville: Broadman Press.

HUNSINGER, George
　1976　　　*Karl Barth and Radical Politics*. Editor. Philadelphia: Westminster Press.

HUNTER, James Davidson
　1983　　　*American Evangelicalism: Conservative Religion and the Quandary of Modernity*. New York: Rutgers University Press.
　1987　　　*Evangelicalism: The Coming Generation*. Chicago: University of Chicago Press.

HUTCHENS, Steven Mark
　1989　　　"Knowing and Being in the Context of the Fundamentalist Dilemma: A Comparative Study of the Thought of Karl Barth and Carl F.H. Henry." Th.D., Lutheran School of Theology.

HUTCHESON, Richard., Jr.,
　1981　　　*Mainline Churches and the Evangelicals: A Challenging Crisis?* Atlanta: John Knox Press.

HUTCHISON, William
　1976　　　*The Modernist Impulse in American Protestantism*. Cambridge: Harvard University Press.

JELLEMA, Dirk
　1957　　　"Abraham Kuyper's Attack on Liberalism." *Review and Politics* 19 (October): 472-485.

JEWETT, Paul
　1954　　　*Emil Brunner's Concept of Revelation*. London: James Clarke and Company.
　1961　　　*Emil Brunner: An Introduction to the Man and His Thought*. Downers Grove: InterVarsity Press.
　1971　　　*The Lord's Day: A Theological Guide to the Christian Day of Worship*. Grand Rapids: Eerdmans Publishing Company. Reprinted by Fuller Theological Seminary.
　1975　　　*Man as Male and Female: A Study in Sexual Relationships from a Theological Point of View*. Grand Rapids: Eerdmans Publishing Company.
　1978　　　*Infant Baptism and the Covenant of Grace*. Grand Rapids: Eerdmans Publishing Company.
　1985　　　*Election and Predestination*. Grand Rapids: Eerdmans Publishing Company.
　1991　　　*God, Creation, and Revelation: A Neo-Evangelical Theology*. Grand Rapids: Eerdmans Publishing Company.

JOHNSTON, Robert K.
 1979   *Evangelicals at an Impasse: Biblical Authority in Practice.*
           Atlanta: John Knox Press.
 1985   *The Use of the Bible in Theology: Evangelical Options.*
           Editor. Atlanta: John Knox Press.
 1991   "American Evangelicalism: An Extended Family." *The Variety of American Evangelicalism.* Edited by Donald Dayton and Robert Johnston. Knoxville: University of Tennessee Press.

JONES, Charles Edwin.
 1974   *Perfectionist Persuasion: The Holiness Movement and American Methodism, 1867-1936.* Metuchen, New Jersey: Scarecrow Press.

JONES, Robert L.
 1985   "Scripture and Theology: An Analysis of Bernard Ramm's Proposal to Adopt Karl Barth's Methodology." Th.M., Western Conservative Baptist Seminary.

JORDAN, Philip
 1982   *The Evangelical Alliance for the U.S.A., 1847- 1900.* Lewiston, New York: Edwin Mellen Press.

JORSTAD, Erling
 1970   *The Politics of Doomsday: Fundamentalists of the Far Right.* Nashville: Abingdon Press.
 1973   *The Holy Spirit in Today's Church: A Handbook of the New Pentecostalism.* Nashville: Abingdon Press.
 1981   *Evangelicals in the White House: The Cultural Maturation of Born Again Christianity, 1960-81.* Lewiston, New York: Edwin Mellen Press.
 1987   *The New Christian Right, 1981-88.* Lewiston, New York: Edwin Mellen Press.

JÜNGEL, Eberhard
 1976   *The Doctrine of the Trinity: God's Being is in Becoming.* Translated by Horton Harris. Grand Rapids: Eerdmans Publishing Company.

KANTZER, Kenneth
 1956a   "Karl Barth." *The Christian Graduate* 9:3: 124-126.
 1956b   "Barthianism." *The Christian Graduate* 9:4:185-195.
 1958a   "Revelation & Inspiration in Neo-Orthodox Theology." *BibliothecaSacra* 115 (1958): 120-127, 218-228, 302-312; 116 (1959): 15-29.
 1958b   "The Christology of Karl Barth." *Bulletin of the Evangelical Theological Society* 2:2: 25-28.
 1960a   "The Authority of the Bible." *The Word for This Century.* Edited by Merril C. Tenney. New York: Oxford University Press.

1975	"Unity and Diversity in Evangelical Faith." *The Evangelicals*. Edited by David Wells and John Woodbridge. Nashville: Abingdon Press.
1976	"Buswell as Theologian." *Presbyterion* 2 (1976): 67-94.
1978	"Evangelicals and the Inerrancy Question." *Evangelical Roots: A Tribute to Wilbur Smith*. Edited by Kenneth Kantzer. Nashville: Thomas Nelson Inc., Publishers.
1986	"Thank God for Karl Barth, But...." *Christianity Today* 30 (October 3): 14-15.

KAUFMAN, Daniel K.
1914   *Bible Doctrine: A Treatise on the Great Doctrines of the Bible*. Editor. Scottdale, Pennsylvania: Mennonite Publishing House.

KEGLEY, Charles William
1962   *The Theology of Emil Brunner*. Editor. New York: The Macmillan Company.

KELLEY, Dean
1972   *Why Conservative Churches are Growing: A Study in Sociology of Religion*. New York: Harper and Row.

KEYLOCK, Leslie R.
1988   "Meet Donald Bloesch." *Moody Monthly* (March): 61-63.

KING, Henry Churchill
1901   *Reconstruction in Theology*. New York: The Macmillan Company.

KLOOSTER, Fred H.
1951   *The Incomprehensibility of God in the Orthodox Presbyterian Conflict*. Franeker: T. Weaver.
1958   "Karl Barth's Doctrine of Reconciliation in *Church Dogmatics*." *Westminster Theological Journal* 20 (May): 170-184.
1959   "Aspects of the Soteriology of Karl Barth." *Bulletin of the Evangelical Theological Society* 2:2: 6-14.
1961   *The Significance of Barth's Theology: An Appraisal with Special Reference to Election and Reconciliation*. Grand Rapids: Baker Book House.
1962   "Karl Barth's Doctrine of the Resurrection."*Westminster Theological Journal* 24 (October): 137-172.
1975   "Jesus Christ: History & Kerygma, I and II." *Presbyterion* 1:23 50, 80-110. Republished in 1977 as *Quests for the Historical Jesus*. Grand Rapids: Baker Book House.
1979   "Predestination: A Calvinistic Note." *Perspectives on Evangelical Theology*. Edited by Stanley Gundry and Kenneth Kantzer. Grand Rapids: Baker Book House.

1984 "Revelation and Scripture in Existentialist Theology." *Challenges to Inerrancy: A Theological Approach.* Edited by Gordon Lewis and Bruce Demarest. Chicago: Moody Press.

1985 "Barth and the Future of Evangelical Theology." Review of *After Fundamentalism*, by Bernard Ramm. *Westminster Theological Journal* 47:2 (Fall): 301-317.

KRABBENDAM, Hendrick
1980 "B.B. Warfield vs. G.C. Berkouwer on Scripture." *Inerrancy.* Edited by Norman Geisler. Grand Rapids: Zondervan Publishing House. Academia Books.

1984 "The Functional Theology of G.C. Berkouwer." *Challenges to Inerrancy: A Theological Approach.* Edited by Gordon Lewis and Bruce Demarest. Chicago: Moody Press.

KRAUSE, C. Norman
1979a *Evangelicalism and Anabaptism.* Scottdale, Pennsylvania: Herald Press.

KROMMINGA, D.H.
1941 *The Sovereignty of God: Being the Proceedings of the American Calvinistic Conference, June, 1939.* Edited with Leonard DeMoore. Grand Rapids: Zondervan Publishing House.

KUHN, Harold B.
1946 Review of *The New Modernism* by Cornelius Van Til. *The Asbury Seminarian* 1:121-122.

1956 "Universalism in Today's Theology." *Christianity Today* 1:24 (September 16): 9.

KUIPER, R.B.
1959 *For Whom Did Christ Die?* Grand Rapids: Eerdmans Publishing Company.

KUKLICK, Bruce
1984 *Churchmen and Philosophers from Jonathan Edwards to John Dewey.* New Haven, Connecticut: Yale University Press.

LADD, George Eldon
1962 "The Resurrection and History." *Dialog* (Autumn, 1962): 55-56.

1967 *The New Testament and Criticism.* Grand Rapids: Eerdmans Publishing Company.

1975 *I Believe in the Resurrection of Jesus.* Grand Rapids: Eerdmans Publishing Company.

LASOR, William Sanford
1976 "Life Under Tension." *Theology, News and Notes*, Special Issue.

LEWIS, Edwin
1934 *A Christian Manifesto*. New York: The Abingdon Press.

LEWIS, Gordon R.
1976 *Testing Christianity's Truth Claims: Approaches to Christian Apologetics*. Chicago: Moody Press.
1987 *Integrative Theology*, Volume One. With Bruce Demarest. Grand Rapids: Zondervan Publishing House, Academia Press.
1990 *Integrative Theology*, Volume Two. With Bruce Demarest. Grand Rapids: Zondervan Publishing House, Academia Press.

LIGHTNER, Robert R.
1965 *Neo-Evangelicalism*. Findlay, Ohio: Dunham Publishing Company.
1979 *Neo-Evangelicalism Today*. Schaumberg, Illinois: Regular Baptist Press.
1986 *Evangelical Theology: A Survey and Review*. Grand Rapids: Baker Book House.

LINDSELL, Harold
1976 *The Battle for the Bible*. Grand Rapids: Zondervan Publishing Company.
1979 *The Bible in the Balance*. Grand Rapids: Zondervan Publishing Company.
1987 *The New Paganism: Understanding American Culture and the Role of the Church*. San Francisco: Harper and Row.

LIPPMAN, Walter
1934 *A Preface to Morals*. New York: The Macmillan Company.

LOETSCHER, Lefferts
1954 *The Broadening Church: A Study of Theological Issues in the Presbyterian Church since 1869*. Philadelphia: University of Pennsylvania Press.

LOEWEN, Harry
1988 *Why I am a Mennonite: Essays on Mennonite Identity*. Editor. Kitchener, Ontario: Herald Press.

LOEWEN, Howard John
1976 "Karl Barth and the Church Doctrine of Inspiration: An Appraisal for Evangelical Theology." Ph.D., Fuller Theological Seminary.

1985   *One Lord, One Church, One Hope and One God: Mennonite Confessions of Faith in North America: An Introduction.* Elkhurst, Indiana: Institute of Mennonite Studies.
1987   "The Anatomy of an Evangelical Type: An American Evangelical Response to Karl Barth's Theology." *Church, Word, and Spirit: Historical and Theological Essays in Honor of Geoffrey W. Bromiley.* Edited by James Bradley and Richard A. Muller. Grand Rapids: Eerdmans Publishing Company.

LOVELACE, Richard
1979   *Dynamics of Spiritual Life.* Downers Grove: InterVarsity Press.
1983   "Renewal and the Future of Evangelicalism." *Renewal* 3:3 (November): 1-12.

MACHEN, John Gresham
1923   *Christianity and Liberalism.* New York: The Macmillan Company.

MACKAY, John A.
1972a   "Toward an Evangelical Renaissance." *Christianity Today* 16:9 (February 4).
1972b   "Ecclesiastical Union But Evangelical Renaissance." *Christianity Today* 16:14 (April 14): 10-12.

MANWARING, Randle
1985   *From Controversy to Co-Existence: Evangelicals in the Church of England, 1914-1980.* Cambridge: Cambridge University Press.

MARSDEN, George
1980   *Fundamentalism and American Culture: The Shapina of 20th Century Evangelicalism, 1870-1925.* New York: Oxford University Press.
1983   "The Collapse of American Evangelical Academia." *Faith and Rationality: Reason and Belief in God.* Edited by Alvin Plantinga and Nicholas Wolterstorff. Notre Dame: University of Notre Dame Press.
1986   *Evangelicalism and Modern America.* Grand Rapids: Eerdmans Publishing Company.
1987   *Reforming Fundamentalism.* Grand Rapids: Eerdmans Publishing Company.

MARTIN, David
1978   *A General Theory of Secularity.* New York: Harper and Row.

MARTY, Martin
1969   *The Modern Schism: Three Paths to the Secular.* New York: Harper and Row.

	1971	*Righteous Empire: The Protestant Experience in America.* New York: Dial Press.
	1976	*A Nation of Behavers.* Chicago: University of Chicago Press.
	1986	*Modern American Religion: "The Irony of It All," 1893-1919.* Chicago: University of Chicago Press.
	1987	*Religion and Republic: The American Circumstance.* Boston: Beacon Press.

MATHEWS, Donald
    1977   *Religion in the Old South.* Chicago: University of Chicago Press.

MAY, Henry
    1959   *The End of American Innocence, 1912-1917.* New York: Knopf.
    1976   *The Enlightenment in America.* New York: Oxford University Press.

MAYER, Frederick
    1949   "Karl Barth and the Christian Conception of Revelation." *Concordia Theological Monthly* 20 (February): 127-134.

McCLENDON, James William, Jr.
    1986   *Ethics: Systematic Theology*, Volume One. Nashville: Abingdon Press.

McINTIRE, Carl
    1944   *Twentieth Century Reformation.* Collingswood, New Jersey: Christian Beacon Press.
    1949   Review of "Through Ecumenical Glasses," by Bela Vassady. *Christian Beacon* I (October 6): 8.
    1958   "The New Evangelicalism." *The Christian Beacon* (January 9): 1-8.

McKIM, Donald K.
    1986   *How Karl Barth Changed My Mind.* Editor. Grand Rapids: Eerdmans Publishing Company.
    1979   *The Authority & Interpretation of the Bible: An Historical Approach.* With Jack Rogers. San Francisco: Harper and Row.

McLOUGHLIN, William G.
    1959   *Modern Revivalism: Charles Grandison Finney to Billy Graham.* New York: Ronald Press.
    1968   *The American Evangelicals, 1800-1900, An Anthology.* Harper Torchbook Series. New York: Harper and Row.
    1970   *The Meaning of Henry Ward Beecher: An Essay on the Shifting Values of Mid-Victorian America, 1840-70.* New York: Knopf.

MEAD, Sidney
    1954   "Denominationalism: The Shape of Protestantism in America." *Church History* 23: (December): 291-320.
    1963   *The Lively Experiment: The Shaping of Christianity in America*. New York: Harper and Row.

MERRIT, Major John G.
    1986   "Fellowship in Ferment: A History of the Wesleyan Theological Society, 1965-1984." *Wesleyan Theological Journal* 21: 1,2 (Spring, Fall): 186-204.

MEYE, Robert
    1991   "Paul K. Jewett: An Appreciation." *Perspectives on Christology: Essays in Honor of Paul K. Jewett*. Edited by Marguerite Shuster and Richard A. Muller. Grand Rapids: Zondervan Publishing House.

MICKEY, Paul
    1980   *The Essentials of Wesleyan Theology: A Contemporary Affirmation*. Grand Rapids: Zondervan Publishing House.

MOBERG, David
    1972   *The Great Reversal: Evangelicalism versus Social Concern*. Philadelphia: J.B Lippincott.

MOHLER, Richard Albert, Jr.
    1989   *Evangelical Theology and Karl Barth: Representative Models of Response*. Ann Arbor, Michigan: University Microfilms International. Ph.D., The Southern Baptist Seminary.
    1990a   "Carl F. H. Henry." *Baptist Theologians*. Edited by Timothy George and David Dockery. Nashville: Broadman Press.
    1990b   "Bernard Ramm: Karl Barth and the Future of American Evangelicalism." *Perspectives in Religious Studies* 17 (Winter): 27-41.

MONSMA, Peter H.
    1937   *Karl Barth's Idea of Revelation*. Somerville: Somerset Press.

MONTGOMERY, John Warwick
    1962a   *The Shape of the Past: An Introduction to Philosophical Historiography*. Ann Arbor, Michigan: Edwards Publishing.
    1962b   "Barth in Chicago: Kerygmatic Strength, Epistemological Weakness." *Dialog* I (Autumn): 56-57.
    1963   "Karl Barth and Contemporary Theology of History." *Bulletin of the Evangelical Theological Society* 6: 39-49.
    1967   *Crisis in Lutheran Theology, Volumes 1 and 2*. Editor. Grand Rapids: Baker Book House.

| | 1969 | *Where is History Going? A Christian Response to Secular Philosophies of History.* Minneapolis: Bethany Fellowship. |
| | 1970 | *The Suicide of Christian Theology.* Minneapolis: Bethany Fellowship. |

MOODY, Dale
- 1947a "The Problem of Revelation and Reason in the Writing of Emil Brunner." Th.D., The Southern Baptist Theological Seminary.
- 1947b "An Introduction to Emil Brunner." *Review and Expositor* 44: 312-330.
- 1949 "The Crux of Christian Theology." *Review and Expositor* 46: 164-180.
- 1950 "Present Theological Trends." *Review and Expositor* 47 (January): 3-20.
- 1962 "The Church in Theology." *The Theology of Emil Brunner.* Edited by Charles W. Kegley. New York: The Macmillan Company.
- 1964 *The Hope of Glory.* Grand Rapids: Eerdmans Publishing Company.
- 1967 *Baptism: Foundation for Christian Unity.* Philadelphia: Westminster Press.
- 1968 *The Spirit of the Living God: The Biblical Concepts Interpreted in Context.*
- 1981 *The Word of Truth: A Summary of Christian Doctrine Based on Biblical Revelation.* Grand Rapids: Eerdmans Publishing Company.
- 1988 "Perspectives on Scripture and Tradition: A Response by Dale Moody." *Perspectives in Religious Studies* 15: (Spring): 5-16.

MOORE, Laurence R.
- 1988 *Religious Outsiders and the Making of Americans.* New York: Oxford University Press.

MUELLER, David L.
- 1958 "Karl Barth's Critique of the Anthropological Starting Point in Theology." Ph.D., Duke University.
- 1969 *An Introduction to the Theology of Albrecht Ritschl.* Philadelphia: Westminster Press.
- 1972 *Karl Barth. Makers of the Modern Theological Mind.* Waco, Texas: Word Books, Publisher.
- 1974 "Changing Conceptions of 'Christian Experience' in Representative Contemporary Protestant Theologians." *Perspectives in Religious Studies* 1:2 (Fall): 165-186.
- 1987 "The Contributions and Weaknesses of Karl Barth's View of the Bible." *The Proceedings of the Conference on Biblical Inerrancy, 1987.* Nashville, Tennessee: Broadman Press.

1988   "The Whale and the Elephant: Barth and Bultmann in Dialogue." *Perspectives in Religious Studies* 15:3 (Fall): 197-214.
1989   "Karl Barth and the Heritage of the Reformation." *Review and Expositor* 81: 45-64.
1990   *The Foundation of Karl Barth's Doctrine of Reconciliation: Jesus Christ Crucified and Risen*. Lewiston, New York: Edwin Mellen Press.

MUELLER, J. Theodore
1934   "The Christian Doctrine in its Modern Setting." *The History of Christian Doctrine*. By Ernest H. Klotsche. Burlington, Iowa: The Lutheran Literary Board.
1963   "The Question of Christian Certainty." *Christianity Today* 7 (August 2): 22.

MUELLER, William A.
1954   "Karl Barth's View of the Virgin Birth." *Review and Expositor* 51: 508-21.

MULLINS, Edgar Y.
1924   *Christianity At The Cross Roads*. New York: George H. Doran Company.
1925   *Baptist Beliefs*. Valley Forge, Pennsylvania: The Judson Press. Original Edition, 1912.
1947   *The Christian Religion in Its Doctrinal Expression*. Valley Forge, Pennsylvania: The Judson Press.

MURCH, James Deforest
1956   *Cooperation Without Compromise: A History of the National Association of Evangelicals*. Grand Rapids: Eerdmans Publishing Company.

MURPHY, Cullen
1981   "Protestantism and the Evangelicals." *Wilson Quarterly* 5:4 (Autumn): 105-116.

NASH, Ronald
1963   *The New Evangelicalism*. Grand Rapids: Zondervan Publishing Company.
1968   *The Philosophy of Gordon H. Clark: A Festschrift*. Editor. Philadelphia: Presbyterian and Reformed Publishing Company.

NELSON, Rudolph
1987   *The Making and Unmaking of an Evangelical Mind*. Cambridge: Cambridge University Press.

NICHOL, John Thomas
1966   *Pentecostalism*. New York: Harper and Row.

NICHOLS, David R.
1984 "The Search for Pentecostal Structure in Systematic Theology." *Pneuma* 6:2 (Fall): 57-76.

NICOLE, Roger
1984 "The Neo-Orthodox Reduction." *Challenges to Inerrancy: A Theological Response*. Edited by Gordon Lewis and Bruce Demarest. Chicago: Moody Press.
1987 "How to Deal with Those Who Differ from Us." *The PCA Messenger* (November): 9.

NOLL, Mark
1982 *The Bible in America: Essays in Cultural History*. Edited with Nathan Hatch. New York: Oxford University Press.
1983 *The Princeton Theology, 1812-1921*. Grand Rapids: Baker Book House.
1986 *Between Faith and Criticism: Evangelicals, Scholarship and the Bible in America*. New York: Harper and Row.

OCKENGA, Harold John
1960 "Resurgent Evangelical Leadership." *Christianity Today*. (October 10): 11-15.
1978 "From Fundamentalism Through New Evangelicalism to Evangelicalism." *Evangelical Roots: A Tribute to Wilbur Smith*. Edited by Kenneth Kantzer. Nashville: Thomas Nelson Publishers.

PACKER, James
1957 Review of *The Triumph of Grace in the Theology of Karl Barth*, by G.C. Berkower. *The Christian Graduate* 10 (June): 101-102.
1958 *Fundamentalism and the Word of God*. Grand Rapids: Eerdmans Publishing Company.
1961 "Barth's Dogmatics." Review of *Church Dogmatics III/1*. *Christianity Today* 5 (January 16): 334.
1986a "No Little Person." *Reflections on Francis Schaeffer*. Edited by Ronald Ruegesegger. Grand Rapids: Eerdmans Publishing Company.
1986b "What Do You Mean When You Say God?" *Christianity Today* 30:13 (September 19): 27-31.
1988 "God the Image-Maker." *Christian Faith and Practice in the Modern World*. Edited by Mark Noll and David Wells. Grand Rapids: Eerdmans Publishing Company.

PALMA, Robert J.
1983 *Karl Barth's Theology of Culture: Freedom of Culture for the Praise of God*. Pittsburgh Theological Monographs, Volume Two. Allison Park, Pennsylvania: Pickwick Publications.
1984 "Thomas F. Torrance's Reformed Theology." *Reformed Review*. 38: 2-46.

PATTERSON, Robert E.
    1979   *Science, Faith and Revelation. Festschrift in Honor of Eric Charles Rust.* Editor. Nashville: Broadman Press.
    1983   *Carl F.H. Henry.* Makers of the Modern Theological Mind Series. Waco, Texas: Word Books, Publisher.
    1990a   "Eric C. Rust." *Baptist Theologians.* Edited by Timothy George and David Dockery. Nashville: Broadman Press.
    1990b   "Modern Science and Contemporary Biblical Interpretation: Ramm's Contribution." *Perspectives on Religious Studies* 17 (Winter): 55-67.

PEARLMAN, Meyer
    1937   *Knowing the Doctrines of the Bible.* Springfield, Missouri: Gospel Publishing House.

PEIPKORN, Arthur Karl
    1979   *Profiles in Belief: The Religious Bodies of the United States and Canada.* Volumes 3,4. New York: Harper and Row.

PIERARD, Richard
    1970   *The Unequal Yoke: Evangelical Christianity and Political Conservativism.* Philadelphia: J.B. Lippincott.

PINNOCK, Clark
    1971a   *Biblical Revelation: The Foundation of Christian Theology.* Chicago: Moody Press. 1985 Reprint: Phillipsburg, New Jersey: Presbyterian and Reformed Publishing Company.
    1971b   *Set Forth Your Case.* Chicago: Moody Press.
    1976   "The Inerrancy Debate Among the Evangelicals." *Theology, News and Notes* (1976, Special Issue).
    1977   "Karl Barth and Christian Apologetics." *Themelios* 2 (May): 66-71.
    1978   "Joyful Partisan of the Kingdom: A Reflection on Karl Barth." *Sojourners* (December): 26.
    1982   Review of *The Word of Truth*, by Dale Moody. *Christian Scholars Review* 11: 159-160.
    1984   *The Scripture Principle.* San Francisco: Harper and Row.
    1986a   "Assessing Barth for Apologetics." *How Karl Barth Changed My Mind.* Edited by Donald McKim. Grand Rapids: Eerdmans Publishing Company.
    1986b   "Schaeffer on Modern Theology." *Reflections on Francis Schaeffer.* Edited by Ronald Ruegesegger. Grand Rapids: Eerdmans Publishing Company.
    1990   "Bernard Ramm: A Postfundamentalist Theologian Coming to Terms with Enlightenment Modernity." *Perspectives on Religious Studies* 17 (October): 42-54.

POLLOCK, John Charles
    1964   *The Keswick Story: The Authorized History of the Keswick Convention.* Chicago: Moody Press.

	1979	*Billy Graham: Evangelist to the World: An Authorized Biography of the Decisive Years.* San Francisco: Harper and Row.
	1983	*Moody.* Chicago: Moody Press.

POLMAN, A.D.R.
    1960   *Karl Barth.* Translated by Calvin D. Freeman. Philadelphia: Presbyterian and Reformed Publishing Company.

POLLEY, Max E.
    1979   "Revelation in the Writings of H. Wheeler Robinson and Eric Rust: A Comparative Study." *Science, Faith and Revelation: An Approach to Christian Philosophy.* Edited by Robert E. Patterson. Nashville: Broadman Press.

POSTAMERICAN
    1975   "A Conversation with Young Evangelicals." *PostAmerican* 4:1 (January): 6-13.
    1978   "Two Sowing Christ." *PostAmerican* 7:12 (December): 3-4.

PREUS, Robert D.
    1960a   "The Word of God in the Theology of Karl Barth." *Concordia Theological Monthly* 31 (February): 105-115.
    1960b   "Prolegomena According to Karl Barth." *Concordia Theological Monthly* 31 (March): 174-183.
    1962   "The Word of God in the Theology of Lutheran Orthodoxy." *Concordia Theological Monthly* 33: 469-483.
    1967   "The Doctrine of Revelation in Contemporary Theology." *Crisis in Lutheran Theology.* Edited by John Warwick Montgomery. Grand Rapids: Baker Book House.

PRICE, Robert M.
    1981   "The Crisis of Biblical Authority: The Setting and Range of the Current Evangelical Crisis." Ph.D., Drew University.
    1988   "Clark H. Pinnock: Conservative and Contemporary." *Evangelical Quarterly* 88: 157-183.

PROCEEDINGS
    1987   *Proceedings of the Conference on Biblical Inerrancy, 1987.* Nashville, Tennessee: Broadman Press.

PRUITT, Ray
    1981   *The Fundamentals of the Faith.* Cleveland, Tenessee: White Wing Publishing House.

QUEBEDEAUX, Richard
    1974   *The Young Evangelicals.* New York: Harper & Row.
    1976   *The Worldly Evangelicals.* New York: Harper and Row.
    1983   *The New Charismatics II.* New York: Harper and Row.

RAMM, Bernard L.
1947 "The Idealisms of Jeans and Eddington in Modern Physical Theory." M.A., University of Southern California.
1949 *Problems in Apologetics*. Portland, Oregon: Western Conservative Baptist Seminary.
1950a "An Investigation of Some Recent Efforts to Justify Metaphysical Statements from Science with Special Reference to Physics." Ph.D., University of Southern California.
1950b *Protestant Biblical Interpretation*. Boston: W.A. Wilde and Company.
1953a *Protestant Biblical Evidences*. Chicago:Moody Press.
1953b *Types of Apologetic Systems: An Introductory Study to the Christian Philosophy of Religion*. Wheaton: Van Kampen Press.
1954 *The Christian View of Science and Scripture*. Grand Rapids: Eerdmans Publishing Company. Reprinted 1984 by Eerdmans.
1956 *Protestant Biblical Interpretation*. Second Revised Edition. Boston: W.A. Wilde and Company.
1957a *The Pattern of Authority*. Grand Rapids: Eerdmans Publishing Company. Reprinted under the title *The Pattern of Religious Authority*.
1957b "The Major Theses of Neo-Orthodoxy." *Eternity* 8 (June): 18-19, 33.
1957c "Karl Barth: The Theological Avalanche." *Eternity* 8 (July): 4-5, 48.
1960 *The Witness of the Spirit*. Grand Rapids: Eerdmans Publishing Company.
1961a *Special Revelation and the Word of God*. Grand Rapids: Eerdmans Publishing Company.
1961b *Varieties of Christian Apologetics*. Grand Rapids: Baker Book House.
1963 "Biblical Faith and History." *Christianity Today* 7:11: 5, 7-8.
1965 "The Labyrinth of Contemporary Theology." *Christianity Today* 9:21: 6-7.
1966a "The Continental Divide in Contemporary Theology." *Christianity Today* 10:1: 14-17.
1966b *A Handbook of Contemporary Theology*. Grand Rapids: Eerdmans Publishing Company.
1970 *Protestant Biblical Interpretation*. Third Revised Edition. Grand Rapids: Baker Book House.
1972 *The God Who Makes a Difference: A Christian Appeal to Reason*. Waco, Texas: Word Books, Publisher.
1973 *The Evangelical Heritage: A Study in Historical Theology*. Waco, Texas: Word Books, Publisher.
1974 "Scripture as a Theological Concept." *Review and Expositor* 71 (Spring): 149-161.
1976 Review of *Holy Scripture*, by G.C. Berkower. Christian Scholars Review 6: 215-216.

1977a	*The Devil, Seven Wormwoods, and God*. Waco, Texas: Word Books, Publisher.
1977b	"Is 'Scripture Alone' The Essence of Christianity?" *Biblical Authority*. Edited by Jack Rogers. Waco, Texas: Word Books, Publisher.
1983	*After Fundamentalism: The Future of Evangelical Theology*. San Francisco: Harper and Row.
1985a	*An Evangelical Christology: Ecumenic and Historic*. Nashville: Thomas Nelson Publishers.
1985b	*Offense to Reason: The Theology of Sin*. San Francisco: Harper and Row.
1986a	"Barth As A Person and As A Theologian." *TSF Bulletin* 9 (May-June): 4-6.
1986b	"Helps From Karl Barth." *How Karl Barth Changed My Mind*. Edited by Donald McKim. Grand Rapids: Eerdmans Publishing Company.

RAND, James Freeman
 1953 "The Barthian Doctrine of Salvation." *BibliothecaSacra* 110: 111-120, 220-226.

REYMOND, Robert
 1968 *Introductory Studies in Contemporary Theology*. Philadelphia: Presbyterian and Reformed Publishing Company.
 1969 *The Justification of Knowledge*. Philadelphia: Presbyterian and Reformed Publishing Company.

RICE, John R.
 1959 "Fuller Seminary's Carnell Sneers at Fundamentalism." *Sword of the Lord* (October 30); reprinted in John R. Rice, *Earnestly Contending for the Faith*. Murfreesboro, Tennessee: Sword of the Lord Foundation.

RICHARDS, George Warren
 1934 *Beyond Fundamentalism and Modernism: The Gospel of God*. New York: Charles Scribner's Sons.

RIVIERE, William T.
 1934 "The Philosophy Underlying Barth's Theology." *BibliothecaSacra* 91: 154-176.
 1936 "The 'Word' and Some Notions of Today." *Evangelical Quarterly* 8: 407. BibliothecaSacra 93: 288-300.

ROBERTS, Richard H.
 1989 "The reception of the theology of Karl Barth in the Anglo-Saxon world: history, typology and prospect." *Karl Barth: Centenary Essays*. Edited by Stephen W. Sykes. Cambridge: Cambridge University Press.
 1991 *A Theology on its Way? Essays on Karl Barth*. Edinburgh: T&T Clark.

ROBINSON, William Childs
    1928   "The Theology of Karl Barth: A Protest and Standpoint." *Union Seminary Quarterly Review* 40 (October): 105-122.
    1935   "The Lost Chord in Current Protestantism." *BibliothecaSacra* 92: 206-218.

ROGERS, Jack
    1967   *Scripture in the Westminster Confession: A Problem of Historical Interpretation for American Presbyterianism*. Grand Rapids: Eerdmans Publishing Company.
    1974   *Confessions of a Conservative Evangelical*. Philadelphia: The Westminster Press.
    1977   *Biblical Authority*. Editor. Waco, Texas: Word Books, Publisher.
    1978   "A Third Alternative: Scripture, Tradition, and Interpretation in the Theology of G.C. Berkower." *Scripture, Tradition, and Interpretation: Essays Presented to Everett Harrison*. Edited by Ward Gasque and William Sanford LaSor. Grand Rapids: Eerdmans Publishing Company.
    1979   *The Authority and Interpretation of the Bible: An Historical Approach*. With Donald McKim. San Francisco: Harper and Row.

ROLSTON, Holmes
    1933   *A Conservative Looks to Barth and Brunner: An Interpretation of Barthian Theology*. Nashville: Cokesbury Press.

ROSENBERG, Ellen M.
    1989   *The Southern Baptists: A Subculture in Transition*. Nashville: University of Tennessee Press.

RUDNICK, Milton
    1966   *Fundamentalism and the Missouri Synod: A Historical Study of Their Interaction and Mutual Influence*. St. Louis: Concordia Publishing House.

RUEGESEGGER, Ronald W.
    1986   *Reflections on Francis Schaeffer*. Editor. Grand Rapids: Zondervan Publishing Company.

RUMSCHEIDT, H. Martin
    1972   *Footnotes to a Theology: The Karl Barth Colloquium of 1972*. Editor. Waterloo, Ontario: Corporation for the Publication of Academic Studies in Religion in Canada.
    1986   *The Way of Theology in Karl Barth: Essays and Comments*. Editor. Allison Park, Pennsylvania: Pickwick Publications.

RUNIA, Klaas
    1958   "Karl Barth on Man in His Time." *Reformed Theological Review* 17 (February): 1-11. 1959" Authority of the Confession: Barthian and Reformed View." *Reformed Theological Review* 18: 6-20.
    1962   *Karl Barth's Doctrine of Holy Scripture*. Grand Rapids: Eerdmans Publishing Company.
    1965   "Karl Barth and His Theology: An Introduction." *Themelios* 2:2; 3:1.
    1967   "Barth's View on Scripture." *Themelios* 4:1.
    1969   "Karl Barth, 1886-1968: His Place in History." *Christianity Today* 14 (December 5): 6-9.
    1982   "Karl Barth's Christology." *Christ the Lord*. Edited by Harold H. Rowden. Downers Grove: InterVarsity Press.

RUSSEL, C. Allyn
    1976   *Voices of American Fundamentalism: Seven Biographical Sketches*. Philadelphia: The Westminster Press.

RUST, Eric Charles
    1947   *A Christian Understanding of History*. London: Lutterworth Press.
    1953   *Nature and Man in Biblical Thought*. London: Lutterworth Press.
    1962   *Salvation History: A Biblical Interpretation*. Richmond, Virginia: John Knox Press.
    1963   *Towards a Theological Understanding of History*. New York: Oxford University Press.
    1967   *Science and Faith: Towards a Theological Understanding of Nature*. New York: Oxford University Press.
    1981   "Theological Emphases of the Past Three Decades." *Review and Expositor* 78 (Spring): 259f.
    1982   *The Word and the Words: Toward a Theology of Preaching*. Macon, Georgia: Mercer University Press.

RYRIE, Charles Caldwell
    1956   *Neo-orthodoxy: An Evangelical Evaluation of Barthianism. Revised 1972*. Chicago: Moody Press.
    1986   *Basic Theology*. Wheaton: Victor Books.

SANDEEN, Ernest
    1970   *The Roots of Fundamentalism: British and American Millenarianism, 1800-1930*. Chicago: University of Chicago Press.

SAULS, Ned
    1979   *Pentecostal Doctrines: A Wesleyan Approach*. Dunn, North Carolina: Heritage Press.

SCAER, David P.
    1979   "Theological Developments Since World War II." *The History of Christian Doctrine,* Revised Edition. By Ernest H. Klotsche. Grand Rapids: Baker Book House.

SCHAEFFER, Edith
    1969   *L'Abri.* Wheaton: Tyndale House.

SCHAEFFER, Francis A.
    1950   *The New Modernism (Neo-Orthodoxy) and the Bible.* Philadelphia: The Independent Board for Presbyterian Foreign Missions.
    1968a   *Escape from Reason.* Downers Grove: InterVarsity Press.
    1968b   *The God Who Is There.* Downers Grove: InterVarsity Press.
    1970   *The Church at the End of the Twentieth Century.* Downers Grove: InterVarsity Press.
    1972   *He Is There and He Is Not Silent.* Wheaton: Tyndale House Publishers.
    1973   "Why and How I Write My Books." *Eternity* 24 (March): 64f.
    1976a   *How Should We Then Live?* Old Tappen, New Jersey: Fleming H. Revell.
    1976b   "Watershed of the Evangelical World." *United Evangelical Action* 35 (Fall): 19-23.
    1979   *Whatever Happened to the Human Race?* Old Tappan, New Jersey: Fleming H. Revell.
    1981   *A Christian Manifesto.* Westchester, Illinois: Crossway Books.
    1984   *The Great Evangelical Disaster.* Westchester, Illinois: Crossway Books.
    1990   *Francis A. Schaeffer: Trilogy: The Three Essential Books in One Volume.* Westchester, Illinois: Crossway Books.

SHELLEY, Bruce
    1967   *Evangelicalism in America.* Grand Rapids: Eerdmans Publishing Company.
    1981   *A History of Conservative Baptists.* Wheaton: Conservative Baptist Press.
    1986   "The Rise of Evangelical Youth Movements." *Fides et Historia* 18 (January): 47-63.

SHEPPARD, Gerald
    1977   "Biblical Hermeneutics: The Academic Language of Evangelical Identity." *Union Seminary Quarterly Review* (Winter, 1977): 81-94.

SIDER, Ronald
    1974   *The Chicago Declaration.* Carol Stream, Illinois: Creation House.

Bibliography

1979   "Evangelicalism and the Mennonite Tradition." *Evangelicalism and Anabaptism*. Edited by C. Norman Krause. Scottdale, Pennsylvania: Herald Press.

SIMS, John A.
1979   *Edward John Carnell: Defender of the Faith*. Washington, D.C.: University Press of America.

SMEDES, Lewis B.
1962   "Does Karl Barth Believe in the Resurrection of Christ?" *The Reformed Journal* 12:4 (April): 21-22. Barth
1966   "G.C. Berkower." *Creative Minds in Contemporary Theology*. Edited by Philip E. Hughes. Grand Rapids: Eerdmans Publishing Company.
1970   *All Things Made New: A Theology of Man's Union with Christ*. Grand Rapids: Eerdmans Publishing Company.
1987   "The Distinctives of Fuller Theological Seminary." *Ministry and the Miraculous: A Case Study at Fuller Theological Seminary*. Editor. Pasadena: Fuller Seminary.

SMEND, Rudolph
1972   "Parrhesia." *Footnotes to a Theology*. Edited by H. Martin Rumscheidt. Waterloo, Ontario: Corporation for the Publication of Academic Studies.

SMITH, Gary Scott
1985   *The Seeds of Secularization: Calvinism, Culture, and Pluralism in America, 1870-1915*. Grand Rapids: Eerdmans Publishing Company.

SMITH, H. Sheldon
1955   *Changing Concepts of Original Sin: A Study in American Theology Since 1750*. New York: Charles Scribner's Sons.

SMITH, Timothy
1956   *Revivalism and Social Reform: American Protestantism on the Eve of the Civil War*. Harper Torchback. New York: Harper Brothers.
1962   *Called Unto Holiness, the Story of the Nazarenes: The Formative Years*. Kansas City: Nazarene Publishing House.
1986   "The Evangelical Kaleidoscope and the Call to Christian Unity." *Christian Scholars Review* 15: 125-140.
1987   "Evangelical Christianity and American Culture." *A Time To Speak: The Evangelical Jewish Encounter*. Edited by A. James Rudin and Marvin R. Wilson. Grand Rapids: Eerdmans Publishing Company.

SMITH, Wilbur
1946   *Therefore Stand*. Shepherd Illustrated Classics Edition, 1981. New Canaan, Connecticut: Keats Publishing.

1950 "Introduction." *Protestant Biblical Interpretation*, by Bernard Ramm. Boston: W.A. Wilde Company.

SMYTH, Newman
1902 *Through Science to Faith*. New York: Charles Scribner's Sons.

SPITTLER, Russel
1976 *Perspectives on the New Pentecostalism*. Grand Rapids: Baker Book House.
1985 "Scripture and the Theological Enterprise: View from a Big Canoe." *The Use of the Bible in Theology: Evangelical Options*. Edited by Robert K. Johnston. Atlanta: John Knox Press.

SPROSS, Daniel B.
1985 "The Doctrine of Sanctification in Karl Barth." *Wesleyan Theological Journal* 20:2 (Fall): 54-76.

SPROUL, R.C.
1982 *Reason to Believe*. Grand Rapids: Zondervan Publishing House.
1984 *Classical Apologetics: A Rational Defense of the Christian Faith and a Critique of Presuppositional Apologetics*. With John Gerstner and Arthur Lindsey. Grand Rapids: Zondervan Publishing House, Academia Books.

STACKHOUSE, Max
1982 "Religious Right: New? Right?" *Commonweal* 29 (January): 52-56.

STEARNS, Miner Broadhead
1948 "Barth and the Barthians." *BibliothecaSacra* 105: 59-81.
1949 "A Conservative Interviews Barth." *BibliothecaSacra* 106: 196-199.

STEVENSON, Herbert
1963 *Keswick's Authentic Voice: Sixty-five Dynamic Addresses Delivered at the Keswick Convention, 1875-1957*. Grand Rapids: Baker Book House.

STIVER, Danny R.
1900 "Dale Moody." *Baptist Theologians*. Edited by Timothy George and David Dockery. Nashville: Broadman Press.

STOB, Henry
1957a "The Mind of the Church." *The Reformed Journal* 7:3 (March): 3-6.
1957b "The Mind of Safety." *The Reformed Journal* 7:4 (April): 4-9.

	1957c	"The Militant Mind." *The Reformed Journal* 7:6 (June): 3-7; 7:7 (August): 3-6; 7:9 (October): 13-17.
	1961	"The Positive Mind." *The Reformed Journal* 11:3 (March): 5-9.
	1962	"Themes in Barth's Ethics." *The Reformed Journal* 12:4 (April): 19-23.

STOEFFLER, Earnest
    1965   *The Rise of Evangelical Pietism.* E.J. Brill.

STONEHOUSE, Ned
    1946   *The Infallible Word.* Edited with Paul Wooley. A Symposium by the members of the Faculty of Westminster Theological Seminary. Philadelphia: Presbyterian Guardian Publishing Corporation.
    1954   *John Gresham Machen: A Biographical Memoir.* Grand Rapids: Eerdmans Publishing Company.

STREIKER, Lowell
    1972   *Religion and the New Majority: Billy Graham, Middle America, and the Politics of the 70's.* With Gerald Strober. New York: Association Press.

SWEET, Leonard I.
    1984   "The 1960's: The Crisis of Liberal Christianity and the Public Emergence of Evangelicalism." *Evangelicalism and Modern America.* Edited by George Marsden. Grand Rapids: Eerdmans Publishing Company.

SWEET, William W.
    1944   *Revivalism in America: Its Origin, Growth and Decline.* New York: Charles Scribner's Sons.

SYKES, Stephen W.
    1979   "The Study of Barth." *Karl Barth: Studies of His Theological Method.* Edited by Stephen W. Sykes. New York: Oxford University Press. The Clarendon Press.
    1986   "Introduction." *The Way of Theology in Karl Barth: Essays and Comments.* Edited by H. Martin Rumscheidt. Allison Park: Pickwick Publications.
    1989   *Karl Barth: Centenary Essays.* Editor. Cambridge: Cambridge University Press.

SZASZ, Morton
    1982   *The Divided Mind of Protestant America, 1880-1930.* University of Alabama Press.

THIESSEN, Henry Clarence
    1949   *Lectures in Systematic Theology.* Grand Rapids: Eerdmans Publishing Company.

THOMPSON, David L.
1984 "Presidential Address: Kuhn, Kohlberg and Kinlaw: Reflections for Over-serious Theologians." *Wesleyan Theological Journal* 19:1 (Spring): 7-25.

THOMPSON, JOHN
1986 *Theology Beyond Christendom; Essays on the Centenary of the Birth of Karl Barth, May 10, 1886.* Allison Park, Pennsylvania: Pickwick Publications.

TIMNER, John
1969 "G.C. Berkower: Theologian of Confrontation and Co-Relation." *The Reformed Review* (December): 17-22.

TRUEBLOOD, Elton
1948 *Alternative to Futility.* New York: Harper and Brothers Publishers.
1952 *Your Other Vocation.* New York: Harper and Brothers Publishers.
1961 *The Company of the Committed.* New York: Harper and Row, Publishers.

VANDER STELT, John
1978 *Philosophy and Scripture: A Study in Old Princeton and Westminster Theology.* Marlton, New Jersey: Mack Publishing Company.

VAN TIL, Cornelius
1931 Review of *Karl Barth's Theology* by A.S. Zerbe. *Christ Today, A Presbyterian Journal* 1:10 (February): 13.
1936 Review of *A Christian Manifesto* by Edwin Lewis. *Presbyterian Guardian* 1: 191.
1937a "Karl Barth on Scripture." *Presbyterian Guardian* 3: 137.
1937b "Karl Barth on Creation." *Presbyterian Guardian* 3: 204.
1937c "Karl Barth and Historic Christianity." *Presbyterian Guardian* 4: 108.
1938a "Changes in Barth's Theology." *Presbyterian Guardian* 5: 221.
1938b "More Barthianism at Princeton." Review of *Christianity in America: A Crisis* by Elmer Homrighausen. Presbyterian Guardian 5 (February): 26-27.
1946 *The New Modernism: An Appraisal of the Theology of Barth and Brunner.* Philadelphia: Presbyterian and Reformed Publishing Company.
1948a "Christianity and Crisis Theology." *Presbyterian Guardian* 17: 69.
1948b "More New Modernism at Old Princeton." *The Presbyterian Guardian* 18: 166f.
1948c Review of *Kirchliche Dogmatik*, II/2 and III/1. *Westminster Theological Journal.* 9: 131-138.

1948d	"Introduction." *The Inspiration and Authority of the Bible, by B.B. Warfield*. Philadelphia: Presbyterian and Reformed Publishing Company.
1949	*An Introduction to Systematic Theology*, Two Volumes. Class Syllabus. Westminster Theological Seminary.
1950	Review of *Karl Barth en de Kinderdoop* by G.C. Berkower. *Westminster Theological Journal* 11: 77-80.
1951	Review of *De striid tegen de analogia entis in de theologie van Karl Barth* by Feisser. *Westminster Theological Journal* 12: 162-166.
1954a	"Dimensionalism or the Word: Comments on the Theology of John A. Mackay." *Presbyterian Guardian* 23: 105f.
1954b	"Has Karl Barth Become Orthodox?" *Westminster Theological Journal* 16 (May): 135-181.
1954c	Review of *Karl Barth's Church Dogmatics: An Introductory Report* by Otto Webber. *Westminster Theological Journal* 16:237.
1955a	*The Defense of the Faith*. Philadelphia: Presbyterian and Reformed Publishing Company. Third Revised Edition, 1967.
1955b	*Christianity and Idealism*. Philadelphia: Presbyterian and Reformed Publishing Company.
1955c	Review of *De triomf der genade in de theologie van Karl Barth* by G.C. Berkower. *Westminster Theological Journal* 18: 58f.
1958a	"Barth's View of Man." *Christianity Today* 2 (February 3): 34.
1958b	Review of *Church Dogmatics* II/2. *Westminster Theological Journal* 21: 75-78.
1959a	"What of the New Barth?" *Christianity Today* 3 (June 8): 5-7.
1959b	Review of *Kirchliche Dogmatik* IV/1,3. *Westminster Theological Journal* 22: 64-69.
1959c	"What About Karl Barth?" *Eternity* 10 (September): 21.
1960	"Karl Barth on Chalcedon." *Westminster Theological Journal* 22 (May): 147-166.
1961	"Christian and Theistic Evidences." Class Syllabus. Westminster Theological Seminary.
1962a	*Barth's Christology*. International Library of Philosophy and Theology. Philadelphia: Presbyterian and Reformed Publishing Company.
1962b	*Christianity and Barthianism*. Philadelphia: Presbyterian and Reformed Publishing Company.
1964a	*Karl Barth and Evangelicalism*. Philadelphia: Presbyterian and Reformed Publishing Company.
1964b	*Christian Theistic Evidences*. Class Syllabus. Westminster Theological Seminary.
1969a	*A Christian Theory of Knowledge*. Phillipsburg, New Jersey: Presbyterian and Reformed Publishing Company.
1969b	*The Sovereignty of Grace*. Phillipsburg, New Jersey: Presbyterian and Reformed Publishing Company.

> 1969c   "Karl Barth: His Message to Us." *The Banner* 104 (July 4): 4-5.
> 1971   "My Credo." *Jerusalem and Athens: Critical Discussions on the Philosophy and Apologetics of Cornelius Van Til.* Phillipsburg, New Jersey: Presbyterian and Reformed Publishing Company.
> 1972   *Common Grace and the Gospel.* Nutley, New Jersey: Presbyterian and Reformed Publishing Company. Contains 1947 Edition of *Common Grace.*
> 1974   *The Great Debate Today.* Phillipsburg, New Jersey: Presbyterian and Reformed Publishing Company.
> 1975   *The New Synthesis Theology of the Netherlands.* Nutley, New Jersey: Presbyterian and Reformed Publishing Company.

VASSADY, Bela
> 1951   *The Main Traits of Calvin's Theology.* Grand Rapids: Eerdmans Publishing Company.
> 1965   *Christ's Church: Evangelical, Catholic and Reformed.* Grand Rapids: Eerdmans Publishing Company.
> 1985   *Limping Along: Confessions of a Pilgrim Theologian.* Grand Rapids: Eerdmans Publishing Company.

VESEY, Laurence
> 1976   *The Emergence of the American University.* Chicago: University of Chicago Press.

VON BALTHASAR, Hans Urs
> 1971   *The Theology of Karl Barth.* Translated by John Drury. New York: Holt, Rinehart, and Winston.

VOSKUIL, Dennis N.
> 1980   "America Encounters Barth, 1919-1939." *Fides et Historia* 12 (Spring): 61-74.

WACKER, Grant
> 1986   "Uneasy in Zion: Evangelicals in Postmodern Society." *Evangelicalism and Modern America.* Edited by George Marsden. Grand Rapids: Eerdmans Publishing Company.

WALDVOGEL, Edith
> 1977   "The 'Overcoming Life': A Study in the Reformed Evangelical Origins of Pentecostalism." Ph.D., Harvard University.
> 1979   "The 'Overcoming Life': A Study in the Reformed Evangelical Origins of Pentecostalism." *Pneuma* 1:1 (Spring): 7-19.

WALLIS, Jim
> 1976   *Agenda for Biblical People: A New Focus for Developing a Life-Style of Discipleship.* New York: Harper and Row.

Bibliography

WALVOORD, John
- 1946   Review of *The New Modernism*, by Cornelius Van Til. *BibliothecaSacra* 103: 488.
- 1957   "What's Right About Fundamentalism?" *Eternity* (June): 6-7, 34-35.
- 1968   "The Pragmatic Confirmation of Scriptural Authority." *The Bible: The Living Word of Revelation*. Edited by Merril C. Tenney. Grand Rapids: Zondervan Publishing House.

WARFIELD, Benjamin Breckenridge
- 1927   *Revelation and Inspiration. The Works of Benjamin B. Warfield*, Volume 1. New York: Oxford University Press. Reprinted by Baker Book House, 1981.
- 1931   *Perfectionism: Part One. The Works of Benjamin B. Warfield*, Volume 7. New York: Oxford University Press. Reprinted by Baker Book House, 1981.
- 1932   *Perfectionism: Part Two. The Works of Benjamin B. Warfield*, Volume 8. New York: Oxford University Press. Reprinted by Baker Book House, 1981.

WEBBER, Robert
- 1978a   *The Orthodox Evangelicals: Who They Are and What They Are Saying*. Edited with Donald Bloesch. Nashville: Thomas Nelson Publishers.
- 1978b   *Common Roots: A Call to Evangelical Maturity*. Grand Rapids: Zondervan Publishing House.

WEBER, Timothy
- 1987   *Living in the Shadow of the Second Coming: American Premillennialism, 1875-1982*. Chicago: University of Chicago Press.

WEISBERGER, Bernard
- 1958   *They Gathered at the River: The Story of the Great Revivalists and Their Impact Upon Religion in America*. Boston: Little, Brown and Company.

WELLS, David
- 1975   *The Evangelicals: What They Believe, Who They Are, Where They Are Changing*. Edited with John Woodbridge. Nashville: Abingdon Press.
- 1985   *Reformed Theology in America*. Editor. Grand Rapids: Baker Book House.

WENGER, John Christian
- 1946   *Introduction to Theology: an interpretation of the doctrinal content of Scripture, written to strengthen a childlike faith in Christ*. Scottdale, Pennsylvania: Herald Press.
- 1979   "The Inerrancy Controversy Within Evangelicalism." *Evangelicals and Anabaptism*. Edited by C. Norman Krause. Scottdale, Pennsylvania: Herald Press.

1981	"The Mennonite Church." *An Introduction to Mennonite History*. Edited by Cornelius J. Dyck. Scottdale, Pennsylvania: Herald Press.

WIEBE, Robert
    1967   *The Search for Order, 1877-1920*. New York: The Macmillan Company.

WILEY, H. Orton
    1943   *Christian Theology*, 3 Volumes. Kansas City, Missouri: Nazarene Publishing House.
    1947   *Introduction to Christian Theology*. Kansas City, Missouri: Nazarene Publishing House.

WILLIAMS, Ernest S.
    1953   *Systematic Theology*, 3 Volumes. Edited by Frank Boyd. Springfield, Missouri: Gospel Publishing House.

WILLIAMS, J. Rodman
    1965   *Contemporary Existentialism and Christian Faith*. Englewood Cliffs, New Jersey: Prentice-Hall.
    1971   *The Era of the Spirit*. Plainfield, New Jersey: Logos.
    1988   *Renewal Theology: God, The World and Redemption. Systematic Theology From a Charismatic Perspective*. Grand Rapids, Michigan: Zondervan Publishing House.
    1990   *Renewal Theology: Salvation, The Holy Spirit, and Christian Living*. Grand Rapids, Michigan: Zondervan Publishing House.

WILSON, Bryan
    1966   *Religion in Secular Society*. London: C.A. Watts.
    1982   *Religion in Sociological Perspective*. New York: Oxford University Press.

WINTER, Ralph
    1970   *The Twenty-Five Unbelievable Years: 1945 to 1969*. Pasadena, California: Christian Mission Books, William Carey Library.

WOOD, Lawrence
    1980   *Pentecostal Grace*. Wilmore, Kentucky: Francis Asbury Press.
    1986   "Defining the Modern Concept of Self-Revelation: Toward a Synthesis of Barth and Pannenberg." *Asbury Theological Journal* 41:2 (Fall): 85-105.

WOODBRIDGE, Charles
    1969   *The New Evangelicals*. Charlottesville, South Carolina: Bob Jones University Press.

WOODBRIDGE, John
  1975   *The Evangelicals: What They Believe, Who They Are, Where They Are Changing.* Edited with David Wells. Nashville: Abingdon Press.
  1983   *Biblical Authority: A Critique of the Rogers/McKim Proposal.* Grand Rapids: Zondervan Publishing House.

WOODWARD, Kenneth
  1982   "Guru of Fundamentalism." *Newsweek* 102 (November 1): 88.

WUTHNOW, Robert
  1983   *The New Christian Right: Mobilization and Legitimation.* Edited with Robert C. Liebman. Hawthorne, New York: Aldine.
  1988   *The Restructuring of American Religion: Society and Faith Since World War II.* Princeton: Princeton University Press.

YANCEY, Philip
  1979   "Francis Schaeffer: a Prophet for Our Time?" *Christianity Today* 23 (March): 17.

YODER, John Howard
  1957   "The Nature of the Unity We Seek: A Historic Free Church View." *Religion in Life* (Spring): 215ff.
  1958   *The Ecumenical Movement and the Faithful Church.* Scottdale: Mennonite Publishing House.
  1962   *Die Gesprache zwischen Taufern und Reformatoren in der Schweiz.* Karlsruhe: Mennonitische Geschichtsverein.
  1964a   *The Pacifism of Karl Barth.* Washington, D.C.: The Church Peace Mission.
  1964b   *Christian Witness to the State.* Newton, Kansas: Faith and Life Press.
  1968a   *Taufertun und Reformation im Gesprach.* Zurich: EVZ Verlag.
  1968b   *Preface to Theology: Christology and Theological Method.* Elkhart, Indiana: Goshen Biblical Seminary.
  1968c   "The Free Church Ecumenical Style." *Quaker Religious Thought* 10: 29ff.
  1970   *Karl Barth and the Problem of War.* Nashville: Abingdon Press.
  1972a   *The Original Revolution: Essays on Christian Pacifism.* Scottdale, Pennsylvania: Herald Press.
  1972b   *The Politics of Jesus: Vivit Agnus Noster.* Grand Rapids: Eerdmans Publishing Company.
  1973   *The Legacy of Michael Sattler.* Translator and Editor. Scottdale, Pennsylvania: Herald Press.
  1975   "The Disavowal of Constantine: An Alternative Perspective on Interfaith Dialogue." *Tantur Year Book* 1975/1976: 47-68.

1977	*The Schleitheim Confession (1527)*. Translator and Editor. Scottdale, Pennsylvania: Herald Press.
1980	"Could There Be a Baptist Bishop?" *Ecumenical Trends* (Graymoor) 9:7 (July/August): 104ff.
1981	"Anabaptist Origins in Switzerland." "Persecution and Consolidation." "A Summary of the Anabaptist Vision." *An Introduction to Mennonite History*. Edited by Cornelius J. Dyck. Scottdale, Pennsylvania: Herald Press.
1984	*The Priestly Kingdom: Social Ethics as Gospel*. Notre Dame, Indiana: University of Notre Dame Press.
1985	"The Use of the Bible in Theology." *The Use of the Bible in Theology: Evangelical Options*. Edited by Robert K. Johnston. Atlanta: John Knox Press.
1987	*The Fullness of Christ: Paul's Revolutionary Vision of Universal Ministry*. Elgin, Illinois: Brethren Press.
1989	*Balthasar Hubmaier, Theologian of Anabaptism*. Edited with H. Wayne Pipkin. Scottdale, Pennsylvania: Herald Press.

ZERBE, A.S.
1930	*Karl Barth's Theology*. Cleveland: Central Publishing House.

INDEX

Aquinas, Thomas 57, 67
Alexander, Archibald 94
Allis, Oswald T. 97
American Council of Christian Churches 32
Anabaptist
    Primary Discussion 243-248
    Other References 212, 42n5, 110n16, 249n9
Anderson, Ray Sherman
    Definition of Evangelicalism 1,167
    Primary discussion 166-175
    Other references 147
Anselm 117, 151, 188, 202, 203, 229
Apologetics
    Importance in Evangelicalism 44-45, 108n1
    Evidentialist, Empiricist 47, 90-97
    Presuppositionalist 47-48, 70-73, 80-81, 95
    Verificationist 142-143, 177, 179, 188-189
    Rationalistic (criticized) 116, 141, 162, 201-202, 245
    See Barth, Apologetics
    See Orthodoxy, Scholasticism
Arminian, Arminianism 10-11, 21, 212
Associations, Societies and Councils
    American Council of Christian Churches 32
    Biblical Witness Caucus (U.C.C.) 36
    Christian Holiness Association 235
    Evangelical Alliance 42n5
    Evangelical Theology Group
        American Academy of Religion 193, 245
    Evangelical Theological Society 29, 65, 91, 97, 108n2, 154
    Federal Council of Churches 13, 137
    Fellowship of Evangelical Lutheran Laity and Pastors...................................36
    Good News Movement (U.M.C.) 36
    Independent Fundamental Churches of America...25
    International Council of Christian Churches...64
    International Council on Biblical Inerrancy..........................34, 42n10, 65, 66
    National Association of Evangelicals 28, 29, 32, 34
    New England Fellowship 28
    Presbyterian Lay Committee 36
    Presbyterians United for Biblical Concern 36
    Society for Pentecostal Studies 233
    Wesleyan Theological Society 34, 103, 235
    World Christian Fundamentals Association...15-16

World Congress on Evangelism 79
World Council of Christian Churches 64, 137, 221, 245
World Evangelical Fellowship..200
See Missionary Organizations, Societies
Augustine 60, 73, 80, 151, 156, 190, 225, 226
Awakening, Great 2, 41n5, 195
Ayer, A.J..93
Azusa Street Revival 19

Ballie, Donald and John 219, 222, 223
Barmen Declaration 240
Barnhouse, Donald Grey 28, 55
Barr, James 2-3, 45
Barth, Karl
    Activism, Actualism 52-54, 56-57, 109n5, 170-171
    Apologetics 53-54, 74-76, 127, 143, 188-189,
                                                   201-202, 224-225
    Analogy of Being 50, 53, 57, 87, 119, 128, 151, 156
    Anselm...117, 150, 188, 229
    Anthropology..53, 157-158, 173-174, 189-190
    Baptism..157, 226
    Contact with Evangelicals 64, 97, 109n7, 109n9, 220, 227
    Development of thought................................57-58, 85-86, 117-118, 149-151,
                                                                228-229
    Ethics 240-241, 244-247, 248n1,
    Election 62, 120, 130-131, 149-150, 158-
                                                                159,163-165, 174, 204-205,
                                                                                    210n19, 231
    Hermeneutics 125, 140, 170, 201
    Holy Spirit 234, 236
    History 52, 54, 55, 62, 87, 93, 100, 128-
                                                          120, 130, 151-152, 156
    Natural Theology 53, 75, 150, 231
    See Barth, Revelation
    Objectivism, criticized 203-205, 236-237
    Philosophical Presuppositions 44, 48, 50-54, 57, 63, 68-69, 74-
                                                            75, 84, 85, 87-88, 112, 116-119,
                                                           133-134, 150-151, 200-202
    Revelation
        View Criticized 50-54, 75-77, 85-88, 92-93, 96,
                                                    98, 127, 134, 151, 171, 179, 181-
                                                    182, 184, 186-188, 237
        View Affirmed 117-119, 120, 121, 125-126, 128
                                                    139-140, 150-151, 154-155, 163,
                                                    165, 169-170, 181-182, 184, 187-
                                                    188, 200-202, 229-230, 232
    Sabbath 157
    Science of theology 75, 119, 144, 150, 172, 182
    Sin, view of 129-130, 174, 189-190

Index 235

Soteriology, Christology 61-62, 117, 119, 132, 149-150,
  (Christomonism)   158-159, 171, 172-173, 184,
                                    203-204, 225, 229-231
Supralapsarianism 130, 159
Time 56, 109n5
Trinity 54, 109n5, 132, 157, 158, 164,
                                    169, 171, 221, 224, 230, 244
Universalism 131, 159, 204-205, 209n10
Veiling, Unveiling 119, 136
Bavinck, Herman 47, 60, 122, 123, 211
Bebbington, Bruce 42
Beecher, Lyman 10
Beegle, Dewey 42n10
Bell, L. Nelson 78
Bender, Harold 244, 249n9
Berger, Peter 13
Berkhof, Louis
  Primary Discussion 59-60
  Other references 20, 43, 164
Berkower, Gerrit Cornelius
  Primary Discussion 121-134
  Criticism of Van Til 55, 133-135
  Other references .... xviii, xix, 20, 57, 113, 114, 150,
                          166, 167, 171, 185, 187, 189,
                   208n4, 209n15, 210n19, 231, 232
Bettis, Joseph 209n10, 241
Bible Conferences, Bible Schools *See* Schools, Colleges,
  Seminaries 15-17
Biblical Realism 222, 246, 247
Biblicism 2-3, 16, 18, 19, 21, 38
Bloesch, Donald
  Primary Discussion 191-204
  Definition of Evangelicalism 195-197, 198
  Leadership in Evangelicalism 191-192, 194
  Other references .... xix, 42n10, 167, 176, 210n23,
                                           248n1
Blumhardt, Christoph 242
Boettner, Loraine 164
Boice, James 109n7
Bolich, Gregory .... xiv-xviii
Bonhoeffer, Dietrich 169, 171
Bouma, Clarence 138
Boyce, James P. 216
Bratt, James 20-21, 42, 59
Brightman, Edgar 142-143
Bromiley, Geoffrey
  Primary discussion 114-121
  Other references .... xvi, xix, 42n10, 55, 114, 141, 147,
                                 160, 166, 185, 208n3
Brown, Colin
  Primary discussion 147-152

Other references 166, 208n2, 209n15
  Brown, Harold O.J. 110n12
  Brown, William Adams 8
  Brunner, Emil 50, 53,85, 86 144, 152-154, 156,
                                                        180, 183, 204, 209n17, 218, 219,
                                                        220, 221, 223, 234
  Bryan, William Jennings 24
  Bultmann, Rudolph 85, 87-88, 92, 117, 182, 190, 227,
                                                                               234
  Buswell, J. Oliver
    Primary discussion 63-65
    Other references 43, 94, 109n8
  Calvin, Calvinism
    Nineteenth Century Decline 8-12
    Evangelical Advocacy 42n9, 50, 59, 60, 61, 80, 108n2,
                                                    126, 137, 151, 166, 180, 181, 182,
                                                    188, 198, 199, 200, 201, 205, 211,
                                                             216, 222, 225-226
  Carnell, Edward John
    Primary discussion 141-146
    Other references 29, 45, 46, 70, 84, 87, 137, 140,
                                                          152, 160, 177, 199, 215
  Carpenter, Joel 2, 27
  Carter, Charles 110n15
  Cartesian 168, 169
  Catholic, Catholicism
    Pentecostals 36
    Fundamentalist Critique 50, 57, 122
    Evangelical Advocacy 194
  Chafer, Lewis Sperry 102, 215
  Charismatic
    Renewal Movements 36-37, 38-39
    Theology 18-19, 233-234
  Chicago Call 193
  Chicago Declaration 35-36, 238, 240
  Christianity Today 29, 30, 33, 65, 73, 78, 79, 85, 91,
                                                   97,115, 117, 118, 120, 145, 148,
                                                   160, 163, 192, 238
  Christian Reformed Church
    History 20, 21, 42n8, 42n9, 59
    Theology, Barth reception 59-62, 121-134, 159-165
  Civil War 7, 8, 14, 22
  Clark, Gordon
    Primary discussion 70-77
    Other references .... xvii, 43, 63, 83, 87, 90, 109n10,
                                                   122, 133, 141, 142, 145, 146, 152,
                                                   159, 164, 184, 185
  Common Sense Realism 6-7, 90
  Connor, W.T. 104-107, 216
  Coats, Thomas 110n13

Index

Cranmer, Thomas 116
Custodial Ideal 5-7, 13
Daane, James
   Primary discussion ....159 - 166
   Other references 176, 208n6, 210n19
Dagg, John L. 11
Darrow, Clarence 24
Darwin, Charles 8
Dayton, Donald
   Primary discussion 238-242
   Definition of Evangelicalism 1, 41n5, 212, 242, 255
   Roots of Pentecostalism 19
"Death of God" Theology 69, 88, 92, 94
DeHaan, Martin 28
Demarest, Bruce 110n12
Denominations
   Anglican (Epsicopal) 10, 115, 160
   Assemblies of God 27, 28, 34
   Baptist, American (or Northern) 4, 10, 11, 14, 17, 22, 26, 27-28, 153
   Baptist, Conservative 26, 138
   Baptist, General Association of Regular Baptists..25
   Baptist, General Conference..177
   Baptist, Southern Baptist Convention 4, 22, 25, 27, 28, 34, 104-106, 214-232
   Bible Presbyterian Church 64
   Brethren in Christ 243
   Christian and Missionary Alliance 19
   Christian Reformed Church 13, 20-21, 34, 45, 59-61, 160-166
   Church of God (Anderson, Indiana) 18
   Church of the Nazarene 27, 28, 34, 102
   Congregationalist (19th century) 22, 10, 11
   Evangelical and Reformed Church 193
   Evangelical Free Church 97, 167
   Free Methodist 18
   Lutheran Church, Missouri Synod 20, 91, 110n13
   Methodist 10, 17-19, 22, 36, 37, 39
   Orthodox Presbyterian Church 25, 46, 63, 70-71
   Pentecostal Holiness Church 39
   Pilgrim Holiness Church 18
   Presbyterian Church, U.S.A. 4, 10-11, 14, 36, 77, 135, 136-137, 153, 193
   United Church of Christ...36, 37, 193
Dialectical Theology........................50-54, 57, 62-63, 67-70, 74, 84, 87, 88, 98-99, 143-144, 151, 154, 162, 171, 201-202, 229
Dispensationalism
   History 15-17
   Influence on Evangelicalism 15-16, 215, 220
   Reception of Barth 99-101, 102
Dobson, Edward 32, 176

Dooyeweerd, Herman 90
Dort, Synod of 61
Du Plessis, David 38
Dutch Reformed
    History 20-21, 42n8, 42n9, 58-59
    Barth reception 43-63, 114, 121-134, 159-166

Ecumenism, ecumenical 136-138, 140, 195, 220-221, 245
Edwards, Jonathan 11, 94, 211
Eerdmans Publishing House 20, 208n2, 208n6
Eller, Vernard 249n8
Ellingson, Mark 1-2, 42n1
Enlightenment 6, 185-186, 189
Epistemology
    Evangelical positions 72-73
    See Apologetics
    See Barth, Philosophical Presuppositions
Establishment of religion 5
Evangelical Alliance 42n6
Evangelical Theological Society 29, 91, 97, 154
Evangelicalism
    Boundary confusion 35-36
    Consensus, Nineteenth Century 5-7
    Definitions 3-5, 41-42
    Distinguishing characteristics 6-7, 41-42
    Dominant traditions 4, 14-22, 42
    Establishment Evangelicals 35, 238, 241
    New Evangelicalism 29-41, 111-114, 135, 147, 192-193
    Renewal Movements 36-39, 191-192
    Young Evangelicals 33, 238, 241
Evolution 8-9, 14, 24, 178

Fackre, Gabriel 37, 80, 193
Falwell, Jerry 65
Family resemblances 6, 42n4
Feuerbach, Ludwig 55
Fideism 94-95, 96-97, 188, 202
Finney, Charles 2, 10-11, 233
Fletcher, William 110n12
Flew, Antony 93
Forsyth, P.T. 106, 181, 217
Frontier 6, 22
Fuller, Charles 28, 135, 138
Fuller, Daniel 109n7
Fuller Theological Seminary 29, 33, 34, 76, 115, 206, 135-175

Fundamentalism
    Bible conferences, Bible schools 14-15, 27-28
    Criticism by Evangelicals 149, 196
        See Orthodoxy, Scholasticism
    Definition, redefinition 3-4, 14, 24, 30-31, 40-41, 43

Index

Dominant Traditions 4, 14-22
Evolution controversies 24
Fundamentalist image 24-25
Fundamentalist pattern 23-25, 26, 39-41, 43, 111, 251
Heresy trials, controversies 9, 13, 14, 21
History, Origins 3-4, 5-22
Resurgence 26-28, 29
Separation 24-26, 43, 111
Two-party system 8, 9-10, 13-14, 26

Garret, James Leo 249n2
Geisler, Norman 42n10, 108n1
George, Timothy 216
Gerstner, John
  Primary discussion 94-95
  Other references 41n3, 43, 46, 97, 108n1
Geschichte 44, 55-57, 62, 85, 87, 93, 172,
                                                                                               191, 209n14, 218
Gilkey, Langdon 231
Graham, Billy 15, 28, 29, 33, 35, 38, 78, 85, 113,
                                                                                               136, 215, 238
Gunton, Colin 109n5

Hamilton, Kenneth 193
Handy, Robert 5, 7
Harris, R. Laird 43, 109n6, 209n14
Hegel, G.W.F. 50-52, 67-68
Henry, Carl F.H.
  Primary discussion 78-88
  Evangelical spokesman 28, 30, 33, 35, 37, 78-79
  God, Revelation and Authority 79-83
  Influenced by 46, 70, 80, 81, 84, 87, 88, 109n10
  Rationality, theory of 79-83
  Reception of Barth 83-88
  Revelation, doctrine of 79-83
  Other references .... xiii, xvii, xviii, 11, 15, 29, 30, 33,
                                                          35, 38, 43, 46, 70, 91, 102, 104,
                                                           107, 111, 113, 116, 118, 133, 137,
                                                           141, 160, 167, 177, 185, 199, 215,
                                                            223, 232, 237, 238
Hepp, Valentinius 122, 123
Hermann, Wilhelm 87, 88
Hinson, E. Glenn 3, 219, 221
Historie 44, 56-57, 62, 85, 93
  See Geschichte
Hodge, Charles 47, 95, 97, 187, 211, 216, 223, 233
Hoekema, Anthony A. 63
Hoeksema, Herman 63, 164
Holiness tradition
  Barth reception 101-104, 233-242
  Definition and History 4, 17-19, 22, 38

Influence on Fundamentalism 16
Influence on Pentecostalism 17-19, 38
Homrighausen, Elmer George 192, 241
Horton, Douglas 85
Hubbard, David Allen 136, 141
Hughes, Philip E. 208n1
Hunsinger, George...241
Hunter, James Davidson 3, 31, 35, 41 n5, 42n10
Hume, David 188

Industrialization 12
Inerrancy, inerrancy debate
   Analyses of Debate 33-35, 42n10
   Anderson, Ray S. 168-169
   Barr, James 2-3
   Berkouwer, G.C. 134-135
   Bloesch, Donald 200-202
   Bromiley, Geoffrey 119, 208n3
   Brown, Colin 151
   Carnell, Edward John 142, 144, 145, 146
   Clark, Gordon 71, 77
   Fuller Seminary 136-
   Henry, Carl F.H. 81-83
   Jewett, Paul 153, 155-156
   Lindsell, Harold 34
   Montgomery, James Warwick 91-92, 94
   Mueller, David 232
   Pinnock, Clark 96, 110n14
   Ramm, Bernard 177-178, 181-182, 187-188, 190
   Rust, Eric 218
   Schaeffer, Francis 66, 69-70
   Southern Baptists 214
   Vassady, Bela 137-140
Independent Fundamental Churches of America...25
International Council on Biblical Inerrancy 34, 66

Jewett, Paul King
   Primary discussion 152-159
   Other references 70, 147, 166, 177, 215
Johnston, Robert K. 3, 34- 35, 41n4, 42n10
Jüngel, Eberhard 109n5, 109n11

Kant, Immanuel
   by Van Til 50-53
   by Francis Schaeffer 67-68
   by Gordon Clark 73
   by Carl Henry 80, 87-88
   by Clark Pinnock 96-97
   by Bernard Ramm 188
Kantzer, Kenneth
   Primary discussion 97-98

Index

Other references 41n3, 45, 109n8, 111, 177, 209n16
Kahler, Martin 190
Kaufman, Daniel 110n16, 244
Kelly, Dean 25
Kierkegaard, Soren
  Influence on Barth, interpreted
    by Van Til 50-52
    by Fred Klooster 62-63
    by Francis Schaeffer 67-70
    by Carl Henry 88
    by Kenneth Kantzer 98
    by Clark Pinnock 96-97
    by Paul Jewett 154
    by David Mueller 229
  Influence on Edward J. Carnell 142
  Influence on Paul Jewett 153
King, Henry Churchill 8
Klooster, Fred
  Primary discussion 60-63
  Other references 83, 123, 150, 176, 209n15
Koop, C. Everett 65
Krabbendam, Hendrick 123
Kromminga, D.H. 63
Kuiper, R.B. 63
Kuyper, Abraham 20, 42n9, 48, 59, 122, 181-182,
  188

Ladd, George Eldon 160, 177, 209n14
Lankford, Sarah 17
Lausanne Covenant 200
Lewis, Edwin 85, 86, 192
Lewis, Gordon 110n12
Liberalism
  Definition, history 8-9
  Other references 84, 227
  See Modernism
Lindsell, Harold 34, 41n3, 176, 215
Lovelace, Richard 193
Luther, Lutheran theology 20, 91, 110n13, 166, 198, 199,
  200, 201, 202

Mackay, John 192, 195
Machen, J. Gresham 17, 46, 50, 66, 94, 146, 209n12
Mackintosh, H.R. 85
Mainline Denominations 23, 25, 27, 114, 136, 192-193
Marsden, George
  Definition of Evangelicalism 1-2, 5, 9
  Scopes Monkey Trial 24
  Fuller Seminary history 135-142
Marty, Martin
  Definition of Evangelicalism 25

Index

Righteous Empire 5, 7 13
Two-Party System 9, 10, 13-14
Mathews, Donald 10
May, Henry 6
Mayer, Frederick 110n13
McClendon, William Jr. 248n2
McGloughlin, William 5, 10
McIntire, Carl 32, 46, 138
McMurray, John 169
Mead, Sidney 5, 6, 42
Mencken, H.L. 24
Mennonite 110n16, 243
Methodist, Methodism
   Fundamentalism 17-19
   Holiness Tradition 17-19
   New Evangelicalism 36-37, 238-239
   Perfectionism 18
   Revivalism 9-10
Mickey, Paul 37, 193
Millenialism
   19th century Evangelicalism 5-6
   Premillenialism 3
      Northern Fundamentalist 16
      Methodist 18
      Pentecostal, Holiness 19
      Dutch Reformed 21
Minear, Paul 246
Missionary Organizations, Societies
   Billy Graham Evangelistic Association 28
   Campus Crusade for Christ 28
   China Inland Mission 27
   Far East Gospel Crusade 28
   Greater European Mission 28
   InterVarsity Christian Fellowship 194
   Navigators 28
   Southern Baptist Missions 27, 28
   Trans World Radio 28
   Wycliff Bible Translators 28
   Youth for Christ 28
Modernism, Modernist
   Historical analysis 8-9, 13
   Fundamentalist controversies 7, 9, 13-14, 21
Modernization 12-13, 18, 22
Mohler, Richard Albert .... xvii, xviv-xx, 110n14, 186, 208n6, 228
Moltmann, Jurgen 225
Monsma, Peter 63
Montgomery, James Warwick
   Primary discussion 91-94
   Other references 43, 97, 209n14
Moody, Dale

Index 243

Primary discussion 220-226
Other references 216
Moody, Dwight L. 15-16
Mueller, David L.
   Primary discussion 227-232
   Other references 223
Mueller, J. Theodore 110n13
Mueller, William A. 227
Mullens, Edgar Y.
   Primary discussion 104-107
   Other references 216
Murch, James Deforest 29-30
Murphy, Cullen 2, 41n1

National Association of Evangelicals 29, 32, 34
Natural Theology
   See Barth, Natural Theology
New Divinity 11
New England Fellowship 28
New Hampshire Declaration of Faith 105
New Measures Revivalism 11
Neo-Orthodoxy, Interpreted by
   Allen, Diogenes 193
   Bloesch, Donald 192, 194, 198
   Carnell, E.J. 143-144
   Henry, Carl 83, 84-86
   Kantzer, Kenneth 98-99
   Moody, Dale 222-223
   Pinnock, Clark 96
   Ramm, Bernard 179, 180, 182
   Ryrie, Charles 99
Niebuhr, Reinhold 9, 85, 86, 89, 142, 192, 194
Nicole, Roger 43, 110n12
Northern Fundamentalist Evangelicalism
   Definition 4
   Historical analysis 15-17, 26

Ockenga, Harold 15, 28, 30, 33, 38, 41n3, 46, 78,
                                                                               113, 135, 137, 138
Old School Presbyterianism 11
   Coalition with Dispensationalism 3, 15, 21
   Influence on Northern Fundamentalism 15, 43, 46, 58, 63
   Doctrine of Scripture 17, 71, 146
Orthodoxy
   Reformed Confessionalism 20-22
   Fundamentalist Evangelical
      Self-Understanding 30-31, 44-45
         by Berkhof, Louis 59-60
         by Clark, Gordon 70-71
         by Klooster, Fred 61
         by Schaeffer, Francis 69

  by Van Til, Cornelius 47-48
 New Evangelical Self-Understanding
  by Berkower, G.C. 123-125, 134
  by Bloesch, Donald 195-196, 199
  by Brown, Colin 149
  by Carnell, E.J. 30-31, 142, 146
  by Daane, James 161
  by Paul Jewett 153
  by Bernard Ramm 177-178, 183-184, 189, 190
 Scholasticism Criticized
  by Anderson, Ray 168-169
  by Berkuower, G.C. 134, 135
  by Bloesch, Donald 196, 201
  by Bromiley, Geoffrey 116
  by Daane, James 162, 164
  by Jewett, Paul 155-156
  by Moody, Dale 222
  by Mueller, David 232
  by Ramm, Bernard 181, 186
  by Rust, Eric 217
  by Yoder, John 245
Overbeck, Franz 52

Pacifism 246-247
Packer, James I. 67, 208n1, 209n16
Palma, Robert J. 175
Palmer, Phoebe Worral 17
Pannenberg, Wolfhart 225, 236-237
Paradox Theology
 Criticized by
  Carnell, E.J. 143-144, 145
  Kantzer, Kenneth 99
  Ramm, Bernard 179
  Sproul, R.C. 95
 Affirmed by
  Bloesch, Donald 198, 200, 202
  Jewett, Paul 156
  Vassady, Bella 139
Parham, Charles 19
Pearlman, Meyer 233
Pelican, Jaroslav 144
Pentecostal, Pentecostalism 4
 Holiness-Pentecostal Tradition 17-19
 Two-Stage Doctrine of Spirit Baptism 5-6, 8
 Influence on Charismatic movement 38-39
 Theologians 110n16, 233-235
Perfectionism
 Characteristic of 19th century Evangelicalism..............................6, 10
  Phoebe Palmer 18
  Charles Finney 10-11
  B.B. Warfield 17

Index

Periodicals
  Christian Century 145
  Christianity Today 29, 30, 33, 65, 73, 78, 85, 91, 97,
                                              115, 117, 118, 120, 145, 148, 160,
                                                                 163, 192, 238
  Moody Monthly 193
  Newsweek 65
  Pneuma 233
  Post American 238
  Reformed Journal 160, 161, 162, 166
  Review and Expositor 221
  Sojourners 237, 238, 239, 241, 248
  Time xii
Pietism
  Definition 211-213, 241-242, 42n7
  Influence on Evangelicalism 10-12, 17-19, 22-23, 42n7, 59,
                                                              101, 194, 198, 211-213
  Reception of Barth 101-110, 211-249
Pinnock, Clark
  Primary discussion 95-97, 110n14, 210n21
  Other references 42n10, 66, 176, 215, 239
Political Engagement
  Chicago Declaration 35, 238, 241
  Christian Right 35-36
  Fundamentalist Evangelical 29-30
  New Evangelical 35-36, 238-240
Praxis, Christopraxis 167, 169, 172
Premillenialism
  See Millenialism
Presbyterians
  See Denominations, Schools and Associations
  Old School 3, 11, 16, 17, 58, 140, 146
  Orthodox Presbyterianism 63-77
  Plan of Union 10
  Revivalism 10-11
  Theologians 10-11, 46, 58, 64, 65, 70, 94, 153,
                                                                                    160
Presuppositionalism 47-48, 70-73, 80-81
  See Apologetics
Preuss, Robert D. 110n13
Price, Robert M. 110n14
Process Theology 198
Propositional Revelation
  Evangelical Affirmation
    by Carnell, E.J. 142
    by Clark, Gordon 72
    by Henry, Carl 80, 81-82
    by Pinnock, Clark 96
  Evangelical Criticism
    by Bloesch, Donald 200
    by Jewett, Paul 154

    by Ramm, Bernard 187
    by Rust, Eric 217-218
    Criticism of Barth 86-87, 96
Pruitt, Ray 233
Puritan 5-6, 8

Quebedeaux, Richard 2, 32, 33

Ramm, Bernard
    Primary discussion 176-190
    Definition of Evangelicalism .... xiii-xiv, 183 -184
    Other references 49, 61, 166, 167, 215, 223
Reformed Confessionalism
    Fundamentalist Evangelical Tradition 20-22, 43-73
    Influence on Evangelicalism 43-44, 46, 58, 63, 111, 122, 124
    See Orthodoxy, Dutch Reformed and Christian Reformed Church
Renewal Movements 36-39, 191-192
Revivalism 5-6, 10-11, 17-19, 21-22
Reymond, Robert 43, 109n6
Rice, John R. 32, 209n13
Richards, George W. 192
Riley, William Bell 15-16, 26, 27
Ritschl, Albrecht 227
Riviere, William T. 55
Roberts, Oral 38-39
Roberts, Richard ....xvii, 109n5
Robinson, H. Wheeler 219
Robinson, William Childs 55
Rogers, Jack 42n10, 123, 160, 166, 208n6,
                                                                                                                              210n21
Rolston, Holmes 55
Rudnick, Milton 3, 110n13
Runia, Klaas 185, 208n6, 210n16, 232
Rust, Eric
    Primary discussion 217-220
    Other references 249n3
Ryrie, Charles Caldwell
    Primary discussion 99-100
    Other references 43, 215

Sandeen, Ernest 3
Scaer, David 110n13
Schaeffer, Francis
    Primary discussion 63-69
    Other references 41n3, 43, 46, 89, 96, 107, 122,
                                                                                                                                150, 185, 199
Schleiermacher, Friedrich 50, 55
Schools, Colleges, Seminaries, Universities
    American Baptist Seminary of the West 191
    Baylor University 191, 220, 227
    Bethel Baptist College and Seminary 176, 191

Index

Bible Churchman's Missionary and Theological College........................207n1
Bible Institute of Los Angeles 28, 176
Bob Jones University 214
Boston University 141
Calvin Seminary 60, 138, 208n4
Covenant Seminary 108n3
Dallas Theological Seminary 97, 99, 100, 102, 108n3, 214, 220
Denver Conservative Baptist Seminary 26
Duke University 227
Eastern Baptist Seminary 26, 108n3, 180
Emmanuel College, Cambridge 115
Faith Theological Seminary 64, 108n3
Free University of Amsterdam 47, 121, 161
Fuller Theological Seminary 29, 33, 34, 78, 115, 135-175, 206
Gordon College, Gordon-Conwell Theological Seminary................27, 108n3
Goshen Biblical Seminary 244
Grace Theological Seminary 108n3
Graduate Theological Union 191
Gregorian University, Rome 221
Harvard University 141, 152
Kansas Bible School 19
Los Angeles Baptist Seminary 176
Mennonite Biblical Seminary 249n9
Moody Bible Institute 15-16, 27, 28, 145, 193
Northern Baptist Seminary 26, 108n3
Northwestern Bible College 26, 27
Oxford University..194, 219, 220
Princeton Seminary 15-16, 21, 27, 46, 49, 101, 137,
140, 142, 146, 160, 192
Regents Park College, Oxford 219, 220
Royal College of Sciences 219
Southern Baptist Theological Seminary 34, 105, 108n3, 215-232
Southwestern Baptist Theological Seminary..34, 105
Trinity College, Bristol 148
Trinity Evangelical Divinity School 97, 108n3
Tyndale Hall, Bristol 115, 207n1
Union Theological Seminary 220
University of Basel 191, 227, 244
University of Chicago 144, 194, 197
University of Dubuque Theological Seminary......................................193
University of Edinburgh 115, 236
Westminster Theological Seminary 21, 46, 47, 58, 84, 101, 108n3,
141, 152, 159
Wheaton College 70, 97, 100, 102, 108n3, 212, 220
Secularization 12-13
Seymor, Charles 19
Shakarian, Demos 38
Shelly, Bruce 2, 28
Simpson, A.B. 19
Smedes, Lewis B. 121, 123, 124, 166, 175, 210n18
Smith, H. Sheldon 11

Smith, Timothy 1-2, 4, 5, 10, 11, 41n5
Smith, Wilbur 94, 138
Smyth, Newman 8
Social Gospel 12, 13, 35-36
Sojourners 237, 238, 239, 241, 248
Southern Evangelicalism 4, 21-23, 214-215
   Impact of Civil War 7, 22-23
   Separation from Northern Culture 25, 22-24
Southern Baptists 21-23, 214-232
   See Denominations, Schools
Sproul, R.C.
   Primary discussion 94-95
   Other references 43, 208n6
Stearns, Miner Broadhead 55, 109n7
Stob, Henry 42n8, 175
Stoeffler, Earnest 42
Stonehouse, Ned 46
Strauss, David Friederich 50, 55
Strong, Augustus 11, 211, 233
Student Volunteer Movement 21
Sweet, William Warren 9
Sykes, Stephen .... xvii, 109n4, 209n11

Taylor, Nathaniel 10-11
Tertullian 48
Theopaschitism 132, 171
Theilicke, Helmut 118, 167-168
Thiessen, Henry Clarence 102
Thirty-nine Articles 116
Tillich, Paul 219, 220, 221, 234
Torrance, Thomas .... xix, 119, 167, 169, 183
Torrey, R.A. 28, 233
Transcendentalism 8
Tribble, H.W. 105, 216
Trueblood, Elton 193
Tulga, Chester 138
Turretin, Francis 164
Two-party System 9-10, 13-14

Unitarians 8
Urgeschichte 52

Van Til, Cornelius
   Primary discussion 46-56
   Theological paradigm 47-48
   Influence on Evangelicalism 46, 66, 89, 108n2, 142
   Criticism by New Evangelicals
      G.C. Berkower 126, 133-134
      James Daane 161, 163
   Other references .... xvii, xviii, 20, 43, 44, 59, 63, 65,
                                      66, 70, 73, 83, 87, 89, 90, 95, 104,

Index

Other references - cont'd 107, 109n4, 116, 118, 122, 123, 126, 133-134, 141, 143, 146, 150, 159, 161, 163, 171, 179, 183, 185, 208n4, 209n11
Vassady, Bela 137-140, 193, 195
Von Balthaser, Hans Ur 55, 57
Voluntaryism 5

Walvoord, John F. 32, 100
Warfield, Benjamin Breckinridge 17, 47, 82, 94, 96, 97, 164, 187, 223
Webber, Robert 41n1
Wenger, John C. 110n16, 243-244
Wesley, John 2, 18
Wesleyan Theology 17-19, 102-104, 110n15, 233-242
Wesleyan Theological Society 34, 103, 235
Westminster Confession 72, 77
Westminster Theological Seminary
  See Schools
Whitfield, George 2
Wiley, H. Orton 102-104
Wilkerson, David 38
Williams, Donald Day 198
Williams, J. Rodman 233-235
Wilson, Robert Dick 47
Women's roles 35, 153, 157-158
World Christian Fundamentals Association 15-16
World Council of Christian Churches 64, 137, 221, 245
World Evangelical Fellowship 200

Yoder, John Howard
  Primary discussion 244-247
  Other references 212
Youth for Christ 28

Zerbe, A.S. 63
Zinzendorf 242
Zondervan Publishing Company 20

www.ingramcontent.com/pod-product-compliance
Lightning Source LLC
Chambersburg PA
CBHW050843230426
43667CB00012B/2128